The Will to Kill

THIRD EDITION

The Will to Kill

Making Sense of Senseless Murder

James Alan Fox
Northeastern University

Jack Levin
Northeastern University

Kenna Quinet
Indiana University Purdue University Indianapolis

PEARSON

Boston   New York   San Francisco
Mexico City   Montreal   Toronto   London   Madrid   Munich   Paris
Hong Kong   Singapore   Tokyo   Cape Town   Sydney

Series Editor: *Dave Repetto*
Series Editorial Assistant: *Jack Cashman*
Marketing Manager: *Kelly May*
Production Editor: *Claudine Bellanton*
Editorial Production Service: *Omegatype Typography, Inc.*
Composition Buyer: *Linda Cox*
Manufacturing Buyer: *Debbie Rossi*
Electronic Composition: *Omegatype Typography, Inc.*
Cover Administrator: *Elena Sidorova*

For related titles and support materials, visit our online catalog at www.ablongman.com.

Between the time Website information is gathered and then published, it is not unusual for some sites to have closed. Also, the transcription of URLs can result in typographical errors. The publisher would appreciate notification where these errors occur so that they may be corrected in subsequent editions.

ISBN-13: 978-0-205-51671-1
ISBN-10: 0-205-51671-8

Library of Congress Cataloging-in-Publication Data

Fox, James Alan.
   The will to kill : making sense of senseless murder / James Alan Fox, Jack Levin, Kenna Quinet. — 3rd ed.
         p. cm.
   Includes bibliographical references.
   ISBN-13: 978-0-205-51671-1
   ISBN-10: 0-205-51671-8
   1. Murder.   2. Homicide.   3. Criminal psychology.   4. Criminal justice, Administration of.   I. Levin, Jack   II. Quinet, Kenna.   III. Title.
   HV6515.F69 2008
   364.152'3—dc21

                                                          2007020915

Printed in the United States of America

10   9   8   7   6   5   4   3   2   1   11   10   09   08   07

CONTENTS

PREFACE

We welcome the opportunity to write the third edition of *The Will to Kill*. In this revision, we have updated a number of topics and have expanded or refined our discussions in critical places throughout the text. Indeed, virtually every chapter has undergone significant revision. Specifically, we have updated sections to reflect legislative changes and recent Supreme Court decisions. All tables, charts, and other statistical references have been updated, at least through 2005 figures. Throughout the book, we have inserted new and recent cases to illustrate various themes, and have updated developments in others.

Like earlier editions, this book is about the circumstances in which people kill one another. In the pages that follow, we review homicide laws, introduce theories purporting to explain why murder occurs, and present statistical data depicting patterns and trends in homicide. Then, we cover a range of topics from domestic and workplace homicide to cult and hate killings; from murder committed by juveniles to serial slayings. In two closing chapters, we examine criminal justice responses to homicide, including the strategies and tactics employed to apprehend, prosecute, and punish killers.

Notwithstanding its broad scope, this book is by design far from comprehensive. As our subtitle "Making Sense of Senseless Murder" indicates, we purposely concentrate on the extraordinary and seemingly inexplicable cases—those involving large body counts, bizarre crime scenes, elements of sadism, and irrational motivation. Thus, the reader will hardly find in the pages that follow detailed accounts explaining why a man who loses his temper impulsively shoots his spouse, why a barroom brawl results in a fatal stabbing, or why an impoverished out-of-work father robs a liquor store. The chapters focus much more on family annihilations, fatal romantic attractions, school shootings, mass poisonings by cultists or medical practitioners, serial killers who torture their victims, and disgruntled ex-workers who go on a rampage.

We have accepted the challenge to concentrate on homicides that don't make obvious sense. This is not to suggest, however, that *The Will to Kill* would not be useful for understanding a much broader range of murders. We believe, on the contrary, that the lessons to be learned from examining senseless and outrageous murders can be easily extrapolated to more ordinary and mundane homicides as well. By dissecting extreme cases, we derive a selection of "pure types" against which most murders can be compared and, hopefully, better understood.

The intriguing and sensational circumstances that surround most, if not all, of the cases of homicide presented throughout this book have made them inordinately important in a public policy sense. These are, after all, the murder cases that have typically made the headlines and the evening news; they are the examples that politicians refer to when they seek to change some aspect of criminal law or to secure funding for programs and policies to reduce violence. These are also the murder cases on which public opinion about homicide is often based.

A data file on homicides in the United States for the years 1976–2005 is used throughout the book. A note at the end of the book describes in detail the elements and contents of this data file. Analysis of these data was supported by grants from the U.S. Department of Justice, Bureau of Justice Statistics.

ACKNOWLEDGMENTS

We owe a special debt of gratitude to the Lipman and Brudnick families for their generous support and encouragement of our work. We also benefited from the institutional support of Northeastern University, Indiana University Purdue University Indianapolis, the Center for Urban Policy and the Environment, and Guardsmark, L.L.C. We would like to thank the following reviewers for their helpful comments: Steven Brodt, Ball State University; Brenda Chaney, Ohio State University; John Heeren, California State University–San Bernadino; and Brian Howarth, Clackamas Community College. Finally, we wish to thank Karen Hanson, Jennifer Jacobson, and David Repetto, our current and former editors at Allyn and Bacon, for their continuing faith in us, as well as our families, whose love is only equaled by their patience.

ABOUT THE AUTHORS

James Alan Fox is the Lipman Family Professor of criminal justice and former dean at Northeastern University in Boston. He has written 16 books and has published hundreds of journal and magazine articles and newspaper columns, primarily in the areas of multiple murder, juvenile crime, school violence, workplace violence, and capital punishment. As an authority on homicide, he appears often on national television, including *The Today Show, Meet the Press, Dateline,* and *20/20,* and is regularly interviewed by the press. He was profiled in a two-part cover story in *USA Today,* as well as in the *New York Times* and *Scientific American.* He has also consulted on police investigations and with television networks on major cases. Fox frequently gives lectures and expert testimony, including over 100 keynote or campus-wide addresses around the country, more than a dozen appearances before the U.S. Congress, and briefings at the White House and the Office of the U.S. Attorney General on trends in violence. Finally, he served as a visiting fellow with the Bureau of Justice Statistics specializing in the measurement of homicide trends.

Jack Levin is the Irving and Betty Brudnick Professor of sociology and criminology and director of the Brudnick Center on Violence and Conflict at Northeastern University in Boston. He has published 27 books and numerous journal articles and newspaper columns, primarily in the areas of serial and mass murder, hate crimes, school violence, juvenile murder, and workplace violence. Levin has appeared on such national television programs as *48 Hours, 20/20, Dateline NBC, The Today Show, Good Morning America, Oprah, The O'Reilly Factor, Larry King Live,* and all network newscasts, and is often interviewed by the national press. He has served as an expert witness or consultant in a number of cases involving murder, cults, hate crimes, and the death penalty, and has been a speaker to a wide range of community, college, and professional groups including the Dallas Woman's Club, the International Association of Chiefs of Police, the American Psychological Association's Symposium on School Violence, the Academy of Psychiatry and the Law, the White House Conference on Hate Crimes, OSCE's Office for Democratic Institutions and Human Rights, and the University of Paris Conference on "Killing the Other."

Kenna Quinet is an associate professor of criminal justice, law, and public safety in the School of Public and Environmental Affairs at Indiana University Purdue University Indianapolis (IUPUI). She is also a research fellow at the Indianapolis-based Center for Urban Policy and the Environment. Her research interests include homicide, particularly medical murder, female offenders, serial and mass murder, and theories of aggression. She also researches suicide and other causes of death, missing persons, and unidentified dead, and evaluates the effectiveness of federally funded criminal justice programs. She has won 15 teaching awards and teaches classes in homicide, criminological theory, public policy, and animal rights. In addition, she is a member of the board of directors of the Indiana Violent Crime and Homicide Investigator's Association, of which she is also a member.

The Will to Kill

1 The Lure and the Law of Homicide

Homicide intrigues virtually all of us. From the sensational and historic double murder trial of ex-football star O.J. Simpson to the travails of the elusive yet fictional Hannibal Lecter of Thomas Harris's *The Silence of the Lambs,* we are drawn irresistibly to the drama, mystery, intrigue, and power of murder and murderers, both real and invented.

It would hardly be an overstatement to suggest that within popular culture, murder has become a cottage industry. In bookstores across the United States, the true-crime section, new since the late 1980s, offers an expanding array of books primarily about serial killers, multiple murders, killer cults, and crimes involving celebrities. *People* magazine, a yardstick for America's enchantments, increasingly places killers on its front cover. Film, trading cards, action figures, even artwork, center on murders and murderers, creating a cottage industry in *murderabilia.*

Fascination with Murder

What is it about homicide that captures our attention? Or perhaps the more fitting question is, what is it about us that explains our captivation? And what kinds of killings are especially appealing to the general public, which seems to have an insatiable appetite for true-crime books and films? It is our obsession with murder—both as news and as entertainment—that prompts print and TV magazines to feature infamous killers of the day.

For most of us, a fascination with murder is entirely benign. Ironically, we are drawn to murder, and especially to its most grisly and grotesque examples, as an escape from the mundane problems we face in everyday life—how to pay the bills, how to avoid being mugged, how to get a long-awaited promotion at work, and so on. Paying the bills, avoiding a mugger, and waiting for an overdue promotion—these are all too real. By contrast, some homicides are so extraordinary that psychologically they might as well be fiction. The killers might as well be characters in a novel or a film. Because they are so unlikely—at least from the point of view of true-crime buffs—they are also a form of entertainment and enjoyment. Homicides yielding large body counts—a massacre in a shopping mall or at a law firm or in the family—may qualify as crossing the line into fantasy. But the most fascinating homicides are those involving extreme forms of sadism—crimes in which victims are tortured, raped, and dismembered. The more grotesque (and therefore removed from ordinary life) a particular killing spree, the more likely it is to entertain us.

A second source of fascination with murder is not so trivial. In fact, there are many people who feel intensely vulnerable to the effects of violence—so much so that they read true-crime stories and watch TV docudramas about murder, not because they seek to escape psychologically, but in order to learn how to avoid becoming victims of homicide. Going beyond their role as members of the audience for murder, some actually seek to overcome feelings of powerlessness, anxiety, and vulnerability by planning careers as crime investigators or forensic psychologists. They hope to learn the techniques of criminal profiling and DNA analysis. The better they understand the murdering mind and the process of criminal investigation, the more they are able to distance themselves psychologically from the killers they fear and to feel safe.

The third and final source of fascination is also the most troubling. There are some individuals—hopefully, few in number—who live vicariously through the exploits of sadistic killers. Fascinated with power but controlled by normal feelings of conscience, these individuals are psychologically incapable of murdering for pleasure, money, or protection. They can, however, learn every detail of a killer's biography, every detail of a killer's modus operandi, and every detail of the investigation by which a killer is brought to justice.

The most infamous and celebrated killers sometimes attract fan clubs, complete with member organizations, newsletters, and even fund-raisers. At the extreme, we occasionally hear about someone, usually a woman, a so-called killer groupie, who dates or even marries an incarcerated murderer. Among the many possible motivations for her attraction, she may regard her man as an important celebrity, a powerful figure worthy of respect and admiration.

The public preoccupation with murder apparently extends to the news media as well, both print and electronic. In a sense, the prime-time news is more like the *crime-time* news, and the events that are the least common in reality appear to be featured more than the rest. According to the Center for Media and Public Affairs, more than one-third of the crime stories presented on the major network evening news broadcasts concern homicides.[1] By contrast, homicide, according to FBI tallies, accounts for only 1 percent of all violent offenses and 0.1 percent of all serious offenses. Furthermore, the murders that seem particularly exploited are those that involve sex, sadism, or celebrity—hardly the norm in stark reality.

The criminal trial of O.J. Simpson, who was accused of having stabbed to death his estranged wife and her companion, provides a major example of this excess. The case contained all of the elements required to gain the attention of the nation and achieve top TV ratings—a well-liked, even heroic, celebrity football player and his beautiful wife, an interracial romance gone bad, rumors of spouse abuse, and charges of police racism. Indeed, the television coverage of the trial was so excessive that someone unfamiliar with American popular culture might have thought that O.J. Simpson was a senator or that the trial was a congressional impeachment proceeding. For a period of time, regular television programming was preempted so that Americans could get their daily dose of courtroom drama. In addition, periodic rundowns of trial proceedings were regularly featured on network newscasts, morning talk shows, and prime-time news magazines.

The advent of *Court TV* ensured that the "O.J. Simpson phenomenon" would continue unabated into the foreseeable future. Television trials, while entertaining millions of people who subscribed to cable news channels, also gave them access to a nondegree education in U.S. law.

Selling Evil

In 1985, the *National Lampoon* spoofed the U.S. glorification of murderers by publishing a series of "Mass Murderer Trading Cards," complete with photos, autographs, and statistics on "all your favorite slayers." As a parody, the *Lampoon* had placed despicable multiple killers in a context generally reserved for superstars. What was meant as social satire in 1985 has since become a social reality. In 1991, a California trading card company published its first series of mass and serial killer cards, spotlighting such infamous criminals as Jeffrey Dahmer, Theodore Bundy, and Charles Manson. Selling for 10 dollars per pack (without bubble gum), it was no joke. Several other card makers soon followed suit, hoping to cash in on the celebrity of multiple murderers.

Even comic books have been used as a vehicle for celebrating the exploits of vicious killers like Jeffrey Dahmer, rather than traditional superheroes. By giving him a starring role once held by the likes of Batman and Superman, the killer is unnecessarily glorified, as in Marshall McCluhan's famous adage, "the medium is the message." The victims' memory is trivialized by being placed in a comic book format. In a more respectable context, the coveted cover of *People* magazine has become a spotlight for infamous criminals. It was bad enough that Milwaukee's confessed cannibal Jeffrey Dahmer was on the cover of *People* multiple times, an honor usually reserved for Hollywood stars and Washington politicians. But this magazine also chose Dahmer as one of its "25 Most Intriguing People of 1991" and later placed him on its list of the "100 Most Intriguing People of the Century."

Consider how *People* magazine has changed since the 1970s, when celebrities selected for the cover included First Lady Pat Nixon, Barbara Walters, Richard Burton, Joe Namath, Ralph Nader, and Mary Tyler Moore—individuals who were honored for their achievements in politics, industry, sports, and entertainment. By the late 1980s, many of the cover stories had turned negative—JFK and the mob, Robin Williams' love affair with his son's nanny, Jimmy Swaggart's sex scandal, Drew Barrymore's alcoholism, Kristy McNichol's drug addiction, the troubled life of Christina Onassis, why everyone hates Robin Givens, the scandal behind the Tawana Brawly rape case, and on and on. And finally, *People's* covers began to feature rapists, murderers, and other criminals: Robert Chambers (the preppie murder case), schoolyard sniper Laurie Dann, Leona Helmsley, Mike Tyson, Joel Steinberg, Jim and Tammy Bakker, Charles Stuart, the Menendez brothers, Amy Fisher, David Koresh, Heidi Fleiss, the Bobbitts, O.J. Simpson, Luke Woodham, Louise Woodward, and, of course, Jeffrey Dahmer.

Television and motion pictures have also helped to turn our criminals into celebrities. Docudramas are often biographies of vicious criminals—many of whom are played by leading actors and actresses, like Mark Harmon as Theodore Bundy, Brian Dennehy as John Wayne Gacy, and Helen Hunt as Pam Smart. In fact, Hollywood starlet Charlize Theron won an Oscar for playing serial killer Aileen Wuornos in the film *Monster.* Having glamorous actors cast in the roles of vicious killers unfortunately infuses these killers with glamour. In addition, a variety of news magazine programs regularly feature the biographies of multiple murderers, delving into every minute detail of their past. Highlighting the way in which they suffered as children places them unjustifiably in the role of helpless victims.

The glorification of mass killers has created a big-money market for almost anything that they say or do: the artwork of John Wayne Gacy, who got the death penalty for killing

33 young men and boys in Des Plaines, Illinois; the paintings of mass murderer Richard Speck, who slaughtered eight nurses in Chicago; the refrigerator in which Jeffrey Dahmer had stored his victims' body parts; songs written or recorded by Charles Manson; the poetry of Danny Rolling, who brutally tortured, killed, and mutilated five college students in Gainesville, Florida; and the writings of Theodore Kaczynski, the Unabomber. The popularity of murderabilia has inspired a market for various third-party souvenirs and products of questionable taste: tee-shirts, aprons, boxer shorts and thongs bearing the images of serial killers like Ted Bundy; calendars featuring Hillside Strangler Kenneth Bianchi; and action-figure toys of infamous murderers like Manson and Dahmer. Arguably over the top, a recent serial killer board game, which comes with its own body bag and features "dead baby" markers, instructs players to kill as many children and babies as possible before being captured by the FBI.

Homicide Law

In everyday usage, the terms *murder, homicide, kill,* plus a variety of more colorful synonyms such as *slaughter, butcher, massacre, slay,* or even slang terms like *knock off, bump off,* and *polish off* are often used somewhat interchangeably. This practice (except for the slang) will be followed throughout most of this book for the sake of convenience, if not readability. It is important, nevertheless, to understand the important distinctions among these concepts.

The term *killing* represents the most general notion of extinguishing life. Although there is nothing inherent in the broad concept of killing that excludes suicide or even animal abuse, our attention shall be limited to homicidal acts, those specifically directed against other human beings. We shall discuss suicides, but only those that are coupled with a homicide. We shall also examine killers who train on animals, but only as a pathway to targeting human prey.

Not all acts of killing are illegal. Most societies authorize agents of the state—police officers and soldiers, for example—to kill under appropriate circumstances. Wartime aggression against an enemy nation as well as state-sanctioned executions of condemned prisoners are not violations of the law, although certain governmental acts of violence can be proscribed by international treaty (e.g., genocide—the attempt to exterminate a racial or ethnic group).

Criminal homicide refers to unlawful and unjustifiable actions or inactions that result in the death of other human beings. Homicidal acts include such clear-cut misdeeds as shooting a semiautomatic rifle at a crowd of people in a shopping mall or poisoning over-the-counter cold medications. As we shall see, stabbing an intruder to death during a burglary is also a homicide but may be legally justifiable (that is, noncriminal), depending on the particular circumstances.

Failures to act (known in the law as *omissions*) can also result in criminal charges if such inactivity helps to precipitate a death. Omissions can be subtle yet are nonetheless illegal, such as when a landlord disregards faulty wiring that causes a fatal blaze, or a parent neglects a child to the point the youngster starves to death, even if the parent had not intended this tragic outcome.

Although it may seem self-evident, a necessary condition for homicide is that the intended victim of a dangerous act or neglectful omission is indeed a living human being. Thus, shooting a gun at a suitcase—hidden underneath bed sheets to look like a sleeping person—constitutes attempted murder, but shooting a gun at someone who had just died in bed of a heart attack technically does not. That is, it is only *factually* impossible to kill someone who isn't where he or she is believed to be, but it is *legally* impossible to kill a corpse. Even though the defense of *legal impossibility* derives from the English Common Law origins of our system of jurisprudence, in recent years U.S. courts have been reluctant to recognize it as an excuse.

The often-debated question of when life begins—be it at birth or at conception—has turned into a wider issue for homicide law than just the legality of medically performed abortions. Pregnant mothers who place their unborn babies at risk by using narcotics have been prosecuted for child endangerment, as well as homicide, should the fetus fail to survive. At present, two dozen states have on their books homicide, laws recognizing unborn children as victims throughout the entire period of pre-natal development. Ten other states recognized fetal homicide as a crime under certain circumstances. And, in 2004, by the closest of margins (one vote in the Senate), the U.S. Congress passed the Unborn Victims of Violence Act recognizing unborn children as victims if injured or killed during the commission of federal or military crimes of violence.

The various situations described above may all constitute homicide, but they do so at varying levels of culpability and, therefore, involve varying levels of punishment. The criminal law recognizes types and degrees of homicide based on such notions as intent, premeditation, gravity, provocation, and foreseeability. The law of homicide is particularly complex and differs somewhat from jurisdiction to jurisdiction. State laws change frequently, moreover, as politically minded legislatures and constitutionally minded courts struggle to fine-tune the definitions and applications of criminal codes. Nevertheless, across the land there are some fundamental commonalities that guide the administration of justice in the area of homicide.

Murder

The first distinction among types of criminal homicide is that between murder and manslaughter. Murder requires malicious intent (or simply "malice"), an aim to cause death or great bodily harm. In addition, malicious intent can extend to acts that are reckless or show "depraved indifference" to human life, such as exploding a bomb inside a school, even if the perpetrator never meant to hurt anyone. Assaults not necessarily designed to be fatal can constitute murder so long as the deadly outcome is a reasonable or foreseeable possibility. Thus, if a victim of an unarmed assault—a blow to the chest—falls down, bangs his head on the sidewalk, and then dies three days later from the head injury, the assailant can be brought up on murder charges. A parent, distraught over a crying, colicky baby, who shakes the infant to silence her and does it so vigorously as to cause death can also be charged with murder, assuming that the parent is aware that this rough form of treatment can be detrimental.

In early English common law, the root of the U.S. legal system, murder was automatically punishable by death. In the post-revolutionary United States, however, legislatures, wishing to mitigate the law's inflexibility and excessive harshness, moved to limit capital punishment only to the most grievous acts of homicide, by establishing degrees of murder, typically first and second degrees for capital and non-capital murder.

In contemporary statutes, the degree of murder, first versus second, essentially turns on whether the offender premeditated the act of violence. Premeditation entails some evidence of planning, deliberation, or scheming, although not necessarily over a prolonged time period. In fact, the extent of deliberation can be a matter of minutes or even seconds. A plan to kill one's spouse after doubling the size of her life insurance policy obviously reveals cunning and cold-blooded deliberation. Yet an act of road rage in which a motorist deliberately chases another vehicle, forcing it off the road into a fatal encounter with a concrete pole, can also reflect sufficient deliberation so as to constitute first-degree murder.

Many states also consider intentional acts of homicide that are especially brutal, cruel, or extreme, to be first-degree murder, even if the crime is not premeditated. On the evening of August 28, 1995, for example, Richard Rosenthal and his wife, Laura Jane, argued heatedly in the backyard of their suburban Boston home. The fight began over a burned ziti dinner and escalated quickly. The 40-year-old insurance executive lost all control over his temper and started beating his wife repeatedly with a rock. He then cut open her chest with a six-inch kitchen knife and impaled her heart and lungs on a stake in the backyard. Although Rosenthal may not have planned the fatal attack, the jury convicted him of first-degree murder because of the "extreme atrocity and cruelty" of the crime.

The so-called felony-murder rule also grants murder status, typically in the first-degree, for any death that results during the commission of a dangerous felony, such as a robbery or arson. Even though the felon may not have planned or intended for someone to die during the crime, the intent and planning surrounding the commission of a reckless crime are by law transferred to the homicide. If, for example, a robber fatally shoots a store clerk because the victim is too slow in handing over the contents of the cash register, the charge is "murder one." He may have planned to use the gun only to intimidate but not to kill; however, the deliberation in committing a dangerous felony like robbery translates into premeditation for the homicide.

The felony-murder rule may even apply when the felon does not directly cause the death, so long as the fatality results from an act or conspiracy in which he or she is implicated. If, for example, the police shoot and mistakenly kill a hostage whom the robber has taken as a shield, the robber may be charged with first-degree murder.

Twenty-nine-year-old Aldrin Diaz was charged with murder following a January 28, 2000, disturbance outside of a Providence, Rhode Island restaurant, even though he never fired his weapon and dropped it when ordered to do so by the police. During the incident, an off-duty cop, rushing to assist fellow officers with his gun drawn, was fatally shot by a uniformed officer who had mistakenly identified the cop in street clothes as one of the combatants. Because Diaz's use of a gun precipitated the chain of events leading to the officer's death, he could have been held legally responsible under the felony-murder rule, although the charge was ultimately dropped.

The felony-murder rule may appear unreasonably strict when, for example, the person charged with murder takes a fall for the one who directed the crime, or, as in the Diaz case, when a police action results in a death. In an attempt to address this concern, some courts have limited the application of the rule to deaths that were foreseeable during the commission of the dangerous felony.

Homicides that reflect malicious intent yet lack premeditation, that do not show extreme cruelty, and that are not committed during the course of a dangerous felony are considered murders in the second degree. For example, a man who impulsively stabs his teenage son to death during an argument over a football game has, given the spontaneity of the act, committed second-degree murder. Homicides committed under the influence of alcohol or drugs are also generally considered second-degree murders, if the intoxication is believed to have reduced the drunken person's capacity to act deliberately and premeditate the deadly assault.

Manslaughter

Homicides that lack malicious intent or reckless disregard for life are considered manslaughters, which in turn are divided into voluntary and involuntary forms. Voluntary manslaughter is the intentional killing of another person under extenuating circumstances, such as provocation or emotional duress (the so-called heat of passion) without time or opportunity for cooling off. A woman who kills her husband upon finding him sexually molesting their daughter has committed voluntary manslaughter. If, on the other hand, she deliberately seeks him out in order to avenge his act of incest, she could be charged with murder, although most juries would likely respond sympathetically.

Also considered manslaughter are deaths that result from fistfights, barroom brawls, or similar conflicts between equal combatants. Of course, picking a fight with someone who is less than your size can easily be considered murder if the disadvantaged victim dies. Voluntary manslaughter also applies when a person uses excessive force in self-defense or wrongly but honestly perceives that self-defense is required given the situation. Thus, for example, shooting a neighbor under a genuine yet mistaken belief that he was a burglar is not murder, but neither is it accidental in the eyes of the law.

In the crime of manslaughter, it is the heat of passion, intense fear, or provocation that negates the malice required for murder. Malicious intent is presumed absent when the killer reacts, understandably yet unjustifiably, to some provocation (such as the discovery of an unfaithful lover or the attack by an inebriated drinking buddy) or duress (such as murdering and cannibalizing another human being in order to stay alive while lost in the wilderness). While one may use deadly force in self-defense or to survive a perilous attack, the use of excessive force (e.g., shooting an unarmed attacker) also constitutes manslaughter.

The provocation necessary to reduce the crime of murder to that of manslaughter must, however, be reasonable in some objective sense. The fact that an offender feels provoked does not automatically constitute the lesser offense.

Vigilantism, for example, may entail a deeply felt emotional reaction to a perceived injustice in society, as in the actions of 36-year-old Michael A. Mullen, but is not recognized as legitimate provocation. In September 2005, Mullen telephoned the Bellingham, Washington, police and confessed to having shot to death two men—Hank Eisses, 49, and Victor Vasquez, 68—whom he had identified from Whatcom County's online registry of sex offenders. Mullen was outraged and upset about a recent widely publicized case involving Joseph E. Duncan, III, a repeated sex offender from Washington State who had been arrested in Idaho for kidnapping and murder. Reportedly, Duncan had bludgeoned to death three victims inside the Groene family home near Coeur d'Alene, Idaho, in order to kidnap for sex 9-year-old Dylan and 8-year-old Shasta. According to a letter sent to the *Seattle Times* to explain his own reasons for targeting sexual predators, Mullen wrote:

> It is true—Joseph Edward Duncan was my already fragil [sic] straw broken. To think it was "our" state to let him go free. Then to stalk & prey on the Groene family. God, the horrors those kids must have witnessed. It made me cry when I heard the news. It made me "VERY" angry when I heard how he bragged to Shasta on how he killed her siblings. It made me sick to think of the abuse Dylan suffered before he died. To just be discarded like garbage. Slade, Dylan and Shasta will not be another helpless ending. I will see to it personally that their deaths and abuse was [sic] not in vain!

Michael Mullen's decision to target locally accessible sex offenders to avenge Duncan's alleged crimes was in part to dramatize the plight of victims like the Groenes. Mullen also indicated his desire to be executed as soon as possible; he wanted to reach the hereafter in time to welcome Duncan's arrival: "I am not proud of taking two lives . . . but my death alone would have meant nothing," wrote Mullen.

There are limits to the levels of provocation that can reduce murder to manslaughter. Words, slogans, insults, gestures, or style of dress and appearance may be socially provocative, yet not so in a legal sense. A hot-tempered individual who fatally attacks someone for uttering a racial slur and a homophobic man who kills in reaction to a proposition from another man have committed murder, even though in both cases the victims may have precipitated their own demise.

Jonathan Schmitz of Lake Orion, Michigan, for example, was convicted of second-degree murder for slaying his friend and neighbor Scott Amedure with a 12-gauge shotgun because the victim had publicly humiliated him. Amedure, age 32, had revealed his sexual attraction to Schmitz during a 1995 taped episode of the Jenny Jones television talk show, entitled "Same-Sex Secret Crushes." During the program, the host elicited Amedure's whipped cream and strawberries fantasy involving Schmitz. The heterosexual defendant testified that he was embarrassed and mortified in front of a crowd and had been led to believe by the staff of the show that his secret admirer was a woman.

The critical factor in assessing Schmitz's criminal responsibility was the three-day time span separating the defendant's public embarrassment from the subsequent shooting. Because of the "cooling off" period, the jury rejected Schmitz's claim that he killed during an insane rage provoked by his victim's public admission. Schmitz's conviction was overturned on appeal because of errors in the jury selection process. Yet, in his subsequent retrial, a second jury convicted him of second-degree murder, rejecting his "crime of passion" defense. For his crime, Schmitz will serve a sentence of 25 to 50 years.

In recent years, homicides inspired by a victim's sexual orientation, race, religion, or gender have come under particular scrutiny in both the criminal court as well as the court of public opinion. Known as bias or hate crimes, such offenses are typically dealt with at the state level by enhancing the defendant's sentence—that is, by increasing his prison time beyond what he would have received had he not selected his victim based on a protected characteristic like race or sexual orientation. In addition, as a violation of the victim's civil rights, bias-motivated offenses may also result in additional charges under federal hate crime statutes. Thus, a perpetrator who commits a hate-inspired manslaughter might spend as much time incarcerated as someone who commits second-degree murder.

A death resulting from negligence is considered involuntary manslaughter. The law punishes those whose recklessness or negligence causes loss of life as well as those who fail in their duty to act in a manner that may prevent someone from dying. For example, on February 20, 2003, a swiftly-moving blaze killed 100 people and injured over 200 more at a West Warwick, Rhode Island club when a pyrotechnic display used by the rock band Great White accidentally ignited sound-proofing material behind the stage. Daniel Biechele, Great White's tour manager and the man who set off the pyrotechnics, pled guilty to 100 counts of involuntary manslaughter and was sentenced to four years in prison. Jeffrey and Michael Derderian, the two brothers who owned the Station Nightclub, pled no contest to charges of involuntary manslaughter. Jeffrey Derderian was sentenced to three years of probation and 500 hours of community service, while his brother Michael was ordered to serve four years in a minimum-security prison and three years probation. The short prison terms and probation were difficult for many who lost spouses or children to accept, especially in view of the large death toll, yet the absence of malice certainly influenced the legal outcome.

Following the February 29, 2000, fatal shooting of a 6-year-old girl by her first-grade classmate in Mount Morris Township, Michigan, 19-year-old Jamelle James, who lived with the young perpetrator, was charged with involuntary manslaughter. Although he was not present at the scene of the shooting, court papers alleged that James had carelessly left the murder weapon, a loaded 32-caliber semiautomatic, within easy reach of the 6-year-old shooter. It is also involuntary manslaughter if a physician carelessly writes out a prescription for the wrong medication or the improper dosage, thereby causing the death of a patient.

The duty to act can extend to some rather dark places, as illustrated by the bizarre "dominatrix trial" of Barbara Asher, aka Mistress Lauren M., following the July 2000 disappearance of 53-year-old Michael Lord. According to the prosecution theory, Lord suffered a heart attack while strapped to a rack in a Quincy, Massachusetts condominium in which Asher performed her "bondage and discipline" professional services. The prosecutor argued that Asher deliberately chose not to seek medical help for the dying man out of fear that her illicit business would be exposed. It was further alleged that Asher, with the assistance of a friend, dismembered Lord's body, disposing of it in a trash dumpster in Maine. At trial, the state failed to produce any physical evidence to support its argument or even to prove that the victim had visited Asher's dungeon of domination. Despite its distaste for the defendant's trade, the jury acquitted Asher due to lack of proof.

Like the felony-murder doctrine, the misdemeanor-manslaughter rule applies if a death occurs while the offender is engaged in a misdemeanor, an act less serious than a felony. In Worcester, Massachusetts, for example, a homeless man and woman, both marginally retarded, were charged with involuntary manslaughter following an abandoned 1999 warehouse blaze in which six firefighters perished. Not only had the homeless squatters caused the fire with careless burning of a candle, but they apparently failed to report the fire as it spread rapidly. Because the defendants were both marginally retarded, a plea bargain was offered and accepted, placing the two on five years probation.

Defenses to Criminal Homicide

The law recognizes both defenses and excuses that limit an individual's criminal responsibility for committing homicide. In certain defenses (sometimes referred to as justifications), defendants admit to having carried out the killing but maintain that under the circumstances (e.g., the exercise of police powers or citizen use of self-defense) what they did was proper under the law and therefore noncriminal. Thus, a claim of self-defense would suggest that an individual committed the act but was justified in doing so. In excuses, by contrast, defendants admit what they did was wrong but maintain that under the circumstances (e.g., duress, mistake, entrapment, insanity, intoxication, extreme youth or senility, diminished capacity, or various psychiatric syndromes), they were not fully responsible for the criminal act they perpetrated.

In July 2003, 86-year-old George Russell Weller hit the gas pedal instead of the brake in his 1992 Buick and careened into a crowded farmer's market in Santa Monica, killing 10 people ranging in age from 7 months to 78 years. In addition, he injured more than 50 pedestrians. Although Weller had tested negative for drugs and alcohol and had passed a vision and written driving exam three years earlier, evidence came to light that his driving skills had for some time been impaired. Ten years earlier, Weller had crashed his car into a retaining wall. More recently, he damaged his own garage on at least two occasions. Weller's horrendous accident brought the issue of elderly drivers and the law to the forefront of public debate.

Weller never accepted responsibility or showed genuine remorse. Evidence suggested that he had actually been in control of the car and was steering his way through the crowd; perhaps he could have avoided hitting many of the people. On the day of the accident, moreover, he had had a minor accident a short distance away and was possibly fleeing the scene when he crashed into the farmer's market. After the carnage, as people lay dead or dying, Weller was heard chastising the victims because they didn't get out of his way and also asking witnesses to imagine how *he* felt.

Despite his age, Weller was charged and convicted of 10 counts of vehicular homicide with gross negligence. By his November 2006 sentencing date, Weller's health had so deteriorated that Superior Court Judge Michael Johnson ordered the frail defendant to serve five years but no jail time, a decision that upset the families of Weller's victims. Judge Johnson noted that Weller's actions and apparent indifference to the suffering he had caused clearly warranted prison time, yet was persuaded against incarceration for practical reasons. Not only would prison life kill the man, but it would burden the state with the cost of his medical care. Thus, in the final analysis, old age and senility did not excuse Weller from responsibility for his actions. Come sentencing time, however, age did play a role in assessing the appropriate punishment.

In contrast to excuse defenses that lessen or eliminate responsibility for criminal conduct, certain homicides are considered completely legitimate. Killings by public officials in the course of executing their duties and job responsibilities are generally considered justifiable, although in reaction to recent abuses of power the police have been restricted from using deadly force against unarmed, nondangerous suspects fleeing the scene of a felony. Four white New York City police officers were charged with, but acquitted of, second-degree murder after firing a 41-shot barrage of bullets at an unarmed West African immigrant, 22-year-old Amadou Diallo, on February 4, 1999, during an anticrime sweep through the Bronx. The jury felt that the officers were justified in using deadly force when they mistakenly yet reasonably believed Diallo had reached for a gun. The victim was actually reaching for his wallet, presumably in order to produce some identification.

Homicides are considered justifiable if they are in reaction to a level of provocation so great that deadly force is necessitated in order to defend oneself, other innocent people, or even one's home and property. To constitute self-defense, however, only that amount of force sufficient to repel an attack or intrusion is permitted by law. Generally, one cannot fend off a fist with a gun, unless the weapon is required to counterbalance any disadvantage in size or strength. Thus, a child or diminutive adult may be justified when using a gun to defend against a knife assault by a larger assailant. However, if excessive force is in fact used in defense of self or others, then manslaughter charges may result.

In general, self-defense is only justified if no other reasonable means of escape or retreat exists. If the victim of an attack can safely flee, rather than use lethal force, then this opportunity must be taken. However, some states allow homeowners to defend their "castle" by using deadly force, and juries have typically been sympathetic to the "castle doctrine" over the retreat requirement.

Many states allow deadly force if a resident reasonably believes it is needed to protect self or others from harm or to prevent a suspect from committing a violent crime. Once the threat is over, the resident must allow the police to take control. The citizen cannot keep a would-be robber or rapist in the basement to mete out his or her own form of justice and, in most cases, cannot pursue the assailant beyond the reasonable "curtilage" area surrounding the home. In December of 2001, Indianapolis homeowner Michael Clements pursued a burglar, Leon Williams, Jr., who had unlawfully entered Clements's home. Clements chased Williams down the street away from the house and shot him in the back. A jury convicted Clements of aggravated battery and carrying a weapon without a license, and he was sentenced to six years in prison. In pursuing the intruder beyond his home, Clements had changed roles from that of victim to that of assailant.

Even though the law generally permits individuals to use force in the defense of property, it is the element of personal danger (not property rights) that underlies this prescription. Thus, a resident or retailer is not permitted to set a death trap in order to catch a burglar or some other intruder. Even so, the sympathies of jurors often run contrary to the law. In 1986, Prentice Rasheed, a store owner in the Liberty City section of Miami, set a makeshift booby trap to ward off burglars, resulting in the electrocution of a drug-addicted intruder. The grand jury, seeing him more as hero than villain, elected not to indict Rasheed for manslaughter.

In spite of the long-standing prescription that individuals attempt to avoid confrontation, the State of Florida in 2005 opened wide the rules for using deadly force in self-defense when the legislature enacted a so-called Shoot First Law. By this provision, citizens are no longer required to retreat from a public space when they feel threatened. Previously, people acting in self-defense outside of their home or workplace were required to use any reasonable means at hand to escape. The new law permits them to "meet force with force," establishing the right to shoot a presumed assailant if there is a reasonable perception of danger. This highly controversial law prompted the Brady Campaign to Prevent Handgun Violence to fight the move by impacting upon the Sunshine State's tourism industry. The Brady Center produced warning cards and distributed them to visitors arriving at Florida airports:

> Thinking about a Florida Vacation? Please Ensure Your Family is Safe.
>
> A new law in the Sunshine State authorizes nervous or frightened residents to use deadly force.
>
> In Florida, avoid disputes. Use special caution in arguing with motorists on Florida roads.
>
> Police and prosecutors are concerned about the potential for unnecessary violence.
>
> TRAVELERS: BE VERY AWARE OF FLORIDA'S SHOOT FIRST LAW.

A one-year follow-up of Shoot First cases in Central Florida published by the *Orlando Sentinel* newspaper identified 13 shootings resulting in six deaths and four injuries.[2] All but one of those shot were unarmed. The reasonableness of the perceived threat apparently has opened a perplexing gray area in the law. In one episode, 43-year-old Michael Brady of Winter Haven was cleared of any responsibility for fatally shooting Justin Boyette as the 6' 2", 270-pound man, who had been drinking at Brady's neighbor's home, approached on his lawn. Brady claimed to have been frightened by Boyette's menacing gestures. Friends of the victim argued that Boyette was just trying to be friendly.

Following Florida's lead and with encouragement from the politically powerful National Rifle Association, several other states, including Oklahoma, Texas, Alabama, Georgia, Idaho, Indiana, Kentucky, Kansas, Mississippi, and South Dakota, passed their own Shoot First or Stand Your Ground laws. The Texas and Oklahoma shoot-first provisions are even more forgiving and broad than Florida's. In those states, citizens can use deadly force in self-defense or in defense of a third person in order to prevent imminent kidnapping, murder, sexual assault, or robbery. Such force may also be used to protect property (if during the night) and to prevent arson, burglary, robbery, theft, or criminal mischief. Time will tell whether this approach to empowering victims results in more innocent lives lost, rather than saved.

Regardless of the law in Florida or elsewhere, people sometimes perceive personal danger where there is none. In Louisiana in 1994, for example, a 16-year-old Japanese exchange student, Yoshihiro Hattori, was shot and killed by Rodney Peairs. Dressed up like John Travolta in the film *Saturday Night Fever,* Hattori went to the wrong address looking for a Halloween party to which he had been invited. As Mrs. Peairs saw him approach their house she told her husband to get his gun. Hattori was gesturing wildly and had a camera in his hand, trying to explain to Mr. Peairs that he was there for a party. The Japanese exchange student likely did not understand Mr. Peairs's demand to "Freeze!" Although the case prompted local petitions for tighter gun control and sparked public outcry in the victim's home country of Japan, a jury acquitted Mr. Peairs. It seems that his wife panicked and he feared for her safety and the safety of their three children. The jury thought this was a reasonable response to a perceived threat, even if the perception was incorrect.

The legitimate use of deadly force as self-defense is also limited to the immediate time frame when danger is imminent. An attempt to fight back, for example, following an assault that had occurred the previous day becomes an act of aggression or vengeance and can be punishable as murder.

In such instances, we might sympathize with the avenger. We may feel that his or her culpability is limited, even though the act of revenge cannot be tolerated or legitimated in a civilized society. Thus, the law provides a range of excuses that reduce the wrongfulness of the act. Contrary to justifiable homicide, in which the claim is "I killed him, but it was my responsibility, right, or duty," in excusable killings, the reasoning is "I did it, but I couldn't help myself."

Historically, mental illness (being too confused), intoxication (being too drunk), and age (being too young) have been used to negate or reduce culpability, the logic being that these conditions limit or even eliminate criminal responsibility or punishability. More recently, legislatures and courts have grappled with novel theories of how free will may be restricted, including defenses based on such conditions as battered woman syndrome (BWS), premenstrual syndrome (PMS), postpartum depression (PPD), and post-traumatic stress disorder (PTSD). The list of potential defenses is seemingly endless. In recent years, even some sociological defenses, such as black rage, urban survivor syndrome, and gay panic, have been raised in attempts to excuse criminal responsibility, although with very little success.

In one bizarre case, 44-year-old Scott Falater of Phoenix, Arizona, raised a somnambulism (sleepwalking) defense as an excuse for his rather bad night in January 1997 when he stabbed his wife of 20 years with a hunting knife 44 times before holding her head under water until she drowned. The defense argued that lack of consciousness would fail to meet the intent requirement of the law. The jury rejected entirely his explanation and excuse.

Defendants have also raised cultural customs and religious beliefs as excuses for criminal conduct, but also with mixed success. The First Amendment of the Constitution protects the free exercise of religion, yet this right can sometimes come in conflict with another person's rights, including the right to life. Laurie Grouard Walker, a practicing Christian Scientist from Sacramento, California, for example, was convicted of involuntary manslaughter following the 1984 death of her 4-year-old daughter, Shauntay, from meningitis. Consistent with her religious beliefs, Walker had chosen prayer—rather than medicine—as a means of treating her daughter's flu-like symptoms. Although California, like many other states, provides a statutory exemption to criminal prosecution in the practice of religion, the California Supreme Court held that the rights of the child preempted the exemption. A federal judge later overturned Walker's conviction, but on procedural, not religious, grounds. By contrast, in a similar case in Massachusetts (the home of the Christian Science Church), the state's Supreme Judicial Court, citing religious freedom as a basis, overturned the manslaughter convictions of David and Ginger Twitchell, who also had relied unsuccessfully on faith healing to treat their 2-year-old son, Robyn.

Law and culture sometimes come in conflict, forcing an individual to make a very difficult choice. In January 1985, after learning of her husband's adultery, Fumiko Kimura, a 33-year-old Japanese immigrant, walked with her 4-year-old son and infant daughter into the Pacific Ocean off Santa Monica to save them from the shame that her husband had brought upon the family. Kimura was pulled to safety and charged with the deaths of her two children. Although customs of her cultural heritage could not excuse her actions entirely, her lack of malice did result in a light sentence of one year in jail and five years' probation.

Homicide Law in Practice

The levels and types of homicide are summarized in Table 1.1. When homicide cases come to trial, however, the jury is typically offered a range of possible verdicts. If a defendant is charged with first-degree murder, for example, jurors are typically presented with the option of convicting on a lesser charge—second-degree murder, manslaughter, or possibly even assault with a deadly weapon. On many occasions, a jury will find a defendant guilty of a lesser charge than the facts would dictate or even not guilty altogether because of their sympathies surrounding the case.

Jury nullification, as it is called, is particularly common when smaller or weaker victims are charged with using excessive force to kill an abusive partner or a feared predator.

TABLE 1.1   Types of Homicide

Classification	Elements	Example
First-degree murder	Homicide with malicious intent and with premeditation or extreme cruelty	A man decides to kill his wife, rather than divorce her, to ensure that he maintains sole custody of their children
Second-degree murder	Homicide with malicious intent but without premeditation or extreme cruelty	A man kills his wife during an argument over how best to discipline their children
Felony-murder	Homicide during the course of a dangerous felony	A man commits arson in order to collect insurance, not knowing that his wife is home and will die from smoke inhalation
Voluntary manslaughter	Willful homicide with provocation or from excessive force	A man kills his wife when he finds her spanking their child with a belt
Involuntary manslaughter	Non-willful homicide resulting from negligence	Driving while dialing his cell phone, a man slams into a tree, killing his wife who is seated next to him
Misdemeanor-manslaughter	Homicide during the course of a misdemeanor	As a prank, a man yells "fire" in a crowded theater, and his wife dies in the subsequent rush to escape
Justifiable homicide	Killing a fleeing felon or in self-defense	A man kills his wife as she attempts to strangle their child
Excusable homicide	Homicide with diminished capacity based on mental illness, age, and other conditions	A man kills his wife under a delusion that she is demonically possessed

Even if the facts fall short of self-defense, the jury can still choose to excuse. The infamous subway vigilante Bernhard Goetz was cleared by a New York City jury of homicide charges for his December 22, 1984, shooting of several black youngsters who had accosted him on the train. Even though the teens were unarmed, the jurors apparently identified with Goetz's fear in the situation and excused his quick-on-the-trigger response. Goetz was acquitted of all charges except a minor gun offense.

In the vast majority of criminal prosecutions, the case never reaches a jury. The charges may be dropped without a trial because of insufficient evidence, or the case may be decided by a trial judge. But most often, the defendant accepts a negotiated guilty plea. In such instances, the charge may be reduced from what the facts would indicate in exchange for the defendant's plea. Also, in crimes involving two or more accomplices, one defendant will often plead a lesser charge in exchange for giving testimony against his or her accomplices.

The physician's prescription blunder, which, as noted earlier, would constitute involuntary manslaughter, may also result in a civil action—a malpractice claim or even a wrongful death suit. In fact, virtually all criminal homicides can result in two kinds of trials, which can proceed in succession—civil suits brought by families of the victims to recover financial damages as well as criminal prosecutions leading to prison time. Unlike the criminal proceedings, the burden of proof in the civil action is far less demanding—guilt must be shown by preponderance of evidence rather than beyond a reasonable doubt. Thus, for example, it is not inconsistent or even uncommon to encounter defendants like ex-football star O.J. Simpson being found not guilty in criminal court but civilly responsible.

The criminal prosecution of O.J. Simpson, the most watched trial in U.S. history, provides an important lesson for understanding the application of homicide law to real-world cases. As critical as were the eyewitness testimony, the DNA evidence, and the credibility of the defendant's alibi in shaping opinion inside and outside the courtroom, issues of race, class, and gender also had an impact. Some observers speculated that the jury, in acquitting Simpson, had sought to send a message about racism and police misconduct. Others argued that the defendant's wealth had bought him the best defense—The Dream Team—that money could buy; still others claimed that Simpson's celebrity earned him special treatment.

Notwithstanding the actual rule of law, the political context surrounding a homicide— issues of race, gender, and class, among others—ultimately determines, as Susan Estrich persuasively argues, how the criminal law is applied to the facts, how a case is charged by a prosecutor, how a jury responds to a defendant's strategy, and how an appellate court considers procedural challenges.[3] For these many reasons, therefore, the punishment may not exactly fit the crime.

ENDNOTES

1. Center for Media and Public Affairs, *Media Monitor,* Vol. 8, January/February 1999, Washington, DC.

2. Henry Pierson Curtis, "Gun Law Triggers at least 13 Shootings." *Orlando Sentinel,* June 11, 2006.

3. Susan Estrich, *Getting Away with Murder.* Cambridge, MA: Harvard University Press, 1998.

CHAPTER

2

Explaining the Will to Kill

✁ While legal scholars debate issues of intent and criminal responsibility in homicide cases, criminologists tend to take a different approach. They seek to answer the question: Why do people kill one another?

The major schools of thought regarding the causes of crime, and thus the causes of homicide, have included supernatural, free will, biological, psychological, and sociological explanations. Is violence an inherent aspect of human nature? Or, do we learn it from others? Is it simply a product of a choice made by the murderer? Is it the result of poor parenting or inferior schooling?

Society cannot make informed policy decisions and create successful violence intervention and prevention programs without first attempting to understand the causes of violent behavior. If homicidal acts are learned and reinforced in social settings such as the family or schools, prevention policies would be very different from those that are appropriate if the primary causes of violence are biological.

Once we begin to explain acts of murder, it leads us to some inevitable questions: Does explanation translate to justification? At what point, if ever, does the cause of a behavior become an excuse? At what point, for example, does abuse or neglect experienced by the offender actually reduce criminal responsibility? The Supreme Court of the United States recently overturned the death sentence of Kevin Wiggins due to the incompetence of his lawyers (*Wiggins vs. Smith,* 2003). The justices felt that competent attorneys would have presented information regarding Wiggins' "excruciating" childhood. They felt that if the lawyers had properly included this information in his defense, Wiggins might not have received a death sentence for his crimes. So even if an explanation of an individual's behavior does not affect the decision of guilt or innocence, it may still be relevant in determining the severity of the punishment.

Although focused on homicidal behavior, our journey in this chapter will include theories that more broadly explain violent behavior rather than just those violent events that end in death. Except for the life or death consequences, there is often little difference between homicides and aggravated assaults. One crime ends in death and the other does not, often because of proximity to hospitals or police personnel, choice of weapon, or the presence of bystanders. These two crimes have similar offender and victim SES, race, gender, and age characteristics.[1] Therefore, the same theories may be helpful in explaining both types of violent crime.

The Devil Made Me Do It

Only since the late 1800s has our approach to criminal violence been informed by scientific criminological theories. Before that, there were two major schools of thought about the causes of criminal behavior. For most of human history, society accepted supernatural or spiritual explanations.[2] Whether the crime was stealing a goat or murdering a neighbor, the explanation was the same—demonic possession.

The supernatural phase of explanation left a legacy of irrationality, resulting in thousands of witch hunts and executions. Some sources report that by the end of the 1600s, hundreds of thousands of people were executed throughout the world because they were believed to be inhabited by evil spirits. Often these executions included torture, such as burning at the stake or boiling in oil, in part to extract a confession or an admission of consorting with the devil.

By the mid-eighteenth century, the supernatural phase of explanation and its history of chaos, injustice, and torture gave way to the classical school of thought based on the presumption of free will. Yet the devil or other "evil spirit" explanations of homicidal behavior are still with us. In May of 1993, three 8-year-old boys were murdered in West Memphis, Arkansas. Three local teenagers were convicted of these murders under a cloud of rumors about satanic sacrifices, rituals, and cults. When the three young defendants appeared outside the courthouse, local residents threw rocks at them, reminiscent of witch burnings in fifteenth-century Europe. More recently, the defense team for Scott Peterson, a Modesto, California, man accused of the December 2002 death and dismemberment of his wife Laci and her unborn child, suggested that satanic cults might be responsible for the murder.

Claims of satanic influence—"the devil made me do it"—continue to be present in many U.S. murder cases each year and remain a convenient explanation for what we do not understand. In August 2005, four adults in the small, rural Southern Illinois town of Olney set out to kill Lindsey Kasinger, a pregnant 16-year-old girl. Practicing witchcraft after viewing "Harry Potter" movies, the foursome had apparently planned to eliminate Kasinger in order to remove a hex they claimed she had put on them. They had tried removing the curse in séances, by the use of voodoo dolls, and with other spell castings but felt they were unsuccessful. The group's ringleader, Irenia Cotner, 34, convinced her followers that their families would die if they did not act decisively to end the threat. During the early morning hours of August 23, after rehearsing their intended attack with the group, two of its members entered a home where they thought the pregnant girl was living. They were instead confronted by the mother of their intended victim along with Joshua Bennett, a 20-year-old man who was getting ready to be deployed to Iraq. Bennett was slain by a knife wound to the heart and his mother was repeatedly stabbed, but survived. As a result, Cotner was sentenced to 57 years in prison for her role in conspiring to kill the pregnant girl and convincing her companions to break into Kasinger's home, where they took Bennett's life. Courtroom testimony from the defendants suggested that they believed the girl and her baby had to be killed so that the baby's soul would go to hell. More realistically, however, Cotner's claims of being cursed by Kasinger were actually a result of the ringleader seeking revenge for an alleged sexual assault and rejection by the pregnant girl's boyfriend. The charge of satanic influence was merely a convenient cover for persuading members of her group to take on her personal cause and commit murder.

Back to the Classics

In response to the irrationality, anarchy, and injustice of the supernatural phase of explanation and its harsh punishment methods, a school of thought emerged in the eighteenth century that viewed criminal behavior, including homicide, as a product of free will, a rational choice. Marking a return to the principles of early Greek philosophers, the writings of Cesare Beccaria (1738–1794) and Jeremy Bentham (1748–1833) shaped the foundations of the second phase of explanation—classical criminology.[3]

Although the classical school included a number of complexities, its fundamental premise about the cause of criminal behavior was simple: crime is a rational choice made by the offender, who chooses to kill with free will. Rather than believing that the murderer was a witch or possessed by a demon, classical criminology viewed human beings as possessing mental calculators that they used to determine, "Is this murder worth it? What do I have to lose? And what are the costs versus the gains?" Thus, a murderer would strike when, after evaluating all other options, killing seemed to be the best possible solution. In other words, the killer decided that the crime was worth the risk. Government officials believed that in order to prevent crime, criminal codes, laws, and punishments should be created so that each person, knowing the risks, would decide that crime does not pay. For each offense, therefore, there would be a fitting and proportional punishment.

Obviously, many factors such as alcohol, drugs, anger, and mental illness can affect our decisions and choices. The classical school lost favor in part because of its rigid orientation toward punishing the crime and ignoring these individual circumstances. But it also lost momentum when immigration, industrialization, and urbanization during the late 1800s drove crime levels upward. The prevailing view in society was that the classical notions about criminal behavior and punishment were failing.

Although the classical approach was dormant for some time in criminological theory, it made a comeback in the 1970s, retooled as rational choice theory.[4] Are murderers rational? In 1990, 22-year-old Pamela Smart, a media services director at a New Hampshire high school, hired three students (including one who was her lover) to kill her husband, Greg. She was convicted and sentenced to life in prison for his calculated murder. Pamela Smart planned her husband's death in great detail. Her scheme included an affair with a teenage student, a staged burglary, an unlocked front door, disguises, and the decision to use a gun instead of a knife so there would be less blood on her white leather furniture. She even instructed the boys not to kill her husband in front of her beloved Shih Tzu, for fear that it would traumatize the little dog. From Smart's perspective, the murder of her husband was worth about $140,000 in life insurance and the couple's personal property. Smart avoided the death penalty but did receive a life sentence for first-degree murder.

For 42-year-old Wanda Holloway of Houston, Texas, a murder was worth planning if it meant that her eighth-grade daughter Shanna would get to become a high school cheerleader. Holloway asked Terry Harper, her former brother-in-law, to locate a hit-man. Her scheme was to arrange the murder of another girl's mother so that Shanna's chief rival would be too emotionally distraught to try out for the cheerleading squad. For Holloway, a human life was worth trading for a cheerleading spot for her daughter. Fortunately for the intended target, Harper told the police about Wanda Holloway's devious plot. The "cheerleader mom" was convicted of attempted murder-for-hire but served only six months of her 10-year sentence.

Most research on homicides illustrates that they are unlike the planned, premeditated murders discussed above, and rather are spontaneous, seemingly irrational events. How is it that day-to-day frustration so easily boils over into homicide? Are there factors at work that are not apparent to most of us? In *Seductions of Crime,* Jack Katz suggests that there are benefits of crime, even for what appears to be cold-blooded "senseless" murder.[5] Katz argues that the killers in these cases are often defending their own moral worth and social status, committing murder as a last attempt at gaining respectability in situations where humiliation is turned into rage. These offenders believe they can resolve their humiliation by destroying the source—a wife, a boss, fellow students, or society in general.

Research on serial medical murderers has determined that these killers get a thrill from taking the lives of their patients. They are playing God, deciding who lives and dies; and their murders make them feel superior to highly paid, highly trained doctors, to other medical personnel, to the victim, to the medical facility where they work, and to society in general. The killers might hold a marginal position in the structure of a hospital or a medical practice, but their secret homicides mean they are smarter and more powerful than anyone suspects. After all, they have smothered their patients with a pillow and/or have injected poison into their patients' IVs, but nobody suspects. They leave clueless doctors with the task of explaining a series of mysterious deaths to the victim's family.

Using Science to Explain Violence

Emerging in the late nineteenth century, *positivism*—as reflected in biology, psychology, sociology, and economics—employed scientific observation and measurement to explain criminal behavior. This approach was a shift away from free will and rational choice toward determinism. Why do people commit murder? Positivists believe that external factors cause criminal behavior. The first positivistic criminological theories were biological, and these were quickly followed by psychological and sociological explanations.

Most of the criminological explanations of homicide are not theories specific to homicide—they are broader, more general explanations of crimes ranging from shoplifting, drug use, and exam cheating to rape and murder. Moreover, even theories that try to explain why people kill aim to address the whole class of events, not just one case. Thus, we do not have a theory about why Ted Bundy was a serial killer (since theories are not designed to explain single cases), but a theory about serial killers or perhaps, even more broadly, murderers in general.

It is sometimes frustrating that we cannot definitively state what causes crime or violence. Criminology is a "soft" science; there are no certainties, but only likelihoods and probabilities. It is not a certainty that severe child abuse will create a murderer, but abuse is one of many factors that may increase the likelihood that someone will behave violently.

Biology Then and Now

The earliest biological theories of criminal behavior focused on body constitution, heredity, and intelligence. As early as the eighteenth century, scientific researchers were applying the techniques of physiognomy (the study of facial features) and phrenology (the study of bumps on the head) in search of clues to criminal behavior. Although not noted at the time, phrenology or "skull feeling" presents an interesting causal order problem: Did the bumps on the head cause the homicidal behavior? Or did a history of violent behavior leave the offender with bumps on the head? This "which came first" causal order dilemma haunts a number of biological theories, including theories about a possible link between violence and testosterone levels, head trauma, and premenstrual syndrome (PMS).

The apparent breakthrough to uncovering the secrets of criminal conduct came, in 1876, when an Italian physician, Cesare Lombroso, published his famous volume, *The Criminal Man,* advancing the premise of a "born criminal." Lombroso suggested that criminals are *atavistic*—they are a throwback to an earlier, more primitive evolutionary stage of human development, a notion influenced heavily by Charles Darwin's 1871 treatise, *The Origins of Man.* Lombroso, in his detailed empirical study of Italian prisoners, noted that criminals show outward signs of their differentness (known as *stigmata*), such as long arms, large ears, and sloping foreheads.

Although the theory has long since been discredited, Lombroso's work in criminal anthropology spirited a new tradition of empirical research, both in Europe and the United States, earning him the undisputed title as the father of modern criminology. Many followed Lombroso's lead in trying to expand or refute his theories. Richard Dugdale's study of the Jukes family and Henry Goddard's report on the Kallikak clan both suggested that criminal tendency, although not necessarily visible from physical characteristics, is an inherited condition that persists through generations of offspring. Even though the work of both Dugdale and Goddard has been rejected as unscientific, the idea that some people "look" like criminals (e.g., profiling) or that some families are genetically predisposed to violence is still part of contemporary thinking about the origin of criminal behavior.

Ernst Kretschmer and William Sheldon both attempted to use somatotyping, or constitutionalism, to classify body type and physique as indicators or correlates of various forms of human behavior, including criminality. In the 1940s, Sheldon suggested that the mesomorph somatotype (muscular and athletic) was more likely to be found in populations of violent criminals.

As late as the 1950s, Harvard University researchers Sheldon and Eleanor Glueck were including various body measurements in their multidisciplinary studies of the biological, psychological, and social factors distinguishing delinquents and nondelinquents. Although at the time social scientists sharply criticized the Gluecks for including biological traits among the thousands of variables they examined, years later their work was praised as one of the most significant multidisciplinary efforts ever undertaken to explain crime.[6]

Whatever momentum the biological school of criminological theory had retained went on life support during the sociologically dominated, humanistic climate of the 1960s. For most of the twentieth century, the field of criminology was *biophobic.* In more contemporary times, however, the biological approach (not nearly as dogmatic and narrow as in Lombroso's day) appears to have been resuscitated with the aid of new ideas and new technologies, allowing us to probe deeply into the bodies and brains of violent criminals. Modern biosocial theories of crime integrate biological variables such as learning disabilities, food allergies, neurological problems, and genetics within the social contexts of family structure, childrearing, abuse, and other factors.

Presenting a new twist to the "drugs cause crime" argument, various psychiatric drugs widely prescribed to treat depression and attention deficit disorder (ADD) have recently been suspected of triggering murderous behavior. Joseph Wesbecker, on the morning of September 14, 1989, went on a 20-minute rampage at the Standard Gravure printing plant in Louisville, Kentucky, where he had worked as a pressman for over two decades. Opening fire with an AK-47 assault weapon, Wesbecker shot to death eight of his co-workers and then took his own life. Some people tried to blame Wesbecker's deadly outburst on his longstanding struggle with depression. Others placed the blame squarely on the anti-depressant Prozac, which he had been taking for several weeks prior to the massacre.

Besides Wesbecker, there is a long list of other high-profile killers who were treated with psychiatric medications just before they committed senseless murders. On September 27, 1997, Sam Manzie, a 15-year-old boy from Freehold, New Jersey, who was being treated with the antidepressant Paxil, raped and strangled to death an 11-year-old boy in his neighborhood. On May 20, 1999, T.J. Solomon, a 15-year-old student at Heritage High School in Georgia who was taking Ritalin, opened fire on his classmates, wounding six of them. On May 21, 1998, Kip Kinkel, a 14-year-old boy from Springfield, Oregon, who took both Ritalin and Prozac, killed his parents and then launched a shooting spree through his high school. On April 20, 1999, 18-year-old Eric Harris of Littleton, Colorado, who was taking the anti-depressant Luvox, teamed up with his friend Dylan Klebold to perpetrate a horrific rampage at Columbine High School, killing 12 students and a teacher.

The case against psychiatric medications might be stronger if it were not for the fact that killers who were being treated at the time they committed murder typically had many of the usual warning signs associated with such crimes. In almost every case, there was good reason why a psychiatrist had prescribed a psychotropic drug: The killer had been profoundly depressed, disappointed, and discouraged about the future. Moreover, the actions of killers who commit a rampage are typically neither episodic nor spontaneous. Whatever role Prozac may have had in lifting the weight of depression and enabling him to take action, Wesbecker began preparing for mass murder, purchasing guns and making hit lists, six months before starting the medication. At most, the drug may have reduced his inhibitions, but hardly inspired him to kill. The Prozac controversy surrounding cases like Wesbecker's shooting spree affirms the importance of establishing causal order when attempting to explain how various factors may cause a murder.

In a four-year longitudinal study of antisocial boys, researchers at the University of Chicago Medical School discovered a biological propensity for violence.[7] Boys with histories of starting fights, stealing, carrying weapons, and engaging in forced sexual acts had lower-than-expected levels of the stress hormone cortisol (a hormone typically released in response to fear) in their saliva. More than one-third of the boys with low cortisol levels were identified by their peers as the "meanest in their class." Some researchers have also connected antisocial criminal behavior with high levels of the male hormone testosterone. Though studies have frequently confirmed this relationship, there is little evidence yet of a strong causal effect of testosterone on the propensity to commit criminal violence.[8] If the findings about testosterone, cortisol, or other important hormones are valid, then at least some violent children may have a biological predisposition for antisocial behavior, even youngsters who grow up in healthy, nonthreatening families. This predisposition may make them less fearful of the possible punishments for their antisocial behavior and also less amenable to counseling or therapy. At the extreme, some of these violent children may be inclined to commit homicide, regardless of the punishment they anticipate. Even if hormones do not have a profound influence on homicidal behavior, there is growing evidence of a biological basis for differences in the propensity for violence.

In another controversial area of biology, researchers in the 1960s purported to demonstrate that inmates in institutions for the criminally insane were significantly more likely to possess the "XYY syndrome." That is, they believed that as many as 100,000 men—so-called Super Males—were inclined to violence by virtue of an extra Y, or male sex, chromosome.[9]

The XYY anomaly for a while became a popular explanation for extreme forms of violence after it was erroneously reported that mass murderer Richard Speck possessed the extra Y chromosome. In July 1966, Speck had committed the "crime of the century" when he murdered eight student nurses in their Chicago apartment. Newspaper articles and even some scientific accounts reported that Speck's XYY constitution was apparent in such phenotypical characteristics as facial acne, tallness, long extremities, mild mental retardation, and a history of mental illness.

To this day, high school science teachers occasionally repeat the Richard Speck as Super Male mythology. However, we now know that very few violent criminals possess an extra Y chromosome. Those who actually have this genetic abnormality may be treated more harshly and be more likely institutionalized, often simply because of their abnormally awkward and substantial physical features. Thus, the disproportionate presence of XYYs in institutions for the criminally insane may be more a function of the way they look than the way they act.

This is not to say that chromosomes are unimportant in explaining differences in homicidal proneness. Clearly, males have a far greater propensity for committing senseless and extreme acts of violence than do females, a fact which seems to hold true almost universally, across virtually all cultures and time periods. Thus, it is more accurately the normal Y chromosome (the forty-sixth or male chromosome), not the extra Y (the forty-seventh or Super Male chromosome) that might make the vital difference.

Millions of Americans are the victims of some form of brain dysfunction involving epilepsy, mental retardation, ADD, hyperkinesis, minimal brain disorder, strokes, brain tumors, head injuries, or malnutrition. Clinical studies suggest that certain brain diseases or injuries can result in outbursts of anger and occasionally in episodes of violent behavior. In a Polish study, for example, researchers discovered an organic lesion to the central nervous system in 14 of 24 killers. Gross and Wilson similarly concluded that a large body of evidence points to an association between organic brain disorder and impulsive violence.[10] Generally, brain disorder cannot fully explain why a vengeful husband methodically plans the murder of his wife or why the members of an organized hate group commit a series of murders and robberies in the hope of inciting a race war; however, it may help to explain their predisposition toward pursuing violent solutions.

Only days after Richard Speck's mass murder of eight Chicago nurses, Charles Whitman's 1966 University of Texas tower sniper mass murder included 47 gunshot victims, 16 of whom died, including his wife and mother. Whitman's murders are often attributed to a brain tumor that was discovered at autopsy—a brain tumor that supposedly caused him to snap. However, Whitman was not simply the all-American boy who snapped. His murders were planned in advance, he had a history of drug abuse, a childhood filled with violence and exposure to guns, and a discharge from the military. Whitman failed in school, at jobs, and in the military. His one major accomplishment was his marksmanship.[11] The extent to which his brain tumor may or may not have played a role in his mass murder plans illustrates the complexities of disentangling biological, psychological, and social sources of homicidal behavior.

Diana Fishbein's research illustrates that antisocial behavior, including violence, is a result of various genetic and biological factors, but that these factors do not alone cause violence.[12] Rather, they interact with other psychological, environmental, and social conditions to produce aggression. A child born with brain systems that create the need for thrill-seeking, impulsive behavior, and a negative temperament may, under adverse social conditions, become aggressive. These negative conditions—stressors such as poverty or child abuse—act as triggers for violent behavior. Biological predispositions point to the importance of interdisciplinary work in the study of violence.

The policy implications of biological sources of crime can be frightening. The early Lombrosion and inheritance theorists recommended *eugenics*—the idea that some people would need to be sterilized or even euthanized because of their biological deficiencies. Although modern biological policy responses to aggression include less offensive treatments, including drugs and even vitamins, the dangerous notions of preventing violence by selective breeding, sterilization, castration, or euthanasia emphasize the importance of linking theory with sensible public policy. More recent and reasonable biosocial policy interventions include various chemotherapies (e.g., hormones, antidepressants, anticonvulsants), substance abuse treatment, and family and individual therapies. However, even these policy responses come with serious questions: Can we require people to be medicated? Can we medicate them involuntarily?

Another critical policy question spawned by biological theories of violence is that if the offender is a victim of a biological abnormality, to what extent should he or she be held accountable for criminal acts? Although the public may recognize the facilitating role played by various biological predispositions toward aggression, most people still want the offender to be punished, and they still believe the offender made a choice. Recent integrated theories of crime are sensitive to these issues by blending various biological, psychological, and sociological variables along with a component of individual choice.[13]

Psychological Causes of Violence

Biological, psychological, and sociological theories can be difficult to disentangle. For example, what causes someone to be a sociopath, a person who acts completely without conscience or remorse? While the biologist might point to the role of testosterone, cortisol, or adrenalin in the development of the antisocial personality disorder (i.e., sociopathy), some psychologists have long argued instead that antisocial behavior, and especially homicidal proneness, has its roots in early childhood.[14]

In particular, some youngsters are so brutalized—physically or sexually abused, neglected, abandoned, or adopted under extremely harsh circumstances—that they fail to develop a capacity to bond with other human beings.[15] There are differences in the defining characteristics of psychopaths and sociopaths. Psychopathy (the term typically used by psychologists) is usually defined by personality traits, whereas sociopathy (used by sociologists) is a combination of personality traits and behaviors. In any case, both of these terms have been replaced by the umbrella term *antisocial personality disorder* (APD). Illustrating another perspective that is both biological and psychological, Freud embraced the human nature viewpoint when he proposed that people have "an active instinct for hatred and destruction."[16] The psychoanalytic view of human nature suggests that all human beings are predisposed, given particular circumstances, to lash out at other people. Of course, most individuals never succumb to the temptation, especially not in the extreme case of committing murder.

Although few practicing criminologists adhere to Freudian traditions, Freudian theory in the form of "bonding" or "attachment therapy" is still a respected treatment method for troubled children.[17] As is the case with many therapies, positive outcomes are not always the result. In April 2000, 10-year-old Candace Newmaker was smothered during a "rebirthing" session conducted by therapists and her mother. The Freudian-based therapy was intended to give the troubled child a new bond and new beginning with her adoptive mother via the new birth—in this case, a child was suffocated and asphyxiated by five adults who were acting as a quasi-birth canal by crushing the girl with pillows. So far, two of Candace's therapists have been convicted of reckless child abuse in her death, and her mother pled guilty to abuse and neglect and received a suspended sentence.

Proponents of the field of *ethology* (the study of animals in their natural environment) also support the existence of an aggressive instinct—a natural urge to be violent and commit murder. Prominent ethologist and Nobel Prize winner Konrad Lorenz presented a large amount of evidence that animals are aggressive by nature.[18] He described, for example, the battles between male animals as they compete for females and the defensive behavior of a group of animals whose territory is invaded by another creature of the same species. He described the massacre that ensues when different colonies of insects or rodents are mixed together: they literally tear one another apart.

Lorenz argued that because humans evolve from violent animals, they must have inherited their destructive dispositions. Denying the possibility that behavior is primarily a reaction to environmental conditions, he asserted instead that it results from internal and spontaneous forces. External stimulation is often unnecessary. Lorenz assumed that aggression gives animals an advantage in the struggle for survival. He assumed further that human violence could be explained in the same way.

Erich Fromm suggested that Lorenz may have been only half right.[19] Fromm argued that *instrumental aggression*—violence as a means to an end—may indeed have roots in our biological heritage, being necessary for our survival as individuals and as a species. Instrumental aggression is self-defensive, protective, and, therefore, necessary. *Expressive aggression*—violence for its own sake—is, in Fromm's view, another story altogether. What Fromm called human destructiveness—sadistic aggressive behavior as an end in itself—is not instinctual, but completely learned in response to society's failure to satisfy the basic human needs of its members. According to Fromm, destructive aggression increases to the extent that society becomes civilized and therefore more out of touch with the basic human needs of its citizens. This theory loses its strength, of course, when we consider the highly violent nature of many past and present "less civilized" societies.

Recent psychological research suggests that there are many variables involved in explaining aggression, including both personal and environmental factors. This research finds that sensation-seeking personalities are susceptible to boredom, seek engagement in disinhibitive behaviors (e.g., alcohol use, partying), pursue unconventional lifestyles/

experiences (e.g., the use of LSD) and engage in thrill- and adventure-seeking behaviors (e.g., risky sporting activities). More specifically, the researchers find that sensation seekers are more likely to engage in aggressive behavior because it relieves their boredom and because these individuals also suffer from increased levels of hostility and anger. The researchers hypothesize a vicious cycle in which behaving aggressively over time causes others to respond negatively to them, which further contributes to the sensation seekers' hostility and anger.[20]

The work of evolutionary psychologists Daly and Wilson also blends biological and psychological factors. For these researchers, the psychological processes involved in the homicidal act are as much choice as they are a matter of thousands of years of experiences in human decision making. Why do we like sweets? Because thousands of years ago, our ancestors found out that foods with a sweet taste were rich in nutrients. Why are we so threatened by the infidelity of our mate? Is it perhaps because we don't want to spend our time caring for someone else's gene pool? Even personal ads are filled with the request for "no kids." Daly and Wilson's theory would help explain why the infidelity of a wife has historically been considered more serious than that of a husband. Men could spend resources caring for a child who, unbeknownst to them, was not biologically theirs. It is unlikely women could be tricked into doing the same. Humans with a common goal of survival of their genetic heritage make decisions that they believe will support their own self-interests—specifically, their genetic self-interests.[21]

Basing their conclusions about human behavior on animal studies, evolutionary psychologists have similarly contended that human violence is triggered by so-called selfish genes, which are propelled by a biological need to perpetuate themselves in one's offspring. If true, an individual would be less likely to eliminate people who are closely related by heredity—less likely to murder siblings than cousins, and less likely to kill cousins than unrelated strangers. It is self-defeating, according to the evolutionary psychology perspective, for individuals to murder those who share their genetic makeup.

Some researchers have used the sociobiological perspective to explain violence in stepfamilies. Stepparents have absolutely no biological investment in their spouses' children—even if they love them. Thus, we might expect parents to murder their stepchildren at a greater rate than they kill their biological offspring. If the sociobiologists are right, then stepfamilies should be at greater risk of violence than blood relatives. According to Daly and Wilson, the incidence of violence is indeed far greater in stepfamilies than in traditional families where the children are genetically related both to parents and to one another.[22] For example, Daly and Wilson determined that the rate of infanticide (the killing of young children) is 60 times higher in stepfamilies than in biologically connected families.

Daly and Wilson also suggested that homicides perpetrated by stepfathers differ from those by biological fathers not only quantitatively, but qualitatively as well. Biological fathers who kill their offspring are more likely to do so as a desperate act of twisted love before committing suicide. Stepfathers, however, rarely kill their children and then themselves. Moreover, stepfathers are more likely to beat their young stepchildren to death, whereas biological fathers are more likely to kill their youngsters with guns or asphyxiation, methods that do not require brute force.

Children's fables of wicked stepmothers have occasionally come true. Michelle Gauvin, 34, of Lafayette, Indiana was recently sentenced to life without parole for the

March 2005 murder of her 4-year-old stepdaughter, Aiyana. With the assistance of Aiyana's biological father, Michelle had repeatedly tied her stepdaughter to a chair, where she was paddled with a broken cutting board and whipped with a belt. After six months of brutal abuse, Aiyana died of trauma to her head.

We should keep in mind that murder is a rare phenomenon, of course, and the members of most stepfamilies do not harm one another. The theoretical task is to pinpoint the factors that increase the probability that rare instances of deadly violence are more likely to occur. Moreover, as is the case with all of our biological and psychological variables, there are social and environmental contexts that might explain differences in infanticide between biological and stepfamilies.

Is there a violent personality? The psychological perspective considers the relationship between various personality traits and aggressive behavior. Many people have taken the MMPI (Minnesota Multiphasic Personality Inventory) or other personality tests that attempt to measure traits such as introversion, hostility, suspicion, assertiveness, and impulsiveness. There should be no surprise that comparisons of inmate and student population personality inventories often show no significant differences since these are not mutually exclusive categories of people (students can become inmates, and vice versa). Although some researchers, such as the Gluecks, found significant personality differences between offenders and non-offenders, most research has been far less definitive regarding the violent personality. Rather than just one or two personality traits, some recent research has found that a set of personality traits may cluster together to create "negative emotionality," and this cluster of traits is more likely to be present in juvenile offenders. These traits include stress, excessive control, cowardice or bullying, approval seeking, jealousy, low self-esteem, fears of abandonment, moodiness, anger, immaturity, and suspicion.[23]

As we have seen, certain personality traits may manifest themselves, at least in part, in the social context. While one person who is an aggressive risk-taker grows up in a loving home, another person born with a similar set of personality characteristics may be raised in conditions of abuse or neglect. Additionally, if individuals with a personality or genetic predisposition toward risk taking are born into prosperous families, they may have legitimate ways to satisfy their need for thrill and excitement, for example by engaging in certain high-risk sports like skydiving. But if these same people are instead born into poor or dysfunctional families with no legitimate avenues to exercise risk-taking, the outcomes could be deadly and criminal.

Are most murderers mentally ill? If so, what kinds of mental illnesses do they tend to have? And what are the causes of these illnesses? There is some empirical connection between some mental illnesses and criminal behaviors, but the association is not clear. Psychiatric patients report more violent behavior than community residents who are not part of a psychiatric patient group. One possible explanation for the link between mental illness and violent behavior has been offered by the research of Bruce Link and his colleagues (1999). This research proposes that psychotic patients are more likely to feel threatened by others, even if there is no actual threat. In addition, if these patients suffer from delusions that they are being persecuted or controlled by others (e.g., their minds and thoughts are being dominated by forces beyond their control and they believe that there are people who wish to do them harm), they are more likely to engage in violent, aggressive behavior.[24] Psychosis is clearly an extreme form of mental illness; most forms of mental illness are not associated with violence (e.g., depression, bipolar disorders, anxiety, phobias). Indeed, most mentally ill people never hurt or kill anyone.

Furthermore, the link between mental illness and crime may be indirect. If people suffering from mental illness are more likely to self-medicate with drugs and alcohol, it could be that substance abuse is the key to their violent behavior, rather than the mental illness itself. Also, to the extent that violent behavior and mental illness are both linked to such background factors as child abuse, trauma, and neglect, then the apparent association between homicide and mental illness may be spurious or misleading.

Finally, if mental illness were determined to be a strong predictor of violent behavior, then what should our policy response be? Should it be mandatory psychiatric treatment and medication (e.g., chemical lobotomies) for violent offenders? Should these perpetrators be institutionalized in mental hospitals rather than prisons?

Postpartum psychosis (PPP) has been linked to several cases of mothers who murder their children. Andrea Yates, 36, is the Texas mother who drowned her five children, ranging in age from 6 months to 7 years old, because, she said, the voice of the Devil commanded her to do so. Like many cases of PPP, Yates had a history of depression, suicide attempts, and other mental health risk factors. While most women who give birth suffer from some degree of baby blues, 10 to 15 percent of these women have the more severe PPP. The risk factors for PPP include a personal or family history of mental health issues, such as depression, anxiety, obsessive-compulsive disorder, panic attacks, bipolar disorder, marital conflicts, previous episodes of post-partum depression or psychosis, hormonal risks, and certain characteristics of the baby, including the infant's health, personality, and disability.[25] The homicides of children as a result of the mother's PPP, as with many other forms of mental illness, appear to draw on biological, psychological, and situational forces that come together at the time of the birth to produce a pathological state of mind.

A psychological dimension that does appear to be associated with at least one type of murderer, the serial killer, is the presence of some *paraphilias*—sexual attractions to unusual or bizarre objects. Obviously, not all paraphilias are linked to murder (e.g., exhibitionism, cross-dressing, or foot fetishes). However, several sexual proclivities, such as pedophilia and necrophilia, necessitate criminal behavior that may in some cases also lead to murder. Because of his sexual craving for corpses, Jeffrey Dahmer committed a string of brutal murders, after first lobotomizing his victims to create zombie-like sex partners. Although necrophilia is obviously a mental disorder, the State of Wisconsin did not believe that Dahmer's necrophilia was so incapacitating to sustain his insanity plea. While paraphilias represent distortions in what a person perceives to be sexually arousing, they are generally not the kind of profound distortions in thinking or perception that would mitigate criminal responsibility. Paraphilias seem to cluster—in other words, people with one paraphilia (e.g., a sexual attraction to gas masks, fur, or human excrement), typically have more than one.

One of the most hotly debated topics related to criminality is whether low intelligence predicts criminal and violent behavior. As early as the 1920s, Goddard and several other psychologists were applying the new Simon-Binet intelligence quotient (IQ) in their studies of criminal populations.[26] In Congressional testimony, they argued that Americans needed protection from the "worthless" Eastern and Southern European immigrants who scored lower on intelligence tests than their counterparts from Western and Northern Europe. This work reflected a history of feeblemindedness profiling that lasted at least from 1900 through the 1930s. In 1907, Indiana passed the first eugenics law allowing for state-authorized sterilizations; many other states followed with their own, sometimes even more aggressive, laws. Lasting until the 1960s, many states had mandatory sterilization laws for residents of mental institutions, welfare moms, the retarded, and epileptics. Not until 2003 did the state of North Carolina abolish its 74-year-old eugenics law that allowed the state (among other things) to sterilize a woman without her consent based on the conclusion that she was feebleminded. Thus, the IQ debate and the frightful social policy that flows from it have a long checkered past in the annals of criminological theory.

Notwithstanding the questionable policy responses, quality scientific research, such as the work of Sheldon and Eleanor Glueck in *Unraveling Juvenile Delinquency,* has indeed found IQ to be a significant predictor of delinquency. As recently as 1977, criminologists Travis Hirschi and Michael Hindelang observed IQ to be a stronger predictor of delinquency than either social class or race.[27] It is in large part because of racial differences in IQ that the relationship between intelligence and crime is so politically volatile. Research conducted 40 years ago speculated that IQ differences between whites and blacks could be genetic, and that the genetic "inferiority" of blacks, in turn, may be related to their higher rates of poverty and criminality.[28]

While many critics viewed this type of work as misguided and reflective of political ideologies, the publication in 1994 of *The Bell Curve* by two respected Harvard researchers, Charles Murray and Richard Herrnstein, kept the IQ issue alive, at least in the public mind.[29] Murray and Herrnstein reported significant differences in intelligence among races, but they were unable, like their predecessors, to rule out important educational differences and racism as factors that could account for these disparities.

The controversy surrounding whether IQ is a significant predictor of violent crime as well as the debate about the factors influencing IQ remain unresolved, even after a half-century of research. Why would we expect IQ to predict violence? Do we believe that people with a low IQ could be more easily convinced by others to kill someone, or that they are too unintelligent to see viable solutions other than murder? Does low IQ leave people with such limited means of earning money that they kill because of the frustration of being poor or as part of their menial job? Perhaps the strongest possible link between IQ and violence would be in the extent to which IQ affects a person's ability to perceive consequences and make informed choices.[30] As with many other biological and psychological variables, IQ also fails to account for significant gender, seasonal, regional, and age variations in homicide.

Obviously, very low intelligence can restrict a person's ability to understand right from wrong, but the association between low IQ and the will to kill remains dubious. Studies of IQ and crime are generally performed on convicted offenders. And since more than one-third of murders are unsolved, perhaps it is the more intelligent offenders who are less likely to be caught, convicted and, therefore, studied.

Whether they be Freudian factors, personality traits, mental illness, natural aggression, or IQ, the psychological variables reviewed here are characteristics of individuals. Thus, to some extent, criminal justice responses and punishments need to be individually tailored as well. Yet many citizens and policymakers are not comfortable with therapies or sanctions that vary from individual offender to individual offender. However, based on what we know about individual biological and psychological predispositions toward violence, overly rigid punishment responses that treat all offenders in the same way may be questionable in terms of their fairness or appropriateness.

The Social Sources of Murder

Rather than the individual-specific variables of biological and psychological positivism, sociologists look for the origins of crime and violence in the external world. Characteristics of neighborhoods, poverty, subcultural value systems, learning, and lack of social bonds to others reflect the important variables of twentieth-century criminology. Sociological positivism began with theories that attempted to explain the high crime rates in lower-class urban areas. From the early 1900s through the 1950s, criminological theory operated on the assumption that crime is predominantly a problem of lower-class areas and its residents. While these early theories may have been useful in explaining the activities of lower-class boys who joined urban gangs, they were obviously inadequate to explain homicides that did not involve offenders from a lower economic class.

Social disorganization theory focused on the factors that weaken communities— mobility, heterogeneity, and poverty—rather than biological or psychological deficiencies in the residents of those communities. Transience and poverty combine to create conditions such that no matter who lives there, those areas will have higher crime rates.[31] In social disorganization theory, the causes of violent behavior are the very factors that lead to social disorganization. Clearly, this sort of theory would be most useful for explaining felony murders or even homicides that result from an argument on the street corner, but would fail to explain murder committed by middle- and upper-class offenders.

Some researchers have retooled social disorganization theory to incorporate many area-level variables other than mobility, poverty, and heterogeneity. These so-called "social ecology theories" still focus on the characteristics of areas and how some areas may be particularly fertile ground for crime and violence. For example, the recent "broken windows" approach to policing—cleaning up the neighborhood to eradicate conditions that breed lawlessness and disorder—is based in part on ideas from social disorganization theory.[32] These types of community-level explanations are particularly helpful in understanding why certain areas of cities have a disproportionate share of homicides.

In 2006, many cities across the U.S. began to see increases in their homicide rates. These increases were typically not citywide, but rather were concentrated in certain parts of the community. The view that bad neighborhoods can foster conditions that lead to violence amongst residents can be seen in policy responses that mirror the social disorganization perspective. The addition of street lights in high homicide areas, along with neighborhood clean-ups and the destruction of abandoned houses, all point to efforts to reduce the social disorganization of an area. These strategies are often coupled with an increased police presence and more aggressive policing—all strategies to fix an area, replacing disorder with order.

Social scientists have long recognized that absolute levels of unemployment or income do not necessarily translate into a subjective feeling of misery. The impact of economic variables on *feelings* of deprivation or frustration—especially at levels that promote murder—depends at least to some extent on an individual's standards of comparison. On both individual and aggregate levels, criminologists focus on relative deprivation by asking: How much status and salary do individuals enjoy relative to the amount of prestige and money they had five or 10 years earlier? How much money do they earn relative to their friends, neighbors, and other significant people in their lives? To what extent has the unemployment rate risen or fallen over time? How wide is the income gap between rich and poor, and how does income inequality across countries and over time correlate with rates of murder?

Downward mobility—the very process of losing economic ground—may contribute to individuals' feelings of deprivation, even if they are millionaires.[33] As a cohort, those baby boomers who entered the labor force during the late sixties and seventies may experience a sense of losing economic ground even at a time when the unemployment rate is very low. Since the early 1970s, the income gap between the haves and the have-nots has continued to widen, resulting in a shrinking middle class. At the bottom of the socioeconomic ladder, the level of permanent, inter-generational poverty in major U.S. cities, often referred to as the underclass and the "truly disadvantaged," has not abated.[34] According to a recent study by the Economic Policy Institute and the Center on Budget and Policy Priorities, income inequality has been on the rise. During the late 1970s, there was not one state in which the wealthiest 20 percent earned 9.5 times more than the poorest 20 percent. At this juncture, however, the "top to bottom ratio" exceeds 9.5 in nearly half the states and continues to rise in all states but Alaska, Louisiana, and Tennessee. It seems that prosperity has not had the same impact throughout the class structure. Instead, it has pushed rich and poor Americans further and further apart. Downward mobility has been particularly steep for displaced manufacturing workers who, since the 1970s, have found themselves stuck in service-sector jobs that pay less and have fewer fringe benefits. More recently, a bull market made the wealthy even wealthier and further widened the disparity between rich and poor. The median income of families in the top 20 percent of income distribution is now more than 10 times larger than the median income of the poorest 20 percent.[35]

Cross-national comparisons have often failed to uncover any relationship between aggregate rates of unemployment and homicide. At least at the national level, the unemployment rate seems to have little, if anything, to do with differences in murder rates across countries. Comparing income inequality across nations yields quite a different result, however. Specifically, countries with high levels of income inequality, such as the United States, also tend to have high rates of homicide.[36] Still, as income inequality has continued to increase over the past decade in the United States, homicide rates have declined. Thus, income inequality may help explain cross-national differences in homicide rates but does not seem to be a reliable tool for explaining recent fluctuations in homicide rates within the United States.

Principles of psychology and sociology, rather than economics, might explain the differential impact of unemployment and income inequality on murder rates. When joblessness prevails, many citizens feel that everyone is in the same sinking boat. Economic misery may therefore not be tied to feelings of inequity or unfairness (i.e., things are bad, but at least they are bad for everyone). Under conditions of income inequality, however, citizens find themselves in different boats, some much larger and more lavish than others. A few even own luxury yachts while many others have merely rowboats that are rapidly taking on water. Those individuals who are left behind—even if their boats are bigger than ever before—feel as though they are victims of economic injustice. Compared with wealthy segments of their society, they are losing ground and feel relatively deprived.

Strain, Frustration, and Murder

In 2002, Thomas Junta, the father of a youth hockey player, was sentenced to six to 10 years in prison for what has become the latest trend—parents' sports rage. Junta beat another player's father, Michael Costin, to death, because he believed that Costin's son had been unnecessarily rough on the ice against his son. Their sons, as well as other 10-year-olds, witnessed the beating that started inside and ended up outside the rink. Junta claimed self-defense and there was, in fact, evidence of a violent history for the victim. Yet, clearly the judge and jury thought that Junta's anger had spilled over into unjustified rage and violence. This is but one of the many cases in which we find drivers, airplane passengers, and parents losing control over trivial frustrations and resorting to aggression and violence.

The concept of *frustration-aggression* has had a powerful influence on the field of criminology. In 1939, a group of Yale University psychologists focused on the effects of frustration—an unpleasant psychological state resulting from the failure to satisfy some need or desire—on aggressive behavior.[37] They proposed that frustration and aggression are inextricably connected. In what became famous as the "frustration-aggression hypothesis," they argued that frustration always causes some form of aggression, and that aggression is always preceded by frustration. Thus, anything that interferes with an individual's movement toward a goal—whether it is as minor as waiting for a long red light to change or as major as failing to earn enough money to feed one's children—will inevitably lead to the expression of aggression, including murder.

Notwithstanding the original conceptualization, frustration is not necessarily followed by aggression (or else, few of us would make it home each day). When is frustration followed by aggression? When people think they can get away with it, when there are no police around, when they don't care what parents, teachers, or significant others think, when they are drinking, or when the frustration is extreme. All of these scenarios illustrate the obvious contextual factors that facilitate or limit how the state of frustration manifests itself. Thus, although humans may descend from a long line of aggressors, societal pressures or controls can increase or decrease the expression of those instincts.

Though the original frustration-aggression hypothesis may have been overstated, it is not without some validity. Aggressive behavior does tend to increase when people are prevented from reaching a goal they expect to attain. There are people who yell at their children after a bad day at the office; there are men who punch the wall after being dumped by a girlfriend. At the extreme, some individuals have annihilated their ex-spouse and children because of a nasty divorce and custody battle. Others have murdered their supervisor after being fired from a job. A few students have been so frustrated with school that they have gunned down their teachers and classmates.

Clearly, we now know that the progression from frustration to aggression is not inevitable. For a variety of reasons other than biology, many people deal with the frustrations of daily life without harming or killing others. Indeed, commuters are much more likely to wait patiently for a long light to change or seek a faster route home than to shout obscenities or shoot another driver, even though some motorists do vent their feelings of road rage. People are more likely to change jobs or seek training for higher paying work than to stab their boss or a family member. Frustration does not always lead to aggression. More likely, people learn to develop coping skills in responding to the frustrations of everyday life.

Not only does aggression not follow every frustrating episode, but just as clearly, frustration does not precede every aggressive action. There are countless examples of violence that occur in the absence of any especially frustrating circumstances. For example, a soldier engages in combat because he is ordered to do so by his commanding officer. A young child shoots his playmate after seeing a gunfight on television. A hit man for the mob eliminates the leader of a rival "family" because he was paid to do so.

The tendency for frustration to lead to aggression is greatest when the frustration is severe and unexpected—that is, if people are deprived of something important that they were certain of getting such as a promised promotion that falls through at the last moment. The tendency is also greater when people believe they can get away with being aggressive— when they do not anticipate being punished in return or being rejected by their friends and associates. For example, a child is more likely to bully his playmates if he thinks none of them will stand up to him and that his parents will not find out.[38]

In 1960, Stuart Palmer studied 51 convicted murderers to determine whether severe frustrations suffered during childhood might have led them to commit murder later in their lives.[39] To provide a comparison group of similar men who had not killed anyone, Palmer also studied the nearest-in-age brother of each murderer. He found that the 51 convicted killers had indeed experienced more intense frustrations than had their brothers who were not convicted of murder. Specifically, the convicted murderers were more likely to have been dissatisfied with their prestige or status, to have suffered physical defects, to have done poorly in school, and to have had fewer friends. In short, they had led "dismal, unprestigious, frustrating lives." Illustrating an extremely deadly response to frustration, a number of the more infamous mass murderers—including Mark Barton, who slaughtered nine and injured a dozen others at two Atlanta investment offices in 1999 after losing a fortune in the stock market—suffered "reward withdrawal" or status loss before their violent rampages.

In the concept of *strain,* Robert Agnew has transformed the frustration-aggression hypothesis into a much broader concept.[40] In his *general strain theory* (GST), Agnew proposes that criminal violence is a result of strain—frustration, but also anger, disappointment, fear, or depression—that originates in destructive social ties. He identifies four important sources of strain: a) the presence of negative stimuli (e.g., child abuse, peer rejection, school failure, or physical punishment); b) the removal of positive stimuli (e.g., death of a loved one, parents' divorce, or residential mobility); c) perception of inequity (e.g., peers who make more money or get better grades because they have "connections"); and d) failure to achieve desired goals (e.g., missing out on success because of a lack of educational opportunities).

Strain theory was originally an attempt to explain why certain areas have higher crime rates. In his classic analysis, Robert Merton recognized that strain can be institutionalized in the misalignment of institutionalized goals and culturally prescribed means.[41] According to U.S. cultural values learned from an early age, all members of society are expected to strive for economic success. Yet, there is far less emphasis in U.S. society on providing the structural opportunities for achieving that success. This disparity invites what Merton refers to as "innovation": when an individual accepts the cultural emphasis on the success goal, but rejects the socially acceptable means for its attainment. In some cases, an individual will substitute illegitimate (often illegal) but more effective methods of securing wealth and power. For middle-class deviants, the pressure to innovate might take the form of unethical business practices and white-collar crime. But for members of society lacking in education and economic resources, innovation more frequently becomes street crime, including gang membership, drug dealing, property offenses, and violence.

In the spirit of strain theory, Steve Messner and Richard Rosenfeld's recent work, *Crime and the American Dream,* suggested that the breakdown of social institutions regulating behavior (churches, schools, and families) has contributed to elevated levels of crime in the United States.[42] For Messner and Rosenfeld, the economy has become the dominant force controlling behavior and has dwarfed any other institution's ability to curb crime. Families are run like businesses, and roles that don't generate income (e.g., stay-at-home moms) are not valued. In a society where the pursuit of material success is valued above all else, we should not be surprised to witness a crime wave like the crack-related homicide epidemic of the late-1980s.

Cultural Deviance

Cultural deviance theories (also called *subcultural theories*) do not contend that criminals are necessarily strained, but that they obey the norms they were taught—rules of behavior that just happen to differ from those of the law. In other words, criminals learn different codes of right and wrong. Wolfgang and Ferracuti long ago proposed that higher homicide rates among young men, in the lower classes, among blacks, and in the South may have a cultural basis. They are a result of a "subculture of violence," in which violent behavior, even murder, is regarded as an appropriate and rewarded response to a menacing situation (for example, a threatening glance, a jostle, an insulting comment, or the presence of a weapon).[43] In this subculture, violence is a norm to which everyone is expected to comply, and those who do so are accorded high status and respect. According to subculture of violence theorists, under such cultural conditions, murder becomes more likely.

The subcultural explanation for southern homicide patterns is supported by evidence showing that murders occurring in the South are more likely than those in other regions to arise from arguments between people who know each other.[44] These confrontations typically escalate when the reputation or honor of an individual is impugned by an insulting remark. Also supporting the subcultural perspective is evidence that southerners, more than residents of other regions, approve of using defensive violence against people who pose a serious threat to their personal safety, rather than seeking nonviolent alternatives.[45]

There are many different versions of cultural deviance theory, but they all embrace the argument that homicide offenders have learned a set of values and beliefs that promote the use of violence.[46] These individuals are more willing to use physical force to settle disputes and, according to the cultural deviance perspective, this response is learned. The idea that someone perceives a verbal slight as 'fightin' words' is often used in explanations of gang-related homicides. Although most of the fundamental premises of subcultural theory make sense, these theories have received little empirical support, as the variables associated with violence are more likely to be structural or situational than cultural. Rather than a "southern subculture of violence," the source of higher homicide rates in the South could just as likely result from such factors as poverty, income inequality, racial segregation, religiosity, weather, alcohol and drug use, and gun ownership.[47]

Learning to Kill

Some criminologists would argue that it is not primarily the bad neighborhood, strain, or exposure to a subculture that creates the propensity for violence, but rather that people learn to kill one another. Forms of violence vary tremendously from culture to culture, and violent behavior does not occur at all in some, although these instances are more of an anomaly. Few people today would suggest that the propensity to kill is totally inborn, and criminologists recognize the occasional but rare instance of a group that has very little, if any, violence.

Social learning theory offers another approach to explaining individual and social differences in the propensity to commit acts of extreme violence. According to this theory, most aggressive behavior involves skills that we must learn from others.[48] We learn to be violent (or learn to be a victim) not only through rewards and punishments, but also through the role models we imitate. Clearly, significant people around us may serve as models of learning in many other areas of life—for example, in acquiring language, using facial expressions, and dressing for various occasions. In a similar fashion, imitation may also occur in learning violent behavior, even behavior as violent as homicide.

Some have suggested that the mass media generally, and television in particular, could provide powerful models for aggressive conduct. Obviously, the vast majority of people exposed to violent media do not behave violently at all. There are clearly some people who seize upon this sort of media as a model for their own behavior, yet there are likely a number of other stronger causal factors at work for these people. There is very little scientific evidence that supports a causal link between violent or pornographic media and aggressive behavior.[49]

Rather than the media, many learning theories have focused on arguably the stronger influence of the day-to-day interactions that we all have with others. Models for murder can be located in the groups to which an individual belongs. Edwin Sutherland's *differential association theory* contends that criminal behavior is learned during adolescence from an individual's most intimate social relations—his peers, family, and friends. In addition to learning attitudes supporting violence, individuals acquire criminal skills through these associations (no one is born knowing how to roll a joint, hotwire a car, make a bomb, or use a gun). In addition, individuals learn by observing group members who violate the law, from shoplifting and taking illicit drugs to armed robbery and murder. To the extent that people associate with others who regard criminal behavior in a positive light, they are also excluded from associating with those who reject the criminal lifestyle. Just as they learn a host of important values, individuals adopt the criminal attitudes and behavior of their intimate associates.[50]

In a more recent version of social learning theory, Akers blended differential association with conditioning effects of rewards and punishments to explain the development of criminality.[51] In his *differential reinforcement theory*, Akers suggests that the acceptance of violence does not come merely from associating with a particular group of intimates, but from associating with a group whose members reinforce violent behavior and punish law-abiding behavior. According to Akers, offenders learn violence in several different ways from group members—by observing and imitating the deviant behavior of others, by being rewarded and praised by group members for engaging in deviant behavior, and by acquiring attitudes from group members that support and stimulate deviant behavior. The significant level of empirical support for learning theories should give us pause about the criminogenic effects of incarceration—if prisons aren't schools for crime, then perhaps they are at least study halls.

Lonnie Athens also suggests that criminals are trained and conditioned to be violent through a process he calls *violentization.* Athens, a criminologist, grew up in a very violent world, and his theory is grounded in his personal experiences as well as extensive, qualitative interviews with violent offenders. According to this theory, offenders experience their own brutalization early in life and are coached into belligerence by others. They learn to use violence to gain respect and frighten others and, finally, to use violence in order to get what they want and to bond with others who feel similarly.[52]

Self-Control, Social Control, and Murder

Still another theoretical perspective hypothesizes that virtually all criminal behavior is a result of a lack of control rather than a function of learning. *Control theories* envision a set of controls or bonds that work to limit involvement in criminal behavior. But control theory also takes account of the fact that not everyone's moral sense prevents them from committing acts of criminal violence. Hirschi argued that criminality is often controlled by an individual's commitments and attachments to conventional institutions, beliefs, activities, and groups.[53] Many people refrain from engaging in violent behavior because they fear losing their relationships with significant others—with family, friends, and peers. However, members of society who lack strong social ties may also lack the motivation to become law-abiding citizens. In this theory, a person would commit violence or murder when he or she had no controlling influence from attachments to others, commitments to conventional behavior, involvements in conventional activities, and belief in the morality of the law—in a sense, nothing left to lose.

Similarly, Sampson and Laub suggested that the ability of people to form bonds and connections through stable relationships and job and career opportunities may protect them from committing criminal acts and even provide a way for the criminal to go straight.[54] Furthermore, Gottfredson and Hirschi, in their book *A General Theory of Crime,* pointed to the importance of parental love, supervision, and consistent discipline in the formation of self-control. This theory not only seeks to explain why someone might be a shoplifter or serial killer (both would primarily be a function of low self-control and opportunity), but can also be used to explain a host of other maladaptive behaviors such as gambling, alcohol and drug use, financial irresponsibility, interpersonal relationship problems, smoking, and eating disorders. Part of the appeal of the Gottfredson and Hirschi perspective is that the theory incorporates biological, psychological, and sociological variables within a context of opportunities.

An important insight provided by control theory is that commitment or attachment to conventional individuals and institutions inoculates human beings from committing violent offenses. Regrettably, in recent years some Americans have suffered a sharp decline in close bonds with others in their communities. Those areas that have large numbers of individuals lacking in social bonds—the very poor, the drug-addicted, the unemployed, drifters, transients, migrants, and newcomers—also tend to have high rates of crime, including murder.

Years ago, in an early version of control theory, Walter Reckless described the factors that encourage criminal behavior as a set of "pushes and pulls."[55] Consistent with Reckless' perspective, we have discussed in this chapter a number of conditions that can push an individual away from conventional society—for example, being frustrated by poor grades or parental disapproval when not "measuring up" in the conventional sense; having a personality disorder characterized by lack of remorse and empathy; feeling distant from conventional goals, institutions, or individuals; or suffering from repeated head traumas, a disorder that can make everyday functioning difficult. Other factors reviewed in this chapter pull individuals toward murderous behavior—for example, growing up in a subculture in which violence is seen as a virtue; finding social support with a group of friends who engage in criminal behavior; or finding models (fictional or factual) whose murderous behavior is rewarded. In explaining the will to kill, we might then search for the presence of the forces that both pull individuals away from conventional society and push them toward the crime of murder.

A Word of Caution about Cause

Having reviewed in this chapter a wide range of theories, summarized in Table 2.1, all purporting to explain murderous intentions and other violent behavior, we may have left a rather confusing image of the variables responsible for murder. Certainly, each theory has limitations. Most have been criticized, if not condemned, for their shortcomings and flaws.

It is wise to keep in mind that even good theories that have been tested and validated with empirical research cannot account for the full variety of human behavior. Good theories can explain some cases of homicide, but not all forms of homicidal proneness, no matter which variables are used.

The important notion that correlation does not imply causation is virtually a mantra of social science research. For example, blacks have significantly higher rates of committing murder than do whites, but this correlation is not necessarily the impact of race itself; instead, it is likely a result of a host of socioeconomic conditions associated with race.

In addition, correlation also does not guarantee predictability. Men have rates of committing homicide many times higher than women. Yet, though most killers are male, most males do not kill. Theories that reduce a murderous response to the impact of a single variable fail to recognize the complexity of the will to kill. Even elaborate models that predict murder based on demographics, family patterns, peer groups, and other factors fail more than they succeed in identifying killers. The best they can do is to pinpoint those at greatest risk, usually *after* they have already committed serious crimes. What society would do with these high-risk individuals if we could predict their future behavior then becomes an important ethical and policy question.

TABLE 2.1   Selected Theories of Violence and Homicide

Theory and Dates	Selected Proponents	Key Concepts	Policy Implications
Supernatural Through the late 1600s		Demonic possession, evil spirits, witchcraft and the Devil cause crime	Torture and execution drive out evil; chaos, cruelty and anarchy characterize punishments for crime
Classical Mid 1700s–late 1800s	Beccaria and Bentham	Violent behavior is a result of choice and free will, reasoning, decision making, and assessment of pain versus gain	Deterrence through certain, swift and proportional punishment; utilitarian-based notion of justice
Biological Late 1800s–1960s	Lombroso, Garafalo, Goddard, Dugdale and Sheldon	Criminals have a physical and/or genetic inferiority that predisposes them to criminal behaviors; includes atavism, criminal anthropology, genetics, body types, and XYY chromosome	Eugenics; sterilization; feeblemindedness profiling; psychosurgery
Psychoanalytic 1920s–present	Freud	Unconscious motives and repression drive criminal behavior; deviant behavior is linked to inadequate development of personality components in early childhood as a result of abuse, neglect, extreme permissiveness, or unconditional love	Psychoanalysis to relieve overactive id, neurosis, and psychosis
Psychological and Psychiatric Early 1900s–present	Lorenz, Fromm, Skinner, Bandura, Eysenck, and Herrnstein & Murray	Aggression is a response to frustration; aggression is a result of imitation, modeling and rewards for violence; violence is linked to mental illness, personality disorders or low IQ	Counseling, drug therapy, and behavior modification to treat violence as an individual-level phenomenon
Rational Choice Mid 1970s–present	Clarke, Cornish, and Katz	Classical notions of free will combined with positivistic variables; offenders choose to be violent but certain variables influence the ability to make reasoned choices	Target hardening; situational crime prevention; displacement; classical punishment responses with more focus on severe punishments
Social Disorganization and Social Ecology 1920s–present	Shaw & McKay, Bursik, and Sampson	Disorganized areas breed criminal influences	Employment and educational opportunities; neighborhood revitalization; positive role models; strong families and schools

(continued)

TABLE 2.1   Continued

Theory and Dates	Selected Proponents	Key Concepts	Policy Implications
Cultural Deviance 1920s–present	Wolfgang & Ferracuti, Cohen, Miller, and Cloward & Ohlin	Some groups/individuals have different value systems; different socialization forms the foundation for subculture or gang support for violence	Positive role models; legitimate educational and economic opportunities
Strain 1930s–present	Merton, Agnew, and Messner & Rosenfeld	Frustration results from blocked legitimate opportunities; crime and delinquency is an individual adaptation or coping mechanism in response to strain; economic success is a primary form of institutional control	Focus on values and institutions other than financial success (family, church and school); provide psychological and structural opportunities for success
Social Learning 1930s–present	Sutherland, Burgess, Akers, Phillips, and Athens	People learn to commit violent acts; violence continues if reinforced; peer groups influence modeling; highlights copycat offending and media influences	Positive role models and relearning non-criminal values and strategies
Social and Self Control 1950s–present	Reckless, Hirschi, Gottfredson & Hirschi, and Grasmik	People must be socialized to resist pushes and pulls towards crime; delinquency as a result of weakened bonds to society; proper parental supervision, love and discipline develops self-control in children; self-control as the ability to control natural tendencies	Encourage bonding and attachment to conventional others; increase individual stakes in conformity
Integrated 1950s–present	Gluecks, Daly & Wilson, Murray & Herrnstein, Fishbein, Gottfredson & Hirschi, and Sampson & Laub	Biological predispositions create conditional free will; unchangeable latent traits; malleable developmental and life-course approaches	Combined modalities (drugs, counseling, family intervention); educational opportunities; possibilities for marriage, family, and career to redirect criminals

In this chapter, we have offered a taste of the many perspectives and theoretical traditions that have been invoked in attempts to explain and predict violence, in general, and homicide, in particular. Any effort to survey completely and in depth the broad array of theories for homicidal proneness would fill volumes, and already has. In 1988, the National

Academy of Sciences commissioned an expert panel on violence to describe in some detail the multitude of causal theories.[56] Even after the publication of the panel's four volumes of research findings, our understanding and ability to explain, much less predict, extreme violence is still quite limited. Human behavior is complex, and the linkages between biological, psychological, and sociological stimuli and the subsequent homicidal response are much more complicated and difficult to identify than the movements of laboratory mice in search of a piece of cheese at the finish line of a circuitous maze.

After all that has been researched and written on the topic of homicide, which disciplinary tradition has the most to contribute in explaining why some people kill and others do not? Does the abnormal psychology of the murderer or his physical constitution hold greater insights into the mystery of murder? Are the bad schools, bad parents, and/or bad peers more telling?

The simple answer to these difficult questions is: it depends. It is likely that all of these notions have some merit—not to understand all kinds of murder, but perhaps some discrete subset. A focus on head trauma or environmental toxins may help us to comprehend sudden and uncharacteristic outbursts of murderous rage, but will do little to account for cold-blooded acts of murder for hire. Learning theories of social psychology and sociological hypotheses pertaining to social class and social structure are valuable for understanding serious gang violence, but may be inadequate for interpreting infanticide. Violence has many sources, and an integrated theoretical approach that includes an array of biological, psychological, sociological variables will be best suited to explain it.

Regardless of the theoretical approach, we often think of causation in terms of some form of deficiency, deviation, or defect. A "bad seed," diseased brain, poor parenting, maltreatment, drug side effect, running with a bad crowd, exposure to harmful media, poor opportunities, bad days, and bad breaks are all valuable notions, but none alone is generally sufficient to drive a person to kill. Even a person struggling with a combination of biological, psychological, or sociological abnormalities (such as a learning-disabled child raised by an impoverished and unconcerned single parent, who plays violent video games with his delinquent buddies) has an ability to make a choice, though it may be limited by his various handicaps. While our options and opportunities in life are impacted by a host of advantages and disadvantages, virtually all of us have some degree of free will. Human beings have choices in how to respond when the rewards we have come to expect are suddenly withdrawn or unavailable. By nature of heredity and nurture of environment, some individuals are more prone to violence than others, yet free will still exists. The will to kill, though governed by numerous internal and external forces, still includes choice and human decision making, and thus accountability and culpability.

Why does one person harm another? In the case of 58-year-old Mary Kay Gray, it was because her husband shot her pet chicken. In September of 2006, the Oregon woman and her husband had been drinking on Labor Day and doing yard work. After Mr. Gray shot the chicken with a .44, an argument commenced and Mrs. Gray shot Mr. Gray in the shoulder with a .22 caliber rifle. Authorities were not sure whether or not Mr. Gray meant to shoot the chicken but seemed certain that Mrs. Gray intended to shoot her husband. Mr. Gray recovered and Mrs. Gray was arrested on assault charges. The chicken did not survive.

ENDNOTES

1. Marc Reidel and Wayne Welsh, *Criminal Violence: Patterns, Causes and Prevention.* Roxbury Publishing Company: Los Angeles, CA. 2002.

2. George B. Vold, Thomas J. Bernard, and Jeffrey B. Snipes, *Theoretical Criminology.* New York: Oxford University Press, 2002.

3. Cesare Beccaria, *On Crimes and Punishments,* translated by Henry Paolucci. Indianapolis: Bobbs-Merrill, 1963; Jeremy Bentham, *A Fragment on Government and an Introduction to the Principles of Morals and Legislation,* ed. Wilfred Harrison. New York: Oxford University Press, 1967.

4. Derek Cornish and Ronald Clarke, eds., *The Reasoning Criminal: Rational Choice Perspectives on Offending.* New York: Springer-Verlag, 1986.

5. Jack Katz, *Seductions of Crime.* New York: Basic Books, 1990.

6. Robert Sampson and John Laub, *Crime in the Making: Pathways and Turning Points Through Life.* Cambridge: Harvard University Press, 1993; Sheldon Glueck and Eleanor Glueck, *Unraveling Juvenile Delinquency.* Cambridge: Harvard University Press, 1950; Sheldon Glueck and Eleanor Glueck, *Predicting Delinquency and Crime.* Cambridge: Harvard University Press, 1967.

7. Keith McBurnett, Benjamin B. Lahey, Paul J. Rathouz, and Rolf Loeber, "Low Salivary Cortisol and Persistent Aggression in Boys Referred for Disruptive Behavior," *Archives of General Psychiatry* 57 (2000): 21–27.

8. Alan Booth and D. Wayne Osgood, "The Influence of Testosterone on Deviance in Adulthood," *Criminology* 31 (1993): 93–117.

9. Saleem Shah, "The 47, XYY Chromosomal Abnormality: A Critical Appraisal with Respect to Antisocial and Violent Behavior," in W. Lynn Smith and Arthur Kling, eds., *Issues in Brain/Behavior Control.* New York: Spectrum Publications, 1976; Lawrence Taylor, *Born to Crime: The Genetic Causes of Criminal Behavior.* Westport, CT: Greenwood Press, 1984.

10. Mortimer D. Gross and William C. Wilson, *Minimal Brain Dysfunction.* New York: Brunner/Mazel, 1974.

11. Gary M. Lavergne, *A Sniper in the Tower: The Charles Whitman Murders,* Denton, TX: University of North Texas Press, 1997.

12. Diana Fishbein, *Biobehavioral Perspectives in Criminology.* Belmont, CA; Wadsworth, 2001.

13. Diana H. Fishbein, "Biological Perspectives in Criminology." *Criminology* 28 (1990): 27–72; James Q. Wilson and Richard J. Herrnstein, *Crime and Human Nature.* New York: Simon Schuster, 1985.

14. Eric Fidler, "Hormone Level Linked to Antisocial Behavior in Boys," *The Boston Globe,* January 14, 2000, p. A16.

15. K. Magid and C. A. McKelvey, *High Risk: Children Without a Conscience.* New York: Bantam Books, 1988; Robert D. Hare, *Without Conscience: The Disturbing World of the Psychopaths Among Us.* New York: Guilford Publications, 1997.

16. Sigmund Freud, *New Introductory Lectures on Psychoanalysis.* London: Hogarth Press, 1949.

17. URL: www.therapyinla.com for discussions of successful attachment therapy.

18. Konrad Lorenz, *On Aggression.* New York: Harcourt, Brace and World, 1966.

19. Erich Fromm, *The Anatomy of Human Destructiveness.* New York: Holt, Rinehart, and Winston, 1973.

20. Jeff Joireman, Jonathan Anderson, and Alan Strathman, "The Aggression Paradox: Understanding Links Among Aggression, Sensation Seeking, and the Consideration of Future Consequences," *Journal of Personality and Social Psychology* 84 (2003): 1287–1302.

21. Martin Daly and Margo Wilson, "An Evolutionary Psychological Perspective on Homicide," in M. Dwayne Smith and Margaret A. Zahn, eds., *Homicide: A Sourcebook of Social Research.* Thousand Oaks, CA: Sage Publications, 1999.

22. Daly and Wilson, op. cit.

23. Avshalom Caspi, Terrie Moffitt, Phil Silva, Magda Stouthamer-Loeber, Robert Krueger, and Pamela Schmutte, "Are Some People Crime Prone? Replications of the Personality-Crime Relationship Across Countries, Genders, Races and Methods," *Criminology* 32 (1994): 163–195.

24. Bruce Link, John Monahan, Ann Stueve, and Francis T. Cullen, "Real in their Consequences: A Sociological Approach to Understanding the Association Between Psychotic Symptoms and Violence," *American Sociological Review* 64 (999): 316–332.

25. Robin Elise Weiss, "Postpartum Psychosis to blame for murdered Houston children?" URL: http://pregnancy.about.com/cs/postpartumdepress/a/aa062101a.htm, November 6, 2006.

26. Vold and Bernard, op. cit.

27. Travis Hirschi and Michael Hindelang, "Intelligence and Delinquency: A Revisionist Review," *American Sociological Review* 42 (1977): 471–586.

28. William Shockley, "A 'Try Simplest Cases' Approach to the Heredity–Poverty–Crime Problem," *Proceedings of the National Academy of Sciences* 57 (1967): 1767–1774.

29. Charles A. Murray and Richard J. Herrnstein, *The Bell Curve: Intelligence and Class Structure in American Life.* New York: Free Press, 1994.

30. Fishbein, 1990, op. cit.

31. Clifford R. Shaw and Henry D. McKay, *Juvenile Delinquency and Urban Areas.* Chicago: University of Chicago Press, 1972.

32. George L. Kelling and Catherine M. Coles, *Fixing Broken Windows: Restoring Order and Reducing Crime and Communities.* New York: Simon and Schuster, 1996.

33. Katherine S. Newman, *Falling From Grace.* New York: Free Press, 1988.

34. William Julius Wilson, *The Truly Disadvantaged: The Inner City, the Underclass and Public Policy.* Chicago: University of Chicago Press, 1987.

35. Shannon McCaffrey, "Bull Market Leaving Poorest Way Behind, Report Says," *The Boston Globe,* January 18, 2000.

36. Gary LaFree, "A Summary and Review of Cross-National Comparative Studies of Homicide," in M. Dwayne Smith and Margaret Zahn, eds., *Homicide: A Sourcebook of Social Research.* Thousand Oaks, CA: Sage Publications, 1999.

37. John Dollard, Leonard W. Doob, Neal E. Miller, O. H. Mowrer, and Robert R. Sears, *Frustration and Aggression.* New Haven, CT: Yale University Press, 1939.

38. Jeffrey H. Goldstein, *Aggression and Crimes of Violence.* New York: Oxford University Press, 1986.

39. Stuart H. Palmer, *The Psychology of Murder.* New York: Crowell, 1960.

40. Robert Agnew, "Foundation for a General Strain Theory of Crime and Delinquency," *Criminology* 30 (1992): 47–88.

41. Robert K. Merton, *Social Theory and Social Structure.* Glencoe, IL: Free Press, 1957.

42. Steven F. Messner and Richard Rosenfeld, *Crime and the American Dream.* Belmont, CA: Wadsworth Publishing Company, 2001.

43. Marvin E. Wolfgang and Franco Ferracuti, *The Subculture of Violence: Towards an Integrated Theory in Criminology.* London: Tavistock Publications, 1967.

44. Richard E. Nisbett, "Violence and U.S. Regional Culture," *American Psychologist* 48 (1993): 441–449.

45. T. W. Rice and C. R. Goldman, "Another Look at the Subculture of Violence Thesis: Who Murders Whom and Under What Circumstances," *Sociological Spectrum* 14 (1994): 371–384.

46. Christopher G. Ellison, "Southern Culture and Firearms Ownership," *Social Science Quarterly* 72 (1991): 267–283; Jay Corzine, Lin Huff-Corzine, and Hugh P. Whitt, "Cultural and Subcultural Theories of Homicide," in M. Dwayne Smith and Margaret Z. Zahn, eds., *Homicide: A Sourcebook of Social Research.* Thousand Oaks, CA: Sage Publications, 1999.

47. The major cultural deviance theories developed in the 1950s and 1960s were in Albert Cohen, *Delinquent Boys: The Culture of the Gang.* Glencoe, IL: Free Press; R. A. Cloward and Lloyd E. Ohlin, *Delinquency and Opportunity: A Theory of Delinquent Gangs.* New York: Free Press, 1960; Walter Miller, "Lower Class Culture as Generating Milieu of Gang Delinquency," *Journal of Social Issues* 14 (1958): 5–19; Wolfgang and Ferracuti, op. cit.

48. Albert Bandura, *Social Learning Theory.* Englewood Cliffs, NJ: Prentice Hall, 1977.

49. Jonathan L. Freedman, *Media Violence and Its Effect on Aggression: Assessing the Scientific Evidence.* Toronto: University of Toronto Press, 2002.

50. Edwin H. Sutherland, *Principles of Criminology,* Fourth Edition. Philadelphia: J. B. Lippincott, 1947.

51. Ronald L. Akers, *Criminological Theories: Introduction, Evaluation and Application.* Los Angeles, CA: Roxbury Publishing, 2000.

52. Richard Rhodes, *Why They Kill: Discoveries of a Maverick Criminologist.* New York: Knopf, 1999.

53. Travis Hirschi, *Causes of Delinquency.* Berkeley, CA: University of California Press, 1969; Michael Gottfredson and Travis Hirschi, *A General Theory of Crime.* Stanford, CA: Stanford University Press, 1990.

54. Sampson and Laub, op. cit.

55. Walter C. Reckless, "A New Theory of Delinquency and Crime," *Federal Probation* 25 (1961): 42–46.

56. Albert J. Reiss, Jr., and Jeffrey A. Roth, eds., *Understanding and Preventing Violence: Panel on the Understanding and Control of Violent Behavior.* Washington, DC: National Academy of Science, 1993.

CHAPTER

3   The Killers and Their Victims

Unlike television, where the frequency of murders seems to increase unabatedly, the rate of murder in America has been, until recently, on the decline. As shown in Figure 3.1, during the 1990s, the nation enjoyed a steady drop in homicide. In fact, the rate of murder—the number of homicide victims per 100,000 population—declined from a high of 9.8 in 1991 to 5.5 by the year 2000, a level not seen in this country for over 30 years, ever since 1967, to be precise.

The end of the 1990s decade, however, also brought an end to the great 90s slide in murder rates. With the new millennium, the national homicide rate leveled off. During the first half of the decade—from 2000 to 2005, the murder rate was relatively stable, fluctuating only between 5.5 and 5.7 per 100,000 population.

Even the relatively low murder rate in recent years is, of course, still too high, particularly when contrasted with those of earlier times as well as those of other developed nations. Although the 2005 homicide rate of 5.6 may be a welcome change from the national experience of just a decade earlier (when the rate flirted with the 10.0 mark), it hardly can compare with the relative calm of the years prior to the mid-1960s. Thus, although the rate of murder may be at a 30-year low, it would have to drop more to set a 40- or 50-year record for lawfulness. Some have argued that further reductions are beyond reach, characterizing the homicide trend as a "murder rate limbo stick" which arguably can go no lower.

Also sobering is the nation's standing in relation to other countries around the globe. Table 3.1 displays homicide rates for 38 nations. Although such comparisons can be affected

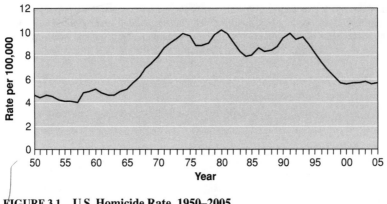

FIGURE 3.1   U.S. Homicide Rate, 1950–2005

TABLE 3.1 Homicide Rates for Selected Countries, 2000

Country	Homicide Count	Population	Homicide Rate per 100,000
South Africa	21,683	43,243,000	50.1
Russia[a] (1999 data)	31,140	145,500,000	21.4
Lithuania	370	3,699,000	10.0
Estonia[b]	143	1,439,000	9.9
Latvia	150	2,410,000	6.2
U.S.A.	15,586	281,422,000	5.5
Spain	1,192	40,500,000	2.9
Finland	148	5,181,000	2.9
Northern Ireland	48	1,692,000	2.8
Czech Republic	279	10,267,000	2.7
Slovakia	143	5,403,000	2.6
New Zealand	99	3,843,000	2.6
Romania[a]	560	22,400,000	2.5
Turkey	1,541	66,600,000	2.3
Poland	854	38,364,000	2.2
Scotland[c]	108	5,115,000	2.1
Hungary	205	10,043,000	2.0
Sweden[d]	175	8,883,000	2.0
Australia	346	19,157,000	1.8
France	1,051	58,747,000	1.8
Canada[e]	542	30,770,000	1.8
England & Wales	850	52,939,000	1.6
Belgium	158	10,239,000	1.5
Greece	158	10,522,000	1.5
Ireland (Eire)	56	3,790,000	1.5
Italy[e]	818	57,680,000	1.4
Netherlands[f]	226	15,941,000	1.4
Slovenia	28	1,990,000	1.4
Portugal	127	10,243,000	1.2
Germany	961	82,143,000	1.2
Japan[a]	1,391	126,862,000	1.1
Norway	49	4,478,000	1.1
Denmark[c]	58	5,330,000	1.1
Malta	4	378,000	1.1
Austria	82	8,127,000	1.0
Switzerland	69	7,210,000	1.0
Cyprus	4	671,000	0.6
Luxembourg	1	436,000	0.2

Notes:

a. Includes attempts
b. Excludes assaults leading to death
c. Includes all deaths initially reported as homicide
d. Includes all deaths initially reported as homicide and assisted suicides
e. Include murder, manslaughter, and infanticide
f. Excludes euthanasia

by variations in the quality of data collection procedures, the table does provide a fairly clear sense of the poor ranking of the United States among reporting nations.

As shown, the United States, even following its 1990s crime drop, has the sixth highest homicide rate and the absolute highest among industrialized nations. Heading the list, South Africa endures high levels of political turmoil and bloodshed (comparable in the United States only in extraordinary and rare cases such as the 1995 Oklahoma City bombing). America's homicide problem is more a matter of interpersonal rather than political conflict.

A popular explanation for the United States' dubious distinction among nations involves lax gun laws and the easy availability of firearms. There are some 250 million firearms in the United States, almost as many as there are citizens. Even so, the non-gun homicide rate for the United States in 2000 (1.9) was still higher than the overall murder rate for Canada (1.8), England/Wales (1.6), Germany (1.2), France (1.8), and Japan (1.1), among others. Thus, guns may be part of the problem, but they are not the entire problem. Since many other countries have relatively high levels of gun ownership and low levels of gun homicide, it seems to be more a function of a willingness in the United States to use a firearm, thus requiring a mindset change rather than just an access change.

Regardless of weaponry, American society is deeply rooted in violence. From the days of the American Revolution to the Wild, Wild West, the country was developed as a consequence of violent conquests. In modern times, moreover, the society applauds and rewards the victor, almost without regard for who is victimized in the relentless pursuit of success, profit, and power. This selfish drive for personal gain has led some social critics to label U.S. culture as "sociopathic."[1] In popular culture as well, movies, music, and even fashion glorify and glamorize violence of all forms. It is often said that America has a love affair with violence—but it may be more like a *marriage*.

At the same time that many conditions of U.S. culture and society have encouraged violence, the traditional institutions of social control—family, community, schools, religion—have grown particularly weak. In their place, we have invested heavily in formal institutions of social control, most notably prisons. With prison and jail populations pushing the two million mark, many times greater than even two decades ago, increasing numbers of dangerous felons are being incarcerated for longer periods of time. Undoubtedly, the downturn in murder rates is partially a result of increased punitiveness for all crimes, yet at a significant price. Each year, approximately 600,000 offenders are released from U.S. prisons. Unless their incarceration reformed them and their transition back into society is positive, much of the crime reduction gained during the 1990s could be lost. The most significant drops in homicide during recent years have come in the large U.S. cities, the very locales that had experienced the most precipitous increases in murder during the late 1980s. To borrow on Newton's law of physics, what goes up generally comes down; and the steeper the rise is, the steeper the subsequent descent. In fact, as shown in Figure 3.2, most of the change, upward and downward, in U.S. homicide rates during the past two-plus decades can be traced to the largest cities—cities with populations over one million such as New York, Chicago, and Los Angeles—which were overrun by crack cocaine markets during the late 1980s and responded with smart policing strategies in the 1990s to help reverse the trend.

Even though the rate of killing moved downward throughout the 1990s, the U.S. public apparently was not fully convinced. In fact, an October 1998 Gallup survey of more than 1,000 Americans found, for example, that a slight majority of respondents still maintained that crime was on the rise, despite the compelling statistics showing otherwise.[2]

FIGURE 3.2   Homicide Rate by City Size, 1976–2005

The media obsession with crime as news and entertainment likely is responsible for this disconnect between perception and reality. Public perceptions of crime trends are based much more on media crime reports than the FBI's Uniform Crime Reports. Seeing is believing, it is said, and images of cold and lifeless bodies at a blood-splattered crime scene shown on the nightly news are far more persuasive in shaping public opinion than are cold and lifeless statistics presented in a newspaper report or a government document. Furthermore, news about crime rates coming down simply is not highlighted in the same way as are stories of mini-epidemics in carjackings, hate crimes, child abductions, school shootings, or whatever the journalist's crime du jour may be. In terms of the mass media, the popular idiom is reversed, "good news is no news," and turned inside out, "bad news is big news."

Because of fast-advancing telecommunications technology, news coverage of crime has become more immediate, more graphic, and more pervasive. Even if there are fewer homicides available to reporters today than in the early 1990s, there are still plenty to lead off the news. Furthermore, should a news station not have a nearby tragedy to feature, satellite feeds from other corners of the nation can easily fill the local news void. More than anything else, the national news picture is about violence, except of course when some other catastrophe, like a terrorist act, a plane crash, or a hurricane, demands center stage.

The evolution of all-news cable channels, such as MSNBC, CNN, and FOX News, among others, has also altered the way in which homicide and other crime stories are covered. In earlier years, when major television networks controlled most of the programming, affiliates would not normally interrupt the viewing schedule for anything other than a major breaking story of national significance (e.g., an attempt to assassinate a top political figure) or a local matter of great importance. But by today's practices, the usually low-rated cable news channels are drawn to continuing coverage of crimes, investigations, or trials to fill their vacuum of airtime. Thus, events such as the Columbine school shooting or even the O.J. Simpson trial, had they occurred 10 years earlier, would not have been covered live by the major networks. Yet, given that the cable news channels now feature continuing coverage of breaking crime news (with music and graphics fitting the big event), the networks feel pressure to follow suit so as not to lose their audience.

Race Differences

More than just exaggerating the risk of murder, television portrayals of homicide also distort the characteristics of killers and their victims. David Fabianic, for example, analyzed the content of two months of crime drama programming in 1995 (including episodes of *NYPD Blue; Murder, She Wrote;* and *Law and Order,* among others) and found that whites constituted nine out of 10 offenders and victims.[3] Motivated by ratings, television dramas feature white victims and perpetrators to appeal to a predominantly white audience. If they were driven more by a desire for realism, homicide offenders and victims would be roughly equally spread between whites and blacks.

Table 3.2 shows demographic patterns—specifically race, sex and age—of victims and offenders over the past three decades combined. In terms of race, slightly more than one-half of homicide offenders are black, and slightly less than one-half of victims are black. Because, of course, the nation's white and black populations are quite different in size (over the three decades represented in the table, 84 percent of the population was white, 12 percent was black, and 4 percent other races), the rates of offending and victimization diverge. As indicated in the table, the rate of homicide (per 100,000 population) committed by blacks (36.9) is about eight times that of whites (4.8), and the rate of victimization is about six times higher for blacks (29.6) than for whites (4.7).

The large race difference among homicide victims and perpetrators has much to do with the kinds of killing in which blacks predominate. Table 3.3 shows the racial split among both victims and offenders in various homicide subtypes. At the extreme, blacks are greatly overrepresented among those who commit felony-related homicides (59.3 percent of offenders) such as robbery, as well as those involved in drug-related incidents (61.7 percent and 65.0 percent of victims and perpetrators, respectively). Much of this extreme overrepresentation is related to the geography of homicide, in that violent crime is associated with the heavy

TABLE 3.2   Homicide Victims and Offenders by Demographic Group, 1976–2005 Combined

		Victims	Offenders	Population	Victims per 100,000	Offenders per 100,000
Overall	Total	100.0%	100.0%	100.0%	7.8	8.7
Race	White	50.9%	45.8%	83.7%	4.7	4.8
	Black	46.9%	52.2%	12.3%	29.6	36.9
	Other	2.1%	2.0%	4.0%	4.1	4.4
Sex	Male	76.5%	88.8%	48.8%	12.3	15.8
	Female	23.5%	11.2%	51.2%	3.6	1.9
Age	Under 14	4.8%	.5%	20.5%	1.8	.2
	14–17	5.0%	10.4%	6.1%	6.4	14.9
	18–24	23.9%	36.6%	10.8%	17.0	29.3
	25–34	28.8%	28.4%	15.7%	14.2	15.8
	35–49	22.8%	17.3%	20.5%	8.6	7.3
	50–64	9.3%	5.1%	14.2%	5.1	3.1
	65+	5.3%	1.7%	12.3%	3.4	1.2

TABLE 3.3   Race Differences by Homicide Type, 1976–2005 Combined

	Victims			Offenders		
	White	**Black**	**Other**	**White**	**Black**	**Other**
All homicides	50.9%	46.9%	2.1%	45.8%	52.2%	2.0%
Intimate	56.6%	41.2%	2.2%	54.4%	43.4%	2.2%
Family	60.7%	36.9%	2.4%	59.2%	38.5%	2.3%
Infanticide	55.9%	41.6%	2.5%	55.4%	42.1%	2.5%
Eldercide	69.2%	29.1%	1.6%	54.5%	43.8%	1.6%
Felony murder	54.7%	42.7%	2.6%	39.1%	59.3%	1.6%
Sex related	66.9%	30.5%	2.5%	54.7%	43.4%	1.9%
Drug related	37.4%	61.6%	0.9%	33.9%	65.0%	1.1%
Gang related	57.5%	39.0%	3.5%	54.3%	41.2%	4.4%
Argument	48.6%	49.3%	2.1%	46.8%	51.1%	2.2%
Workplace	84.6%	12.2%	3.2%	70.5%	26.7%	2.8%
Gun homicide	47.2%	50.9%	1.9%	41.9%	56.4%	1.7%
Arson	58.9%	38.1%	2.9%	55.7%	42.0%	2.3%
Poison	80.6%	16.9%	2.5%	79.8%	18.4%	1.8%
Multiple victims	63.4%	33.2%	3.3%	55.7%	40.8%	3.5%
Multiple offenders	54.8%	42.5%	2.7%	44.6%	53.0%	2.4%

concentration of blacks in urban underclasses. Blacks are also more than one-half the participants in argument-related killings. The link between race and conflict-based homicide has been traced to socioeconomic factors such as low income, poor education, and inadequate employment opportunities.[4]

At the other extreme, blacks are far less overrepresented in domestic homicide—those involving intimates, infanticides, and family killings generally, as well as in sex-related murders. Also noteworthy is the limited representation of blacks as perpetrators of workplace homicides. Employee disgruntlement is not necessarily correlated with race. The limited representation of blacks as perpetrators of workplace homicide may be in part a function of higher black unemployment rates, particularly in the age categories most likely to perpetrate workplace violence. *No job* means *no opportunity* for killing co-workers. Many of the workplace shootings have involved civil service positions (e.g., government and post office workers), which may reflect the greater number of whites holding these jobs. Actually, the representation of blacks as victims in workplace homicide is proportional to their share of the population—about 12 percent.

In recent years, hate crimes motivated by racial bias have received much attention. More than any, the 1991 beating of motorist Rodney King by a group of Los Angeles police officers stirred concern in the United States for racial violence. Although this incident was fortunately not a homicide, the fact that it was captured on video and replayed countless times on television made it a particularly important event, if not a turning point, in U.S. race relations. Seeing the videotaped episode provoked many otherwise skeptical Americans into believing, for the first time, the bitter complaints of black Americans that they were being singled out by the police for brutal treatment. Later in the decade, a national discussion of police brutality and excessive force was broadened to include the use of racial profiling as police policy for determining who is regarded as a suspect and who is not.

Other well-publicized atrocities have reinforced public concern for interracial violence. On June 7, 1998, for example, James Byrd, Jr., a 49-year-old black man from Jasper, Texas, was chained to the back of a pickup truck and dragged to his death by a group of three white supremacists. In New York City, white police officers dragged a black suspect into a precinct men's room, where they sodomized him with a broomstick. Such events have encouraged legislatures to consider new approaches for dealing with insidious mistreatment of minorities.

Despite the increased concern with hate crimes inspired by racism and prejudice, most homicides are actually intraracial rather than interracial. As shown in Figure 3.3, approximately 86 percent of white homicide victims are killed by white assailants, and a somewhat greater percentage of blacks (94 percent) are killed by members of their own race (the small handful of crimes involving races other than whites and blacks is excluded).

This pattern of similarity between victim and offender race, by far one of the most consistent patterns over the years, should not be surprising. Because homicides typically involve a victim and offender who know each other—often on intimate terms—the similarity of race between homicide participants follows from the similarity of race between individuals in most interpersonal relationships. This likeness of victim and offender race holds, moreover, even for relationships that are more distant than family. As shown, among homicides involving friends and acquaintances, 89 percent of white victims and 95 percent of black victims are slain by someone of the same race. Because of the racial homogeneity of most neighborhoods, moreover, it is even true that most stranger killings are intraracial—68 percent for white victims and 87 percent for blacks.

The higher prevalence of blacks killing whites over whites killing blacks should not necessarily be interpreted as a greater propensity toward interracial attacks instigated by blacks. Even if the victim were chosen randomly, blacks would victimize whites more than whites would blacks simply because of the predominance of whites among the potential targets. After all, because the U.S. population is primarily white, it is more likely for a black assailant to run across a potential white victim than it is for a white assailant to encounter a black target.

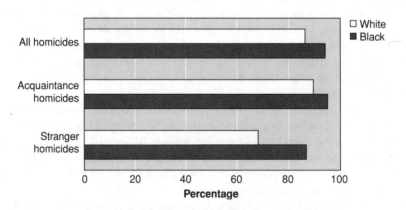

FIGURE 3.3   Percentage Intra-Racial Homicide by Relationship and Victim Race, 1976–2005 Combined

Despite the tendency for most homicides, even those involving strangers, to be intraracial, it is important not to minimize the concern for fatal interracial attacks. The percentage of homicides that cross race lines has increased from about 8 percent of the total three decades ago, to nearly 13 percent of the total at present. This increase does not necessarily reflect growing levels of racial hostility; it also could reflect increased contact between black and white Americans in everyday activities, including work, school, and romantic relationships.

Gender Differences

In addition to race, media images of gender are also frequently distorted. Pritchard and Hughes, for example, examined the factors that affect four measures of print newsworthiness of homicide cases—frequency of coverage, average story length, proportion of front-page placement, and use of photographs.[5] Overall, they found that homicides involving male offenders and female victims receive the most intense coverage.

Gender was a primary force driving the intense media coverage of the February 2006 brutal murder of 24-year-old Immette St. Guillen, believed to have been abducted late at night from a popular bar in the SoHo section of lower Manhattan. Her body was recovered in Brooklyn; she was found naked with her hands bound behind her back with plastic ties and her ankles tied with shoelaces. A gym sock was stuffed down her throat, and her face was wrapped in brown packing tape.

Of course, the brutality of the murder, the location of the crime in the Big Apple, and the fact that the victim was white while the lead suspect was black all added to the potential for sensationalism. Yet it was more the "young, defenseless graduate student" allegedly abducted, tortured and killed by the "big, bad ex-con bouncer" that made news producers salivate.

In the actual pattern of homicide cases over the past three decades, the offenders are indeed most often men. Yet, contrary to the media emphasis on crimes against women, most murder victims are also men.

As was shown in Table 3.2, men are far more likely than women to kill (88.8 percent of offenders are men) and to be killed (76.5 percent of victims are men). Despite changing gender roles that have led to greater involvement of women in violent crimes generally, murder has remained overwhelmingly a male preoccupation. If anything, the gender ratio among perpetrators has widened—nearly doubled—in recent years: from 5.2 males for every female in the mid-1970s to 9.5 males for every female in the mid-2000s.

As with race, most homicides occur in same-sex pairs; over two-thirds of all murders are men killing men. Overall, for the years 1976–2005, 89 percent of offenders were male and 78 percent of their victims were also male, typically killed in disputes over money, drugs, turf, honor, or pride. Cross-sex homicides only predominate when women kill. That is, not only do most male murderers kill men, but most female murderers (81 percent) also kill men.

It is important not to lose sight of the particular physical and situational vulnerability of women in dealings with men. Moreover, the statistical predominance of male victims likely stems from issues of victim precipitation. That is, men are far more likely to start a fight or to place themselves in dangerous or volatile situations resulting in their own death. Yet, the common media focus on "femicide"—female victims especially of male killers—does not reflect the norm in actual patterns of murder.

When women do in fact commit homicide, the nature of the offense is sharply different from those perpetrated by men. Women tend to kill close intimates (husbands, boyfriends, sons, or daughters), while men often attack strangers or mere acquaintances. As shown in Table 3.4, the gender ratio among murderers narrows considerably in family homicides (29.2 percent of offenders are female) and especially infanticides (38.2 percent female offenders). Homicides by women often result from turmoil or stress that may build up over time. Men, by contrast, are often quick to respond violently, killing an acquaintance in a bar who challenges them or even a stranger on the street who insults them. Also shown in Table 3.4, predatory incidents, such as felony-murders, stranger killings, and especially sexual homicides, are overwhelmingly the province of men. Homicides within the family, by contrast, are somewhat more "equal opportunity" by gender.

The instruments of murder selected by men and women are also very different. Men are better trained in the use of firearms, often feel comfortable with them, and therefore favor a gun when there is some murdering to do. By contrast, women prefer methods that are cleaner and more distant. Whereas fewer than 10 percent of gun killings are committed by women, more than 20 percent of homicides by arson and more than a third of murders by poison involve female offenders. Also, women often choose poison or suffocation in cases of family murder, including infanticide.

Unlike guns or brute force, women have more equal access to fire or poison as a means of committing homicide. In fact, because of their traditional role as homemakers and caretakers, women are often better acquainted than men with the harmful effects of various drugs and poisons. It was not difficult, for example, for 64-year-old Sacramento landlady Dorothea Montalvo Puente to poison her elderly boarders in order to cash in their social security checks. It was also not difficult for Puente to cover up the crimes by burying her victims in the yard of her rooming house . . . until 1988, that is, when a local social worker discovered that her missing clients' social security checks were being cashed.

TABLE 3.4   Gender Differences by Homicide Type, 1976–2005 Combined

	Victims		Offenders	
	Male	**Female**	**Male**	**Female**
All homicides	76.5%	23.5%	88.8%	11.2%
Intimate	35.2%	64.8%	65.5%	34.5%
Family	51.5%	48.5%	70.8%	29.2%
Infanticide	54.6%	45.4%	61.8%	38.2%
Eldercide	58.1%	41.9%	85.2%	14.8%
Felony murder	78.4%	21.6%	93.2%	6.8%
Sex related	18.8%	81.2%	93.6%	6.4%
Drug related	90.2%	9.8%	95.5%	4.5%
Gang related	94.7%	5.3%	98.3%	1.7%
Argument	77.8%	22.2%	85.6%	14.4%
Workplace	79.1%	20.9%	91.3%	8.7%
Gun homicide	82.7%	17.3%	91.3%	8.7%
Arson	56.4%	43.6%	79.1%	20.9%
Poison	55.3%	44.7%	63.5%	36.5%
Multiple victims	63.3%	36.7%	93.5%	6.5%
Multiple offenders	85.6%	14.4%	91.6%	8.4%

Over the past two-plus decades, the United States has endured several instances of product tampering, which not only scared the public but also brought about major changes in the packaging of consumer goods. In 1982, seven Chicago-area residents were fatally poisoned when they unknowingly ingested cyanide-laced Extra-Strength Tylenol capsules. The killer responsible for placing the poisoned analgesics on the shelves of local drug stores and supermarkets was never apprehended, which led to some speculation, based at least on statistical patterns, that the murderer was a woman.

Regardless of the Tylenol poisoner's identity and gender, the case no doubt influenced the thinking of Stella M. Nickell of Auburn, Washington, when she conceived a plan to kill her husband, Bruce, in order to collect the proceeds of a $176,000 life insurance policy. In June 1986, 52-year-old Bruce Nickell died after swallowing a poisoned Extra-Strength Excedrin capsule. Susan Snow, age 40, also of Auburn but unknown to Nickell, died after purchasing a contaminated bottle from a local store. She was the unfortunate victim of Stella Nickell's scheme to make the deaths appear to be the work of a random killer.

Murders for hire are also especially appealing to women who see the death of their spouse as a distasteful but necessary step to resolve a difficult situation. By the spring of 1990, 22-year-old Pamela Smart of Derry, New Hampshire, had grown tired of her marriage of less than a year to her 24-year-old husband, Greg. Or maybe it was her affair with a 15-year-old student at the high school where she worked as media services director that had helped Pam sour on matrimony. She wanted to end the marriage but didn't want the stress and complications of a divorce, not to mention the possibility that her adulterous affair with a minor might come to light in the process. Murder would be quicker.

Pam Smart, always concerned about neatness, abhorred the idea of having to perform the unpleasant and messy task herself. Instead, she convinced her young lover that Greg would have to be eliminated for their relationship to continue, and that it was up to him to carry it out. The teen, infatuated and feeling special because of the attention he received from the attractive "older woman," persuaded two of his friends to serve as accomplices. Pam Smart made sure that she wasn't home when the shooting took place, her only requirement for the three young conspirators being that they not kill her husband in front of the dog. She didn't want her "best friend" traumatized.

Reflecting recent thinking in criminology about female offenders, in her book, _When She Was Bad,_ Patricia Pearson argues that women are far more violent than most people assume.[6] Much of this violence is explained away by portraying murdering women as mentally ill, hormonally unstable, or as victims whose actions are driven by forces beyond their control. But Pearson argues that this is a particularly unfeminist view of females. She discusses how indirect female aggression may look different than direct male aggression, but is deadly just the same. In school, girls engage in rumor-mongering and character assassination and provoking boys to beat up (or even kill) other boys or their female rivals through social manipulation. Or they nonchalantly murder newborns and then go about their social lives of attending proms and parties with their dying babies abandoned in trash bins, coolers, and closets. Women assault and kill their ex- and current boyfriends and husbands rather than face being dumped for another woman. A scorned woman may run over her husband with his car or abuse her stepchildren as surrogates for her hostility toward her mate.

When women do engage in direct aggression such as hitting, it is often referred to it in humorous, nonserious, trivializing terms like "catfight" or "hair pulling contests." People joke about aggressive women with PMS. Some people laughed when Clara Harris ran over and murdered her husband in front of his hysterical daughter. Others joked about Lorena Bobbitt excising her cheating husband's penis.

The time may have come to stop portraying violent women as helpless or confused "children" rather than the cold, calculated killers they can be. Women may simply be better than men at hiding their aggression, getting others to do their dirty work, or engaging in less brutal forms of lethal violence.

Certainly Karla Homolka, arrested in Canada in 1993, was convincing as the victim of a battering spouse rather than as a sexual predator. Along with her husband, Paul Bernardo, she participated in the brutal rapes and sadistic murders of three teenage girls—one of whom was her own sister. When police questioned Homolka about Bernardo's possible involvement in the death of one of the girls, they offered her a "sweetheart deal" to talk. What the authorities did not realize was that Karla herself (who admits to performing oral sex on her own unconscious sister and wanting to give her husband her sister's virginity as a Christmas present) was a dangerous sexual sadist who played much more than an ancillary role in the rapes and murders. The deal had already been confirmed by the time police and prosecutors saw videotapes of the murders and heard other evidence about her involvement. Because of this premature negotiation, Homolka was freed from prison on July 4, 2005 (her personal independence day), at the end of her 12-year sentence. Despite widespread outrage, particularly in the Province of Ontario where the crimes had occurred, there was nothing the authorities could do to prolong her incarceration. Homolka settled in the Province of Quebec, where apparently the level of negative public opinion toward her release was not quite as high.

Age Differences

A crime time capsule of the 1990s would likely be decidedly slanted toward murders committed by juveniles. In recent years, the mass media have focused heavily on homicides committed by teenagers—not just the most sensationalistic crimes like the April 1999 Columbine High School massacre, but also the general problem of armed and dangerous youngsters. On March 25, 1996, the usually understated cover of *U.S. News & World Report,* screamed "Teenage Time Bombs: Violent Juvenile Crime Is Soaring and It's Going to Get Worse." Even *People* magazine devoted its June 23, 1997, issue to the rhetorical query, "Kids Without a Conscience?" The report examined a variety of senseless homicides, including the case of a 15-year-old couple who murdered and disemboweled a 44-year-old drinking buddy in Manhattan's Central Park and the story of an 18-year-old New Jersey girl who delivered a baby in the bathroom during her senior prom, dumped the child in the trash, and then returned to dance with her prom date.

Despite the intense attention given to juvenile offenders, as was shown in Table 3.2, only about 10 percent of murderers and victims are under 18 years old. By contrast, young adults, ages 18 to 24, represent over one-third of the offenders and about one-quarter of the victims.

The disconnect between media hype and statistical reality in regard to juvenile homicide has led some observers to allege that journalists as well as politicians have exploited a few highly publicized cases for their own ends. According to attorney and author Peter Elikann, a whole generation of teenagers has been demonized in media and political circles, which cast them as ruthless superpredators.[7]

The superpredator concept was first conceived by John J. DiIulio, Jr. In the book *Body Count,* DiIulio and colleagues commented that, "America is now home to thickening ranks of juvenile 'superpredators'—radically impulsive, brutally remorseless youngsters, including ever more pre-teenage boys, who murder, assault, rape, rob, burglarize, deal deadly drugs, join gun-toting gangs, and create serious communal disorders." [8]

The term superpredator may indeed have been inflammatory and unduly sensationalistic. It may even be technically inaccurate, because juvenile violence is typically impulsive rather than predatory (the true superpredators are more accurately serial killers who prey on scores of innocent victims). Notwithstanding such caveats, the frequent attention given to youth violence and especially murder may have had much to do with the special character— the unmitigated senselessness—of youthful killings. When adults kill, it often involves rather commonplace motivations—jealousy, revenge, and greed. When kids kill, the reasons are often as trivial as a pair of sneakers or even the ownership of a Pokemon card.

Juvenile homicides are quite different from adult killings in several other respects. As shown in Table 3.5, the involvement of youngsters is far greater in gang killings (juveniles are implicated in nearly one-third of gang-related murders). Although less dramatic, homicides that involve multiple offenders (two or more accomplices working together), that are drug related, or that involve arson, guns, or a felony also have a higher-than-average percentage of offenders under age 18.

More than their older counterparts, juveniles tend to travel and kill in groups, sometimes tightly organized gangs with a well-defined hierarchy of authority, but often just informal cliques or bands. It is often the strong influence of peers that motivates murder, rather than

TABLE 3.5   Age Differences by Homicide Type, 1976–2005 Combined

	Victims				Offenders			
	Under 18	**18–34**	**35–49**	**50+**	**Under 18**	**18–34**	**35–49**	**50+**
All homicides	9.8%	52.7%	22.8%	14.7%	10.9%	65.0%	17.3%	6.8%
Intimate	1.5%	46.7%	34.3%	17.5%	1.0%	46.2%	34.9%	17.9%
Family	19.6%	31.9%	26.4%	22.1%	6.0%	49.1%	28.1%	16.8%
Infanticide	100.0%	—	—	—	7.9%	81.3%	9.7%	1.1%
Eldercide	—	—	—	100.0%	10.3%	49.2%	19.1%	21.4%
Felony murder	7.6%	46.9%	21.8%	23.8%	14.8%	72.9%	10.3%	2.0%
Sex related	19.6%	45.1%	16.6%	18.7%	10.7%	73.6%	13.7%	2.0%
Drug related	5.4%	71.4%	19.9%	3.3%	10.6%	76.9%	11.3%	1.2%
Gang related	24.2%	68.4%	6.1%	1.3%	28.9%	69.2%	1.6%	.3%
Argument	5.5%	56.1%	26.3%	12.2%	6.9%	60.2%	23.1%	9.7%
Workplace	.5%	28.0%	32.0%	39.5%	3.7%	53.1%	27.6%	15.5%
Gun homicide	7.4%	59.3%	22.4%	10.9%	11.9%	64.8%	15.8%	7.5%
Arson	28.3%	27.0%	19.2%	25.5%	11.5%	57.7%	23.8%	7.0%
Poison	28.0%	23.3%	16.5%	32.2%	4.5%	50.9%	26.2%	18.5%
Multiple victims	18.2%	46.3%	19.1%	16.4%	9.5%	66.1%	18.5%	5.9%
Multiple offenders	11.3%	55.5%	19.7%	13.5%	18.2%	73.1%	7.5%	1.2%

any particular burning desire of the perpetrator to kill. It is easier psychologically to participate in a horrible crime "because your friends are doing it, too."

Despite the limited involvement overall of juveniles in homicide, the intensive focus on young killers can also be justified based on patterns of growth in their rate of murder. Whereas 7.5 percent of murders during the mid-1980s were committed by offenders under age 18, juveniles during the mid-1990s were implicated in 15 percent of the killings. Correspondingly, the average age of murderers dropped over this time period, from about 31 years old on average in the mid-1980s, down to nearly 27 years old on average in the mid-1990s, trending upward slightly since. A similar pattern of youth movement has occurred among victims, with an average age in the mid-1980s of nearly 35 years old, down to an average victim age of just over 31 years old in the mid-1990s. The parallel trends in the average ages of offenders and victims are understandable because offenders tend to murder victims close to their own age.

The younger the killer, it seems, the greater the shock. Over the past several years, the nation was clearly shaken when, for example, two boys, ages 10 and 11, dropped a 5-year-old out of a fourteenth-story window in a Chicago housing project in retaliation for tattling on them; when an 11-year-old and a 13-year-old killed four students and one teacher at their middle school in Jonesboro, Arkansas; and even when a 6-year-old Michigan boy shot and killed his first-grade classmate. Though it is little consolation for the rise in adolescent homicide over the past 15 years, murder at the hands of younger children—those under age 14—has remained especially rare. On average, about 50 children age 13 and younger, and fewer than 10 children age 10 and younger, commit homicide each year nationwide, and neither tally has shown any indication of increasing. Thus, despite the special senselessness of kiddie murder, it remains little more than a horrifying aberration.

In terms of the age patterns between victims and offenders, homicide is intragenerational. Adults tend to target other adults (husband–wife, co-workers, friends), and adolescents tend to target their contemporaries as well. The major exception, of course, is in cases of infanticide (victims under the age of 5), in which the perpetrator tends to be a parent or some other caretaker (e.g., babysitter), but certainly not a playmate. Figure 3.4 provides perspective on the match between victim and offender age. In this plot, depicting homicides in 2005, the greater the density of points (each representing a separate incident), the more commonplace the victim–offender age combination. Aside from the sizable left-hand cluster of children killed by adults (infanticides) and the more modest number of elders murdered by younger perpetrators (eldercides), the plot thickens along the diagonal, showing that most offenders and their victims are similar in age.

As frequently described by social scientists, numerous characteristics of lifestyle tend to change dramatically as a person moves through the life course from infancy into adolescence, and from adulthood into retirement age. The same can be said for styles of death by homicide. Figure 3.5 shows that three key homicide characteristics—whether a gun was used, whether the offender was known to the victim, and whether the homicide was felony-related—vary considerably by age of the victim.

Firearms are rarely needed in murders of young children, but gun use increases steadily throughout the teenage years, peaks at nearly 80 percent for older adolescents, and then declines steadily with advancing victim age. The vulnerability of elders, as with young children, produces a large proportion of deaths with weapons other than guns. Also, children are almost always murdered by someone they know, in contrast to victims of older ages who,

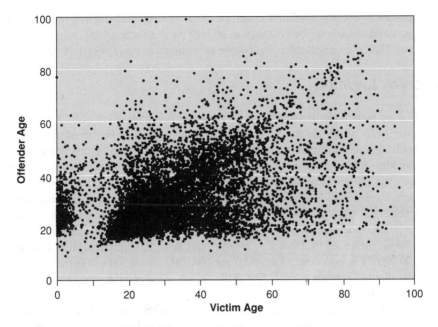

FIGURE 3.4   Age of Homicide Victims and Offenders, 2005

nearly half the time, are killed by strangers or unidentified assailants. For elders, the percentage of known perpetrators is particularly low, which has much to do with the unusually high percentage of older victims who are killed during the course of a felony, such as a holdup. For victims aged 50 and over, the proportion of murders resulting from robberies and other attacks by strangers increases, while murders resulting from interpersonal disputes decline.

Some criminologists have noted that the elderly have the highest levels of fear of violence yet the lowest risk of victimization. Their low victimization rate results, however, from the fact that senior citizens are rarely killed by family members or friends and often live alone with few

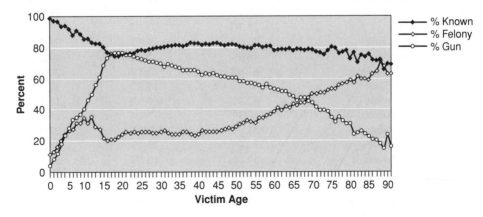

FIGURE 3.5   Homicide Characteristics by Victim Age, 1976–2005 Combined

occasions for deadly conflict. By contrast, elders have relatively high rates of felony-murder victimization and homicides by strangers, often dying in an attack that younger victims would survive. Thus, the fears of elders may not be as irrational as many observers have suggested.[9]

Differences by Location

Besides patterns in terms of race, sex, and age, homicides vary considerably by location—specifically urbanness and geographic region. As noted earlier, most of the recent shifts in homicide rates occurred in larger U.S. cities, rather than small cities, suburbs, or rural communities. Table 3.6 shows that urban areas also tend to be overrepresented in homicides that are gang related, drug related, and felony related. By contrast, homicides in the family—including infanticides and killings by romantic intimates—as well as murders on the job are spread more evenly across location types, with particular prevalence in the suburbs.

Focusing next on individual cities, the 2005 homicide rates for the 50 largest municipalities, presented in Table 3.7, clearly reflects wide variability, from a high of 42.0 per 100,000 for Baltimore to a low of 1.7 per 100,000 for Honolulu. Together these Top 50 represent about 15 percent of the U.S. population, yet accounted for over 35 percent of the nation's murders in 2005.

A certain measure of caution is needed in interpreting the homicide rate of any single jurisdiction for any particular year. Because many cities have homicide counts that are near or below 100 annually, some fluctuation tends to occur over time as a result of various random factors—such as how many shooting victims are able to survive their injuries so as not to be among the murder statistics. Table 3.7 is merely a snapshot in time when some cities may have had unusually high murder tolls while others experienced relatively low levels. For example, Kansas City tallied 126 homicides in 2005, a whopping 40 percent increase over the 89 killings that occurred in 2004. However, such a large one-year change often represents an

TABLE 3.6   Location Differences by Homicide Type, 1976–2005 Combined

	Large City	Small City	Suburban	Rural
All homicides	57.3%	11.5%	21.0%	10.2%
Intimate	40.7%	14.5%	28.0%	16.8%
Family	38.7%	13.2%	29.1%	19.0%
Infanticide	47.9%	15.0%	25.5%	11.6%
Eldercide	46.9%	13.5%	24.2%	15.3%
Felony murder	61.0%	11.1%	20.3%	7.7%
Sex related	48.4%	12.2%	27.2%	12.2%
Drug related	67.4%	9.9%	18.1%	4.5%
Gang related	69.3%	13.1%	16.9%	0.7%
Argument	53.4%	12.7%	21.0%	12.9%
Workplace	31.4%	13.4%	37.2%	17.9%
Gun homicide	59.3%	10.6%	19.8%	10.4%
Arson	54.8%	13.1%	21.7%	10.4%
Poison	38.9%	15.7%	29.3%	16.0%
Multiple victims	47.4%	11.9%	27.0%	13.7%
Multiple offenders	61.7%	10.2%	19.1%	8.9%

TABLE 3.7   Homicide Rates for 50 Largest Cities, 2005

City	Population	Homicides	Homicide Rate
Baltimore	641,097	269	42.0
Detroit	900,932	354	39.3
St. Louis	346,005	131	37.9
Washington	550,521	195	35.4
Kansas City	447,915	126	28.1
Philadelphia	1,472,915	377	25.6
Cleveland	458,885	109	23.8
Oakland	400,619	93	23.2
Atlanta	430,666	90	20.9
Milwaukee	586,500	121	20.6
Memphis	678,988	137	20.2
Nashville	557,034	95	17.1
Dallas	1,230,303	202	16.4
Houston	2,045,732	334	16.3
Chicago	2,873,441	448	15.6
Tulsa	386,414	58	15.0
Phoenix	1,466,296	220	15.0
Columbus	730,329	102	14.0
Miami	388,295	54	13.9
Indianapolis	800,304	108	13.5
Boston	567,589	73	12.9
San Francisco	749,172	96	12.8
Los Angeles	3,871,077	489	12.6
Charlotte	677,122	85	12.6
Minneapolis	376,277	47	12.5
Jacksonville	795,259	91	11.4
Sacramento	457,347	52	11.4
Las Vegas	1,281,698	145	11.3
Albuquerque	490,631	53	10.8
Fresno	460,758	49	10.6
Denver	564,552	59	10.5
Tucson	529,447	55	10.4
Oklahoma City	531,688	54	10.2
Fort Worth	613,261	60	9.8
Louisville	623,735	55	8.8
Long Beach	479,729	42	8.8
Omaha	412,128	31	7.5
San Antonio	1,256,584	86	6.8
New York	8,115,690	539	6.6
Arlington	365,380	24	6.6
Mesa	452,340	29	6.4
Virginia Beach	446,448	20	4.5
Seattle	579,215	25	4.3
San Diego	1,272,148	51	4.0
Austin	693,019	26	3.8

(continued)

TABLE 3.7   **Continued**

City	Population	Homicides	Homicide Rate
Portland	540,389	20	3.7
Colorado Springs	374,482	12	3.2
San Jose	910,528	26	2.9
El Paso	601,839	14	2.3
Honolulu	908,521	15	1.7

Source: Federal Bureau of Investigation, *Crime in the United States–2005.* Washington, DC, 2006.

aberration in local fluctuations, rather than a trend. As predicted, the Kansas City murder tally dropped back to 115 in 2006, a more usual level.[10]

In an analysis of city murder trends over the past two decades, Fox showed that whenever a city experiences a sudden spike in murder of 20 percent or more, there is about a 75% chance that the next year will show an improvement.[11] Called *statistical regression to the mean,* the more a city's homicide count drifts up or down from its usual level, the more likely it is that the following year will bring a return toward the norm.

In addition to the advised caution in interpreting short-tem spikes in local homicide counts, observations concerning city murder statistics need to take into account any special circumstances that might impact significantly on the murder statistics. The city of New Orleans is noticeably—and understandably—absent from the city homicide rates in Table 3.7. Notwithstanding the homicides that occurred in the aftermath of Hurricane Katrina, crime statistics were not available for the second half of 2005. The absence of New Orleans is especially noteworthy since the Big Easy typically appeared at or near the top of the city homicide rankings. In fact, projecting the second half of 2005 based on the homicides reported for the first half of the year plus seasonal patterns from the previous 10 years, New Orleans would have been expected to finish the year with 265 murders and a chart-topping rate of 56.2 per 100,000. Also experiencing a "Katrina effect" was the city of Houston, which became home to thousands of hurricane evacuees. Houston's homicide tally for 2005 was 23 percent higher than 2004, largely owing to the nearly 10 killings per month above average that the city experienced in the four months after the catastrophic storm to the east.

Given the extent of variability among cities, many analysts have been tempted to treat these rankings as measures of comparative safety or dangerousness. The news media, in particular, often attempt to approach these city-by-city rates as indicators of relative security and quality of life. Using homicide rates in this manner, however, is as tricky as it is enticing. These 50 cities vary considerably in terms of both demography (i.e., population characteristics) and geography, making any attempt to identify the safest or deadliest U.S. cities to be problematic, at best.

The most difficult aspect of making sense of city homicide rankings involves the extent to which the municipalities include or exclude suburban communities. New York City, for example, consists of much more than the Manhattan downtown areas; it encompasses residential neighborhoods in Queens and Staten Island. The population in a city like San Antonio may have boomed in recent years, but the million-plus population count is, in large part, a result of sprawling city limits. Cities such as Seattle and Boston are densely populated and urbanized, compared with, for example, Virginia Beach. Quite clearly, density and urbanness tend to correlate with crime levels, regardless of overall population count.

In addition to the issue of population density, the use of residential population figures may, in certain cases, distort the homicide victimization rates. Many cities contain large numbers of nonresidents (e.g., commuters, tourists, seasonal visitors, out-of-state college students, homeless people, and even hurricane evacuees) who may be at some risk of homicide for certain periods of time yet are excluded from the population base used in calculating the city's homicide rate.

Besides these qualifications, an unusual demographic distribution (by race, sex, or age) can impact a city's murder rate. Most notably, the top four cities in Table 3.7 (Baltimore, Detroit, St. Louis, and Washington, D.C.) all have high concentrations of black residents, as do most of the top-ranked cities for murder. It is not race itself that accounts for this pattern, but the socioeconomic conditions that tend to be associated with a sizable minority population. In a study of crime rates in the largest U.S. cities, Cohen, Fox, and Wolfgang found that the strong statistical correlation between violent crime rates and the percentage of blacks in the population vanishes when controlling for the percentage of families below the poverty line, the percentage of children in broken homes, and other dimensions of social disorganization.[12]

Another common approach to analyzing murder rates is to examine variations among states. As shown in Table 3.8, state homicide rates for 2005 ranged from a high of 9.9 (per

TABLE 3.8   State Homicide Rates, 2005

State	Population	Homicides	Homicide Rate
Louisiana	4,523,628	450	9.9
Maryland	5,600,388	552	9.9
Nevada	2,414,807	206	8.5
Alabama	4,557,808	374	8.2
Arizona	5,939,292	445	7.5
New Mexico	1,928,384	143	7.4
South Carolina	4,255,083	315	7.4
Mississippi	2,921,088	214	7.3
Tennessee	5,962,959	432	7.2
Missouri	5,800,310	402	6.9
California	36,132,147	2,503	6.9
North Carolina	8,683,242	585	6.7
Arkansas	2,779,154	186	6.7
Georgia	9,072,576	564	6.2
Texas	22,859,968	1,407	6.2
Virginia	7,567,465	461	6.1
Michigan	10,120,860	616	6.1
Pennsylvania	12,429,616	756	6.1
Illinois	12,763,371	766	6.0
Indiana	6,271,973	356	5.7
Oklahoma	3,547,884	187	5.3
Ohio	11,464,042	585	5.1
Florida	17,789,864	883	5.0
Alaska	663,661	32	4.8

(continued)

TABLE 3.8   Continued

State	Population	Homicides	Homicide Rate
New Jersey	8,717,925	417	4.8
Kentucky	4,173,405	190	4.6
New York	19,254,630	874	4.5
West Virginia	1,816,856	80	4.4
Delaware	843,524	37	4.4
Kansas	2,744,687	102	3.7
Colorado	4,665,177	173	3.7
Wisconsin	5,536,201	194	3.5
Washington	6,287,759	205	3.3
Rhode Island	1,076,189	34	3.2
Connecticut	3,510,297	102	2.9
Wyoming	509,294	14	2.7
Massachusetts	6,398,743	175	2.7
Nebraska	1,758,787	44	2.5
Idaho	1,429,096	35	2.4
South Dakota	775,933	18	2.3
Utah	2,469,585	56	2.3
Minnesota	5,132,799	115	2.2
Oregon	3,641,056	80	2.2
Montana	935,670	18	1.9
Hawaii	1,275,194	24	1.9
Maine	1,321,505	19	1.4
New Hampshire	1,309,940	18	1.4
Vermont	623,050	8	1.3
Iowa	2,966,334	38	1.3
North Dakota	636,677	7	1.1

Source: Federal Bureau of Investigation, *Crime in the United States–2005.* Washington D.C., 2006.

100,000 population) in Louisiana (even with the partial reporting from New Orleans) to a low of 1.1 in North Dakota. As with the city tabulations, these state differences to some extent reflect the degree of urbanness and population density. For example, the bottom five states (Maine, New Hampshire, Vermont, Iowa, and North Dakota) are especially rural and sparsely populated. At the same time, some regional differences are fairly significant and hard to miss. For example, six of the 10 highest murder-rate states are within the Southern region of the nation. As illustrated in Figure 3.6, there are some clearly defined clusters of low and high homicide rate areas within the nation. Specifically, in 2005, the New England, North Central, and Mountain regions generally had rates under 3.0 per 100,000, whereas the Southern states were almost all within the highest rate category.

Homicide patterns among states translate, of course, into overall regional differences, as shown in Table 3.9. In relation to population share, homicides are more prevalent in the South, even though the region is not as urbanized as others. Over the 1976–2005 time period combined, the South was home to 40.9 percent of all homicides but only a third of the U.S.

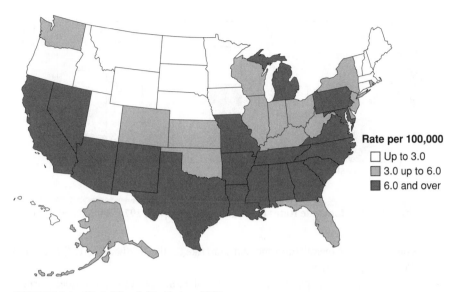

FIGURE 3.6   State Homicide Rates, 2005

population. The Southern pattern is especially pronounced in gun homicides (43.0 percent), and is also overrepresented in homicides involving an argument (45.5 percent) or within the family (48.0 percent). Figure 3.7 confirms the role of firearms in the higher rate of homicide within the South. As shown, the gun homicide rate for this region (6.6 per 100,000 population)

TABLE 3.9   Regional Differences by Homicide Type, 1976–2005 Combined

	Northeast	**Midwest**	**South**	**West**
All homicides	17.0%	19.1%	40.9%	23.0%
Intimate	12.4%	17.7%	48.9%	20.9%
Family	13.0%	18.2%	48.0%	20.9%
Infanticide	18.2%	22.3%	34.2%	25.2%
Eldercide	17.0%	19.6%	41.8%	21.6%
Felony murder	17.9%	19.6%	37.5%	25.0%
Sex related	12.4%	19.8%	35.5%	32.2%
Drug related	18.2%	16.7%	39.6%	25.6%
Gang related	3.2%	15.5%	6.0%	75.3%
Argument	14.0%	17.1%	45.5%	23.3%
Workplace	9.9%	22.0%	38.5%	29.6%
Gun homicide	15.4%	19.1%	43.0%	22.6%
Arson	32.1%	24.3%	27.4%	16.2%
Poison	16.6%	23.4%	31.5%	28.5%
Multiple victims	16.4%	20.2%	37.0%	26.5%
Multiple offenders	17.0%	19.6%	37.4%	26.0%
Population	20.8%	24.6%	32.7%	21.9%

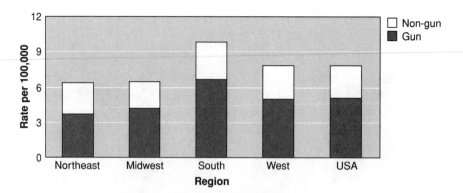

FIGURE 3.7   Homicide Rates by Region and Weapon, 1976–2005 Combined

is higher than the overall (gun and non-gun) rate for the Northeast and Midwest (6.3 and 6.4 per 100,000 population, respectively).

Doerner has applied the subculture of violence theory, described earlier, to account for the elevated Southern murder rates.[13] That is, in the South where rates of gun ownership are relatively high, violence is often seen as an acceptable way to resolve disagreements. Rather than taking it to court, Southern combatants often take it outside, in the long-standing tradition of a duel.

The Geography of Meth

Given the recent increase in the production, sales, and use of crystal methamphetamine (i.e., meth) in nonurbanized areas of the United States, rural America may be beginning to witness an increase in drug-related crimes, including homicide, similar to the urban crack crime waves of the late 1980s and early 1990s. In fact, while the percentage of urban homicides classified as drug-related dropped from 10 percent to under 6 percent during the 1990s, the percentage of rural murders that were drug related increased from about 2 percent to 3 percent over the same time span. Recent work by the Center for Urban Policy and the Environment notes that drug surveys find approximately 5 percent of the U.S. population has ever used meth; these statistics have climbed for adults but remained stable for youth. The number of meth addicts and persons being treated in emergency rooms for meth-related problems continues to increase. Some estimates suggest that meth addicts are responsible for as many as 6 million U.S. crimes each year, including burglaries, vehicle thefts, and credit card frauds.[14]

Meth has already taken a terrible toll, largely because of the many homemade labs that have exploded, killing the cooks and their family, friends, and neighbors. Indiana, a rural state where the number of meth labs doubled every year from 1997–2002, saw continued increase through 2004; when 1,549 clandestine meth labs were closed down by the police. The numbers for 2005 were the first measurable decline (1,300 lab closures) since the meth epidemic invaded this heartland state.[15]

Unfortunately, this reduction in the number of homegrown meth labs (due to successful law enforcement efforts and the restriction of the sales of cold medicines) has been replaced by the importation of meth, primarily from Mexico; the imported meth is even more potent than the homegrown version. As the drug comes into the country under the control of drug gangs, we may also see increasing violence related to the business of selling and distributing meth, similar to the territorial and money disputes associated with other drug crazes.

There have also been deaths associated with the noxious effects of the chemicals used in producing crystal meth (e.g., anhydrous ammonia), as well as drug overdoses. In some cases, meth cookers are now facing murder charges when they cause explosion deaths. Also, those who provide meth to someone who dies from an overdose can be charged with murder. And, unfortunately, there is no shortage of meth murders. A 10-year old girl was murdered in Crothersville, Indiana in January 2005 because she accidentally stumbled upon some meth cookers, and they killed her so she couldn't tell anyone what she had seen. Her body was found five days after she disappeared, hands tied behind her back, drowned in a creek. In another case, two Oregon women, strung out on meth, decided to rob a meth dealer one night in 2003. With the help of two accomplices, they made arrangements to buy crack and then killed the seller. They also murdered a 17-year-old runaway who was living with the dealer. One of the murderers admitted she spent most of her share of the robbery cash on video poker. In another case of a murderer under the influence of meth, a Vincennes, Indiana man, Daniel Ray Wilkes, 37, claimed that he had been awake for a week when he killed an Evansville woman and her two young daughters. Wilkes had met the mother in drug rehab, and after he moved in with her, he began using meth again.

Not unlike the consequences of crack, the growing popularity of crystal meth has created "parentless" children living with drug-addicted adults and sometimes being murdered by them. Many states are now recognizing that a significant number of their child maltreatment deaths are related to the meth use of the parents. In many communities, there aren't enough foster care openings for the "meth orphans" after their parents have gone to jail or prison or die. Also, chemicals used to produce meth can spread through the walls, creating a toxic environment for children. We may see a lagged crime effect as meth babies and children exposed to meth come of age.

The Role of Firearms

Any discussion of the rate of murder in the United States and how to prevent interpersonal violence must consider the role of guns. Unfortunately, the available gun research is difficult to decipher and highly charged, politically. Regardless of the findings concerning the link between guns and crime and the tone of the debate, few people tend to change their positions.

Do guns cause or at least facilitate homicidal behavior? Are homicidal people more likely to own guns? Should the government limit gun ownership or instead, as John R. Lott, Jr. argues in his controversial book, *More Guns, Less Crime,* encourage people to arm themselves? Lott suggests that the loss of lives to gun-involved homicides, suicides, and accidents is not as great as lives saved by the actual use of guns and their deterrent effect. Using many sources of gun data, Lott finds no benefits of waiting periods, gun buybacks, or even background checks and suggests that there are clear benefits in states where citizens can carry concealed firearms. Lott's research even shows that mass public shootings are less likely to occur in places where a citizen victim may be armed.[16]

While there is little agreement about what to do with guns in the U.S., there is basic consensus about figures on gun ownership. Approximately 40 percent of adults in the United States own a firearm. In total, there are at least 250 million guns in the hands of private citizens, approximately 76 million of them handguns. Whereas in the past most purchases of firearms were shotguns or rifles, most gun sales today involve handguns. Although the number of guns continues to increase in the United States, the prevalence of gun ownership has declined—in other words, fewer people own more guns.[17]

Guns have played a significant role in the recent U.S. homicide rate trends. As will be discussed in depth in Chapter 5, virtually the entire increase in the nation's homicide rate during the late 1980s involved young males—primarily minority youth—who killed using firearms. Likewise, most of the decline in killing over the past decade represented a drop specifically in gun-related incidents.

On a global scale, gun ownership does not necessarily boost a nation's homicide rate. Countries like Finland, Israel, New Zealand, Norway, and Switzerland have high levels of gun ownership, similar to U.S. patterns of ownership, and these countries have low levels of homicide. For example, Switzerland has a rate of gun ownership that is more than two times as high as Germany, but a homicide rate that is 40 percent lower.[18] Even if all guns were somehow removed from the United States, the homicide rate would still rank somewhere in the middle of the international homicide rankings. The nation's homicide rate is a function of the presence and availability of guns as well as the willingness to use them to settle personal disputes. In fact, it is not that the violence rate in the United States is so much higher than other developed countries—it is just that the rate of *lethal* violence in the United States has historically exceeded that of other nations.[19]

American gun owners may use their firearms in self-defense as many as thousands of times a year (perhaps hundreds of thousands of times or more, depending on which data source one believes). According to the National Crime Victimization Survey (NCVS), would-be assault victims use guns to defend themselves 110,000 times a year. At the other extreme, renowned gun scholar, Gary Kleck, has estimated that guns are used to defend U.S. citizens as many as 2.5 million times a year. Kleck's research also suggests that 1,500–2,800 criminals a year are lawfully killed by citizens with firearms.[20]

Gun laws formerly on the books in Texas prohibited citizens from carrying a concealed firearm. As a result, on the October day in 1991 when 35-year-old George Hennard massacred 23 people at a Lubby's Cafeteria in Killeen, none of the patrons had possession of a gun. One woman had removed her gun from her purse earlier in the day, and the weapon was locked in her car parked in the Lubby's parking lot when the slaughter occurred. She watched as both of her parents were murdered.

It is easy to cite cases, like the Lubby's mass murder, in which a gun may have prevented enormous bloodshed. On the other hand, research has also shown that the presence of a gun in the home tends to increase the risk of a family-related homicide or suicide.[21] As with most areas of debate in regard to crime control strategies, there are few clear-cut answers.

Public policy recommendations regarding guns run the continuum from a total ban on private ownership to encouraging all adult Americans to carry a firearm. The 1993 Brady Law, which mandated background checks and initial waiting periods as well, may or may not have had the desired effect on gun crimes; there is evidence on both sides of the argument. Other gun control strategies include reducing the supply and availability of guns, limiting who can own guns (e.g., restricting convicted felons, domestic abusers, or the mentally ill from purchasing) and controlling how or where guns may be used (e.g., banning guns in certain places, or requiring trigger locks). Such strategies may help to keep guns away from the small proportion of gun owners who choose to use their guns to commit murder.

Even if a jurisdiction maintains and enforces strict gun laws, it may still experience a significant problem related to gun violence. For example, whereas about two-thirds of homicide victims nationally are killed with firearms, in Washington D.C., a city with relatively stringent gun laws, 77 percent of homicides involve guns. This compares to cities like Chicago, with 68 percent gun-related homicides, and Atlanta (a city with relatively lax gun restrictions), with 69 percent gun-related homicides. However, although Washington D.C. tightly restricts gun ownership, the jurisdiction is surrounded by areas with less restrictive gun regulations, specifically Maryland and Virginia. The overriding conclusion of this murky relationship between gun availability and gun crime is that, even though guns increase the lethality of criminal assaults, the nation's high homicide rate is much larger than a matter of guns.

Breaking the Mold

Despite all the patterns in murder victimization and offending described in this chapter, many homicides still run counter to the norm. For example, Aileen Wuornos was executed in October 2002 by the state of Florida because she killed seven strangers in the style of male serial killers such as Theodore Bundy. In the small town of Plainfield, Wisconsin, Edward Gein was in his fifties when he began committing a hideous series of crimes including murder, cannibalism, grave robbing, and necrophilia. Most of the recent multiple shootings in schools around the country have been committed by white youngsters in suburban or small towns. Incidents like these help to make the study of homicide ever fascinating and challenging. The challenge is to make sense out of seemingly senseless acts of murder.

ENDNOTES

1. Charles Derber, *The Wilding of America: How Greed and Violence Are Eroding Our Nation's Character.* New York: St. Martin's Press, 1996.

2. Patrick O'Driscoll, "Poll: Media Distort Public Perception," *USA Today,* November 19, 1998.

3. David Fabianic, "Television Dramas and Homicide Causation," *Journal of Criminal Justice* 25 (1997): 195–203.

4. William Julius Wilson, *The Truly Disadvantaged: The Inner-City, the Underclass and Public Policy.* Chicago: University of Chicago Press, 1987.

5. David Pritchard and Karen D. Hughes, "Patterns of Deviance in Crime News," *Journal of Communication* 47 (1997).

6. Patricia Pearson, *When She Was Bad.* New York: Penguin Books, 1998.

7. Peter Elikann, *Superpredators: The Demonization of Our Children by the Law.* Plenum Press, 1999; Howard Spivak and Deborah Prothrow-Stith, "Stop Demonizing Our Youth," *The Boston Globe,* July 27, 1997.

8. William J. Bennett, John J. DiIulio, and John P. Walters, *Body Count: Moral Poverty and How to Win America's War against Crime and Drugs.* New York: Simon & Schuster, 1996.

9. James Alan Fox and Jack Levin, "Homicide against the Elderly: A Research Note," *Criminology* 28 (1991): 317–327.

10. Christine Vendel, "You still have a problem." *Kansas City Star,* January 1, 2007, p. A1.

11. James Alan Fox, "Roasting Chicken Little: Epidemic Thinking about Crime." Presentation at the 113th Annual Meeting of the International Association of Chiefs of Police, Boston, MA, October 16, 2006.

12. Bernard Cohen, James Alan Fox, and Marvin E. Wolfgang, *The Memphis and Shelby County Crime Report— 1996.* Guardsmark, Inc., 1996.

13. William G. Doerner, "A Regional Analysis of Homicide Rates in the United States," *Criminology* 13 (1975): 90–101.

14. James Alan Fox, David Kass, and William Christeson, "Meth Crime Rises as Budget Axe Falls," Fight Crime Invest in Kids, Washington DC, March 2006.

15. Eric Wright, Harold Kooreman, Rachel Thelin, and Marion Greene, "Methamphetamine Use in Indiana: Consumption Patterns and Consequences," in *The Consumption and Consequences of Alcohol, Tobacco, and Drugs in Indiana: A State Epidemiological Profile.* Indiana State Epidemiological and Outcomes Workgroup, Center for Urban Policy and the Environment, Indiana University, Indianapolis, 2006.

16. John R. Lott, Jr., *More Guns, Less Crime: Understanding Crime and Gun Control Laws.* Chicago: University of Chicago Press, 1998.

17. Gary Kleck, *Point Blank: Guns and Violence in America.* Hawthorne, NY: Aldine de Gruyter Publishers, 1991.

18. John R. Lott, "More Guns, Less Crime: Understanding Crime and Gun Control Laws," *American Experiment Quarterly,* Summer, 1999.

19. Franklin E. Zimring and Gordon Hawkins, *Crime is not the Problem: Lethal Violence in America.* New York: Oxford University Press, 1997.

20. Kleck, op. cit.

21. Linda L. Dahlberg, Robin M. Ikeda, and Marcie-jo Kresnow, "Guns in the Home and Risk of a Violent Death in the Home: Findings from a National Study," *Journal of Epidemiology* 160 (2004): 929–936.

4 Intimate and Family Murder

The family unit encompasses a wide constellation of relationships, many of which are linked by bloodlines. Understandably yet tragically, the around-the-clock opportunity for conflict and discord within families often causes that same blood to spill. Notwithstanding all the positive and nurturing aspects of family life, it is quite telling that the study of homicide has so many expressions within the family unit—instances when affection turns unhappily to aggression, including *domicide* and *spousicide* (spouse killings), *patricide* and *matricide* (the murder of fathers and mothers, respectively), *fratricide* and *sororicide* (killings of brothers and sisters, respectively), and *infanticide* (murders of young children), among other less common forms of intrafamilial homicide. That criminologists have established so many labels to describe killings by and of family members indicates the diversity of this phenomenon.

As shown in Table 4.1, more than 100,000 Americans were killed by family members or other intimate partners from 1976 to 2005. On average, nearly 4,000 of such homicides occur annually. About 65 percent of the intimate-partner/family killings involve spouses, ex-spouses, or boyfriends/girlfriends, with 65 percent of these homicides in turn involving current or former marital partners as opposed to current boyfriends/girlfriends.

Killing for Profit

Murder in the family and other intimate relationships spans a wide range of motives, from jealousy to revenge, from attention-seeking to mercy. It is one of the most insidious motives, if only for its selfish cold-bloodedness, when the family unit occasionally becomes a vehicle for profit. Murders involving strangers, as we would expect, frequently involve the profit motive. Yet greed knows no limits. Blood may be thicker than water, but not always when cash is involved.

On Halloween 1974, as other Houston residents prepared treats for the neighborhood children, Ronald Clark O'Bryan replaced the white sugary powder inside several Pixy Sticks with cyanide, one of which he placed in his own son's bag of goodies. O'Bryan's dastardly plan was to kill his own eight-year-old son and collect on a $20,000 insurance policy. He had hoped that rampant concern (unfounded, as there are no cases of children dying from Halloween candy poisoned by strangers) for treat tampering as a form of adolescent Halloween trickery and the discovery of similarly contaminated candy in other children's

TABLE 4.1   **U.S. Intimate-Partner and Family Homicides, 1976–2005 Combined**

Relationship	Cases	Percentage
Spouse	39,088	34.9
Ex-spouse	2,613	2.3
Parent	9,726	8.7
Child	17,052	15.2
Sibling	6,505	5.8
Other family	14,075	12.6
Boyfriend/girlfriend	22,828	20.4
Total	111,887	100.0

bags (which fortunately was not eaten) would provide a convenient cover-up to his selfish deed. O'Bryan's plan failed. He was convicted of first-degree murder and himself poisoned to death ten years later in the form of Texas' lethal injection ritual.

Another episode of cold, calculating family murder sent shockwaves reverberating through Beantown, Massachusetts. On October 23, 1989, the Boston police received an urgent call from a man using his car phone to report that he and his pregnant wife had just been shot by a stranger who had jumped into the backseat of their car. The caller, identified as 29-year-old Charles Stuart, claimed that he and his wife had been attacked by a black intruder dressed in a jogging suit as they drove home from a birthing class in a predominantly black Mission Hill section of the city. Charles Stuart survived the attack, but his wife and unborn child were not so fortunate.

Bostonians quickly rushed to support Charles Stuart with an unparalleled outpouring of sympathy. Everyone in Boston had heard the tape of his heart-wrenching call to 9-1-1. Everyone was shaken by his sorrowful eulogy to his wife Carol read at the funeral he was too sick to attend. Even the most die-hard cynic was moved when, despite the severity of his injuries, Stuart begged to be taken across town to cradle his dying infant son in his arms. With the skill of a Shakespearean actor, Stuart played the role of a grieving husband/ father.

By January 1990, however, as the police investigation into the homicide continued feverishly, Charles Stuart's story started to crumble. It was eventually discovered that he had indeed shot his wife to death after she refused to abort the pregnancy. Stuart had sensed that fatherhood would put a major chink into his ambitious career plans. Once the hoax was discovered, Stuart jumped off a bridge to his death rather than face public outrage, not to mention state prison.

In the very same year as the Stuart murder, millionaire José Menendez and his wife Mary were shot to death execution-style as they slept in their posh Beverly Hills home. José Menendez, a Cuban refugee, had built his fortune in the video distribution business, and the police suspected, based on the crime scene and the victim's business dealings, that the murder may have been a Mafia hit.

As the police tracked down leads in the case, the Menendez children, 19-year-old Erik and 22-year-old Lyle, split the first portion of their large inheritance and began to pursue the lifestyle of rich bachelors. After seven months, however, as the organized crime theory dissolved, the police scrutinized apparent inconsistencies in the Menendez brothers' alibis. The two brothers eventually broke down under police interrogation and admitted to the murders. Erik and Lyle Menendez were convicted of murder, after two jury trials in which their claim of having been abused by their father seemed far less plausible than the motive of greed.

Greed can also motivate women to kill their intimates. Toni Cato Riggs was convicted of first-degree murder and conspiracy and sentenced to life without parole after she hired her brother to murder her husband, Anthony. He was a Gulf War veteran who had only been home a few weeks when he was gunned down by Toni's brother so that she could collect his $150,000 life insurance proceeds. At first, there was not enough evidence to charge Toni Riggs with the homicide. Years later, however, she became involved in drug smuggling and confessed to undercover agents posing as drug dealers that she had in fact carefully planned her husband's death.

Obsession and Jealousy

The killer's desired reward in domestic murder cases is often something other than money: securing the love and affection of another person. Tufts University professor William Douglas, a middle-aged family man, had grown so helplessly obsessed with prostitute Robin Benedict that he wanted her all to himself. Embezzling funds from various federal grants, Douglas placed Benedict on his research payroll to compensate her for sexual exclusivity. As time progressed and Douglas' obsession grew deeper, however, Benedict resisted his jealous possessiveness.

On March 5, 1983, Douglas, unable to accept the thought of his beloved Robin sexually entwined with another man, bludgeoned the 21-year-old call girl to death with a sledgehammer and dumped her body in a trash bin off Route 95, south of Boston. Although her body was never recovered by the police, the prosecution forged ahead with murder charges against the disgraced biochemist. Faced with a murder rap, Douglas pled guilty in exchange for a reduced charge of manslaughter.

The figurative romantic triangle has three points, and at each nexus we find a person with sufficient motivation for murder. Occasionally, the triangle's apex—the unfaithful two-timer—is murdered for his or her infidelity by a jealous and spiteful mate or lover. Forty-five-year-old Clara Harris, a dentist, tried everything to keep her husband, David, 41, from leaving her for another woman. She scheduled liposuction and breast augmentation surgery, went to a tanning salon, hired a personal trainer, lost 20 pounds, lightened her hair, and wore more provocative clothing. When none of this worked, Harris repeatedly ran over her husband in a hotel parking lot, while his daughter (her stepdaughter) looked on in horror. Harris claimed the whole episode was an accident; however, a videotape of the incident, recorded by the private investigator hired by Harris to follow her philandering husband, showed her running over him multiple (perhaps as many as five) times. Harris was convicted of murder and sentenced to 20 years in prison and given a $10,000 fine. In January of 2007, a civil jury also awarded $3.75 million to Harris' in-laws as a result of their wrongful death suit against their son's killer.

The Texas jury sent a clear message that it is hardly acceptable to kill an unfaithful mate rather than face rejection. Harris, like many rejected spouse-killers, seemed to think that by killing her husband she could preserve their relationship forever. More often, however, it is one of the competing rivals (not the two-timer) who is killed in order to clear the path for romance. On April 29, 1997, 33-year-old Craig Rabinowitz of Merion, Pennsylvania, an affluent suburb outside of Philadelphia, reported to the police that he had discovered his wife, Stefanie, dead in the bathtub, apparently the victim of an intruder. But in the following weeks, his story dissolved in the face of forensic evidence revealing a web of obsession and financial debt that served as a powerful motive for murder. Rabinowitz had secretly fantasized sharing a life with an exotic dancer nicknamed "Summer," and spent more than $100,000 on trips and private couch dances with the object of his desire. Unable to maintain his innocence any longer, Rabinowitz confessed to killing his wife, not only to remove her as an obstacle to romantic bliss, but to receive almost $2 million in life insurance to pay off his personal and business debt.

Romantic triangles can also lead to the violent expulsion of an outside threat to an existing relationship. While money and passion combined to drive Rabinowitz to murder his wife, affairs of the heart are often sufficient in themselves to inspire a homicide. When David Graham, a popular high school student/athlete from Mansfield, Texas, confessed to his sweetheart, Diane Zamora, about his sexual tryst with sophomore Adrianne Jones, Zamora flew into an uncontrollable rage. As Graham tried to calm her, Zamora jealously insisted that Jones had to be killed. In order to prove his remorse and devotion, Graham conspired with Zamora in the December 1995 beating and shooting death of Jones. The two lovers then went off to become cadets in military academies and vowed to keep the crime as their dark secret. However, Zamora later broke the pact by admitting her involvement to her roommates.

Heterosexuals do not have the market cornered on domestic violence or homicide. There are several cases of intimate violence among gay couples. In December of 2002, in Ocean City, New Jersey, 24-year-old Dorothy Haines murdered and dismembered her lover, Suzanne Stiehl, 39. Haines pled guilty to aggravated manslaughter and received 27 years in prison. Although Haines, an exotic booth dancer, had a history of alcoholism, bipolar disorder, and severe brain injuries that on two occasions resulted in comas, her murderous actions appeared to have been planned (she had on a previous occasion dug an experimental grave). Haines also bragged about the murder afterwards and was rational enough to put body parts in several different locations.

In 1997, in Richmond, Virginia, a lesbian love triangle resulted in the brutal murder of one of the girls. Stacey Hanna, 18, was murdered by Kelley "Turtle" Tibbs (the ringleader) and Tibbs's longtime girlfriend, Tracy Bitner. Two other girls were also there the night Stacy was dragged into the woods and was kicked, slashed, and stabbed to death in a violent, bloody frenzy.[1]

Also in Virginia, John "Smoke" Davis, 24, of Norfolk, pled guilty to killing his partner, Ronald Luper, 36, in a July 2005 fight after a barbecue. The couple had a violent history, including knife fights. The fight that led to Luper's death also included a screwdriver and a hammer, and at one point Luper tore off Davis' lip with his teeth. Davis grabbed his gun and shot his boyfriend twice.

In a scandalous episode in Columbia, Missouri, Jesse Valencia, a 23-year-old openly gay college student, was murdered by his deeply-closeted lover, Steven Rios, a married man and a patrolman on the local police force. Apparently, Officer Rios had a history of soliciting sex from both men and women while on duty and had stalked several crime victims while working on their cases. In June 2004, as Valencia tried to end the affair and threatened to expose Rios to the police brass, Rios choked Valencia into unconsciousness and then slashed his throat, dumping the body in an alleyway before returning home to his wife and new baby.

Power, Control, and Abuse

The extraordinary cases of family and intimate homicide described thus far involve a selfish and cold-blooded scheme to commit murder in order to achieve a financial or romantic goal. Most instances of homicide within intimate relationships, however, are more likely to represent an expression of power or a defensive response to it, rather than an instrumental means for satisfying some other personal objective.

More often than not, the use of lethal force by a spouse is not the first violent episode within the relationship. One recent study examined 250 cases of women murdered by their intimate partners and found that nearly two-thirds had been assaulted by their mate in the past. In cases like these, murder is not so much a spontaneous, unpredictable act or a behavior out of character for the perpetrator but the culmination of a consistent and growing pattern of abuse within the relationship.[2]

While the jury in the criminal trial of ex-football star O.J. Simpson may, for example, have been unconvinced that he had murdered his estranged wife, Nicole Brown, and her friend Ronald Goldman, it was incontrovertible that he had assaulted and terrorized her in the years leading up to her violent death. The jury, like millions of Americans, heard 9-1-1 tapes of her desperate pleas for help while O.J. Simpson stormed her apartment. Notwithstanding his guilt or innocence, the potential for lethal violence had clearly been evidenced.

The most troubling and perplexing cases of domestic violence involve relationships held together not so much by intimacy and affection but by intimidation and aggression. In some marriages, the husband's sense of ego and self-worth depends on his ability to control, dominate, and manipulate his wife and children—not just to be in charge of traditional male responsibilities such as the family finances but to have complete and absolute authority over the household. Should his position of authority be questioned by what he perceives (or misperceives) as insolence or disobedience from his subordinate partner, he may use violence or the threat of violence to enforce his rule and reestablish command. The frequency and level of violence within such a relationship typically escalate as the abuser/controller constantly expands and tests the limits of aggression, possessiveness, and control. His wife may threaten to leave for the sake of the children, if not for herself, yet he may try to exploit her needs and feelings of guilt by begging for forgiveness and promising to change. Unfortunately, in some cases the only change to occur is for the violence to increase in its brutality as he attempts to tighten his control.

Despite widespread efforts in this country to emancipate victims of domestic violence, we have not successfully resolved all the legal, financial, and emotional ties that can strangle a woman as much as her abusive spouse can. Many women remain in a violent and potentially lethal relationship out of emotional or financial dependency or a perception, even if a false one, that staying together is better for the children.

Domestic violence expert Lenore Walker has characterized the response of some abuse victims as *learned helplessness*.[3] Frustrated in her ineffectual struggles to repel early episodes of abuse, a woman may come to develop a sense of resignation that she is helpless in controlling her own fate or that of the children. Seeing no way out while perhaps hoping things will improve, she may stay in the abusive marriage, sometimes until the level of violence becomes deadly.

Similar to the so-called *Stockholm syndrome* used to describe the compliant behavior of wartime hostages, some domestic abuse victims who feel trapped in a violent relationship can become even more closely bonded to their attacker.[4] Initially, she may strive to please and appease her abuser as a means of sheer survival. As she becomes more isolated from others, she may grow increasingly dependent on her abuser for whatever bits of attention and meager rewards he concedes her. In extreme cases, she can identify so closely with her controlling mate that she focuses exclusively on his real or imagined good points, unable psychologically to see him in a more accurate light.

As an alternative response to sustained abuse, a woman may grow in her determination to survive. Rather than give up hope and give in to their victimizers, many women find the courage and will to fight back—figuratively, if not literally—by seeking help and refuge from friends and family or legal and social services.[5]

Although the survival instinct may be healthier both physically and emotionally, on occasion attempts to escape and survive can instigate retaliatory acts of lethal violence. A move to terminate the relationship occasionally becomes the innocent precipitant to murder, sparked by what Dutton has called *abandonment rage*.[6] For example, in a study of a group of nearly 300 women murdered by their intimates, researchers found that 42 percent of victims had either separated or threatened to separate from their assailant.[7] It is the fear of this kind of deadly outcome that ultimately keeps many women in violent relationships.

When a woman does attempt to break away from an abusive partner, he may see her effort to take over control of the relationship as nothing less than a capital offense, punishable by death. In 1991, for example, 39-year-old James Colbert of Concord, New Hampshire, killed his estranged wife and three daughters before taking his own life by leaping off a bridge into the water below. Learning that his wife had started a new relationship, Colbert reasoned, "If I can't have her and the kids, then no one can." As an ultimate expression of control, Colbert—and definitely not his wife—would be the one to decide when, where, how, and on what terms their marriage would end.

Although the most typical scenario involves lethal violence as the offensive climax to escalating abuse by a husband, in about 40 percent of domestic murders it is the wife who deals the fatal blow. Sometimes the woman is the aggressor in the marriage; in these cases, the woman murders in response to her husband's infidelity, kills him to collect life insurance, or kills in order to be with her lover. But, more than men, domestic homicides committed by women are frequently a self-protective response to intimidation, threats, and physical, emotional, or sexual abuse.[8]

In a 1977 murder case made famous in the TV film *The Burning Bed* starring actress Farrah Fawcett, 30-year-old Francine Hughes of Dansville, Michigan, poured gasoline around the bed where her ex-husband Mickey lay sleeping off his latest drinking binge. After lighting a match and setting her former husband ablaze, she boarded her children into the car and drove straight to the police station where she confessed. To the detectives, it had seemed like a simple case of domestic homicide. But after hearing testimony detailing 14 years of battery and death threats, the jury surprised the legal community, if not the nation, by finding Hughes not guilty by temporary insanity.

Ever since the Burning Bed case, the courts have struggled with the battered woman syndrome as a defense to murder.[9] A chronic abuse victim feels trapped as a consequence of her prolonged history of physical, sexual, or psychological punishment. In the tradition of English common law, in order to invoke self-defense, the risk of aggression has to be immediate and with no reasonable means of escape. Yet increasingly, the courts have excused or at least lessened responsibility when violence was not imminent but a day-to-day, continuing threat. As for the requirement of taking flight, the courts have begun to recognize that legal ties and financial dependencies, if not feelings of sheer terror, often prevent what ordinarily would appear to be opportunities for escape.

Partially due to the efforts by battered women advocacy groups, the incidence of domestic homicide has fallen nationally over the past quarter century. Overall, the number of homicides of husbands and wives has declined steadily from just under 2,200 in 1976 to fewer than 800 in 2005, a drop of nearly two-thirds.

But domestic violence services are not necessarily helpful to all women. Research by Laura Dugan and her colleagues suggests that some domestic violence interventions may not work, and may even make things worse.[10] Dugan found that some resources, such as warrantless arrest provisions and economic assistance for victims, may indeed have reduced the incidence of domestic violence homicides. However, warrantless arrests had a positive effect only for white victims, both married and unmarried. In these cases, making it easier for a woman to escape a violent relationship may protect both the woman and her batterer.

Other policies, however, appear to have worsened the predicament for certain victims. Protective orders issued in court, for example, may have increased the risk of homicide for some demographic groups (e.g., unmarried black male and female partners). It is critically important, therefore, when implementing any domestic violence reduction policies, that both the protective effects as well as the potential for backlash/retaliation be considered.

Some critics have suggested that the downturn in spousal homicide is little more than a demographic artifact, resulting from changes in domesticity—or living arrangements—rather than any real progress in reducing violence between marital partners. By this theory, as divorce rates have risen and rates of marriage have declined, fewer men and women are "eligible" to be murdered by their spouses. As some support for this view, the number of unmarried women murdered by boyfriends has increased somewhat over the past three decades, from about 350 in 1976 to more than 500 in 2005. Although this growth is consistent with the expanded number of unmarried women in the population, it does suggest that non-marriage as well as divorce has put fewer women at risk, at least for spousal homicide.

Over the latter half of the 20th century, divorce laws were indeed liberalized. By contrast to an earlier era when the marital ties could not be easily broken without proof of cause, such as mental or physical cruelty or adultery, no-fault divorce laws have permitted couples to split before the level of discord reaches extreme and violent proportions. Yet for relationships in which violence is indeed a form of control, the easy availability of divorce can be a cruel illusion. The "if I can't have you, no one can" threat would generally prohibit an amicable no-fault divorce. Fortunately, improvement in the economic status of women has eroded the control men have historically had over their spouses.

Another factor behind the decline in intimate homicide is that the social stigma associated with being an abused spouse (as well as a divorcee) has greatly diminished. During a less enlightened era, victims of domestic abuse often internalized blame and guilt for their own victimization. "If only I were a better wife, a better cook, a better lover, he wouldn't get mad and beat me." Today, as the topic of domestic violence has been brought more into the open, victims are less likely to feel responsible for their plight and thus more likely to make a move to exit the relationship.

Besides divorce, more immediate legal and social interventions—such as restraining orders, mandatory police arrest procedures, abuse hotlines, shelters for battered women, and support groups and counseling for victims of domestic violence—have helped provide some abused women with a viable escape route. More than ever, a woman has alternatives to picking up a loaded gun and shooting her loaded husband. As shown in Figure 4.1, it is ironically the men who have benefited the most from intervention strategies designed to protect women. The steepest decline in intimate homicides has been in women killing their partners (husbands, ex-husbands, or boyfriends), down from about 1,300 in 1976 to about 300 in 2005, a remarkable 75 percent decline. Given the expanding array of legal and social interventions, murder is less often the only or last resort for a woman to protect herself from a current or former intimate who abuses or stalks her.

By contrast, the improvement in the number of women killed by their intimates has been more modest and relatively recent. From 1976 to 1993, the incidents of women killed by intimates fluctuated between 1,400 and 1,600, with no indication of a trend in either direction. Apparently, men were unconcerned about the increasing array of interventions available to victims of domestic violence. In fact, some men were inspired in a decidedly violent way in the face of restraining orders and other initiatives by their wives or girl-friends to escape.

We read frequently of domestic disputes that escalate rapidly to deadly proportions, especially if a gun is available. In fact, 66 percent of homicides by intimate partners involve a gun. The firearm may have been purchased ostensibly to protect and defend the family from an outside intruder, but ultimately it is fired offensively against a loved one in a moment of rage or revenge. In their analysis of cases in Tennessee, Washington, and Ohio, for example, Arthur Kellermann and his colleagues found that a gun in the home increased the likelihood of domestic homicide by nearly a factor of three.[11]

It is only in the past few years, since 1993, that the number of men killing wives and girlfriends has declined as well, from almost 1,600 in 1993 to under 1,200 in 2005.

FIGURE 4.1   Intimate-Partner Homicides by Sex of Victim, 1976–2005

Although research finds no effects of the Brady Law on gun violence, this downturn coincides with the implementation of the Brady Law, which mandated background checks (and for the first few years, waiting periods as well) prior to purchases of firearms. It is difficult to establish whether this gun legislation made any difference, but it is noteworthy that virtually the entire decline (about 90 percent) in women murdered by their partners since 1993 has been in gun-related incidents.

The availability of social and legal interventions to abuse victims is, unfortunately, not equally extensive in all parts of the country. The decline in the percentage of homicides involving intimate partners has occurred primarily in urban areas. It is in these same locales where the greatest emphasis has been placed on providing resources such as shelters for battered women. In many suburbs and especially rural areas, a victim of abuse may not have access to such escape routes and may even remain in a dangerous and potentially lethal relationship to avoid the stigma within her small community.

In the final analysis, people often wonder in cases of cold-blooded spousal homicide, "Why didn't he just get a divorce?" For some killers, lethal dissolution of their marriage has far greater benefits—monetary and otherwise—than the legal alternative in divorce court. Clearly, some estranged husbands and wives are motivated to keep all of the marital assets, leaving aside any extra profit from life insurance. Another "asset" they may not want to share is custody of the children. In 2002, for example, 43-year-old Harold Stonier of Concord, Massachusetts, paid a significant sum of money to a hitman who turned out to be an undercover agent. Stonier apparently wanted his wife dead, even if it meant paying a sum greater than what he may have forfeited in a divorce settlement. According to his taped statements, he did not want to lose custody of his son, Jamie. The only way to ensure he got custody, Stonier reasoned, was to eliminate his wife. Liberalized divorce laws may therefore have had a greater impact on husbands killing wives than on wives killing their husbands.

Family Annihilation

Most family homicides involve a single perpetrator (usually the husband/father) and a single victim (usually his wife). Even when only one person is attacked, others in the household—typically the children—become secondary victims, suffering indirectly by witnessing violence and by having to live with its consequences—that is, having a murdered mother and an incarcerated father.

On occasion, however, the domestic murderer doesn't stop with just one victim but may extend his carnage through the entire family. Although the children may have little or nothing to do with his grudge or grievance, they may still be linked in his mind with the primary victim—after all, they are *her* children. In what has been called murder by proxy, innocent people are sometimes targeted in order to punish the primary victim even further.[12]

Although his castle was little more than a ramshackle home, Ronald Gene Simmons was the king in his kingdom. He ruled the household, his wife, children, and grandchildren with absolute control, a pattern not so uncommon in rural southern communities like Dover, Arkansas. Simmons dictated where his family members could go, when, and with whom. By Christmastime 1987, however, he was losing his grip—not on reality but on his family. Simmons' family life seemed to be crumbling around him. Although the kids still obeyed, they now did so without a shred of respect for their father. They had grown rude and insulting toward him. To a former military man like Simmons, this "verbal abuse" was sheer insubordination. But insubordination was nothing compared to desertion. Simmons was aware that his wife was on the verge of leaving him and taking the kids with her. In a final desperate act of control, Simmons executed his entire family, not only his wife, children, and grandchildren who lived with him, but also his older children and their families in succession as they came to the house to visit for Christmas. By the end of a five-day siege, Simmons had killed 14 family members in the largest family massacre in U.S. history. Even then, he wasn't quite finished. After annihilating his family, he launched a 45-minute rampage through the nearby town of Russellville, where he killed two and wounded four others. Simmons was executed by lethal injection in 1990.

Family massacres are generally committed by a head of household who perceives that he has total say over his clan, in life and in death. He feels entitled by his position to determine his family's destiny. However, a few family annihilations have also been committed by children as a violent reaction to this same type of parental domination and control. In 1976, for example, 18-year-old Harry De La Roche, Jr., methodically executed his mother, father, and two brothers in their beds in order to free himself of his dad's domination. Home from college for Thanksgiving vacation, De La Roche could not bring himself to face his father with his decision to quit school. Murder would be the easier way out.

Annually, approximately 300 parents are slain by their children or stepchildren, and more than half of these parricides involve a child or stepchild under the age of 25. Of these younger perpetrators, as shown in Figure 4.2, most incidents involve fathers killed by their sons or stepsons (51 percent), followed by mothers slain by sons or stepsons (35 percent), fathers by daughters (8 percent) and mothers by daughters (6 percent).

Criminologist Kathleen Heide has proposed a three-category typology for parricides.[13] According to her view, the crime is most frequently committed in response to severe physical or sexual abuse. As with preemptive attacks by battered wives, these acts of parricide are often more defensive than offensive. The defensive strike can also come on behalf of another person, typically protecting a mother from her abusive husband or boyfriend. In January 2000, for example, an 8-year-old Tennessee boy confessed to stabbing his mother's boyfriend to death, after witnessing a pattern of physical violence directed against her.

Heide's other two classifications involve psychological rather than situational disorders. Some children who murder their parents do so under the influence of a severe mental

FIGURE 4.2   U.S. Parricides by Type, 1976–2005 Combined

illness, such as schizophrenia. Still others simply have bad character, classifiable as an antisocial personality disorder (or, for especially young offenders, a conduct disorder). In Allentown, Pennsylvania, for example, two chronically delinquent brothers—ages 15 and 17—who fashioned themselves as white supremacist skinheads, killed their father when he refused to let them drive the family car. They also murdered their mother and their 11-year-old brother.

Infanticide

Very young children virtually never commit murder, of course, but they are clearly at risk for being murdered. Overall, 600 to 700 children under the age of five are killed each year in the United States, with boys having a slightly greater level of victimization than girls. Although the number of such cases appears to have risen over the past two decades, the increase is actually no greater than corresponding changes in the population of young children.

Infanticide is a remarkably different event from most other forms of homicide. Because of the small stature and physical vulnerability of young children, firearms are rarely used—or needed—to kill them. Most commonly, victims of this tender age are killed with hands or fists through strangulation, suffocation, beating, or shaking. Infanticide typically occurs during a fit of anger by an adult against a defenseless baby or following a chronic pattern of child abuse that turns fatal. In November 2006, an Ohio mom, China Arnold, 26, was charged with murdering her 3-week-old-baby by cooking her in the microwave. This is not the first mom to kill her child with a microwave—in 2002 a Virginia woman was sentenced to 5 years in prison for killing her month-old son in the microwave, and there are a number of cases of this sickening practice committed against family pets.

As shown in Figure 4.3, the majority of the perpetrators of infanticide are parents, not stranger abductors or intruders. Other than parents, the next largest category of perpetrators consists of male friends or acquaintances, very often the mother's boyfriend. Overall, fewer than 5 percent of infanticides are committed by babysitters or nannies.

The internationally publicized murder trial of 19-year-old English au pair Louise Woodward in the 1997 "shaken baby" death of 8-month-old Matthew Eappen of Newton,

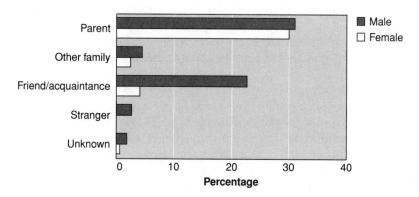

FIGURE 4.3   U.S. Infanticides by Offender Type, 1976–2005 Combined

Massachusetts, gave many parents pause to think about the caretakers to whom they entrusted their young ones. Babysitters have been known to murder children for reasons of ill-temper and poor training, but these cases are few and very far between. Although parents are, of course, wise to investigate fully those in whom they place so much trust, murder is generally the least of their concerns (especially compared with the much higher likelihood of accidental death).

Because of the overwhelming statistical tendencies in cases of infanticide implicating parents, the focus of the investigation into the death of 6-year-old JonBenet Ramsey of Boulder, Colorado, during Christmas 1996 centered, rightly or wrongly, on the girl's parents, John and Patsy. When they refused to cooperate with the police, suspicion grew. And when Patsy could not be ruled out as the author of a ransom note found at the scene of the crime, many people became convinced that JonBenet's mother had murdered her young daughter. The JonBenet Ramsey case remains unsolved and Patsy Ramsey has since died from ovarian cancer. In August of 2006, a mentally ill false confessor, John Mark Karr, claimed that he killed JonBenet but, as is often the case in high-profile crimes, he only wanted to insert himself into the middle of a media circus. Karr desperately wanted the attention and, unfortunately, for a few days, he got his wish. He has now slid back into obscurity.

Although child abductions by strangers do sometimes occur, in general parents have a much greater range of motivations for committing infanticide than do acquaintances or strangers. Because of our steadfast belief that parents should be protectors rather than executioners, we tend to accept alternative explanations for child homicide, despite the strong statistical pattern favoring parents as suspects. This was what 23-year-old Susan Smith of Union, South Carolina, counted on when she and her estranged husband went before a national television audience in October 1994 and begged tearfully for the lives and safety of her two sons, 3-year-old Michael and Alex, age 14 months.

According to the distraught mother, a black stranger had jumped into her Mazda Protégé while she was stopped at a traffic light. The carjacker had reportedly ordered her out of the vehicle and then sped off with Smith's two boys still trapped in the backseat. The police were cautiously skeptical, however, because of some discrepancies in her description of the incident. Within days, after failing a polygraph test, Susan Smith confessed that she had rolled the car into a nearby lake with her children strapped helplessly inside. Smith had a very troubled childhood and had experienced the suicide death of her father when she was a child. In addition, she had attempted suicide, and had been molested by a stepfather as a child and continued to have a consensual sexual relationship with him when they were adults. Obviously these factors do not justify Smith's actions, but they do help us to understand some of the factors that contribute to a mother being capable of the murder of her two children.

In the weeks that followed, Smith's motive for drowning her sons was revealed, and it certainly didn't place her in a sympathetic light. Smith was told in a letter from her new boyfriend that he would not stay with or marry her because she had children. Smith apparently chose to sacrifice her offspring in the pursuit of romance.

In some instances of infanticide, a young parent responds violently when unable to handle the stress of a difficult crying baby. Some instances may be aided by hormonal changes after childbirth, ranging from the baby blues to clinical postpartum depression or even psychosis. In recent years, some movement has even been seen in raising a postpartum defense to murder charges.

In March 2002, Andrea Yates of Houston, Texas drowned her five children, ages 7, 5, 3, 2, and 6 months, in a frenzied religious hallucination. Yates was spared the death penalty, but was sentenced to life in prison with eligibility for parole after 40 years. Although she admitted planning the murders in advance, Yates pled not guilty by reason of insanity due to an obviously severe case of postpartum psychosis (PPP). She had a history of institutionalization, suicide attempts, and previous postpartum depression. Yet jurors believed that Yates knew what she was doing was wrong and therefore failed to qualify for insanity under Texas law.

In November of 2005, the Texas court of appeals threw out Yates' murder convictions. During her trial, a prosecution expert witness had testified in error that Yates had been inspired to kill her children by an episode of the television program *Law & Order.* It was determined later that no such episode ever aired. Yates received a new trial, and in July 2006, she was found not guilty by reason of insanity. She will spend her time in a state mental hospital until she is no longer a threat. Yates' husband divorced her and remarried, but has continued to stand by his former wife, asserting that she was severely mentally ill, but not criminal, at the time of the deaths of their children.

Another Texas mother who murdered her children as a result of schizophrenia was found not guilty by reason of insanity. In 2003, Lisa Diaz drowned her 3- and 5-year-old daughters, and then cut herself in what is believed to be a failed suicide attempt. She was committed to a Texas psychiatric hospital in 2004, but then released in November 2006.

Unlike Diaz's short time in secure treatment, offenders in these cases are often required to spend as much time in the mental institution as they would have in prison; however, it is not always mandated. As is often the case with the mentally ill who kill, proper treatment makes them ready to return to society. Diaz was not imprisoned but was mandated to receive outpatient mental healthcare.

Again in Texas, another high-profile case of infanticide resulted in a verdict of not guilty by reason of insanity for Dena Schlosser, 38. In 2004, Schlosser severed her 10-month-old baby's arms at the shoulders to give them to God. Schlosser's husband filed for a divorce and is raising the couple's two other daughters. Schlosser was diagnosed with PPP, depression, and a brain tumor. Also on a mission for God, Deanna Lacey, a devoutly religious east Texas housewife, stoned her two sons, ages 8 and 6, to death, and permanently injured a third son, 14 months old, in 2003. She had a history of psychiatric problems and thought that she and Andrea Yates had been chosen by God. Lacey was found not guilty by reason of insanity and sent to a Texas mental hospital. Her husband loyally stood by her throughout the proceedings.

Occasionally, as in Susan Smith's case, the use of lethal force against a young innocent is far more selfish and reprehensible than just the inability to cope with parenthood. Sadly, children are sometimes exploited for a number of self-serving reasons—for profit, for love, even for attention. In what is known as Munchausen syndrome, adults and children have been known to feign illness or even self-inflict sickness or injury for the sake of attention.[14] For some people who may otherwise feel insecure and unloved, the attention they receive from family, friends, even the medical professionals when they are sick can become psychologically addictive, so much so that the sympathy is worth the suffering. In a derivative condition, Munchausen syndrome by proxy (MSBP), parents and other caretakers have been known to cause injury or illness to a child, an elderly parent, or other dependent in order to claim center stage and inject themselves into an exciting or emergency situation.

For Marybeth Tinning of Schenectady, New York, the sympathy afforded a grieving mother grew irresistible. Craving attention, she learned that the support given to a new mother only lasts so long. When her third child, baby Jennifer, died shortly after birth following a week-long struggle with hemorrhagic meningitis, she also learned that the attention surrounding a death could be as sustaining as that surrounding a birth. For the span of some dozen years, Marybeth gave birth to a series of children, all of whom eventually died, usually of what had been diagnosed as SIDS (sudden infant death syndrome) or "crib death." Marybeth responded routinely following each loss of another child. She called all her friends and relatives to announce the latest reduction in the Tinning family, expecting the customary round of pity and attention. Her death announcements had become as emotionally arousing for her as the birth announcements; both would make her the center of attention. Marybeth began theorizing—almost bragging—about a genetic defect that she was passing on to each of her babies. But as children numbers six, seven, and eight died, sympathy for Marybeth started turning into suspicion.

For five years after the death of their eighth child, Marybeth and her husband, Joseph, remained childless. After years with an "empty nest," the Tinnings were ecstatic over the birth of their ninth child, Tami Lynne, in August of 1985. The baby girl was beautiful, healthy, and full of life, yet those closest to the Tinnings quietly predicted that there would soon be another funeral to attend.

According to Marybeth, early in the morning of December 20, she went to check on her baby and found her lying on her stomach, motionless and breathless. Despite efforts to restore her breathing, Tami Lynne was pronounced dead. Unable to ignore what had become painfully clear, Marybeth's sister-in-law this time went to the police with her suspicions. Tami Lynne was autopsied carefully and thoroughly, with new and improved methods for distinguishing SIDS from induced asphyxiation. According to the coroner's report, the baby had not died of natural causes but instead had been suffocated. Despite the fact that implicating evidence from earlier deaths had long since been buried, there was enough direct and circumstantial evidence to charge and convict Marybeth with murder.

In Munchausen syndrome by proxy, the victims are exploited as pawns to fulfill the perpetrator's emotional needs. Infanticides, as we have seen in other cases, can also result from a desire for more practical rewards, such as profit, companionship, or even vengeance.

On Father's Day in 1999, Amy Shanabarger of Franklin, Indiana, returned home from her job as a grocery store cashier only to find her 7-month-old son Tyler dead, lying face down in his crib. After an autopsy, the coroner determined that the cause of death was SIDS. Just hours after the funeral, however, the boy's father confessed to the police that he had suffocated the infant while his wife was at work, by wrapping his head in plastic. Ronald Shanabarger, 29, admitted his motive was revenge against his wife, planning the homicide even before the child was conceived. He was angry and resentful that in 1996, before they were married, Amy had refused to cut her vacation cruise short to comfort him following the death of his father. According to the confession, Shanabarger fathered the child, waited until his wife bonded with the infant, and then murdered him so that his wife could experience the same kind of pain she had insensitively ignored years earlier.

In cases where one parent was aware that another parent or adult was abusing their child and did not take action to protect the child, the former can be charged under "failure to protect" laws. These laws have typically been used against mothers. This controversial statute holds mothers (and potentially fathers and other adults) responsible for the abuse (or worse) committed against their children. The purpose is to protect children but in reality, the mother is sometimes also a battered woman who cannot protect herself or her children. She may believe that if she reports the domestic violence being committed against her children, that the batterer will kill her children (and her). According to Schernitzki, women who failed to protect their children could in some cases be subject to more severe penalties than the abuser himself.[15] A more reasonable target of the failure to protect legislation may be non-battered partners.

In October of 1994, Pauline Zile, 24, of Ft. Lauderdale, Florida reported her 7-year-old daughter, Christina Holt, missing from a shopping mall. The girl's body was discovered five days later, and Zile confessed that she had lied about the abduction story. In fact, her husband, the girl's stepfather, had beaten Christina to death. Because she had witnessed the beatings and helped create the false kidnapping story to protect her husband, Pauline Zile was convicted of murder and sentenced to life in prison.

Critics of the failure to protect laws note that they are more likely to be used against mothers than fathers—that it is the mother that is held to a higher responsibility for protecting a child. In a recent Michigan case, Lisa Holland, 33, was convicted of first-degree murder and sentenced to life in prison for killing her 7-year-old adopted son. Her husband was sentenced to 30–60 years for allowing the abuse to continue for years. The boy had come into the Holland home as a foster child in 2000 (as did three of his siblings) and was dead by 2005. According to testimony by the father, the mother had tortured and abused the boy for years and kept him tied in the basement. After she hit him in the head with a hammer, he did not eat, drink, walk, talk, or have control of his bladder. When the boy finally died, the father dumped the body in the woods.

Chapter 3 described a controversial study by economists Donahue and Levitt linking the 1973 *Roe v. Wade,* Supreme Court decision that legalized abortion to declining rates of violence decades later. Along similar lines, economists Kalist and Molinari found a more direct statistical connection between the availability of Medicaid-funded abortion and rates of infanticide. Specifically, their analysis indicated that the rate of infanticide is between 13 and 20 percent lower in states that provide public funding for abortion.[16] Regardless of one's moral position on the long-standing debate over abortion and state-funding of abortion-on-demand, restrictions on a woman's right to terminate pregnancy—which opponents often call "murder"—could actually, if Kalist and Molinari are right, result in higher rates of infant homicide.

Motherhood by Proxy

Some women who become pregnant will murder the baby to hide their pregnancy and childbirth, but some women want to be a mother so desperately that they will murder to become one. Infant abductions used to occur primarily in hospitals, but those types of abductions are on the decline. In an effort to prevent intruders from stealing newborns from nurseries, many hospitals stopped relaying birth announcements and added multiple levels of security. As is true in other crime prevention arenas, however, so-called target hardening approaches sometimes only displace the crime, inadvertently forcing strongly motivated perpetrators to seek alternative means to fulfill their goal. In the case of baby stealing, many thieves have resorted to taking other women's babies before they are born or after they go home.

Although most of the several hundred infant abductions committed since 1983 do not involve the use of violence of any kind, more recently, a particularly heinous form of abduction—newborn kidnapping by Cesarean section—has emerged.[17] These are cases of women who abduct a pregnant woman and, typically by fairly primitive means (e.g., car keys), cut the baby from the mother's womb. These are desperate attempts at motherhood with varying motives. Some of the women want the attention that pregnant women enjoy—motherhood by proxy. Others are attempting to trap a man.

There are several cases of C-section kidnappings from the past two decades, reflecting the bizarre range of motives and tactics used by women desperate for a newborn of their own. One very recent case of abduction by Cesarean section—fortunately an unsuccessful one—demonstrates the extent to which some women will go to "become a mother." In February of 2005, 9-months-pregnant Sarah Brady, 26, of Ft. Mitchell, Kentucky, received a call supposedly from Sarah *Brody* who claimed to have baby gifts that had been delivered to her by mistake. Sarah Brody was actually Katie Smith, 22. The two women chatted by phone, and Sarah Brady then went to Smith's house to pick up the package. Sure enough, there was a box filled with baby items from Sarah's baby registry. As it turns out, Smith also appeared to be heavily pregnant. Later in the day, Smith called again and said another package had arrived. Brady returned to Smith's apartment to get the second package. On this visit, Smith attacked Brady with a knife, and the two women struggled for at least 20 minutes. As is often the case in knife fights, the assailant became a victim: Brady fought back, hit Smith on the head with an ashtray, wrestled the knife from her and stabbed her three times.

When police arrived and took a close look at the Smith's apartment, they found a fully decorated and stocked baby nursery and surgical tools for a C-section delivery. Smith had falsely claimed to be pregnant on at least three other occasions and had worked as a nanny in several homes (where she had stolen ultrasound pictures). Smith died from her injuries (ruled to be a justifiable homicide due to self-defense), and Brady delivered a healthy baby girl days later. Because of cases such as this, many stores that offer online baby registries are beginning to change their systems to hide detailed information about the prospective mothers.

Killing for Love?

One of the less common yet especially insidious forms of family homicide involves the victimization of elders who, because of advanced age, infirmity, or dependency, are vulnerable to family members. Sons, daughters, and other relations have been known to abuse elders for emotional reasons, or even murder them greedily to hasten an expected inheritance.

Within families, murder can also be an expression of love and compassion. Despite the laws prohibiting euthanasia, occasionally children kill elderly and dying parents, and parents kill sickly children to spare them the misery of living. Sometimes it is a case of assisted suicide in which the victim is too weak to execute the fatal procedure. Other times, a loving family member may make a decision for the victim in a merciful act of homicide.

Family annihilations of perfectly healthy loved ones can also reflect the same notion of love, albeit twisted and inspired by depression. To the murderer, life on earth may be so miserable that he feels his loved ones will be better off dead. In what psychiatrist Shervert Frazier termed *suicide by proxy,* the killer sees his loved ones as an extension of himself.[18] He feels personal responsibility for the well-being of his wife and children and sees no other way out of his predicament.

Lawrence DeLisle, age 29, of Lincoln Park, Michigan, had become so overwhelmed with despair that he deliberately drove his station wagon straight into the Detroit River in an effort to murder his entire family—his wife, three kids, and himself. After hitting the water, his survival instinct overtook his self-pity and he successfully swam to safety, as did his wife. The children were not so lucky, however. Unable to extricate themselves from their seat belts, they drowned within minutes. Despite his suicidal intentions, DeLisle was convicted of three counts of murder.

While it is easy to be suspicious of DeLisle's motives, other family murderers have been better able to follow through on their suicide mission. By May 1990, 37-year-old Hermino Elizalde, described by friends and neighbors in Chicago as a devoted father, had become hopelessly despondent over his recent firing. He was even more concerned about his ex-wife's attempt to exploit his lapse in employment to win custody of their four daughters and one son, after she accused him of mistreating them. Rather than losing his beloved children, he decided to keep them together at all cost . . . at least spiritually. Elizalde doused his sleeping children with gasoline, lit a match, and set them afire one at a time. When he was sure they were dead, he set himself on fire. By killing them all, Elizalde felt assured that they would be reunited in a better life after death.

Murder–Suicide

There is no national tracking system for murder-suicide, and thus most of the data on this type of event is based on a review of coroner and medical examiner records as well as news accounts. Comstock and her colleagues studied cases of murder-suicide in the state of Oklahoma from 1994–2001.[19] They found that the typical offender was a white male over 30 years of age who killed a current or former intimate partner. Men are much more likely than women to kill themselves after murdering their partner and/or children. These relationships were characterized as possessive, and the typical circumstance was divorce/estrangement. Eighty percent of the victims were female, two-thirds were current or former intimate partners and 20 percent of victims were children of the perpetrator.

What causes some intimate partners to commit suicide after the homicide of a partner? The search for risk factors reveals that a history of perpetrator depression, a previous history of battering and the presence of a firearm all increase the likelihood of murder-suicide. When a perpetrator threatens to kill the woman and/or other family members, threatens the family with a weapon, engages in stalking behavior, has had orders of protection filed against him, and uses alcohol and drugs, these should be warning signs for the possibility of a murder-suicide.[20]

The death toll is high in some murder-suicides, particularly those involving male perpetrators. In July 2006, Trevor Branscum, 37, killed his four sleeping children with his hunting rifle and then killed himself. The children ranged from 5–12 years of age. Branscum had had an argument with his wife. She then left the house, and he killed the children in what appeared to be an attempt to punish his wife over their dispute. The Violence Policy Center recently released a summary of the 264 U.S. murder-suicides (claiming 591 lives) that occurred in the first six months of 2005. The Center, a nonprofit group that promotes gun control, found that 90 percent of the murder-suicides involved a firearm, 94 percent of offenders were male, and 75 percent occurred in the home. The study also found that most offenders had a history of depression. Six states had more than 10 murder-suicides during the six-month study, including Pennsylvania (18); Texas (18); California (17) Florida (15) North Carolina (14) and Tennessee (11).[21] These state patterns reflect population distribution to some extent (e.g., Texas, California, and Florida); in addition, some have suggested that murder-suicide may be more common in immigrant families, so we may see trends over time in states that have large immigrant populations.

Although the media seems to focus its coverage more on the murder-suicide cases that involve younger couples, recent research by Donna Cohen found the rate of murder-suicide to be twice as high among the over-55 age group than among younger couples.[22] Extrapolating from Florida cases, Cohen estimated that there are approximately 1,000–1,500 episodes of murder-suicide each year in the U.S. (involving about 2,000–3,000 deaths). Her research also suggested that this phenomenon (older couple murder-suicides) may be on the rise. In older couples, it is most common for the husband to be the perpetrator and the wife to be the unwitting victim, typically shot while asleep. Many episodes may stem from the husband's inability to cope with a care-giving role. He may rationalize his crime as an act of love or compassion, but it may actually have a more personal motive.

To any casual observer of current events, the occurrence of family murder seems endless. Yet despite the tragedies in so many households across the country, the number of family murders has actually declined, from nearly 4,000 victims annually in the late 1970s to just under 2,000 in 2005. The percentage of all homicides traced to familial relationships has dropped as well. Though the trend may be in the right direction, the thousands of instances each year when men, women, and children are murdered by people they love, be it for power, passion, or profit, offend our sense of the sanctity and safety of marriage and family. The words "until death do us part" should be a loving promise, never a loathsome threat.

ENDNOTES

1. Sally Chew, *A Fatal Lie: A True Story of Betrayal and Murder in the New South,* New York: St. Martin's, 1999.

2. J. McFarlane, J. Campbell, S. Wilt, C. Sachs, Y. Ulrich, and X. Xu, "Stalking and Intimate Partner Femicide," *Homicide Studies* 3 (1999): 300–316.

3. Lenore E. Walker, "Battered Women and Learned Helplessness," *Victimology: An International Journal* 2 (1977): 525–534.

4. Dee L. R. Graham, Edna Rawlings, and Nelly Rimini, "Survivors of Terror: Battered Women, Hostages, and the Stockholm Syndrome," in Kersti Yllo and Michele L. Bograd, eds., *Feminist Perspectives on Wife Abuse.* Newbury Park, CA: Sage Publications, 1998.

5. Edward W. Gondolf and Ellen R. Fisher, *Battered Women as Survivors: An Alternative to Treating Learned Helplessness.* New York: Lexington Books, 1988.

6. Donald G. Dutton, *The Domestic Assault of Women: Psychological and Criminal Justice Perspectives.* Vancouver: University of British Columbia Press, 1995.

7. Kathryn E. Moracco, Carol W. Runyan, and John D. Butts, "Femicide in North Carolina: A Statewide Study of Patterns and Precursors," *Homicide Studies* 2 (1998): 422–446.

8. Ann Goetting, "Homicidal Wives: A Profile," *Journal of Family Issues* 8 (1987): 332–341.

9. See R. K. Thyfault, "Self-Defense: Battered Women Syndrome on Trial," *California Western Law Review* 20 (1984): 485–510.

10. Laura Dugan, Daniel S. Nagin, and Richard Rosenfeld, "Exposure Reduction or Retaliation? The Effects of Domestic Violence Resources on Intimate-Partner Homicide," *Law and Society Review* 37 (2003): 169–198; Laura Dugan, Daniel Nagin, and Richard Rosenfeld, "Do Domestic Violence Services Save Lives?" Washington DC: National Institute of Justice, Issue No. 250 (2003) (NCJ 196548).

11. A. L. Kellermann, F. P. Rivara, N. B. Rusforth, J. G. Banton, B. T. Reay, J. T. Francisco, A. B. Locchi, B. A. Prosdzinski, B. B. Hackman, and G. Somes, "Gun Ownership as a Risk Factor for Homicide in the Home," *New England Journal of Medicine* 267 (1993): 1084–1090.

12. Shervert H. Frazier, "Violence and Social Impact," in J. C. Schoolar and C. M. Gaitz, eds., *Research and the Psychiatric Patient.* New York: Brunner/Mazel, 1975.

13. Kathleen M. Heide, *Why Kids Kill Parents: Child Abuse and Adolescent Homicide.* Columbus, OH: Ohio State University Press, 1992.

14. Charles V. Ford, "Munchausen Syndrome," in Claude T. H. Friedmann and Robert A. Faguet, eds., *Extraordinary Disorders of Human Behavior.* New York: Plenum Press, 1982; Richard Firstman and Jamie Talan, *The Death of Innocents.* New York: Bantam Books, 1998.

15. Rebecca Ann Schernitzki, "What Kind of Mother Are You? The Relationship Between Motherhood, Battered Woman Syndrome and Missouri Law," *Journal of the Missouri Bar* 56 (2000): 1–11.

16. David E. Kalist and Noelle A. Molinari, "Abortion and Infant Homicide," Unpublished manuscript, Shippensburg University of Pennsylvania, February 2004.

17. Ann W. Burgess, Timothy Baker, Cathy Nahirny, and John Rabun, "Newborn Kidnapping by Cesarean Section," *Journal of Forensic Science* 47 (2002): 827–830.

18. Shervert H. Frazier, op. cit.

19. R. Dawn Comstock, Sue Mallonee, Elizabeth Kruger, Kim Rayno, April Vance, and Fred Jordan, "Epidemiology of Homicide-Suicide Events: Oklahoma, 1994–2001," *The American Journal of Forensic Medicine and Pathology* 26 (2005): 229–235.

20. Julie E. Malphurs and Donna Cohen, "A Statewide Case-Control Study of Spousal Homicide-Suicide in Older Persons," *The American Journal of Geriatric Psychiatry,* 13 (2005): 211–217; Jane Koziol-McLain, Daniel Webster, Judith McFarlane, Carolyn Rebecca Block, Yvonne Ulrich, Nancy Glass, and Jacquelyn C. Campbell, "Risk Factors for Femicide-Suicide in Abusive Relationship: Results from a Multi-site Case Control Study," *Violence and Victims* 21 (2006): 3–21.

21. The Violence Policy Center, "American Roulette: Murder-Suicide in the United States." Washington, DC. May, 2006.

22. Donna Cohen, "Homicide-Suicide in Older People," *Psychiatric Times* 17 (2000): 49–52.

5 The Young and the Ruthless

The decade of the 1990s may long be remembered for its technological advances—the expanding power of personal computers, the ubiquity of the Internet, and the proliferation of wireless communications. Yet to those who closely monitor crime trends, the 1990s will be remembered as the decade when the murder rate fell.

By the end of the 1990s, the rate of killing in the United States had sunk to levels not seen for 30 years. As citizens across the country celebrated New Year's 2000 with incredible fanfare and relief that the Y2K computer bug was little more than a scare, police departments rejoiced in their own sense of victory.

Criminologists had warned of an impending juvenile crime wave created by a new breed of "superpredators." [1] Despite the dire forecast, as the 1990s drew to a close, city after city reported spectacularly low homicide rates. Boston closed out 1999 with as few as 31 murders, compared with 152 in 1990. Philadelphia's homicide toll reached below the 300 level for the first time in well over a decade. New York City, despite a slight increase in 1999, tallied 667 murders, substantially below its 1990 peak of 2,245. Chicago recorded 641 killings, its lowest level in many years.

While these reductions, as well as declines in many other cities, were worthy of celebration, the murder rate was not at a 30-year low point for all segments of the population. Only when we look much more closely into the trends do we begin fully to understand the great crime drop of the 1990s.

An "Epidemic" of Youth Homicide

The overall rate of offending (the number of offenders per 100,000 population) for all age groups combined has experienced substantial fluctuations—peaks and valleys, ups and downs—over the last few decades. Similar to the pattern shown earlier in Chapter 3 for the rate of homicide victimization, the rate of offending peaked in the 1980s at nearly 12 per 100,000, declined by about 25 percent by the mid-1980s, rose sharply through 1991 to another peak of 11 per 100,000, and declined thereafter to a low of just over six offenders per 100,000 population.

Probing deeper into these trends by comparing different age groups uncovers a very different picture. As shown in Figure 5.1, the rate of murder at the hands of adults age 25 and older declined slowly yet steadily through the 1980s and 1990s, without any rise during

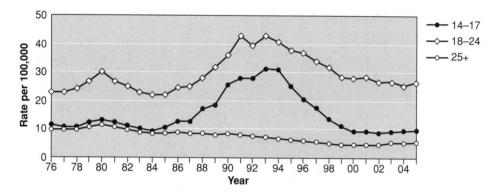

FIGURE 5.1   Homicide Offending Rates by Age, 1976–2005

the violence-filled years of the late 1980s. All of the changes in homicide were among younger offenders. From 1985 to 1993, the rate of killing among young adults age 18 to 24 rose 93 percent, before dropping by nearly a third by 2000 and then continuing slightly downward through the first half of the new decade. Young adults have traditionally had the highest rates of offending, and this gap grew even wider in recent years.

The most remarkable change, however, occurred among teenagers. Prior to 1985, teens committed homicide at the same low rate as their parents' generation. However, since the mid-1980s, the pattern of offending for adolescents has much more resembled that of their older siblings. From 1985 to 1993, the rate of murder committed by teenagers tripled, from 9.8 to 30.2 per 100,000, before its sharp decline in the latter half of the 1990s.

What happened in the mid-1980s that drove the youth homicide figures into record territory? Although there are many factors that would underlie such a sharp trend as this, the most compelling and important was the emergence of crack cocaine as a popular street market drug in cities across the U.S. Although the pharmacological effects of crack cocaine were worrisome, involving a lessening of impulse control as well as unpredictable effects on the body, the real damage to our society came from crime problems surrounding the dynamics of the crack drug market.[2]

When the crack market developed, the usual economic forces of supply and demand created fierce and violent competition for business. The demand for crack, which, unlike other drugs, was sold in small single-hit quantities, was so great that dealers had to recruit large numbers of street merchants to distribute the contraband. In light of this intense demand, teenagers were aggressively recruited and enlisted as street sellers. Not only were they willing to take on the risks for some quick cash (and free drugs), but they did so at a lower level of compensation. It was also perceived that, if caught, they would be treated more leniently by the courts.

Because of the violence associated with the trade, guns were an essential tool for survival. Youngsters trafficking in crack cocaine armed themselves for added muscle as well as for protection.[3] As soon as some teenagers were armed, their peers—even those uninvolved in crack as sellers or users—began to acquire guns as well.[4]

A virtual teen arms race spiraled out of control, instigated by, but not limited to, crack activity. Some kids carried guns for offensive purposes, others for self-defense, and still

FIGURE 5.2   Gang-Related Homicides, 1976–2005 Combined

others for status among their friends and rivals. The arming of U.S. youth created a volatile mix of impulsivity and firepower, as trigger-happy young people used their weaponry for reasons large and small—from the elimination of a rival gang member to the execution of someone who insulted them.

As shown in Figure 5.2, the entire increase in teen homicide was gun-related. From 1985 to 1993, the number of teenagers who killed with a gun quadrupled, before tailing off in recent years. There was no appreciable increase in juvenile homicides by other means.

It has long been true that many teenagers are impatient, imprudent, and impulsive, willing to act spontaneously without fully thinking through the consequences of their actions. The availability of a gun in the hands of quick-triggered kids clearly had an impact on the murder rate.

The increase was also related to gang activity. As shown in Figure 5.3, the number of homicides associated with street gangs soared in the late 1980s and early 1990s. In detailed analyses of homicide reports in Chicago and Los Angeles, Cheryl Maxson has shown that

FIGURE 5.3   Teen Homicide Offenders by Weapon, 1976–2005

gang killings represented an increasing number and percentage of all murders from the mid-1980s to the mid-1990s.[5] During the 1980s, several national gangs (e.g., the Bloods and the Crips) expanded their membership, as more and more kids were attracted to what these and other prominent gangs had to offer. Many observers have characterized the growth of gangs as a process of intimidation—as a gang member you were protected from attacks.

The definition of *gang,* not to mention *gang-related homicide,* can be problematic. At what point does a group of kids involved in delinquent activities become a gang? Would we include in our definition a homicide involving a gang member as an offender, a victim, or both? Would we include one gang member killing another in a love triangle? Or, would we include a gang member killing his parents? Are these all gang-related homicides?

For our purposes, street gangs are to be distinguished from a host of other youth groups in which delinquent behavior occasionally flares, as well as prison gangs, organized crime groups, skinheads, and terrorist cells. Most, but not all, street gangs consist of males from minority backgrounds—Black, Latino, or Asian—who range in age from pre-teenagers to adults in their 30s. Gang members typically live in proximity to one another and have strong neighborhood ties. Much of gang warfare erupts as a result of a shared desire to protect local territory from the encroachment of outsiders. But the antisocial behavior of gang members ranges widely from acts of vandalism and petty theft through incidents of assault and murder. According to an estimate by the National Youth Gang Center, there are some 21,500 youth gangs consisting of 731,000 members in the United States.

Street gangs have changed dramatically over the last 30–35 years. They have proliferated in numbers, but also in their ability to spread fear and terror throughout a community. During the 1950s and 1960s, gangs were noted for committing relatively minor offenses. They spoke about the need to protect their turf, but rarely followed up by committing major crimes of violence.

In sharp contrast, today's gang members are older, more likely to carry firearms, and more willing to be violent in pursuit of their objectives. Gangs continue to serve as the primary distributors of illicit drugs. They infrequently associate with domestic terrorist groups. But they are more likely to be connected with organized crime (e.g., Mexican drug organizations, Asian criminal groups, and Russian organized crime groups) and with influential prisoners. Violent street gangs have become more commonplace around the country. Over one five-year-period in the 1990s, for example, there were several thousand people murdered by gang members in Los Angeles County alone. By 2006, Los Angeles had an estimated 700 gangs consisting of some 40,000 members, and gang-related crimes increased in the city by 14 percent over the previous year.

One of the most significant trends in gang activity during recent years involves the growth and spread of immigrant gangs around the country. Not unlike their European counterparts before them, recent newcomers to the United States from Latin American countries tend to be segregated in their residences by virtue of language and unemployment. In some Latino neighborhoods, gangs develop in order to provide vulnerable residents with the support and protection not available to them from the larger society.

The focal point of a nationwide crackdown by the FBI, the gang MS-13 (aka *Mara Salvatruchas,* or Salvadorian gang, began in the Los Angeles area during the 1980s, but has since spread to 33 states where antigang efforts are less effective and jobs are more plentiful. The gang's criminal activities have included stealing and exporting automobiles, burglarizing houses and stores, selling illicit drugs, smuggling weapons, carjacking, intimidating witnesses, selling firearms, and committing aggravated assault, rape, and murder.

Originally, members of MS-13 consisted almost exclusively of immigrants from El Salvador who had fled from the nation's civil war, settled in the city of Los Angeles, and formed a gang to protect themselves from the threatening activities of other, more established groups. Over the years, as MS-13 has become increasingly violent, the federal government has deported many of its members, only to see them return illegally and rejoin the gang. Since the 1980s, MS-13 has proliferated, becoming a loose network of essentially independent groups of immigrants and encompassing members not only from El Salvador but also Ecuador, Guatemala, Honduras, and Mexico.

Another influential Latino street gang, this one operating in Northern California, is known as SUR-13 (aka Surenos 13). Its members wear identifying red clothing to distinguish them from their principal rival, the Nortenos, whose gang color is blue. Both gangs are especially active in Oakland and San Francisco. They are believed to be offshoots of Mexican prison gangs, though their members come from a range of ethnic groups. Like so many other gangs, the Surenos and Nortenos express pride in their group by wearing their colors and tatooing gang symbols on their bodies. Teenaged members steal from local liquor stores, while older members push drugs on the streets. There is some evidence, moreover, that the two gangs are responsible for an increase in the murder of African Americans as well as Latinos.

Even with a fairly broad definition of what constitutes a gang (most police departments use their own discretion as to whether a homicide is gang related), gang homicides are still relatively uncommon—nationally, approximately 5 percent to 7 percent of the total homicides committed each year are classified as gang related.[6] However, the impact of gangs on urban homicide is significantly greater. For example, the *2004 National Youth Gang Survey*, which solicited responses from police departments across the country about the spread of gang activity in their jurisdictions, found that more than half of the combined homicides in Los Angeles and Chicago—historically two gang hot-spots—were considered to be gang related. In addition, about one-quarter of all homicides in 171 cities with populations above 100,000 (excluding Los Angeles and Chicago) were considered to be gang related.[7]

Of course, the overall representation of gang homicides would increase somewhat if the same standards applied to inner-city youths were applied to middle-class suburban teenagers who commit crimes in a group. Most people would probably not consider the so-called Trenchcoat Mafia at Columbine High School a gang, yet two of its members (Dylan Klebold and Eric Harris) shot to death 13 people.

But there are many other functions to gang membership aside from protection. Gangs provide an alternative socializing mechanism, as the institution of the family is weakened. By joining a gang, a child can feel special, feel as if he belongs to something important, and be a member of a group that praises him. Moreover, it is a source of excitement and even economic resources. Where illicit drugs are sold, impoverished inner-city gang members gain not only a quick way to make large amounts of money but also a way to serve an apprenticeship in a growing business—the drug industry.[8]

One of the features that tends to distinguish juvenile murder from killings perpetrated by older offenders is the involvement of group dynamics. As shown in Figure 5.4, not only

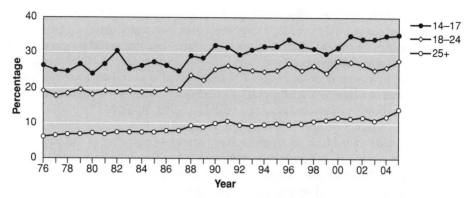

FIGURE 5.4 Multiple Offender Homicides by Age, 1976–2005

are teen murderers significantly more likely to commit homicide with the help of accomplices, but the percentage of juvenile murders involving two or more perpetrators has grown.

Individuals—especially children—often act differently in a group setting than they do on their own. Sometimes peer pressure can encourage someone to conform to a prosocial norm, but frequently it can provide strong encouragement to do the wrong thing. In group settings, the activity may be secondary to interpersonal dynamics. A group leader may feel good that others are willing to follow his lead even into areas of behavior that are cruel and vicious. At the same time, the followers can feel good about the praise they receive from the leader (and other group members) for participating and showing allegiance. In group settings, so-called mob psychology can sweep participants into committing even horrible crimes that no one in the group really wants to do. In situations of a "shared misunderstanding," each group member wrongfully believes that everyone else but him actually desires to commit an offense.[9] Concerned about their reputation among friends, they all participate.

The group effect can operate within large mobs of people—such as in the widely publicized episodes of wilding or even in lynchings—and in collections as small as a pair of accomplices. Following the arrest of two Vermont teenagers, 17-year-old Robert Tulloch and 16-year-old James Parker, for the January 2001 brutal murder of Dartmouth College professors, Half and Susanne Zantop, numerous theories were proposed for a possible connection between the victims and the perpetrators. Some observers suggested that it may have been a hate crime related to the victims' German roots. Others speculated that they all had been members of the same hiking club. These and other proposed linkages proved wrong. The victims were selected just because they had something the assailants wanted—cash, to help fund their dream of traveling to Australia.

Rather than a connection between victims and offenders, it is instead the close bond between the two assailants that holds the key to understanding this tragic episode. Tulloch exalted in his leadership position, feeding off the admiration of his younger partner, while Parker sought the praise and approval of his older mentor. Had Tulloch and Parker been apart, arguably this crime would never have occurred. In tandem, they brought out the worst in each other.

The subculture of violence notion described earlier, if updated and modernized, is quite helpful in understanding the readiness for violence among many young urban dwellers. For inner-city youth, the American Dream, which appears absolutely unattainable, can be little more than a cruel nightmare. Alienated from mainstream society, minority youngsters instead often obey the code of the streets, in which respect is the fundamental and most vital commodity of daily life. In order to earn respect and then guard against losing it, according to sociologist Elijah Anderson, a youngster must comport himself at all times in a manner showing that he's ready and willing to be violent. According to Anderson, being disrespected is a fate worse than being murdered.[10]

Another feature that strikingly distinguishes juvenile murders from those committed by older individuals is the particularly senseless character of the youthful impulses and motivations. By contrast to the inspirations of profit, jealousy, and control that characterize most adult homicide, children often, if not typically, kill for trivial reasons—a leather jacket, a romantic brush-off, a challenging glance, or no reason in particular. In a Los Angeles suburb, for example, two teenage girls murdered their best friend because they were jealous of her slender figure, waist-length auburn hair, good looks, and popularity with boys. In Miami, a 12-year-old boy killed a homeless man over a dispute involving a piece of pizza. And in Independence, Missouri, a teenager murdered a Good Humor man because the vendor refused to give him a free frozen treat.

Criminologists who have focused heavily on the problem of rising teen homicide rates have been criticized for unfairly painting an entire generation with the same broad brush.[11] Despite a growing number of juvenile murderers, it absolutely remains the case that the vast majority of youngsters do not even come close to committing homicide. Even among the highest rate group—young black males—for every youngster who commits homicide, literally hundreds never will.

Those who do commit homicide tend to differ from those who do not in several important respects besides demographics. Kenneth Busch and his colleagues, for example, studied the case histories of 71 juvenile murderers and compared them with similar data for a sample of 71 nonviolent delinquents, matched for age, race, sex, and social class. Overall, the young murderers were significantly more likely to have come from a violent family, to have abused alcohol, to have had severe educational deficiencies, and to have participated in gang activities.[12] More generally, the large body of research on violent youth has suggested a wide range of risk factors including: poor medical care and nutrition during early age as well as poor prenatal care; drug and alcohol dependency; inadequate supervision and ineffective parenting; emotional, physical, and sexual abuse; poverty; learning disabilities and academic problems; isolation from peers or contact with delinquent peers; and exposure to violent media and entertainment, among many others.[13] Yet none of these conditions, even in combination, is sufficient to produce homicidal behavior. Risk factors represent predispositions, not predestination.

Explaining the 1990s Decline

Just as the increase in the U.S. homicide rate in the late 1980s and early 1990s can be linked to the crack epidemic, the subsequent decline can also be associated, at least in part, with a contraction or maturation of the crack market.[14] Typical of most fads in the marketplace—from Furbies in the toy world to skirt length in the fashion industry—the crack market passed through a natural evolutionary process. Although there had been street warfare over market shares in the early years of the drug, by the 1990s, the turf lines were being settled through survival of the fittest and the fiercest. Certain drug sellers were able to muscle or shoot out the competition—many of the losers had been incarcerated, had been killed, or had moved away from their neighborhood in a big city—and the crack frenzy began to dissipate. Also, by virtue of some widely publicized horror stories about the dangers of crack (e.g., the death of basketball star Len Bias), the demand for crack dwindled.

The crack market had largely devastated a particular cohort—those born from 1968 to 1974, especially blacks. When the crack market first hit the streets in the mid-1980s, these young people were old enough to be up to taking the risk, but not old enough to know better. Thanks to what is known as the "big brother effect," those born after the early 1970s were scared away from crack by the devastation they saw in their older siblings and others in their communities. As a result, the rate of homicide by young black males in particular plummeted in the mid-1990s. As shown in Figures 5.5 and 5.6, while similar trends existed for white and black males, the rise and subsequent fall in homicide were especially steep among young black males.

On a statistical basis, murder by juveniles actually has fallen since 1993, but it fell from a level that was an all-time record when the crack epidemic wreaked havoc on U.S. youngsters, especially minority youth in urban centers such as New York, Chicago, and Baltimore. It would be a serious mistake, however, to frame the decline in crack-related violence as solely a market-driven trend that law enforcement passively watched from the sidelines. Rather, police agencies, in implementing community-oriented strategies, had much to do with decreasing the violence associated with crack, as well as guns and gangs. In Boston, for example, the police negotiated a cease-fire with warring gangs after getting everyone's attention by sending away to prison a major gang leader on federal weapons charges. The New York City police confiscated guns from the hands of teenagers through aggressive (aka "zero-tolerance") stop-and-frisk strategies.

It would also be a mistake to leave the impression that the decline in youth murder was solely a result of the decline in the drug wars or due to police intervention. The level of youth violence subsided not only for murder but over a range of behaviors from simple assault to rioting, first in large cities but eventually in smaller cities as well. Perhaps precipitated by the incredible growth of violence associated with big-city drugs, many people around the country

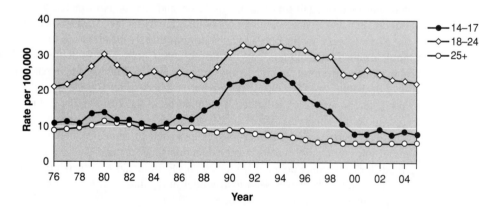

FIGURE 5.5 Homicide Offending Rates by Age, White Males, 1976–2005

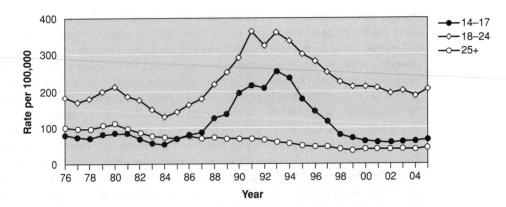

FIGURE 5.6   Homicide Offending Rates by Age, Black Males, 1976–2005

became desperate for solutions. Afraid to walk the streets in their own neighborhoods or go shopping downtown, they became sick and tired of feeling like victims. In urban centers across the country, residents sought to re-establish a sense of community as they began to recognize that they could make a difference in the lives of local youth. At the grassroots level, parents, teachers, psychologists, religious and business leaders, social workers, college students, and the police worked together to repair the moral, social, and economic damage done to young people over a period of 20 years and to take the glamour out of destructive behavior. Through a myriad of new programs, adults gave back to teenagers what they had lacked for more than two decades—supervision, structure, guidance, and hope for the future.[15]

Local schools were at the center of effective community efforts to reverse the scourge of teenage violence, often taking on responsibilities previously performed by the family. High school principals adopted a strict policy regarding students who carried firearms to school, making classrooms safer from the threat of gun violence. In addition, by means of effective conflict resolution programs built into the curriculum, many local schools began teaching their students what parents used to teach: to have empathy for victims, to control their anger, and to manage their impulsive behavior. Finally, schools provided what was lacking after the school day ended—adult supervision, guidance, and control. No wonder, then, that for most of our children and teenagers, the school hours were by far the safest hours of the day.

Schools were not the only local institutions that stepped forward to fill guiding roles. Churches ran athletic and gun-buy-back programs. Community policing placed more officers in strategic positions in high-crime areas. Probation officers rode in patrol cars to keep an eye on youthful probationers. Increasing numbers of local college students served as mentors, tutors, and peer mediators in neighborhood schools. Parents and teachers volunteered more to supervise after-school programs in athletics, drama, and art. Local businesses generated more summer jobs, at least some of which led to careers with the companies. More community centers opened their doors to local teenagers. Municipalities beefed up funds for community policing, with residents forming more partnerships with police.

In Boston, which was seen as a model in dealing with teenage crime, the murder count plummeted from 34 teen offenders in 1990 to only 3 in 1998.[16] Over the same period, the city saw a proliferation of programs geared toward at-risk teenagers. The wake-up call for Boston's community leaders came during a funeral service in 1992 at the Morning Star Baptist Church. As a crowd of mourners looked on in horror, a gang of local youths chased another teenager into the church, where they repeatedly stabbed him into submission. Shocked by this crime, a group of local Boston ministers decided that enough was enough, and that it was time to act. Rather than wait for troubled youngsters to come to their churches, they decided to take their congregations to the streets and the gangs, working with the police to identify the most recalcitrant young offenders and to provide alternative programs for those teenagers whose lives could be turned around.

Boston's attack on juvenile violence during the 1990s was multifaceted, emphasizing prevention, tough and effective law enforcement, and formation of partnerships with local residents. The community policing effort increased communication between police and neighborhood youth. Perhaps taking their cue from Boston's churches, other local institutions—businesses, government, universities, schools, police, and parents—were suddenly more willing to get involved in the lives of local youth. The juvenile crime rate in Boston finally began to reverse direction, and sharply so.

The Boston model continues to influence public policy nationwide. Although generating much political controversy concerning the separation of church and state, President George W. Bush's emphasis on allowing federal funding for faith-based organizations has been an attempt to bring the church into the loop of providing services for at-risk youth as well as ex-offenders, the homeless, the hungry, substance abusers, those with HIV and AIDS, and welfare-to-work families.

It should be clear, then, that the range of explanations for the sizable and steady drop in homicide rates during the 1990s is extremely broad. Criminologists frequently cite changes in drug markets, the expansion of prison populations and community policing initiatives, intensified prevention and enforcement efforts, demographic change, and increased involvement of community leaders and ordinary citizens in grassroots crime fighting campaigns as key contributors. A few other, less obvious, theories have also surfaced.

Anthony Harris and colleagues at the University of Massachusetts have, for example, suggested that growth in medical technology and the spread of medical services may have contributed to lessening the extent of carnage related to assaults with guns and other deadly weapons.[17] They attempted to show empirically that the lethality of criminal assault—the likelihood that aggravated assault victims survive rather than die from their injuries—can in part be linked to emergency care response.

On a very different tack, economists John Donahue and Steven Levitt proposed a rather hotly debated hypothesis, controversial both methodologically and politically, that declining rates of violence in the 1990s were a lagged or delayed effect of the legalization of abortion arising from the 1972 Supreme Court decision *Roe v. Wade*. "Teenagers, unmarried women, and African Americans are all substantially more likely to seek abortions," they wrote in a 1999 paper. "Children born to these mothers tend to be at higher risk for committing crime 17 years or so down the road, so abortion may reduce subsequent criminality through this selection effect."[18]

Their proposition, therefore, was that following *Roe v. Wade*, thousands of unwanted fetuses were aborted instead of being born into less-than-ideal environments, producing two decades later a reduction in the pool of at-risk, violence-prone individuals. Despite some persuasive logic, Donahue and Levitt appear to have grossly overstated the impact of legalized abortion. The change in law, for example, cannot account for the steady decline in rates of homicide by adults, ages 25 and older—individuals who would have been born prior to the landmark abortion decision. It also cannot account for the steep rise in homicide rates after the mid-1980s or for the fact that youth homicide rates plateaued in the early 2000s almost at the same level as they were prior to the mid-1980s surge. The rise-up then fall-back pattern is more consistent with transient factors than with a permanent policy change.

Even as the abortion–violent crime link was being debated in academic circles, the theory received a public airing through Levitt's widely read book, *Freakonomics*.[19] Conservative talk-show host William Bennett, who had served as the Secretary of Education during the Reagan administration, confronted a firestorm of protest when he tried facetiously—and unwisely—to take the theory to its logical end: that the rate of crime in America could be hugely curtailed if every conceived black baby were aborted.

Whatever the actual causes, the rate of youth homicide is back where it was before the deadly crack wars in the late 1980s and early 1990s. Furthermore, the nation's murder rate in general seems to have stabilized—largely unchanged from 1999 through 2005. This is not the time, however, to rest on our laurels or to conclude that youth violence is no longer a problem. To the contrary, there are indications that gang-related murder is once again on the rise. As shown in Figure 5.3, the number of gang killings has nearly doubled since 1999, back to the level witnessed during the early 1990s. This sharp increase can be traced primarily to the Los Angeles area and to a lesser extent to Chicago. But, as we learned painfully during the last wave of gang violence, what starts on the West Coast can eventually spread across the nation.

There are several reasons why gang violence has re-emerged. First, many of the gang leaders who were sent away to prison in the 1980s and early 1990s are returning back to their old neighborhoods and their old gang affiliations. At the same time, young recruits who did not witness the bloodshed in those earlier years are attracted to the excitement, thrill, and status of gang membership. Finally, many cities have slashed their budgets for antigang initiatives, believing that the problem has been resolved. Hopefully, cities will respond quickly, before gang violence gets anymore out of hand.

The powerful stimulant methamphetamine (aka "meth"), discussed earlier in Chapter 3, has, in many cities across the country, taken the place of crack cocaine as the illicit drug of choice. In certain areas—for example, St. Paul, Minnesota, and Sacramento, Fresno, and San Francisco, California—law enforcement officials are already talking about a meth epidemic that has opened new markets for profiteering street gangs.

Not unlike the crack cocaine trade during the late 1980s and early 1990s, much of the violence associated with meth can be attributed to its street market. So-called super labs have long produced large quantities of methamphetamine across the country, especially in out-of-the-way rural areas. But there are also a number of street gangs in urban areas that make smaller quantities in "stovetop" laboratories or, to an increasing extent, import quantities of the drug for re-sale locally. In California, for example, meth is being sold by members of gangs such as the Hells Angels, the Fresno Bulldogs, and the Elm Street Gangsters. Also in California cities, meth is distributed by Hispanic gangs such as Nuestra Familia and by gangs consisting of ethnic Chinese, Vietnamese, and Samoan members. In addition, there are growing numbers of Caucasians who have recently taken up the business by cutting and selling small quantities of meth on the streets of major cities.

Dial M for Media

Despite the highly successful effort in Boston and elsewhere to reduce the level of teenage violence, especially that relating to street gangs and guns, the problem has hardly been resolved. Although crack- and gang-related violence may have taken a nosedive, the nation must still contend with long-term issues, from supervision and television (too little of one and too much of the other) to adolescent angst and alienation.

It is easy enough to implicate the mass media—especially motion pictures, television, and video games—for the occurrence of hideous violence on a national level. Certainly, there is at least some evidence collected over several decades that a steady diet of media-depicted violence can help to desensitize young people, distorting their perceptions of social reality, and even inspiring heinous, brutal crimes. And the average child now grows up observing tens of thousands of murders and more than 100,000 acts of violence on TV. Cumulatively, this has an effect, although the exact size and nature of the effect have been debated for almost as long as television has existed.

Communication research conducted for decades suggests that people who watch many hours of television every day tend to overestimate the percentage of the world population that is white and male, underestimate the level of poverty in our country, and exaggerate the amount of violence they are likely to encounter. Heavy viewers also tend to overestimate the proportion of jury trials in our courts and the number of miracle cures performed by doctors. They are socialized to accept a false view of reality because this is precisely what they see on TV every evening beginning at 8 P.M.

According to George Gerbner, children who view TV excessively tend to develop what he has labeled a "mean world view."[20] Wherever they look—in their neighborhood after dark, on the streets on the way to school, on the playground with their peers—they see violence and the threat of violence. They grow up feeling intimidated, threatened, and paranoid. In line with the television version of life, they exaggerate their likelihood of becoming a victim of violent crime.

Everywhere you turn on TV, you find violence. Because violence is entertaining, it sells; it keeps the ratings high; it keeps programs on the air.[21] The list of programs featuring violence seems endless—*America's Most Wanted, Criminal Minds, 48 Hours, CSI, Crossing Jordan, 24, Law and Order*, not to mention all local and network newscasts. Actually, our entire popular culture has increasingly become a culture of murder and violence. "Gangsta rap" lyrics often extol the virtues of shooting women and attacking whites, gays, and the police. Some heavy metal musically expresses themes in which blacks, immigrants, gays, and women are brutalized. White Power rock calls for a racial holy war, one which white Christians would ultimately win.

Even more troubling, perhaps, are new forms of hero worship, which has always been an integral part of the process whereby young people—adults in training—are socialized to internalize society's most cherished norms and values. Over the decades, we have celebrated members of society who have reached the pinnacle of success in their fields by honoring them in movies, documentaries, magazine profiles, and even on trading cards. More recently, we have extended our celebration to what some consider our new antiheroes, those who have distinguished themselves in the worst possible ways by reaching the pinnacle of "success" as murderers. We celebrate evil.

Professional wrestling could be a metaphor for the way that we now honor wrong-doing. Prior to the 1990s, wrestling matches represented morality plays, featuring good against evil. During the 1980s, for example, Hulk Hogan was widely regarded as a paragon of virtue—until he was caught pumping himself up with steroids. By the mid-1990s, professional wrestling was looking more and more like an episode of the *Jerry Springer Show*—Hulk had become Hulk "Hollywood" Hogan, and he was joined by a lengthy list of filthy fighters with names like "The Undertaker" and "Chainsaw Charlie." Most of the good guys were gone from the ring and were replaced by a host of evil wrestlers battling evil wrestlers.

Celebrating evil and murder in popular culture, as described in Chapter 1, may be having a particularly profound impact on teenagers who want to feel important but are routinely ignored by parents, peers, and teachers. The lesson for youngsters may be: Behave yourself and adults won't notice; go on a rampage at school, and you become a big-shot superstar.

Almost 60 percent of our children and teenagers lack adequate parental supervision, living with a single working parent or in a household where both parents hold full-time jobs.[22] Although many youngsters may enjoy substitute forms of supervision provided by extended family, neighbors, or day care, as many as 5 million have no regular monitoring by adults. As a result, many children come home from school to an empty house, grab milk and cookies from the refrigerator, and watch anything they want on their own TV. If their sets lack cable channels showing their choice of a grotesque movie, they can always run down to the video rental center a block away and rent a nasty R-rated or unrated movie. Or, they can play a violent video game in which they rehearse—in a virtually realistic manner—stabbing, shooting, bombing, or running down other people. Or, they can surf the Internet, visiting an array of pornographic, violent, and hate-filled Websites.

In some respects, violence in television and film, which has been the focus of most of the debate, is relatively tame. It represents a passive form of entertainment, as compared to the more active participation provided by video games. Rather than just lie on the living room couch and witness a massacre on television, children can cybernetically kill on demand—and learn to enjoy it—through one of many violent action games available to them in computer game stores or on the Internet. Moreover, the intrinsic incentives and rewards, such as accruing a top score from killing, advancing through game levels while developing homicidal mastery, and defeating an opponent in an Internet-based competition, reinforce the will to kill, at least in the game setting. Although these games are fantasy, with multimedia sound and advanced graphics, the line between virtual reality and stark reality can become rather thin. Finally, role-playing games and the 360-degree perspective of more recent advances in gameware have taken another step toward realism.

It has been a challenge for adolescent development scholars to keep their research agenda up to pace with the fast-changing world of gaming technology. Even so, the weight of the evidence, involving a range of methodological approaches, suggests that frequent involvement in playing violent video games tends to impact negatively on a youngster's attitudes, thinking, and behavior.

A recent experimental study from the Indiana University School of Medicine has even uncovered an impact of playing video games with violent themes on the gamer's brain activity. The researchers compared randomly-formed groups of adolescents who played violent and nonviolent video games for a half-hour period of time. MRI scans of the area of the brain responsible for emotional arousal indicated significantly greater activity among subjects in the violent game playing group than those in a comparison group.[23]

Reviewing the results of dozens of research studies on the effects of playing violent video games, psychologist Craig Anderson reported a statistically significant link between exposure to the games and increases in aggressive behavior, aggressive thinking, aggressive affect, and cardiovascular arousal, as well as decreases in helping behavior.[24] To whatever extent the evidence can implicate a causal connection, there are concerns, both in Congress and in U.S. livingrooms, over the long-term impact of this thriving and relatively unregulated industry.

Of course, alarm among parents and politicians alike over the effects of violent entertainment of all forms on impressionable children is hardly new. As early as the 1960s, parents and child advocates were alarmed about exposing young viewers to unrealistic images of "cleaned-up violence." That is, because television programs and motion pictures of the day failed to depict the destructive aspects of punching, stabbing, and shooting, youngsters were growing up believing that violence didn't have consequences. In order to placate anxious parents, moreover, a voluntary code of the motion picture industry—movie ratings—was established to give them an opportunity to censor their children's viewing choices.

Beginning in the 1970s, the problem of sanitized film violence was replaced by a much more troubling phenomenon. In order to lure young people to the box office, producers frequently gave them exactly what they wanted—more graphic sex and violence. The movie rating system soon became a media version of "forbidden fruit"—more a guide for children in determining what they really must see than a guide for parents on what their children must *not* see. Experimental studies of factors influencing viewer selection have found that teenaged boys, in particular, prefer programs and films with an R rating or a parental warning, regardless of their content.[25] From the perspective of a young viewer, if you're not part of the mature audience, then you must be part of the immature audience, and what self-respecting, red-blooded American adolescent wants to be labeled that?

Parental warnings and violence ratings have been extended to television shows and video games under the assumption—or rather hope—that they will assist parents in choosing age-appropriate entertainment options. But as with films, the more mature ratings tend to boost the desirability of proscribed material among immature youngsters who are eager for adulthood.

Experiments have also shown that a steady diet of R-rated films in which violence and sex are fused together actually desensitizes youngsters to the plight of rape victims and tends to make young males more aggressive. For teenagers who are having trouble making the transition into adulthood, such films may also confuse them into believing that they cannot have sex without violence—that the one is inseparable from the other.[26]

The impact of media violence can be aggravated or mitigated, depending on the circumstances in which children grow up. It isn't that the mass media are so powerful; it is that our other institutions—our families, our schools, our churches and synagogues, our neighborhoods, our businesses, our political system—have become so weak with respect to raising children.

In Japan, by contrast, television programs are much more violent than their American counterparts. Yet the level of street violence in Japan remains comparatively low. Part of the reason involves the continuing power of Japanese traditional values on its youth. But another important difference is that Japanese parents hardly use television as a babysitter the way that it is more typically used in the United States. In Japan, children watch television with an adult—a parent, a grandparent, a family friend—who monitors, guides, interprets, and explains. This is the crucial difference.[27] Thus, the fundamental issue is not just what children are watching, but who is watching the children.

In the United States, rather than provide creative alternatives to parental supervision, politicians and entertainment industry leaders have sought to develop a method for allowing parents to continue working full-time while still having remote control over their children's access to violent television. As of January 2000, all new TV sets (with at least 13-inch screens) must come equipped with a V-chip (V for violence), with which parents can theoretically filter out the most offensive programs from their children's after-school viewing options.

It may be naive, however, to expect that unsupervised teenagers—left alone in front of their V-chip controlled TV sets—will instead tune into *National Geographic*, read Shakespeare, or take up chess. More likely, they will bypass their parents' attempts at absentee censorship by renting a grotesque film on videotape, playing a violent video game, or listening to the hate-filled lyrics of some rap and heavy metal on the family CD player. Or, they might just go over to a friend's house whose parents don't use a V-chip. The lesson is clear: technology cannot adequately substitute for genuine attention and involvement from parents and other significant adults in the daily lives of children.

In the final analysis, even with enhanced rating systems and parental controls, it is important not let the entertainment industry off the hook for its willingness to pander to and profit from the darker side of human behavior. At the same time, we should be careful not to place inordinate blame on the entertainment industry for the unacceptably high levels of youth violence in America. We should be similarly wary of single-issue critics who contend that the problem of kids today is the media, plain and simple. If anything is simple, it is the fallacy in such a simple-minded point of view.

It is true, of course, that experimental research has suggested a link between exposure to violent entertainment and attitudes tolerant of aggression. Yet, we must also keep in mind that experiments are often limited in terms of real-world generalizability. Even if children are stimulated neurologically or appear somewhat desensitized in affect after viewing violent content or playing violent games, there are questions—and in the minds of some critics, *lots* of questions—whether this translates into lasting change in behavior. In addition, if violent entertainment were at the very root of the youth violence problem, as antimedia zealots claim, how can we account for the decline in rates of juvenile violence in the 1990s? Undoubtedly, there was no reduction in the spread or popularity of violent entertainment.

The media has, at times, been used as a convenient scapegoat, and censorship as an easy solution. Public concerns, political considerations, self-interests, and fear have often encouraged us to point fingers at a profitable industry, while ignoring some of the fundamental causes of violence that are much more difficult to resolve.

Looking Ahead

Citizen concerns over the impact of television, motion pictures, video games, and the Internet on children continue to be strong. Even so, some of the sense of urgency has faded as the violent crime rate plummeted well below levels reached during the bad old days of the early 1990s. Unfortunately, however, in the face of rosy crime statistics, many Americans may have come to believe falsely that we have won the war against youth violence.

Complacency would be a terrible mistake. We dare not relax our efforts in the area of youth crime because there comes a new crop of teens every five years—today's teen will be tomorrow's young adult, and today's child will be tomorrow's adolescent—with each new cohort of teens looking to express its passion for rebellion and thirst for excitement. In addition, demographic change could potentially make matters worse. The next few years will continue to bring an expansion of the teen population as the "baby-boomerang" generation (children of the baby boomers) matures into adolescence.

There are tens of millions of children in America under the age of 13, more than at any time since the original baby boomers were in grade school. This newest group of youngsters will be teenagers before too long. Over the next few years, the number of teenagers, particularly blacks and Latinos, will continue to expand, which may indeed bring increased problems of teen suicide, venereal disease, drug abuse, joblessness, and, of course, violence.

Given the difficult conditions in which many of these youngsters grow up—with inferior schools, disrupted homes, and violence-torn neighborhoods—many more of them will be at risk in the years ahead. In fact, after a decade of welcomed decline, many cities across America are beginning to report spikes in local rates of murder and other forms of disorder, particularly youth-related, gang-related, and gun-related violence. Nationally, the murder rate has inched upward during the mid-2000s, prompting concern that inches could turn into feet or yards. Some observers have wondered if another youth crime wave is developing.

In city after city, budgets for educational enrichment programs, youth athletics leagues, and other critical youth investment approaches have been cut. In addition, the number of police officers per-capita in cities across the country declined by almost 10 percent from 2000 to 2005.[28] To some extent, therefore, the recent upturn in youth crime and gang activity should not come as a surprise.

The hopeful news is that there is still time to stem the tide—to prevent another sustained wave of youth violence. But we must act now while this baby-boomerang generation is still young and impressionable and will listen to what a teacher, a preacher, or some other authority figure has to say. If we wait until these children reach their teenage years and another wave of youth killings is upon us, it may be too late to do much about it. It is far easier and considerably less expensive to build the child than to rebuild the teenager. It is more effective to "prehabilitate" early than to rehabilitate later. At the same time, we should never be willing to give up on an entire generation of youngsters, even if they have reached their teenage years lacking what might have helped place them in the mainstream. Indeed, most teenagers with a juvenile record do not grow into adult offenders.

Even if youth homicide were to increase in the years ahead, the overall murder rate should continue to decline. This is because the fastest-growing segment of the population consists of senior citizens. The 65 million baby boomers, hardly babies anymore, are fast becoming card-carrying members of AARP, doing their part to bring down the crime rate just by aging. It is important, however, that we not be fooled by the graying of America, and be blind to the problems of youth. The future of U.S. society may depend on our collective ability to reach unsupervised youngsters, to make them feel that someone besides a drug dealer cares about them.

ENDNOTES

1. John J. DiIulio, "The Coming of the Super-Predators." *The Weekly Standard* (November 27, 1995): 23–28.

2. Alfred Blumstein, "Youth Violence, Guns, and the Illicit Drug Industry," *Journal of Criminal Law and Criminology* 86 (1995): 10–36.

3. Joseph F. Sheley and James D. Wright, *In the Line of Fire: Youth, Guns and Violence in Urban America.* New York: Aldine, 1995.

4. David Hemenway, Deborah Prothrow-Stith, Jack Bergstein, Roseanna Ander, and Bruce Kennedy, "Gun Carrying Among Adolescents," *Law and Contemporary Problems* 59 (1996): 39–53.

5. Cheryl Maxson, "Gang Homicide: A Review and Extension of the Literature," in M. Dwayne Smith and Margaret A. Zahn, eds., *Homicide: A Sourcebook of Social Research.* Thousand Oaks, CA: Sage Publications, 1999.

6. Malcolm Klein, Cheryl Maxson, and Jody Miller, "The Modern Gang Reader," *Journal of Criminal Justice* 23 (1995): 572–572.

7. National Youth Gang Center. (2006). National Youth Gang Survey Analysis, www.iir.com/nygc/nygsa.

8. Jeffrey Fagan and Deanna L. Wilkinson, "The Functions of Adolescent Violence," in Delbert S. Elliott, Beatrix A. Hamburg, and Kirk R. Williams, eds., *Violence in American Schools: A New Perspective.* New York: Cambridge University Press, 1998; Felix M. Padilla, *The Gang as an American Enterprise.* New Brunswick, NJ: Rutgers University Press, 1992.

9. David Matza, *Delinquency and Drift.* New York: Wiley, 1964.

10. Elijah Anderson, *Code of the Street: Decency, Violence, and the Moral Life of the Inner City.* New York: W. W. Norton, 1999.

11. Franklin E. Zimring, *American Youth Violence.* New York: Oxford University Press, 1998.

12. Kenneth G. Busch, Robert Zagar, John R. Hughes, Jack Arbit, and Robert E. Bussell, "Adolescents Who Kill," *Journal of Clinical Psychology* 46 (1990): 472–485.

13. Rolf Loeber and David P. Farrington, eds., *Serious and Violent Juvenile Offenders.* Thousand Oaks, CA: Sage Publications, 1998; David P. Farrington, "Predictors, Causes and Correlates of Male Youth Violence," in Michael and Mark H. Moore, eds., *Youth Violence.* Chicago: University of Chicago Press, 1998.

14. Andrew Lang Golub and Bruce D. Johnson, *Crack's Decline: Some Surprises among U.S. Cities.* Washington, DC: National Institute of Justice, 1997; Alfred Blumstein, "Disaggregating the Violence Trends," in Alfred Blumstein and Joel Wallman, eds., *The Crime Drop in America.* New York: Cambridge University Press, 2000.

15. Jack Levin, "An Effective Response to Teenage Crime Is Possible—and Cities Are Showing the Way," *Chronicle of Higher Education* 35 (May 7, 1999): 14.

16. Janet Reno, *Youth Violence, a Community-Based Response—One City's Success Story.* Washington, DC: U.S. Department of Justice, 1996.

17. Anthony R. Harris, Stephen H. Thomas, Gene A. Fisher, and David J. Hirsh, "Murder and Medicine: The Lethality of Criminal Assault, 1960–1999," *Homicide Studies* 6 (2002): 128–166.

18. John J. Donahue and Steven D. Levitt, "Legalized Abortion and Crime." Stanford Law School Working Paper, Stanford, CA, June 24, 1999.

19. Steven D. Levitt and Stephen J. Dubner, *Freakonomics: A Rogue Economist Explores the Hidden Side of Everything.* New York: Morrow, 2005.

20. George Gerbner, *Television and Its Viewers: What Social Science Sees.* Santa Monica, CA: Rand Corporation, 1976.

21. James T. Hamilton, *Channeling Violence: The Economic Market for Violent Television Programming.* Princeton, NJ: Princeton University Press, 1998.

22. James Alan Fox, *Trends in Juvenile Violence: A Report to the United States Attorney General on Current and Future Rates of Juvenile Offending.* Boston: Northeastern University, March 1996.

23. Yang Wang, Vincent P. Mathews, Andrew J. Kalnin, Kristine M. Mosier, David W. Dunn, and William G. Kronenberger, "Short Term Effects of Violent Video Game Playing: An fMRI Study." Indiana University School of Medicine, Indianapolis, IN, 2006.

24. Craig A. Anderson, An Update on the Effects of Playing Violent Video Games. *Journal of Adolescence* 27 (2004), pp. 113–122.

25. Joanne Cantor and K. S. Harrison, "Ratings and Advisories for Television Programming." In *National Television Violence Study, Vol. 1.* Thousand Oaks, CA: Sage Publications, 1996.

26. Neil M. Malamuth and Edward Donnerstein, *Pornography and Sexual Aggression.* New York: Academic Press, 1984; Edward, Daniel Linz, and Steven Penrod, *The Question of Pornography: Research Findings and Policy Implications.* New York: Free Press, 1987.

27. Jack Levin and William C. Levin, *The Human Puzzle: An Introduction to Social Psychology.* Belmont, CA: Wadsworth, 1988.

28. James Alan Fox, "Roasting Chicken Little: Epidemic Thinking about Crime." Presentation at the 113th Annual Meeting of the International Association of Chiefs of Police, Boston, MA, October 16, 2006.

6 Well-Schooled in Murder

Just as the United States was beginning to enjoy plunging rates of youth violence and murder, a new phenomenon emerged on the radar screen. On October 1, 1997, 16-year-old Luke Woodham walked into a Pearl, Mississippi, high school just hours after having killed his mother. Pulling a gun out from under his trench coat, the chubby, bespectacled youngster immediately murdered two schoolmates and then sprayed bullets into a crowd of students, injuring seven more. His motive? To take over the school, kill all the students, and escape to Cuba. Woodham and his friends were outcasts who worshipped Satan.

In the aftermath of the Pearl, Mississippi, shooting spree, parents, teachers, and students around the country became extremely anxious about school safety. Their fears were more than confirmed by subsequent events. Exactly two months later, on December 1, 1997, 14-year-old Michael Carneal, a freshman at Heath High School in West Paducah, Kentucky, opened fire on an informal prayer circle held in the school's lobby, killing three girls and wounding five other students. Then on March 24, 1998, two boys, 11-year-old Andrew Golden and 13-year-old Mitchell Johnson, pulled the fire alarm at their Jonesboro, Arkansas, middle school and then began shooting at students and teachers as they filed out of the building. When the gun smoke cleared, four students and a teacher (all female) were dead, and many more injured.

Months later, it happened twice more in the same week. On Tuesday, May 19, a Fayetteville, Tennessee, high school senior shot and killed a classmate over a romantic rivalry. Then on Thursday, May 21, Kipland Kinkel, a 15-year-old freshman from Springfield, Oregon, armed with a .22 caliber semiautomatic rifle, turned his high school cafeteria into a battlefield, after having been suspended a day earlier for bringing a gun to school. At Thurston High, Kinkel killed two students and wounded 22 more. At home, he had killed his parents.

The next school year (1998–1999) saw fewer episodes of school-related homicide, yet featured the single event that burned deeply in the consciousness of the nation and virtually defined schoolyard terrorism. On April 20, 1999, Dylan Klebold and Eric Harris shot and killed 12 students and one teacher and wounded 23 others during a carefully planned siege on Columbine High School in Littleton, Colorado.

School violence in the seventeenth and eighteenth centuries was primarily limited to cases of teacher-on-student violence as teachers used severe corporal punishment on students. By the twentieth century, we can find cases of student-on-student violence (mostly physical fights) and the last 25 years have seen the transition to student-on-teacher violence. School violence is actually not a new phenomenon, and even incidents involving multiple victims have been part of U.S. school history. In Michigan in 1927, Andrew Kehoe, a 56-year-old disgruntled school board member, murdered his wife and then launched several bombs in the small community, including at the local elementary school. Forty-five people were killed (three times the Columbine death toll), mostly elementary school children; another 58 were injured. Kehoe also killed himself with a car bomb. Kehoe did not act solely out of impulse: upset over taxes, his wife's poor health and the loss of his farm, Kehoe had apparently planned the bombings for some time. After the bombings, a sign was discovered on Kehoe's property, believed to have been a message of explanation from the mass murderer: "Criminals are made, not born."

As noted in Table 6.1, there was a lull in the number of school shootings from 2001 to 2003, only to be followed by yet another dramatic increase in the number of incidents and victims from 2003 to 2004 (mirroring to some extent the increases in homicide in general in the United States). We see another 50 percent decline the following year (2004–2005) and continued significant declines through 2006. Then, the 2006–2007 school year was off to a scary start. With less than half of the school year completed, there were already eight homicide incidents involving 12 victims (and only one of those, the Amish schoolhouse shooting, was a multiple-victim incident).

In decades past there were outsider adults involved in a number of multiple-victim school shootings, but that offender trend had all but disappeared—until recently. In 2006, a 53-year-old man, Duane Roger Morrison, lurked around the Colorado Platte Canyon High School grounds in Bailey, Colorado, not far from Littleton, Colorado, the site of the

TABLE 6.1   School-Related Homicides

School Year	Incidents	Victims
1992–1993	43	45
1993–1994	42	45
1994–1995	17	17
1995–1996	25	30
1996–1997	22	24
1997–1998	26	35
1998–1999	12	25
1999–2000	19	21
2000–2001	15	16
2001–2002	2	2
2002–2003	11	11
2003–2004	32	37
2004–2005	15	21
2005–2006	5	5
Fall 2006	8	12

Adapted from "School Associated Violent Deaths," The National School Safety Center, Westlake Village, CA.

Columbine shootings. On the morning of September 27, he entered the school with a revolver and a semiautomatic pistol (and a backpack that he falsely claimed held a bomb) and took six female student hostages, whom he sexually assaulted. Morrison released four of the hostages later in the day but killed one girl when she tried to escape, and then killed himself. Morrison had asked about the whereabouts of specific girls, whom he may have researched on MySpace.com. An outdoors and gun enthusiast, Morrison was a carpenter who had also built and owned haunted houses. He had no connection to the town of Bailey and, according to law enforcement, was living out of his Jeep. Although his 14-page suicide note to his brother made no reference to his school shooting plans, he had clearly planned the assault in advance.

Only a week later, in another incident with a sexual motive, 32-year-old local milkman Charles Carl Roberts IV, the married father of two, took hostages at a one-room Amish schoolhouse in Lancaster County, Pennsylvania. Roberts sent the male students and adult females away and kept 10 young Amish girls in the schoolhouse. Roberts had a shotgun and handgun, tools and equipment for binding the girls, barricade equipment, and candles, toilet paper, and other supplies indicating he planned to be there for a while. Roberts also brought tubes of sexual lubricant with him, and when he called his wife from the scene, he indicated that he had been dreaming about molesting girls for years. Police swarmed the schoolhouse sooner than Roberts had anticipated—he did not get the chance to molest any of the 10 girls but he shot all of them at close range, killing five. The Amish community members tore down the one-room massacre site and built a new school for their children. The Morrison and Roberts cases are unique not only because they involved adult shooters and sexual motives, but also because they occurred in the fall. Most violent school massacres have usually occurred in the spring, but those are typically cases of youth shooters who have had an entire school year of frustrations under their belt.

Blaming Parents

Elevated juvenile crime rates and well-publicized episodes of school violence have prompted many Americans to question the role of family and parenting. Under the assumption that bad kids are products of bad homes—parents who are neglectful and psychologically or physically abusive—many communities have enacted parental responsibility laws in an attempt to threaten parents with fines or jail time into taking their job more seriously.

Although the important role of parenting cannot be denied—there is often evidence of neglect, if not overt abuse, in the backgrounds of school shooters—much of the time teenagers become violent despite the best efforts of parents. Until a child is 8 or 9 years of age, it is still realistic to expect the family to exercise a large measure of control over his or her behavior. By the time a youngster has reached the age of 10 or 11, however, adolescence has set in, making an already troubled child incredibly susceptible to making bad and sometimes violent choices.

It would, of course, not be possible to hold Bill and Faith Kinkel legally responsible for their son Kip's violent outburst at his high school in Springfield, Oregon, just a short drive up Route 5 from Silverton where the first parental responsibility law was passed. They were executed by their boy in stage one of his deadly assault, yet this has not prevented them from being charged in the court of public opinion. In the aftermath, public sentiment was accusatory: How could they have given their son permission to buy a gun—not one but several, including a semiautomatic rifle? Why didn't they instead get him some help?

The truth is that the Kinkels did try to get their son the help that he needed. For years, they tried to provide him with whatever was required to overcome his learning and social deficiencies. Throughout his childhood, Kip Kinkel never fulfilled his parents' hopes and expectations. Dyslexic and physically awkward, Kip struggled academically and socially. He surely wasn't as talented as his older sister, Kristin, and could never measure up in the eyes of his parents, both of whom were highly regarded schoolteachers. With each failed attempt to find activities and pursuits in which he could excel, Kip Kinkel's frustration only grew more intense. Regrettably, Kip did seem to have a passion for bomb-making and guns, much of which he learned over the Internet. His cyber-contacts not only provided him with the inspiration but also reinforced his darkening character and mood. As the demands of high school and the perceived disappointment of his parents increased, Kinkel turned his attention to the school shootings in Pearl and Jonesboro. He yearned to feel important, to satisfy his parents' standards, and to be accepted by his classmates.

Copycat Shootings

The recent rash of school shootings has raised questions about what's different about kids today that would explain this kind of behavior. Actually, in many respects, kids today are no different than youngsters from earlier generations. There has been teenage alienation as long as there have been teenagers. There has been school bullying as long as there have been schools. What is different is today's culture and the weapons to which youngsters have access.

Thirty years ago, an angry high school student would not even have considered the idea of bringing a gun into the classroom. Instead, he might have thoughts about breaking a few windows or spray-painting graffiti in order to vent his anger. The notion of turning the school into a battleground would never come to mind. Sadly, because of widely publicized school shootings around the country, youngsters have been given new deadly examples to follow. And getting a gun—even a semiautomatic—is no problem.

In the aftermath of the highly publicized school shootings, most children identified with the pain of the victims. They grieved for the slain students whom they only knew through television reports, discussed their fears with parents and classmates, and hoped that history would not repeat itself in their own school.

Yet more than a few students—those like Kip Kinkel who felt alienated and frustrated—apparently identified instead with the power of the perpetrators—the foundation for the copycat phenomenon. Some may have fantasized, or worse, about following in their "hero's" footsteps. Not only was the new breed of youthful mass killers featured on the covers of most national publications, but there were even Websites published on the Internet that served as a tribute to their bold heroism and martyrdom.

It is no coincidence that until very recently, nearly all recent episodes of school multiple murders have involved white teenaged boys from small towns. Although this may reflect lesser preparedness in rural areas, the copycat effect is strongest when there is close similarity between hero and follower. A youngster from Oklahoma might identify with the plight of a kindred spirit from Arkansas or Kentucky, whose shooting spree is covered in the news. By contrast, for a black youngster living in a Chicago project, the same episode may not be something with which he could identify. Black teenagers involved in school shootings/killings are more likely to be involved in single-victim incidents that involve interpersonal disputes and gang rivalries.

At the very least, the copycat phenomenon can determine the timing and form of a murderous attack. If the publicized killers strike a school, then they provide the idea to murder in the classroom rather than at a shopping mall or a law firm. If the killers use a firearm, then those who imitate are also likely to use a gun rather than a knife, explosives, or a hammer. Finally, the copycat effect is short-lived, causing a number of similar attacks to be committed over a limited period.

Thus, many vicious murders cluster together in time. For example, in the 1997–1998 school year, when Kip Kinkel went on his shooting spree, there were eight multiple-victim homicides at U.S. schools—compared to two during the previous academic year. For a few disturbed individuals, the media hype and publicity given to killers can provide a source of role models for their own behavior, even inspiring them to realize their dreams of stardom and grandeur. There are fads among killers, just as there are fads among dress designers. Duane Morrison's sexual assault on Platte Canyon High School was followed only a week later by Roberts' planned sexual assault and multiple murder at the Amish schoolhouse. Both killers were adult males, both targeted girls, both had sexual assault on their minds, and both attacked in a rural schoolhouse.

In September 1988, 19-year-old James Wilson of Greenwood, South Carolina, went on a shooting spree at a local elementary school, killing two innocent children. When the police searched his home, they discovered that Wilson had pinned to his wall a photo of his hero taken from the cover of *People* magazine. His hero was 30-year-old Laurie Dann, a woman who a few months earlier had committed a similar crime at a school in Winnetka, Illinois.[1] Dann had a long history of mental illness and assaults against others. Clearly troubled, she had attempted to murder her husband with an ice pick, poisoned sorority members at Northwestern University, and mailed poisoned items to many other people over the years. Dann killed an 8-year-old boy at the school and injured five others. Dann also shot and injured another man at his house after the school shootings and took her own life at the home.

In general, the copycat phenomenon tends to occur when a mass murder receives much media attention. For example, within days of the widely publicized shooting spree by gunman Colin Ferguson on a Long Island commuter train in December 1993, two men were arrested for making threats of violence against Long Island railroad employees and passengers. Similarly, mass killer George Hennard, Jr., who, in October 1991, shot to death 23 people as they were having their lunch at a Luby's cafeteria in Killeen, Texas, had just watched a videotaped documentary about James Huberty's 1984 rampage at a McDonald's restaurant in San Ysidro, California.

Even motion pictures about fictional killers, such as *Exorcist 3, Warriors,* and *Natural Born Killers,* have inspired copycat murders around the country. Just prior to his killing spree in Gainesville Florida, for example, Danny Rolling had seen the film *Exorcist 3.* Based on characters and scenes in the movie, he called himself Gemini and decapitated one of his victims.

Twenty years ago, a child might have been inspired by his or her friends down the block. Now, thanks to the pervasiveness of television, he is just as likely to follow the lead of teenagers in Pearl or Springfield. Like their adult counterparts, troubled teenaged killers can be inspired by other killers, but they may also be inspired by fictional portrayals in films and video games. Kip Kinkel had been fascinated with the popular movie version of Shakespeare's *Romeo and Juliet.* In the small town of Moses Lake, Washington, 14-year-old Barry Loukaitis shot to death two students and a teacher after reading Stephen King's short story about a school massacre and watching the film *Natural Born Killers.* One could argue, however, that only kids with significant levels of mental illness would find messages in the media and then act on those violent fantasies. Of the millions of children and teens who consume violent media, only a handful haunt the halls of a school with homicide in mind.

In June 1998, after a seemingly relentless string of school shooting episodes, summer vacation mercifully arrived. Over a two-month summer vacation, would the contagion effect dissipate? When school opened in the fall, parents were scared. In fact, a 1998 poll conducted by the Shell Oil Company found that three-quarters of parents surveyed were very anxious about school shootings and violence, topping the list of school-related concerns, well ahead of worries about peer pressure, declining academic standards, poor quality of teaching, and limited availability of educational equipment and supplies. Even though fewer students were dying at school than had died in the early 1990s, the attention the media had given to a handful of multiple-victim events had created the beginnings of a moral panic.[2]

Explaining School Massacres

Despite parental concerns arising from the previous year's bloodshed, the 1998–99 school year was relatively uneventful, that is until April 20, 1999, when a school shooting of such immense proportions occurred that it radically, if not permanently, altered public thinking and debate about student safety and security. After months of planning and preparation,18-year-old Eric Harris and 17-year-old Dylan Klebold armed themselves with guns and explosives and headed off to Columbine High School in Littleton, Colorado, to celebrate Adolf Hitler's birthday in a manner befitting their hero. By the time their assault ended with self-inflicted fatal gunshots, a dozen students and one teacher lay dead.

In understanding the horrific actions of schoolyard snipers, it is as important to examine friendships as it is to delve into family background. At Columbine, Harris and Klebold were generally seen as geeks or nerds, from the point of view of any of the large student cliques—the jocks, the punks, etc. Though excluded from mainstream student culture, they banded together and bonded with several of their fellow outcasts in what they came to call the "Trench Coat Mafia." The image they attempted to create was clearly one of power and dominance (the very characteristics of masculinity that all teenage boys pursue)—the gothic incivility, the forces of darkness, the preoccupation with Hitler, the celebration of evil and villainy. Harris and Klebold desperately wanted to feel important; and in the preparations they made to murder their classmates, the two shooters got their wish. In a case of folie a deux, they plotted and planned for over a year, colluding and conspiring to put one over on their schoolmates, teachers, and parents. One of their videotapes shows them talking about how the shootings would finally get them the respect they deserved. They amassed an arsenal of weapons, strategized about logistics, and made final preparations—yet, until it was too late, not a single adult got wind of what Harris and Klebold intended to do. One can only wonder why not.

As is the case with some of our most heinous team serial killings, birds of a feather may kill together. Harris, the leader, would likely have enjoyed the respect and admiration from Klebold, who in turn would have felt uplifted by the praise he received from his revered buddy. In their relationship, the two boys got from one another what was otherwise missing from their lives—they felt special, they gained a sense of belonging, they were united against the world. As Harris remarked, as he and his friend made last-minute preparations to commit mass murder: "This is just a two-man war against everything else."

As with other forms of crime, it is unlikely that there is a single cause of school shootings, nor a single factor shared by all school shooters. However, research has isolated some risk factors. Recent work suggests that school shooters suffer a series of deprivations in their lives, such as lack of encouragement and self-esteem, and that those marginalizing experiences finally explode in the highly competitive school environment. Many school shooters share a history of childhood instability and marginalization from caregivers and guardians, planting the seeds of neglect. These shooters—almost entirely white males—are often isolated and unpopular amongst their peers. They associate with other kids similarly marginalized, and their anger takes on a morally righteous tone.[3] The school shooters lack any sort of cultural capital—popularity, athletic abilities, physical fighting abilities, socioeconomic standing, and relationships with girls—so instead, they prove their masculinity through extreme violence. Boys are socialized to be aggressive, violent, and dominant; if they are the butt of harassment, bullying, taunts, and humiliation, they find someone to pick on, too. In some cases, they may even blame their parents for their miserable lives.[4]

The hazing rituals of secondary schools in the U.S. are painful and brutal for those on the receiving end and are obviously too much to take for some kids who are already troubled. Childhoods filled with neglect, abuse, disappointments, poor peer choices (if they even have any real friends); being shorter than the norm or having appearances perceived as effeminate; suffering neurological problems or school failures; and having access to weaponry—all of this may boil over and explode.

Trends in School Shootings

When the scourge of school shootings emerged, some criminologists speculated that it was just the next phase of the youth violence epidemic. What had started in the inner city, according to this view, had spread to middle-class America. The issue of lethal violence inside of schools struck a nerve with the public.

Unlike crack and gang violence that had infested primarily minority neighborhoods in the urban core, school shootings occurred in suburbs and rural communities that had been largely immune from the urban bloodshed. Indeed, this may help explain why such extraordinary murders occurred where they did. The residents of towns like West Paducah, Springfield, Littleton, and Pearl felt impervious to crime, violence, and poverty—what they regarded as big-city problems. As a result, they never prepared for the possibility that teenagers in their town might become so alienated and marginalized as to go on a shooting spree at school in order to get even with parents, teachers, and classmates. Whereas urban schools initiated programs and policies in the areas of conflict resolution, peer mediation, and counseling, small-town and suburban schools tended to remain complacent.

Political observers capitalized on this uneven public response to youth homicide in cities versus elsewhere as a clear indication of racism. Most people, they said, seemed apathetic when, to an increasing extent, black kids were shooting each other; but once murder spread to the hinterlands, the demand for action was heard loud and clear. Although this allegation is likely valid—even today, gang-related shootings at school receive little media attention—there was another major change in the pattern of school violence that cried out for media and public attention: the emergence of multiple-victim events, or what has come to be known as mass murder.

A search for the number of school homicides annually will generate different results, in part because of different definitions of what counts as a school homicide. The National School Safety Center classifies a death as a school homicide if it occurs on the property of a public or private K–12 school (so any homicide that occurs on school grounds would be counted); while a student is on the way to or from a regular school session (e.g., bus stops, walking home from school); on the way to or from a school-sponsored event (e.g., athletic events, school dances); or as the "obvious direct result" of a school incident, function, or activity.[5] It is important to note that this definition includes many events that some people might not think of as school homicide, including adult domestic homicides (e.g., husband comes to a school to shoot his wife who works there), felony-murder robberies that occur long after a student has left school but is still technically on the way home (e.g., on the subway), and police action shootings (a fleeing felon is shot by police on school property during the weekend). This definition does not include homicides occurring at the nation's colleges, and does not count the death of the offender if he or she commits suicide. Likewise, there are a number of school shootings each year that do not result in any deaths and will not appear on school homicide lists.

On August 30, 2006, Alavaro Castillo, 19, of Hillsborough, North Carolina, shot and killed his father before driving to his former high school armed with smoke bombs, a shotgun, and a rifle, intending to open fire during lunchtime. Castillo had made a videotape after he shot his father proclaiming, "Look at me. I'm not even crying. I just killed him, and I feel fine." The videotape shows the father's corpse, draped by a sheet. After killing his father, Castillo dropped the videotape into the mail on his way to the school. The local paper received the tape after the shootings. It showed Castillo watching violent movies, including *Scarface, The Predator, The Shining, Natural Born Killers,* and a documentary about the Columbine shootings. Castillo also claims to have been the victim of child abuse. Although he killed his father and intended to enter the school shooter hall of shame, no one at the school was killed or injured.

Most school homicide incidents are still single-victim/non-mass-murder events reflecting rival gang member fights, interpersonal disputes, domestic homicides, and robberies. On June 28, 2006, James Lamont Bagsby, 15, was arrested for shooting and killing Anthony Michael Ramirez, 11, and wounding his brother, Joseph Ramirez, 13, in the San Bernardino, CA, schoolyard of the Dr. Martin Luther King, Jr. Middle School. He was also charged with nine counts of assault with a deadly weapon for shooting at other children on the basketball court. Bagsby had been in a group home for juveniles in Victorville and had escaped. He allegedly approached the boys at the school and asked them if they were part of the San Bernardino gang. When they said they were not, he opened fire. Police say that the boys did not provoke the attack and were not part of any gang. Bagsby is being held at San Bernardino Juvenile Hall, and chief deputy district attorney John P. Kochis says that Bagsby will be tried as an adult and could be sentenced to life in prison.

These sorts of events, like homicide in general, nearly disappeared during the school year of 2001–2002, and overall crime rates declined during this brief period as well. The "September 11 effect" for a short time brought people together and focused their attention on a much greater enemy than their own personal issues.

The trend in school homicides has been roughly parallel to the decline in youth killings more generally. The majority of school homicide incidents continue to be in large, inner city schools and involve gang violence. James Tate and six others were charged with the April 14, 2003 New Orleans shooting death of 15-year-old Jonathan "Caveman" Williams inside the school's gymnasium. In addition to the murder, three others were wounded. Tate pled guilty to manslaughter and conspiracy to commit second-degree murder and received a 15-year prison sentence. This school shooting was actually more typical of most school homicides—it was basically an assassination, as the offenders thought the victim had murdered a cousin of one of the co-conspirators.

Though homicides arising from a conflict between one victim and one perpetrator are newsworthy at the local level, these episodes rarely make national news, whether or not the participants are black, white, or Latino. Yet the events of the 1997–98 school year got everyone's attention, all the way to the White House, which established a Presidential Advisory Committee in the wake of an episode in Clinton's home state of Arkansas. As the body counts grew larger, murder grabbed the attention of the nation.

Paradoxically, research that monitors violence-related behaviors among high school students in the U.S. has noted that almost all forms of violence *declined* from 1991–2003. Students were less likely to report carrying a weapon to school (12 percent in 1993 declined to 6 percent by 2003) and were less likely to report physical fighting at school. Interestingly, although schools were becoming safer, students and their parents did not perceive that this was the case, as they were more likely to report that they stayed home from school because of fear for their safety.[6] It is likely that our twenty-first-century media hype and "breaking news" coverage of school shootings contribute to unreasonable fear among parents, students, teachers, and staff. These multiple-victim events were terrifying, but still extremely rare.

Mass murder at school by disgruntled pupils was a scary new wrinkle. A decade earlier, schoolyards were the targets of imbalanced adults looking to hurt society where it hurt the most. School snipers were likely not to be teenagers but middle-aged adults like Laurie Dann, the 36-year-old resident of Glencoe, Illinois, who, in May 1988, went on a rampage with a .22-caliber handgun in a Winnetka elementary school. Actually, there were 12 different school shootings in 1988 through early 1989, the last of which was Patrick Purdy's January assault on the Cleveland Elementary School in Stockton, California. He murdered five Southeast Asian children as they played at recess.

It is not coincidental that the recent shootings occurred at schools, rather than at some other location. Notwithstanding research findings suggesting that most schools do not experience serious forms of violence, the school day itself can present certain issues and risks. Not only do children congregate in large numbers while at school, thereby creating occasions for conflict, but the school setting can sometimes breed feelings of inadequacy, anxiety, fear, hostility, rejection, and boredom. For most kids, the hazing rituals of school will make them feel sad, humiliated, and depressed. Some will find a group of outsiders to cling to, others will be suicidal, and some will develop substance abuse problems or find another way to cope until the humiliation of school is over. Most of them don't harm anyone. But, for some vengeful or alienated children, school can represent an ideal place, both logistically and symbolically, for getting even or settling a score. Just like the adults who turn their disappointments into rage and commit workplace massacres, some students (and some adults) blame the school for most of their disappointments and take their revenge there.

With just two exceptions (Laurie Dann and Brenda Spencer), none of the recent school shooters has been female, but, of course, many of the victims have been. No search of school shootings can turn up a case where the motive was to wipe out boys, but there are several cases where the offender was specifically targeting females. Marc Lepine went hunting the halls of a Montreal, Canada engineering school in 1989. He thought women had no place in an engineering program—that it was a man's world. By the end of his slaughter, there were 14 dead female engineering students. The recent Amish school shooting had 10 female hostages and five were killed; the Platte Canyon case involved six female hostages, one of whom was murdered.

Should these school shootings be considered hate crimes? A recent article on schoolgirls as targets, particularly in rural settings, noted that in the 21 rural school shootings since the 1970s, girls were a majority of victims.[7] Research by Jessie Klein also shows a disturbing pattern: in 12 school shooting cases occurring from 1997–2002, almost all of the shooters targeted girls whom they had perceived had rejected them.[8] Klein finds that rather than "bullying" by other males, the primary motives in 11 out of these 12 shootings were actually related to the slain girls—rejection and jealousies that turned into homicidal rage. Klein argues that dating violence and sexual harassment are generally ignored in schools. Apparently, teachers and other students expect boys to be boys, and that includes their expressions of aggression and domination generally.

We have seen two cases where females targeted schools. One was Laurie Dann, who was discussed previously. The second was Brenda Spencer, 16, who in 1979 opened fire (with the rifle her father had given her for Christmas) on a Cleveland elementary school across the street from her house, killing two adults and injuring eight children and a police officer. Spencer was sentenced to 25 years to life and is eligible for parole in 2009. When interviewed later, Spencer claimed she did it because "I don't like Mondays. This livens up the day."

Although none of the more recent multiple-victim school shooters has been female, research and case analysis suggests that the girls may be gaining on the boys with regards to their likelihood of committing violent acts. In 1983, for example, the boy-to-girl ratio of those committing violence was 7-to-1; by 1998, the ratio had declined dramatically to 3-to-1.[9] Given overall trends in female juvenile violence, some hint that it may only be a matter of time before a multiple-homicide by a schoolgirl shocks the nation.

Girls have been the offenders in single-incident school murders. In September of 2005, Kanisha Neal, 15, was murdered by a 16-year-old female (unnamed because of her age) after a football game in Silver Springs, Maryland. Two groups of girls had been trading insults at the game, and a fight broke out between the two girls. The 16-year-old juvenile female plunged a 3½-inch knife blade into Neal's heart. Found guilty of murder in the second degree, the female offender was remanded to the custody of the Maryland Department of Juvenile Services. She will not be sentenced for a certain period of time, her release date depending on her rehabilitation while in custody.

Despite these horror stories, our nation's children are relatively safe given the number of contact hours they spend at school. Our 92,000 U.S. public schools and 52 million students are two times as likely to be violent crime victims while off of school grounds rather than at school. The number of youngsters who report taking a gun to school has declined, as well the number who report being threatened with a weapon. Comparing the dozens of school children killed each year in school-related violence with the millions who attend, there is literally a one in two-million chance that a school-aged child will be murdered while at school. Of course, when it does happen, the repercussions spread far beyond the grounds of that school or the borders of that community.

Responses to School Shootings

After Columbine, schools around the nation went on red alert. Many heightened security—installing metal detectors, surveillance cameras, entry control devices, and even armed guards—to try to protect the school setting from the latest threat. Although these responses to the school violence panic are quite understandable, they have cost school districts hundreds of millions of dollars since 1999, and yet, most of this technology can do little to deter the truly motivated and determined student from seeking revenge. Metal detectors and other security measures are hardly foolproof; there are many ways in which a student can smuggle weapons past these devices. Besides, a vengeful student can still kill his victims in the schoolyard (as in Jonesboro, Arkansas) or even on the bus. Security might even be regarded as a challenge to be overcome by a rebellious student who would like to show up the administration. Overreliance on a law enforcement approach may also give us a false sense of security, causing school officials to think that the problem has been resolved.

Administrators also responded with tough zero tolerance policies against weapons or even menacing words, putting students on notice that guns, knives, or threats of violence would not be tolerated. Applied rigidly, this has resulted in the suspension of elementary school children in Georgia for making a list of people they wanted to hurt (including the Spice Girls and Barney, the purple dinosaur), a girl in Colorado who brought the wrong lunch bag to school (it contained an apple and a paring knife), and a second-grader in Maryland who made a gun out of construction paper. On other occasions, this no-nonsense stance may have inspired additional feelings of alienation. Six months after the Columbine massacre, another student at the now infamous high school in Littleton was overheard threatening to finish the job.

In the aftermath of the Columbine tragedy, much of the focus (and finger-pointing) was on warning signs that were reportedly missed or ignored. For example, Harris and Klebold had made a movie about blowing up the school. Over two years *before* the events of September, 11, 2001, their original plan had included hijacking an airliner and crashing into the New York City skyline. Mitchell Johnson gave his Jonesboro, Arkansas, classmates advance warning that "something big" was going to happen the next day at school. Yet all of the warning signs were disregarded.

Barry Loukaitis, who killed a teacher and two students during a February 2, 1996, shooting spree in his algebra class at Frontier Junior High in Moses Lake, Washington, was fascinated with books and movies about rampaging youth (see Table 6.2.). But Loukaitis did more than just consume stories of violence; he also wrote them. Before

TABLE 6.2 **Characteristics of Selected School Shootings**

Name and Age of Shooter(s)	Location and Date/Time	Victim Count and Type	Weapon Type and Source	Family and Personal Situation	Mental Health	Cultural Influences and Background	Precipitant	Other
Charles Carl Roberts IV, 32	West Nickel Mines School, Penn. Oct. 2, 2006	5 female students killed, some students shot 12 times	Shotgun, handgun, personal weapons from home	Married, two children	Claims had molested children in past and planned to molest Amish girls	Home-schooled; father was retired police officer, mother worked at Christian.org	Angry with God and depressed over death of stillborn daughter nine years earlier	Killed himself at the scene
Duane Morrison, 53	Platte Canyon High School, Bailey, Colo. Sept 27, 2006, 11:40 A.M.	1 female student killed, several female victims sexually assaulted	Semi-automatic pistol and revolver	An itinerant carpenter, unmarried, minor criminal history	Had made threats against a retail store	Gun and outdoor enthusiast	Unknown	Killed himself at the scene, sent 14 page suicide note to his brother
Jeff Weise, 16	Red Lake H. S., Minnesota Federal Indian reservation March 21, 2005	10 killed; a female teacher, grandfather's girlfriend and 3 of 5 students killed were female; 5 other students injured	.40 caliber handgun and shotgun (grandfather's police-issued weapons), bulletproof vest and police car	Father committed suicide after a police stand-off, mother in nursing home after serious car accident	Had received psychiatric help, abused by mother, lived with grand-father who did not want him	Interested in Neo-Nazi web forums, Goth, Nazi philosophy, idolized Columbine shooters; Liked film *Elephant*	Tried to starve himself to death before the shootings, was being home-schooled, had not been to school for 5 wks	Killed himself at the scene after he was shot by tribal policeman

John McLaughlin, 15	Rocori High School, Cold Spring, MN	2 male students killed	.22 caliber pistol, father had cache of weapons at home	Father was Sheriff's deputy	Insanity plea after guilty verdict was rejected by the judge	Faked mental illness and hallucinations from scenes in movies (e.g., *Sixth Sense*, *A Beautiful Mind*)	Said he only meant to wound one student	Convicted of 1st and 2nd degree murder, sentenced to life plus 12 years
Eric Hainstock, 15	Weston High School, Cazenovia, Wisc., Sept. 29, 2006, 8 A.M., Home-coming day	Killed one male principal, tried to shoot another teacher	Handgun and shotgun, stolen from parents	Lived with father/step-mother, father charged with child abuse, house/yard in disarray	Was described as a troubled child, had attended anger mgt. class at school	Was a special ed student because of emotional, behavioral and learning problems	Was repeatedly bullied by homophobic remarks, angry because teachers did not stop harassment	Disciplinary warning for smoking on school grounds day before shooting
Luke Woodham, 16	Pearl High School, Pearl, Miss. Oct 1, 1997, 8:10 A.M.	2 female students (one was ex-girlfriend) and murdered his mother, 7 other students wounded	Rifle, home	Father left family when Luke was 11	Erratic coping skills, lack of empathy, sensitive to insults, killed and tortured family dog	Marilyn Manson, Hitler, Nietzsche	Was encouraged by a friend to seek revenge against ex-girlfriend and mother	Asst. principal used gun from his car to subdue Woodham, Woodham serving life in prison

(continued)

TABLE 6.2 Continued

Name and Age of Shooter(s)	Location and Date/Time	Victim Count and Type	Weapon Type and Source	Family and Personal Situation	Mental Health	Cultural Influences and Background	Precipitant	Other
Andrew Golden, 11 & Mitchell Johnson, 13	Westside Middle School, Jonesboro, Ark. March 24, 1998 12:35 P.M.	1 teacher and 4 students killed (all female), 10 (many females) wounded	3 rifles, 7 handguns, stolen from relatives	Johnson's parents divorced, Golden's parents both at home, Johnson allowed to drive to school the day of shootings	Johnson—a bully and aggressive, Golden—tough and mean-spirited and had killed a neighbor's cat	Tupac Shakur, Mortal Kombat	Both rejected by girlfriends, Johnson teased for being fat	Johnson had vowed to kill all of the girls who had ever broken up with him, both to be released at age 21
Kipland Kinkel, 15	Thurston High School, Springfield, Ore. May 21, 1998, 8 A.M.	2 students killed, more than 20 students wounded, both parents killed	Semi-automatic rifle, 2 pistols, presents from father	Both parents at home, both parents were teachers, smart, popular older sister	Depressed, took Ritalin, then Prozac, loner; had a history of hearing voices, setting fires	Marilyn Manson, Nirvana, Internet junkie; extensive bomb, grenade, gun, knife and explosives collection at his home	Had to repeat first grade, expelled from high school, about to be sent to troubled youth program	Sentenced to life without parole
Eric Harris, 18 & Dylan Klebold, 17	Littleton, Colo. Columbine High School, April 20, 1999, 11:25 A.M.	1 teacher and 12 students killed, 23 wounded	Handgun, rifle and 2 shotguns, some bought by friends	Both from two-parent families	Harris took antidepressant Luvox; Klebold shy and sad	Marilyn Manson, Hitler, Doom, and Quake	Teased by jocks, labeled "Trench Coat Mafia," called faggots	Planned months in advance

going on his deadly rampage, Loukaitis had submitted to his English teacher a poem about killing:

Murder
It's my first murder
I'm at my point of no return
I can't let him live now
He'd go to the cops for sure
So I finish.
I look at his body on the floor
Killing a bastard that deserves to die
Ain't nothing like it in the world
But he sure did bleed a lot

Many of the warning signs were even more direct. Mitchell Johnson, Andrew Golden, and Luke Woodham all told friends in advance and in no uncertain terms that they planned to shoot classmates. Whether the confidantes took the shooters' words of warning seriously, the powerful code of silence obeyed by many teenagers may still have discouraged them from "snitching," even if it would have meant preventing a murder.

Ignored warning signs and threats, on the one hand, and falsely accused students, on the other, have placed school administrators in a quandary. How aggressively should they respond to rumors of a threat, and how can they distinguish misguided but harmless attention seekers from the truly dangerous outcasts? In one recent case, clearly someone should have done something. As many as 39 people knew of Jeff Weise's plans to assault Red Lake High School on an Indian reservation in Minnesota. For two years, Weise had discussed his plans for the 2005 shooting with his friends and many others. This shooting, the second-worst school shooting in U.S. history, left 10 dead and another five injured. On March 21, 2005, Weise, then 16, killed his grandfather, Daryl Lussier, 58, who was a tribal police officer, and his grandfather's companion, Michelle Sigana, 32. He then took his grandfather's police-issued weapons, a .40 caliber handgun and a 12-gauge shotgun, and drove to Red Lake High School in a federally owned squad car. Once there, he began his 10-minute rampage on the school, wounding seven students and fatally shooting a security guard, five students, one teacher, and then himself.

The FBI has found that Weise may have frequented a neo-Nazi web forum and confirmed that he favored Goth culture and Nazi philosophy. Classmates also say that they had seen him drawing graphic, violent pictures. Weise's cousin reported that Weise had received psychiatric help in the year before the shooting. Weise had a troubled childhood—his father shot himself to death four years earlier and not long after, his mother was placed in a nursing home after a serious car accident that put her in a wheelchair for life. Police are still investigating other motives.

In early 2006, Jefferson County Sheriff Ted Mink released nearly 1,000 pages of documents from the Columbine files. These documents included the diaries of Harris and Klebold, the journal of Harris' father, Wayne Harris, and the writings that Harris and Klebold left in each other's yearbooks and their school work. In the documents the boys display intense levels of nihilism, anger, and contempt for their schoolmates. Their diaries explain that they felt like outcasts because they were different from everyone else. They also show that the boys tracked the provisions of state and federal gun laws to learn how to acquire weapons. Harris followed anti-gun control groups and even wrote a class paper that noted how easy it would be to bring a gun to school. Other documents also suggest that they dropped several clues before their attack. In fact, Klebold wrote a story for his English class depicting a man who kills nine high school students and expressed his personal sympathy for and understanding of this man. The boys' journals show that they were both preoccupied with guns, bombs, murder, and the Nazis, which explains their decision to carry out their shooting on Hitler's birthday.

The sheriff, concerned that they might stimulate a copycat shooting, decided not to release the disturbing "basement tapes" made by Eric Harris and Dylan Klebold. The tapes have been chronicled by reporters and family members who have viewed them, and many believe the tapes should be publicly released so they can be further analyzed by psychologists.

In 2005, 24-year-old Danny Ledonne created *Super Columbine Massacre RPG,* a video role-playing game centered on the Columbine shootings. Ledonne claimed that before Columbine he was headed down the same path as Harris and Klebold; however, after the tragic event, he turned his life around. Ledonne began to see a therapist, got involved in filmmaking and martial arts, and graduated from high school and then college. Though many people criticize his game and claim it glorifies Harris and Klebold, Ledonne explains that the game is meant to promote understanding and discussion of school shootings and how they can be avoided. For this reason, he has also developed an online forum, called the SCMRPG project, so players can discuss the game. He claims that he tried to be true to the actual events of the shooting while still maintaining respect for the victims. The cartoon role-playing game incorporates photographs of Harris and Klebold, pictures taken from newspapers and television stations, and excerpts from their writing. Ledonne first distributed the game online for free anonymously until he was discovered and revealed his identity publicly. The game is no longer available on Ledonne's website but can be found on other sites.

The Bureau of Alcohol, Tobacco, and Firearms hoped it had the answer by teaming up with a California software company to test out a computerized threat assessment program for violent students. High-tech right down to its name, the "Mosaic 2000" system evaluates students on a scale from 1 to 10, to identify the few bad apples before they wreak havoc on their classmates.[10] This approach is actually just the latest in a growing list of checklists and guidebooks, available from such diverse groups as the American Psychological Association and the U.S. Department of Education, which attempt to aid school personnel in picking up on the supposedly telltale warning signs of impending violence.[11] Even the FBI is getting into the act, working with educators to develop a list of 60 red flags to help school personnel profile potentially violent students.[12]

Predicting violent behavior, especially in rare and extreme forms, is enormously difficult. In terms of the few bad apples theory, there are lots of apples that are not quite perfect in color, size, or shape but are fine just beneath the skin. There are lots of kids who look, act, or dress like our image of the schoolyard shooter—they might wear black trench coats, scary tattoos, or gang headgear. Yet very few of them will translate their deviant adolescent attitudes into dangerous acts of violence. The few accurate predictions will be far outnumbered by the many false positives.

In addition, any attempt to single out the potential troublemakers could actually do more harm than good, by stigmatizing, marginalizing, and traumatizing already troubled youth. "Don't play with Johnnie—he's a bad apple." Already ostracized and picked on by his peers, Johnnie will now sense that even the teachers and the administration are against him. The "bad apple" label could even become a self-fulfilling prophesy, encouraging doubly alienated children to act out in a violent manner.

Stressing how to identify characteristics of the individual troublemaker also lets schools off the hook. By turning the problem of schoolyard homicide into a lesson in abnormal psychology, the blame can be located outside of the school setting. From this perspective, students have to change, not the schools. A recent study of city schools suggests that elementary-level administrators who have failed to institute anti-violence policies and programs are especially likely to take the "abnormal psychology" approach.[13] They tend to regard their students as victims of inadequate upbringing, family conflict, excessive exposure to media violence, and parental abuse and neglect (that is, bad apples not falling far from the tree). Under such circumstances, anti-violence programs in the schools would be mistakenly considered a waste of scarce economic resources.

Focusing on the individual child also ignores the fact that students often act far differently in group settings than when they are alone. To understand the course of events in Jonesboro, Littleton, Red Lake, and Pearl, we must examine the relationships and interactions among the perpetrators as closely as we scrutinize their personal backgrounds and individual pathologies. To children, the expectations and approval of close friends can be all-important, especially when parents and other adults are not around. The issue may not be one of a few bad apples, but of a poorly tended orchard.

One of the best approaches to reducing the potential for violence through prediction may be to reduce the caseload of teachers and guidance counselors.[14] Smaller classes and increased staffing would allow school personnel to observe even subtle issues, which cannot be easily determined from a simplistic checklist, an anonymous phone call, or an elaborate computer algorithm. More important, our focus should not be on the potentially violent kid, but on the unhappy kid (although at times these may be one and the same). We should use warning signs, but use them to reach troubled youngsters, long before they become troublesome. If we wait until a student has murderous intentions, we have waited much too long.

Healthy and Safe Schools

It is likely that eventually we will find that the recent spate of school massacres is an aberration rather than a permanent feature of U.S. public education. Fads come and go, especially those involving youthful perpetrators. In many respects, crime contagion spreads and expires very much like fads in fashion, dance, and games. At this juncture, the thousands of angry, alienated children who are ostracized and bullied have several violent role models to copy. Once the contagion passes, the same children may return to less malicious yet equally vengeful actions like breaking windows, stuffing school toilets, and putting stink bombs in lockers.

Despite the school violence hype and panic, schools actually are the safest place for kids to be.[15] With structure and regular supervision, the rate of violence in schools (literally one homicide per two million schoolchildren) is lower than it is on the street corner, in shopping malls, even at home. Youngsters are more likely to be killed riding their bike to school than they are to be murdered by an armed classmate.

Yet concern with school violence is not completely misplaced and may even motivate much positive change. As noted in the school violence research of Garcia and Kennedy, officials charged with developing school safety plans have begun to recognize that costly weapon detection systems and cumbersome entry control devices are not the school violence panaceas that many had hoped they would be.[16] In fact, administrators now acknowledge that these technologies are fairly ineffective at preventing serious school violence and in some instances may violate students' rights. Since only about one-third of school shootings occur in the actual school buildings—many more occur in parking lots, breezeways, bus stops, and athletic fields—we would be misdirected to spend all of our capital improvement money on the actual school building.

Principals have looked to invest in other strategies—mainly school resource officers, security guards, mental health personnel, and prevention programs. For example, many high school and middle school principals have recognized violence prevention as a priority and adopted effective conflict resolution and peer mediation programs, have encouraged after-school programs, have instituted anti-hate curricula, and have worked to bring community resources into the school in the form of tutors and mentors. There are also efforts underway to bring about structural changes that would give more attention to children who desperately need it. Such measures include reducing the size of the schools and the size of the classes, extending the school day, providing meaningful alternative school programming for suspended and expelled students, reinstating extracurricular activities that have fallen victim to budget cuts, hiring more school psychologists and guidance counselors, expanding school resource officer programs, recruiting parents to help patrol crime prone areas such as parking lots and athletic fields, and bringing other volunteers from the community to meet with needy students.

One of the most promising strategies adopted by administrators around the country in the aftermath of the school slaughters was to respond directly and aggressively to bullying. Rather than ignoring incidents of harassment and intimidation or recommending that victims stand up and fight back, educators are intervening in two ways to prevent bullying: by implementing programs designed to increase sensitivity and empathy among students and teachers to the plight of victims, and by training staff to recognize even subtle forms of intimidation. Given the recent identification of boys (and men) who are targeting female victims, we may also want to consider programs that teach kids to cope with rejection in interpersonal relationships. As is the case with domestic violence that escalates to homicide, the period after rejection can be very dangerous.

The American Psychological Association (APA) has issued several warning signs for possible school violence, which include: loss of temper on a frequent basis, frequent physical fighting, significant vandalism or property damage, increased use of drugs and alcohol, detailed plans to commit violent acts including threats/plans to hurt others, carrying a weapon to school, and violence towards animals. Unfortunately, as is the case with many warning signs lists (e.g., serial killers, domestic homicides, cults), we only recognize the risks after the damage has been done. We are not very good at predicting who will become a school shooter before the violent acts occur; rather, we engage in retrospective postdiction by doing post mortems of the cases. In addition, these lists throw a wide net and identify a significant number of false positives, which could do further damage by labeling kids who likely would have never acted out as problems.

Our responses to school violence have included public service announcements (which are ineffective at best), zero tolerance policies that can further marginalize troubled kids, door-lock and entry control policies (which might make it difficult for children to flee the building), police in schools, proposals to arm teachers (a questionable idea, given that even police in combat situations have low levels of accuracy—25 to 30 percent), threat assessment and tactical response teams, safety plans, parental responsibility laws, and increased security for school buildings.

In addition, and perhaps instead, we need better firearm restrictions for juveniles, extended school days for latch-key kids, a reinvestment in extracurricular activities that includes "things to do" for all types of students, and decreases in school size and class size so that teachers can encourage peaceful resolutions of interpersonal conflicts (the primary circumstance in school shootings) and can have the time to identify victims of bullying and refer kids who need mental health services.

As many urban schools did in the 1980s, schools throughout the United States need conflict resolution and peer mediation curricula, alternative programs for expelled and suspended kids, enhancement of school resources including counselors, and psychologists, and student resource officers.[17] In order to save the next generation, perhaps we should provide such classes for our youth with as much zeal as we teach driver's education and woodshop. These programs need to begin in elementary school, because by high school it may be too late. In addition, we need parents to be involved and pay attention. Children should not be able to go undetected over a period of weeks while they build bombs in their parents' houses.

And finally, several school shootings have included racist, homophobic, and misogynistic motives. For example, the Columbine shooting was done to commemorate Hitler's birthday, other shooters aspire to be neo-Nazis, and many male shooters target females only. We need to begin treating some of the hostilities brewing in our nation's schools before they grow into hate crimes.

Without destroying the civil liberties of young people and harming many innocent students with false accusations, we may never be able to identify each and every would-be shooter before he opens fire in a crowded classroom. Even if reliable predictions were possible, we may not be able to intervene effectively in all cases. By contrast, focusing on changing schools and identifying troubled schoolchildren has much broader potential. In the process of improving school climate, we can enhance the health and well-being of all children and, at the same time, hopefully avert murder.

On to College

On April 16, 2007, almost exactly eight years after Columbine, Seung-Hui Cho killed 32 students and faculty members on the campus of Virginia Tech in Blacksburg, before killing himself. He used a pair of semiautomatic firearms. The shooting spree took place in two separate incidents, two hours apart—the first in a residence hall and the second in a building that houses the School of Engineering.

The mass murder was not the first episode reflecting Cho's emotional and behavioral problems that had drawn attention, even though no one could have anticipated the extent of his dangerousness. In 2005, the 23-year-old senior had been accused of stalking two young women and was ordered by the court to receive outpatient mental health services. More recently, one of his instructors urged him to seek psychotherapy when he wrote violent passages in a couple of written assignments.

The scope of the Virginia Tech massacre may have been unprecedented, but the idea of a college student opening fire on his peers was hardly unexpected. It was only a matter of time that shootings associated with middle and high school students would graduate to the college level. Many of the miseries suffered by students long before they matriculate have continued to influence their thinking about their peers and about themselves. The impact on a student who was bullied throughout his early years of schooling does not necessarily dissipate later in life.

Cho's single act of carnage—one that shocked the nation—had roots that started forming years earlier. He was an immigrant from South Korea whose family had relocated to the United States when he was eight. Apparently his lack of facility with the English language and his extreme shyness were enough to make him the daily object of ridicule and scorn throughout his days in middle and high school. By the time he had moved into his room in a residence hall at Virginia Tech, Cho was already filled with hatred and resentment, perhaps toward his peers, Americans, or all of humankind.

Cho had most of the characteristics discovered in younger school shooters. He had long suffered from depression, had been severely bullied, blamed all of his problems on fellow students, had few if any friends on whom he could depend for encouragement and support, and had access to semiautomatic weapons.

He also had a model for his massacre in the now legendary Columbine slayings. Though the slaughter in Littleton, Colorado, had occurred eight years earlier, Harris and Klebold had remained in the minds of alienated and marginalized students around the country—including Cho—as bullied students who fought back and achieved some degree of infamy.

In between his two killing sprees on campus, Cho anticipated his own demise. He had a two-hour period when he was able to mail a package of materials—his writings, photographs, and a videotaped "manifesto"—to NBC News. The photographs showed Cho aiming his guns in a threatening pose. They depicted the killer as a strong and powerful individual who could not easily be ignored. The videotape consisted of a rambling, incoherent, and disjointed message in which he sought to justify his rampage as a rational response to those individuals who destroyed his life. They had many chances to change their ways, he offered, but chose not to do so. Therefore, the victims of his killing spree were, in Cho's mind, actually responsible for his angry mass shooting. Unfortunately, NBC released both the photos and the videotape, assuring that Cho's image would live in infamy and that the potential of the copycat effect would remain in effect for years to come.

ENDNOTES

1. James Alan Fox and Jack Levin, *Overkill: Mass Murder and Serial Killing Exposed.* New York: Plenum Press, 1994.

2. Crystal Garcia, "School Homicides." Presentation at Indiana University-Purdue University Indianapolis, February 2006.

3. Stephen Thompson and Ken Kyle, "Understanding Mass School Shootings: Links between Personhood and Power in the Competitive School Environment," *The Journal of Primary Prevention,* Online edition, September 30, 2005.

4. Jessie Klein "Cultural Capital and High School Bullies: How Social Inequality Impacts School Violence," *Men and Masculinities* 9 (2006): 53–75.

5. National School Safety Center, 2006. URL: www.schoolsafety.us.

6. N. Brener, R. Lowry, L. Barrios, T. Simon, and D. Eaton, "Violence-Related Behaviors Among High School Students–United States, 1991–2003," Centers for Disease Control and Prevention, *Morbidity and Mortality Weekly Report* 53 (2004): 651–655.

7. Gail Russell Chaddock and Mark Clayton, "Patterns in Rural School Shootings: Girls as Targets," *Christian Science Monitor,* October 4, 2006.

8. Jessie Klein, "Teaching Her a Lesson: Media Misses Boys' Rage Relating to Girls in School Shootings," *Crime, Media, Culture* 1 (2005): 90–97; Katherine Newman, *Rampage: The Social Roots of School Shootings.* New York: Basic Books, 2004.

9. David Satcher, "Youth Violence: A Report of the Surgeon General." Rockville, MD: U.S. Government Printing Office, 2001.

10. Lisa Richardson, "Schools Testing Threat Analysis," *The Los Angeles Times,* December 18, 1999, p. B3.

11. American Psychological Association, *Warning Signs.* Washington, DC, 1999; U.S. Department of Education, *Early Warning, Timely Response: A Guide to Safe Schools.* Washington, DC, 1998.

12. Janet Bingham, "FBI Puts 'Risk List' Out for Schools: 60 Factors to Help ID Violent Students," *The Denver Post,* November 9, 1999, p. A1.

13. Jack Levin and Heather Beth Johnson, "Youth Violence and the Urban Public School Response," *Journal of Research in Education* 7 (1997): 3–7.

14. Denise C. Gottfredson, *School Size and School Disorder.* Baltimore, MD: Center for Social Organization of Schools, Johns Hopkins University, 1985.

15. Elizabeth Donohue, Vincent Shiraldi, and Jason Ziedenberg, *School House Hype: School Shootings and the Real Risks Kids Face in America.* Justice Policy Institute, September 15, 1998.

16. Crystal A. Garcia and Sheila S. Kennedy, "Back to School: Technology, School Safety and the Disappearing Fourth Amendment," *Kansas Journal of Law and Policy* 12 (2003): 273–288.

17. Garcia, op. cit.

7 Serial Killers

Thanks in part to a fascination with anything that is "serial," whether it be murder, rape, arson, or robbery, there has been a tendency to focus a good deal of attention on the timing of repeated murders. Thus, the FBI distinguishes between spree killers who take the lives of several victims over a short period of time without a cooling off period and serial killers who murder a number of people over weeks, months, or years, but in-between their attacks live relatively normal lives.[1] In 1990, for example, Danny Rolling brutally murdered five college students in Gainesville, Florida, at three different crime scenes over a 72-hour period, and therefore technically qualifies as a spree killer. Similarly, Andrew Cunanan, in 1997, murdered four victims—two in Minneapolis, one in Chicago, and another in New Jersey—over the period of a few days. He too would appear to fit the definition of a spree killer.

The problem is that the distinction between spree and serial can easily break down. Staying on the loose after killing his four victims, Cunanan turned up in Miami two months later when he shot to death fashion designer Gianni Versace. Cunanan's revised body count—five victims—was accumulated over a period of months, not days. Is he still a spree killer or is he a serial murderer? Or, does it really matter that much?

It turns out that Danny Rolling had slaughtered three people in Shreveport, Louisiana, fully eight months before his Gainesville attacks. Should Rolling be labeled a serial killer? Or, should he instead be regarded as a mass killer for murdering the three Louisiana victims in a single assault? Again, does it really matter?

The point is that rigidly focusing on the timing of attacks, while interesting, is far less important to our understanding of multiple homicide than attempting to assess the killer's motivation. It might also be valuable to distinguish full-time from part-time repeat killers, whether they choose to murder their victims over a short or long period of time. Over a three-week time span in October 2002, the DC Snipers—John Allen Muhammad and Lee Boyd Malvo—gunned down 10 strangers, all chosen randomly, from a "sniper's nest" situated in the trunk of their blue Chevy sedan. During this entire period, aside from eating and sleeping, their time was apparently consumed by planning, executing, escaping, and hiding from the police. For most serial killers, murder is a part-time hobby. They typically return to their normal activities—holding a job, attending classes, playing with their children— after every murder they commit.

It should also be noted that we tend to overlook certain types of serial killers, even when their body counts are high. Most media attention is focused on sexual sadists. Little attention is given to mothers who kill their children, nurses who poison their patients, or armed robbers who repeatedly take the lives of their victims.

Because of the massive publicity devoted to such crimes as the grisly slayings of at least 17 males by cannibalistic necrophile Jeffrey Dahmer, the term serial murder has become part of everyday vocabulary. Serial killers like David Berkowitz (Son of Sam), Kenneth Bianchi (The Hillside Strangler), and Theodore (better known as Ted) Bundy are featured in prime-time TV docudramas and mass market paperbacks, no longer just in obscure detective magazines. Stretching the limits of decency, moreover, serial killers have, as described in Chapter 5, clearly become a fixture in our popular culture, featured in both trading cards and comic books as well as on T-shirts. Further glamourizing and romanticizing their crimes, journalists and true-crime writers often assign colorful nicknames to their murderous activities (see Table 7.1).

It is difficult to gauge the full extent of serial homicide. Because of complexities in linking murders committed by the same perpetrator but at different times and even different places, no precise estimate of the prevalence of serial killers is even possible. Still, in sharp contrast to the rampant interest and enormous fascination with serial murderers, we can be confident that the rate of serial homicide is far from epidemic. Although a large percentage of all killers featured in TV dramas, news magazine programs, and true-crime books commit serial murder, the death toll linked to serial killers in reality represents only about 1 percent of all murders in the United States, a couple hundred victims per year at most. At the same time, it is sobering to recognize that just a handful of murderers, about one to two dozen annually, can account for as many as 100 to 200 victims.

Using a variety of published sources, we compiled a list of 558 serial killers operating in the United States during the twentieth century in order to gain a sense, albeit imperfect, of the trends and patterns in serial murder.[2] Some killers work as pairs or teams in their predatory activity; overall, this collection of 558 assailants represents 494 unique individuals or partnerships.

Determining the number of victims murdered by these offenders is, however, virtually impossible, as the full extent of their murder tolls oftentimes can only be suspected. Using minimum victim counts, the 558 offenders, as a group, are responsible for at least 3,850 homicides, and most likely many more. In fact, using more speculative upper estimates, the offenders may account for as many as 5,650 murders.

In addition to these known serial killers, a number of unsolved cases across the nation continue to baffle investigators. Furthermore, despite recent advances in technology and communication, law enforcement officials may still be unaware of the presence of many other serial killers. The unsolved or open cases and the undetected cases, taken together, could account for hundreds of additional victims.

Notwithstanding their limitations, these data on 494 known killers or killing teams can be used to examine long-term trends in serial homicide. Figure 7.1 displays counts of serial killers, partnerships, and teams during each decade of the century. The overall trend is relatively level for the first half of the century, hovering around 10 serial killers per decade. The pattern emerging during the second half of the century is radically different. In the 1960s, the number of killers or killing teams reached nearly 40. Over the course of the next two decades, the 1970s and 1980s, the number of killers or partnerships quadrupled, surpassing the 150 mark in the 1980s.

While the sharp increase during the 1980s clearly suggests significant shifts in the prevalence of serial murder, these results are vulnerable, at least in part, to alternative

TABLE 7.1   Selected Serial Killer Monikers

Killer(s)	Moniker
Richard Angelo	The Angel of Death
David Berkowitz	Son of Sam
Kenneth Bianchi & Angelo Buono	The Hillside Stranglers
William Bonin & Vernon Butts	The Freeway Killers
Ian Brady & Myra Hindley	The Moors Murderers
Jerry Brudos	The Shoe-Fetish Slayer
Ted Bundy	Ted
David Carpenter	The Trailside Killer
Richard Chase	The Vampire of Sacramento
Douglas Clark	The Sunset Strip Slayer
John Norman Collins	Coed Murderer
Adolfo De Jesus Constanzo	Godfather of Matamoros
Dean Corll	The Candy Man
Juan Corona	The Machete Murderer
Jeffrey Dahmer	The Milwaukee Monster
Albert DeSalvo	The Boston Strangler
Nannie Doss	The Giggling Granny
Larry Eyler	The Interstate Killer
Albert Fish	The Cannibal
John Wayne Gacy	Killer Clown
Carlton Gary	The Stocking Strangler
Ed Gein	The Ghoul of Wisconsin
Vaughn Greenwood	The Skid Row Slasher
Donald Harvey	Angel of Death
William Heirens	The Lipstick Killer
Theodore Kaczynski	Unabomber
Patrick Kearney	The Trash Bag Murderer
Edmund Kemper III	The Co-Ed Killer
Paul Knowles	The Casanova Killer
George Metesky	The Mad Bomber
John Allen Muhammad & Lee Boyd Malvo	The DC Snipers
Dennis Rader	The BTK Strangler
Richard Ramirez	The Night Stalker
Melvin David Rees	The Sex Beast
Gary Leon Ridgway	The Green River Killer
Danny Rolling	The Gainesville Ripper
Timothy William Spencer	The Southside Slayer
Carol Eugene Watts	The Sunday Morning Slasher
Wayne Williams	The Atlanta Child Murderer
Randall Woodfield	The I-5 Killer

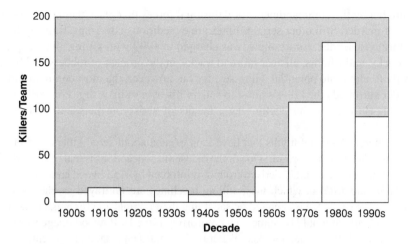

FIGURE 7.1   Serial Killers/Teams by Decade, 1900–2000

explanations related to improvements in data accessibility, improved quality of record keeping, as well as increased ability of law enforcement to identify linkages between victims slain by the same killer or killers. Notwithstanding these rival explanations, the trend in serial killings into the 1980s is quite consistent with a more general rise in violent crime, including homicide, suggesting that the apparent increase in serial murder is more than just an artifact of increased reporting and improved detection.

Even with the heightened interest in serial murder, the number of cases during the 1990s was lower than the previous decade (generally tracking the drop in murder overall). Whatever the true extent of decline during the 1990s and whatever the reasons for it, the problem of serial murder remains a difficult and perplexing one for law enforcement and, of course, for the general public that could be victimized by these predators. Even with about 10 serial killers per year captured by the police plus an unknown number of others undetected or on the loose, the fear and suffering provoked by serial murderers is extraordinary, warranting an attempt to understand who these offenders are and why they kill.

A Profile of Serial Killers

There is a multitude of different motives that provoke serial killers and help them to justify their actions. Some, such as Marybeth Tinning discussed earlier in Chapter 4, have slain a series of children to satisfy a pathological need for attention and sympathy. As described later in Chapter 12, a few serial killings have occurred in the context of cult activity. A charismatic cult leader like Charles Manson or Adolfo De Jesus Constanzo inspires his followers to commit homicides, often ritualistic or excessively brutal in nature, both to achieve some political or spiritual goal as well as to nourish the leader's excessive need to be in charge. A few serial killers are driven not by a charismatic cult figure but by the commandments of delusional forces that place them on a relentless mission of murder. Still other serial killings are expeditious cover-ups. Railway Killer Angel Maturino Resendez, for example, was charged in 1999 with killing nine people in Texas, Kentucky, and Illinois, all near railroad tracks, in the process of robbery and burglary, primarily to eliminate potential witnesses. By far, however, the most common form of serial murder surrounds the killer's quest to satisfy his own sadistic urges or excessive need for control. He exploits his victims as a means of satisfying personal, and often sexual, desires.[3]

There are several myths that have long existed about serial killers, and other legends that are rather recent in origin.[4] One of the oldest misconceptions is that of the serial murderer as a human monster, surely derived from or reinforced by Hollywood creations such as Jason of *Friday the 13th,* in which these killing machines are portrayed as glassy-eyed lunatics whose entire existence is centered on satisfying their compulsion for human destruction.

Actually, it would be somewhat comforting if the Hollywood image were at all accurate. If serial killers indeed looked like crazed maniacs and acted in a patently bizarre fashion, they would be easily avoided on sight. Unfortunately, in very many respects, most serial killers are extraordinarily ordinary, and, as such, extremely deadly.

Quite opposite to the Hollywood stereotype, a more modern image describes these killers as unusually handsome and charming, perhaps generalizing from one of the most celebrated cases of modern years, that of Theodore Bundy, who murdered dozens of women from Washington State to Florida and was indeed a "lady killer," in more ways than one. Richard Ramirez, the so-called Night Stalker of Los Angeles, also was sought after by numerous adoring women, even in prison, and actually married one.

Aspiring to marry a convicted and imprisoned serial killer may say much more about the mental health of the bride-to-be than the charm of the killer himself. Marrying someone in prison is one way an insecure woman can be assured that her man is not cheating on her (at least with other women). He may be behind bars, but not in the bars looking for a good time. She always knows where he is, even at 3 A.M.

It is tempting to focus only on the defects of the killer groupies—their lack of self-esteem and bad judgment—to explain their attraction to serial killers. Some of them find a mission in their relationship. They must tell the world that their man is innocent, that he is only a victim of injustice, not a hardened criminal. Others may be reticent about making a commitment, but can claim a relationship on a superficial level. Still other women may feel special because their man shared his most personal and intimate thoughts. Only she sees his gentler side.

Aside from the needs of killer groupies, however, what deserves to be acknowledged as well is society's complicity in making these murderers into attractive and appealing celebrities. In some cases, serial killers have received more national publicity than rock stars or rap artists. Moreover, most serial killers are extremely manipulative. They know exactly how to lure vulnerable women into a relationship, just as they understood how to lure their poor victims into a position of total vulnerability in order to take their lives.

It would be wrong, however, to characterize all, or even most, serial killers as debonaire, charming, and handsome. Some are decidedly undesirable by conventional standards, and still others suffer from intense shyness. In fact, for some serial killers, murder can be their only strategy for seeking sexual gratification and even "enjoying" the "company" of others.

Leonard Lake, a middle-aged recluse who lived in the woods just east of San Francisco, was painfully aware of his limitations when he outlined on videotape, with chilling calmness and clarity, his motives for abducting women. Preparing to build an elaborate underground bunker in which to imprison young women as sex slaves, Lake described in logical, although patently selfish, terms why he felt the need to proceed with what he called "Operation Miranda":

I am a realist. I am 38 years old, a bit chubby, with not much hair, and I'm losing what I have. I am not particularly attractive to women—or I should say particularly attracting to women. And all the traditional magnets—the money, the position/power—I don't have. And yet I am still very sexually active, and I am still very much attracted to a particular type of woman who almost by definition is totally uninterested in me.

Dirty old man, pervert, I'm attracted to young women, sometimes even as young as 12, although to be fair certainly 18–22 is pretty much an ideal range as far as my interests go. I like very slim women, very pretty of course, petite, small breasted, long hair, if I am allowed. And, such a woman, by virtue of her youth, her attractiveness, her desirability to certainly the majority of mankind, simply has better options. There is no particular reason why such a woman should be interested in me.

But there is more to it than that. It is difficult to explain my personality in 25 words or less, but I am in fact a loner, I enjoy the peace, the quiet, the solitude, I enjoy being by myself. And while all my relationships with women in the past have been sexually successful, socially they have almost always been a failure. I've gone through two divorces, innumerable women, 50–55, I forget exactly the count, I counted recently. I'm afraid the bottom line statement is the simple fact that I'm a sexist slob.

I enjoy using women, and of course women aren't particularly interested in being used. I certainly enjoy sex. I certainly enjoy the dominance of climbing on a woman and using her body. But I'm not particularly interested in the id, the ego, all the things that a man should be interested in to complement a woman's needs. Now I can fake these emotions, and I can fake them very well. In the past, I've been very successful at attracting fairly interesting and attractive women simply because I did fake fairly well an interest in their needs and their requirements. So momentarily I had what I wanted and they thought they had what they wanted. But in the long term I don't want to bother.

What I want is an off-the-shelf sex partner. I want to be able to use a woman whenever and however I want. And when I'm tired or satiated or bored or not interested, I simply want to put her away, lock her up in a little room to get her out of my sight, out of my life, and thus avoid what heretofore has always been the obligation to entertain or amuse or satisfy a particular woman or girlfriend's whims of emotional whatevers.

Such an arrangement, of course, is not only blatantly sexist, but highly illegal. There's no doubt about it. It violates all of the human rights and blah blah, blah blah blah. To spare posterity my concept of other people's morality, I'm explaining my morality—what I feel, what I want. And as of this moment I am going to try to get it.

With the help of his buddy Charles Ng, Lake constructed a holding cell inside a bunker next to his home in which he kept a steady supply of slaves. He used them as long as they were appealing and satisfying, then violently discarded them as human trash. Surely, Lake could have hired prostitutes to fulfill his sexual needs and housekeepers to perform the other assorted chores. But there was much more to his fantasy: ownership. He sought to possess total power over his victims as if they were indeed his slaves.

Although Leonard Lake was as intelligent as he was self-absorbed, it is also part of the modern mythology that serial killers are typically brilliant—like Hannibal Lecter from Thomas Harris's novel, *The Silence of the Lambs.* Although some serial killers, such as California's Lawrence Sigmund Bittaker, have genius-level IQs, others clearly have sub-par intelligence.

Grover Godwin collected data about 107 serial killers and their 728 victims from a variety of sources including local police departments, the FBI, and newspaper reports, but predominantly from the Homicide Investigation and Tracking System (HITS) database in Washington State.[5] All of the cases he examined had been solved. Godwin determined that only 16 percent of the serial murderers he studied had attended college and only 4 percent graduated with a bachelor's degree. The majority were employed in blue-collar jobs working for other people. Regardless of social class, IQ, or level of educational attainment, however, most serial killers—at least those who successfully remain at large for long time periods—typically do possess a certain degree of cunning, criminal savoir faire needed to accumulate a significant body count. Many of them are exceptionally skillful in their presentation of self, so much so that they are beyond suspicion and thus are difficult to apprehend.

The most prolific serial killers also tend to be the most organized psychologically. They methodically stalk their victims for the best opportunity to strike so as not to be seen, and they smartly dump the bodies far away so as not to leave any clues. The discovery of a body in a dump site does not provide investigators with the crime scene where most of the forensic evidence—hairs, blood, fibers, semen—is located. In a sense, becoming a serial killer is a process of self-selection. A confused assailant who kills in a frenzied way cannot successfully plan, execute, and cover up the crime. The most dangerous, cunning murderers are a great challenge for law enforcement authorities. Notwithstanding advances in forensics, computerized offender tracking, and even behavioral profiling, when these crimes are solved, luck generally plays a significant role.

It may not be fair to law enforcement to characterize these apprehensions as lucky, because they still involve the police doing their job. While killers like Theodore Bundy and Gary Heidnik may have been caught in routine traffic stops and Berkowitz was linked to the Son of Sam killings due to a parking ticket, these are obviously important police activities—even if not requiring tremendous technical skill—and highlight the significance of a police presence in our society.

There is also some evidence that the most organized killers can begin to deteriorate over time. Bundy began his killing career with a duffle bag filled with weapons, disguises, and tools and had several ruses he used to lure women (e.g., his arm was in a sling and he needed help loading something into his car). By the time he committed the Chi Omega sorority house murders at Florida State University, however, Bundy used a log he found at the crime scene as his murder weapon and left bite marks on his victim's body. Apparently, Bundy's transformation was from a highly organized to a quite disorganized killer.

The notion that serial killers subconsciously wish to be caught and for this purpose carelessly leave telltale clues at crime scenes or act impetuously and recklessly may hold in detective novels but has little validity when applied to most real cases. When serial killer Andrew Cunanan traveled from the midwest to the east coast in a series of stolen cars, many law enforcement experts speculated that his incautious actions, such as using his victims' cell phones, indicated a latent desire to be apprehended. Despite this wishful thinking on the part of investigators, Cunanan remained at large for months, claiming five victims—two in Minnesota, one each in Illinois and New Jersey, and finally celebrity designer Gianni Versace in Miami. Even as the police cornered him on a Miami houseboat, Cunanan still controlled when, where, and how the killing spree would end. On July 23, 1997, as police and media helicopters circled above, the 27-year-old killer took his own life rather than be taken alive. Perhaps it was a death wish, but clearly not an arrest wish.

Another widely held belief—but one that is true—is that serial killers are typically white males in their late 20s or 30s. Table 7.2 provides a basic demographic profile based on our database of 558 serial killers operating in the United States from 1900 to 2000. In terms of age, our analysis indicated that 41 percent of all serial murderers began killing in their 20s and another 29 percent started murdering in their 30s, with an average of just over 30. This is an age distribution much older than murderers in general. It is quite rare for a teenager or young adult to have acquired an insatiable taste for murder. It is equally uncommon for such a youthful offender to have developed the level of skill and cunning needed to carry out a prolonged career of killing without being caught after one or two murders or attempted murders.

Overall, 86 percent of the serial killers in our database were male and 82 percent were white. The percentage of serial killers who were black (15 percent) was roughly the same as

TABLE 7.2   Characteristics of Serial Killers

Characteristic		Percentage
Sex		
	Male	84.3
	Female	15.7
Race/Ethnicity		
	White	81.9
	Black	14.3
	Hispanic	3.5
	Other	0.4
Age		
	Under 20	12.8
	20–29	41.2
	30–39	29.4
	40–49	12.3
	50+	4.3
Alone/Partnership		
	Solo	80.5
	Pair	12.7
	Team	6.9

their representation in the population and considerably below the substantial percentage of blacks among single-victim killers (more than half). However, the involvement of black serial killers may have been understated proportionately as a consequence of racially disparate linkage-blindness. Serial murder, like murder generally, tends to be intraracial (i.e., whites killing whites and blacks killing blacks); serial killings of black victims, especially those who are impoverished and marginalized politically, are less likely to be connected, prioritized for investigation, and subsequently solved.

The disproportionate involvement of males in serial homicide in part reflects, of course, their greater numbers in murder rates generally. Curiously, however, according to these statistics, the gender ratio among serial killers (86 percent male) was slightly less pronounced than for murder generally (about 88 percent); a finding that is at odds with the prevailing view among most researchers that almost all serial killers are men.

This seeming discrepancy between our data and the common view can, however, be understood as a difference in definition. While we have cast serial homicide in the broadest terms to encompass any personal motive for repeated homicide (including profit and revenge, as well as dominance), other criminologists restrict their attention almost exclusively to sexually motivated killers, virtually all of whom are indeed men.

Even when the serial murders committed by women are heinous, cruel, and sexually predatory, the tendency is still to portray them as victims. Karla Homolka fully and willingly participated in the brutal rapes and murders of three girls, one of whom was her own younger sister, to satisfy her own sexual fantasies. Gwendolyn Graham and Catherine Wood, convicted of killing five elderly people in a nursing home (and suspected of as many as 10 deaths in total), used their murders as foreplay, sneaking away afterward into vacant rooms to have sex and discuss fondly their victims' dying moments. Aileen Wuornos, a Florida prostitute who murdered seven men, told the jurors during her trial that she hoped their daughters would be raped.

Dozens of women have murdered children, stepchildren, husbands, mothers, and fathers for the benefit of collecting on their life insurance. Given the reluctance to label the most brutal female killers as serial predators, profiles of the female serial killers may be off the mark. Much more weight appears to be given to a female killer's past history of child and domestic abuse, portraying her as a victim, as mentally ill, and as not responsible for her actions.[6] Criminologists are only now beginning to recognize the existence of a female sexual predator. Women, like men, can develop deviant psychosexual needs. Women can only begin to achieve equality with men if their predatory, violent, and murderous behavior is acknowledged as a product of their free will to kill and punished accordingly.

One of the most striking dissimilarities between serial murder and criminal homicide generally is the nature of the victim–offender relationship. Unlike single-victim murder, which commonly arises from some dispute between partners, family members, or friends, serial murder is typically a stranger-perpetrated crime. According to Godwin, some 90 percent of serial killers' victims were total strangers to their assailants; only 3 percent were friends and 1 percent were family members. To some extent, the abundance of stranger victims reflects the predatory patterns of these killers as well as the greater ease with which stranger attackers can escape apprehension and therefore be free to amass a large tally of kills.

In addition to their lack of a prior relationship with their assailants, serial murder victims also tend to share one important trait—their vulnerability. Although virtually anyone can be targeted, serial killers tend to prefer children, prostitutes, and the elderly as victims. To some extent, this may reflect their sexual desires. But this victim preference also reflects the relative ease with which the offenders can abduct and slay certain targets. Pedophile Wesley Allen Dodd of Washington State encountered little difficulty in snatching children from parks and other public spaces. Arthur Shawcross made a habit of trolling Rochester's red-light district, not needing even an ounce of force to find streetwalkers willing to enter his web of control.

Like the serial killers who take their lives, victims also tend to be white—in Godwin's study, 81 percent. The age range is quite broad, reflecting the disparate classes of favored victims. The gender characteristics of serial killer victims are quite different from those of killers generally. Given the strong sexual element in the motivations of male serial murderers, their victims tend to be female—fully 67 percent. Despite the greater number of females slain, moreover, some serial killers are gay or bisexual and purposely target male victims for rape and murder. In Godwin's study, 20 percent of the victims were males who were raped by their attackers.

One of the most striking and intriguing aspects of serial murderers is the nature of their motivation. Although it has been loosely described as "motiveless," there is indeed one—to satisfy an intense appetite for power and sadism. The serial murderer tends to kill not for love, money, or revenge but just for the fun of it—because it makes him feel good.

The typical serial killer is someone like Hillside Strangler Kenneth Bianchi, who, along with his cousin Angelo Buono, raped, tortured, and murdered 10 young women in the Los Angeles area in the late 1970s. The Hillside Strangler moniker is quite telling. Unlike most other types of murderers, the serial killer hardly ever uses a firearm. Too easy, too clean, and much too distant, a gun would only rob him of his greatest pleasure: exalting in his victim's suffering.

Some observers have suggested that to a sexual sadist a gun is phallic, and shooting bullets like an ejaculation.[7] Yet few, if any, serial killers have ever used a gun to sodomize a victim—fists, vegetables, and other objects, but no gun barrels. The sadistic serial killer enjoys the whole experience of murder—squeezing a throat rather than a trigger—squeezing from his victim's body her last breath of life, killing her slowly and with great suffering on her part.

Some serial killers feed their need to feel important and powerful by taunting the police and making the headlines. During the 1970s, a serial killer in Wichita, Kansas, phoned a local newspaper reporter directing him to a section of the public library where he located a letter in which the writer claimed credit for the recent massacre of a local family. In his letter, the killer wrote: "The code words for me will be . . . Bind them, Torture them, Kill them." He signed the letter: BTK Strangler, for bind, torture, and kill.

From that point on, the BTK moniker was commonly used by newspaper reporters in their articles about the killer's string of seven murders. In January 1978, BTK sent a poem to a reporter at the *Wichita Eagle-Beacon,* in which he wrote about a victim he had slain a year earlier. In February of the same year, BTK wrote a letter to a Wichita television station complaining about the lack of publicity he had received for his murders. "How many do I have to kill," BTK asked, "before I get my name in the paper or some national attention?"

In addition, the killer compared his crimes with those of Jack the Ripper, Son of Sam, and the Hillside Strangler.

Until recently, it was believed that BTK's killing spree had ended in 1991. Then, after more than 13 years, BTK resurfaced once again to terrorize the Wichita community. In March 2004, he sent a letter to the *Wichita Eagle* in which he claimed credit for the unsolved death of Vicki Wegerle, who was killed in September 1986. As evidence of his complicity, BTK enclosed with his letter a photocopy of Wegerle's driver's license and photographs of her body.

BTK was again communicating with the police and the media. The killer's sudden reemergence indicated that he was feeling insecure about being out of the spotlight. He apparently hadn't taken anyone's life in several years and wasn't getting much attention from the public.

BTK turned out to be 59-year-old Dennis Rader, a church council president and former Cub Scout leader, a compliance officer in his neighborhood who had terrorized the city of Wichita over three decades. Among the items that Rader sent to the media was a computer disk which, unbeknownst to the killer, contained an electronic imprint that could be traced back to its source—a computer in Christ Lutheran Church. After learning that Rader had access to the church computer, police were able to gain the cooperation of the suspect's daughter Kerri Rader, whose DNA specimen tied her father to some of the crime scenes.

Because the state of Kansas had no death penalty at the time Rader committed his crimes, he was able to escape execution. But on June 28, 2005, BTK was given the most severe sentence possible under Kansas law—10 consecutive life terms with no possibility of parole for 175 years.

Like Kenneth Bianchi and his favorite cousin and killing partner Angelo Buono, many serial killers operate in teams—as many as 20 percent. They encourage each other to do the wrong thing and are more likely than their counterparts who operate alone to torture their victims. For Lawrence Bittaker and Roy Norris, killing was a team sport. They called it the "birthday game," seeking to kill teenage girls of different ages (13, 14, 15, etc.), like trophies. Bittaker and Norris preferred blondes and tortured them in their specially equipped van, which they called "Murder Mac." The pair tape-recorded the torture sessions so they could relive them later in their spare time.

Some teams include mixed couples. Doug Clark, the so-called Los Angeles Sunset Strip Killer, did the murdering and decapitating, while his girlfriend, Carol Bundy (no relation to Theodore), assisted. She even prepared the severed heads of victims for him to use as sex objects in the shower. She would do anything for her guy and for the sake of their love. Similarly, Janice Hooker helped her husband, Cameron, abduct young women for his sex torture sessions. So long as her husband had sex slaves around the house, he would leave her alone.

The Murdering Mind

Many people assume that anyone who kills for fun, pleasure, or sport must be psychotic and out of touch with reality. Indeed, some serial killers have been driven by severe mental illness, such as Herbert Mullen of Santa Cruz, California, who killed 13 people in a span of four months in order to avert an earthquake—or at least that's what the voices told him.[8]

By contrast, Godwin found little evidence of serial killers suffering from profound mental disorders. Only 28 percent of all the murderers in his study had a history of receiving any kind of treatment for mental illness; even fewer (20 percent) had a history of being treated for alcoholism or drug abuse. Most serial murderers are not insane in a legal sense or psychotic in a medical sense. Though they know right from wrong, know exactly what they are doing, and can control their desire to kill, they typically choose not to do so. Even the serial killers who remember childhood abuse, experience hallucinations, and "discover" multiple personalities at trial time may be suffering from mental disorders manufactured by defense attorneys who employ the insanity plea as a last resort.

.   Psychologically, most serial killers are sociopaths (or antisocial personality types). They possess a disorder of character rather than of the mind, involving a lack of conscience and feelings of remorse, an inability to feel empathy for others, pathological lying, a manipulative style, impulsivity, and a total concern for maximizing their own pleasures in life.[9] Other people are seen merely as tools for fulfilling their own needs and desires, no matter how perverse or reprehensible. The serial killer is more bad than mad—simply put, he is evil.

In addition to their sociopathic personality disorders, serial killers have often been characterized as suffering from low self-esteem. Although some killers are undoubtedly motivated by their feelings of inadequacy, the relationship between low self-esteem and violence has little empirical support. Rather, anecdotal evidence suggests that many serial killers (including the medical murderers in Chapter 8) may suffer from narcissism or "self-love." They have very inflated senses of themselves and they demand that the rest of the world recognizes their greatness. They have a God-like complex and believe that the rules do not apply to them.[10]

Some serial killers clearly hate women. When Robert Charles Brown, 52, was apprehended by the state of Colorado in 2006 he claimed his murders were triggered by his disgust for women and their lack of morality. Brown likely murdered as many as 48 women across nine states and two countries beginning when he was a 17-year-old medic in the U.S. Army in Korea. He was likely successful for so long because, like many other serial killers, he had a lot of different jobs over the years that required travel; basically he was always a drifter. The son of a Sheriff's deputy, Brown was characterized as a handsome, bright loner. One of his favorite pastimes was to wear a Halloween mask, with which he delighted in scaring women and children outside their homes. Ironically, Brown was born on Halloween in 1952.

Some killers are not only remorseless but are even proud of their conquests and boast to the press, to the relatives of their victims, even to each other with considerable pleasure. Almost half of all serial killers collect souvenirs of their crimes.[11] Joel Rifkin, for example, who in 1993 confessed to murdering 17 prostitutes in New York, kept his victims' underwear, shoes, sweaters, cosmetics, and jewelry in his bedroom. Jeffrey Dahmer proudly displayed pictures of his victims on the walls of his apartment and kept body parts in his refrigerator.

Missouri's Robert Berdella, a 40-year-old man who held captive six male sex slaves, had a particularly rich collection of souvenirs, including two human skulls and over 200 photographs of his victims in a variety of degrading poses before and after death, and with various vegetables inserted into their body cavities. He also chronicled his "human experiments" in a detailed diary of his tortures.

Berdella's collection of souvenirs served several important purposes. First, for a man who had otherwise led an unremarkable life, his treasures made him feel accomplished.

They represented the one and only way in which he had ever distinguished himself "as a real pro." More important, the souvenirs became tangible reminders of the "good times" Berdella had spent with his "playmates." With the aid of his photographs, he could still get pleasure, even between captives, from reminiscing, daydreaming, fantasizing, and masturbating. In fact, serial killers have lasting memories as well as incredibly vivid and elaborate fantasies. Through murder and mayhem, they literally chase their dreams.[12]

Many serial killers have various paraphilias—sexual attractions to unusual or bizarre objects. Rather than just a fetish (a sexual attraction to a nonhuman object such as feces or shoes), some have multiple paraphilias including cannibalism, pedophilia, and necrophilia. At what point does their paraphilia become a mental disorder that they cannot control? Almost never in a court of law, as illustrated by the rejection of Jeffrey Dahmer's plea of insanity based on his necrophiliac and cannibalistic desires.

Even though serial killers tend to be sociopaths, totally lacking in concern for their victims, some actually do have a conscience and the capacity for remorse but are able to neutralize or negate their feelings of guilt. There is a powerful psychological process—known as dehumanization—that allows many serial killers to slaughter scores of innocent people by viewing them as worthless and, therefore, expendable. By targeting marginalized groups—prostitutes, the homeless, runaways—they can rationalize (if they need to for their own sense of emotional comfort) that they are doing something good for society . . . or at least nothing that bad.

Jeffrey Dahmer actually viewed his crimes as a sign of love and affection. He told Tracy Edwards, his final victim who managed to escape and led the police to Dahmer's apartment of horrors, that if he played his cards right, he too could give his heart to Jeff. He meant it literally of course, but, according to Edwards, he said it in an affectionate, not a threatening, manner.

Many serial killers skillfully compartmentalize the world into two groups—those whom they care about and everyone else. Kenneth Bianchi, for example, could be kind and loving to his wife and child as well as his mother and friends, yet be vicious and cruel to those he considered expendable. He and his cousin started with prostitutes, choosing victims for whom they had very little concern. Later, when comfortable with killing, he branched out to middle-class, more respectable targets.

According to Stephen Giannangelo, serial killers are also eased into their murderous avocation by the clumsiness and impulsivity of their first kill.[13] He likens the first murder to the sexually inexperienced teenager who fumbles in the backseat of a car as he attempts to have sex with his date. For a serial killer, what might begin as a rape or an assault is transformed, in the excitement of the moment, into an act of homicide. Almost inadvertently, the killer crosses the threshold separating fantasy from fact. Whatever shame he may feel for having committed a serious offense is completely overshadowed by the "rush" that he acquires from finally discovering what he needs.

It has been estimated that 1 in 20 males in our society could be considered sociopathic. Of course, most sociopaths are not violent: they may lie, cheat, steal, harass, or womanize, but rape and murder are not particularly appealing to them. The other critical ingredient to the profile of the serial killer is a strong tendency toward sexual sadism. More generally, these men have a craving for power and control. They tie up their victims in order to watch them squirm, and torture their victims to hear them scream. They rape, sodomize, degrade, bludgeon, and mutilate their victims in order to feel powerful, dominant, and superior.

One of Lawrence Bittaker's victims pleaded, "Please, if you're going to kill me, tell me so that I can pray first." Bittaker was exhilarated by his victim's begging. He assured her that she would not die and then slammed an icepick in her ear. He just loved the control.

The sexual sadist derives intense pleasure through the pain, suffering, and humiliation of another person. In a pure sense, sexual sadists enjoy the act of inflicting pain upon another, non-consenting victim. Yet the pleasure may also flow from the result—the screams and degradation of the recipient, rather than from just the act itself. Sexual sadists can also relish vicariously when another person (an accomplice or even an actor in a film) causes a victim to suffer. Thus, a pair or team of serial killers can enjoy not only personal satisfaction from raping and torturing a victim, but the feeling of superiority can be enhanced by the power of the partnership.

The essence of the sadistic drive lies in the desire to achieve total domination and mastery over another person. From this point of view, the pleasure derived from killing depends, at least in part, on the sadist's role in having caused the victim to suffer. An alternative argument holds that the sexual or psychological pleasure that a sadistic killer derives from the act of torturing his victim may be more a result of observing the victim's agony than from the actual infliction of pain. This hypothesis appears to be supported by experimental research in which aggressive sex offenders become sexually aroused when shown simulated scenes of men inflicting pain on women.[14]

This begs the question, however, of whether the arousal stems from observing the victim's suffering or from identifying vicariously with the aggressor. Regardless of whether the critical component is the stimulus (the direct infliction of pain) or the response (the victim's suffering itself), the fundamental objective in the actions of the sadistic serial killer is to achieve complete mastery over his victims. In other words, humiliation, enslavement, and terror are vehicles for attaining total domination over another human being.

Power and control may be critical themes in the character of serial murderers, yet these traits are also common in many successful people in the worlds of business, politics, and even academics. The willingness to win at all cost, no matter who is hurt in the process, may insulate many winning individuals from looking back at those they exploit along the road to success. A vital difference between serial killers and those who backstab only figuratively may be access to legitimate opportunity.

At the same time, the sadistic sexual fantasies of the serial killer may also pattern the form of his search for power. It appears that many serial murderers, from an early age, become absorbed deeply in a rich fantasy life involving images of sex and violence. As they mature into adolescence, their fantasies become more and more consuming, increasing in their power as internal drive mechanisms that motivate them to cross the line into murderous behavior.

Robert Prentky and his colleagues compared the nature and prevalence of sexual fantasy between groups of sexually motivated serial killers and single-victim murderers also with sexual motivation to their crime. Based on self-report interview data, the serial murderers were more apt to describe a strong and intrusive fantasy life involving violent themes and paraphilias (deviant sexual practices or obsessions).[15]

Not all children who fantasize about sadistic forms of violence grow up to be serial killers. The fact that most serial murderers do not initiate their murder sprees until well into their adult years indicates the important role of adult experiences—failures in relationships and at work—in the making of a serial killer. Many individuals who have suffered profoundly as children grow into healthy and nonviolent adults. They benefit later from positive experiences with peers, romantic partners, and co-workers who give them the support and encouragement that they lacked when they were young.

This was unfortunately not true of Danny Rolling, who turned to murder at the age of 36, killing three in his hometown of Shreveport, Louisiana, and five more in Gainesville, Florida. Not only had Rolling been the victim of an abusive parent, but his adjustment and personal problems continued through adolescence into early adulthood. A brief marriage ended in divorce, his adult relationship with his parents continued to be severely strained, and he couldn't manage to hold a job. Instead, he drifted first from job to job, next from state to state, then from prison to prison, and finally from murder to murder.

Amazingly, given the abuse and horror of their childhoods, serial killers rarely kill themselves. Their own suffering is not internalized but rather externalized—they blame others. Occasionally, a serial killer will attempt suicide. Gary Heidnik attempted to take his own life 13 times. How can someone who is so skilled at killing others be so inadequate at killing himself? Clearly, the answer is that he did not want to die. Herbert Baumeister, an exception to the rule, committed suicide in 1996, but only after the discovery of thousands of bone and teeth fragments on his family's estate in Westfield, Indiana.

Although only four of Baumeister's victims were positively identified, the fragments were of at least 11 bodies. A father, husband and businessman, he may have also been the I-70 killer during the late 1980s, as his business often took him from Indiana to Ohio over this highway. Baumeister's victims were gay men whom he had picked up in gay bars in Indianapolis. This case is also an example of how serial killers can remain undetected and uninvestigated for so long when their victim pool is a marginalized group. It is unlikely that Baumeister's murderous career would have gone on so long if he had elected to slay college students or professors.

Childhood Origins

Whenever the case of an infamous serial killer is uncovered, be it a cannibalistic sadist or a not-so-merciful mercy killer, journalists and behavioral scientists alike tend to search for clues deep within the killer's biography that might explain his or her seemingly senseless or excessively brutal murders. Many writers, for example, have emphasized Theodore Bundy's concerns over having been born illegitimate, and biographers of Hillside Strangler Kenneth Bianchi capitalized on his having been an adopted child.

The BTK Strangler, Dennis Rader, admitted to investigators that his attraction to violence and death began early in life. He recalled that at the age of eight he would get aroused watching his grandmother kill chickens by strangling them with a leather shoestring. He also admitted to shoplifting issues of *True Detective* magazine as a kid. Rader had rich fantasies involving images of bondage and sexual violence. Even in high school, he wasn't sexually excited about girls unless he imagined tying them up.

Researchers are not of one mind, however, in explaining what produces the psyche of the serial murderer. Some stress genetic or biological factors in accounting for such defects as sociopathy. Moffit and Henry suggest, for example, that damage to the right hemisphere of the brain may be responsible for losses of "social sensibilities," including lack of empathy and difficulties with bonding.[16] Other investigators point instead to early childhood experiences and repeated psychological trauma during development, such as insufficient bonding of the child to his parents or even physical and psychological abuse. Children who are abused, neglected, or abandoned tend to grow into needy adults with difficulty bonding with others, a so-called "attachment disorder." Lacking control over their own lives as children, many remain insecure as they mature, continuing to possess an intense need to control their environment. From an early age, they are unable to trust others, and instead learn to manipulate people in order to fulfill their needs.

Interestingly, shyness has been identified as a factor that may protect against delinquency, perhaps as a trait that limits the number of peer contacts. However, shyness—and particularly shyness with women—is a characteristic that appears in many case histories of male serial killers.

There is a long tradition of research on the childhood correlates of homicidal proneness. For example, John Macdonald long ago hypothesized a triad of symptoms—bedwetting, firesetting, and cruelty to animals—which he viewed as reactions to parental rejection, neglect, or brutality.[17] Although the so-called Macdonald's Triad was later refuted in controlled studies, the connection between parental physical/sexual abuse or abandonment and subsequent violent behavior remains a continuing focus of research. On an anecdotal level, moreover, it appears that many serial killers have as children reportedly expressed sadistic behavior toward animals.

Indeed, a number of more recent studies have purported to support the hypothesis that violent individuals are also abusive toward animals.[18] For example, Kellert and Felthous found significantly more childhood animal cruelty among aggressive criminals than among either nonaggressive criminals or noncriminals.[19] Moreover, tracking the criminal records of 153 animal abusers compared with 153 nonabusers, sociologist Arnold Arluke and colleagues determined that the animal abusers were five times more likely to commit acts of human violence including murder, rape, and assault.[20]

Yet, as described in the case studies of Steve Egger's *The Killers Among Us,* serial murderers don't just abuse animals, but torture and dissect them.[21] Egger's description of serial killer Jerry Marcus notes how the killer set pregnant cats on fire and poured hot water on hungry dogs—and after these sadistic acts he felt pride and joy. Jeffrey Dahmer started his killing spree on neighborhood pets when he was a child. He had a pet cemetery, and a long history of animal decapitation and vivisection. It appears that much more attention should be given to those who abuse animals, as there is ample evidence that in many cases, the animals just get bigger. People of any age who achieve joy via the suffering of any living creature may come to have a long future of child abuse, partner violence, rape, or murder.

It is often suggested that because of deep-rooted problems stemming from childhood, serial killers suffer from a profound sense of powerlessness, which they compensate for through extreme forms of aggression to exert control over others. The biographies of most serial killers reveal significant physical and psychological trauma at an early age. Based on in-depth interviews with 36 incarcerated murderers, Ressler and his colleagues found evidence of psychological abuse (e.g., public humiliation) in 23 cases and physical trauma in 13 cases.[22] Eric Hickey reported that among a group of 62 male serial killers, 48 percent had been rejected as children by a parent or some other important person in their lives.[23] Of course, these same types of experiences can be found in the biographies of many "normal" people as well. More specifically, although useful for characterizing the backgrounds of serial killers, the findings presented by Ressler and Hickey lack a comparison group drawn from nonoffending populations for which the same definitions of trauma have been applied. Therefore, it is impossible to conclude that serial killers have suffered as children to any greater extent than others have.

The emphasis on child abuse as a "cause" of murderous rage has become the latest excuse of serial killers who attempt to deflect blame for their actions. Unfortunately, murderers who might exploit the "child abuse syndrome" to their own advantage frequently receive a sympathetic ear. As a sociopath, the serial killer is a particularly convincing and accomplished liar. As a professional trained to be supportive and empathic, his psychiatrist may be easily conned. The case histories of such malingerers as Kenneth Bianchi and Arthur Shawcross, both serial killers who fooled mental health professionals with fabricated tales of child abuse, remind us to be skeptical about the self-serving testimony of accused killers eager to escape legal responsibility for their crimes.

As a related matter, more than a few serial killers—from David Berkowitz to Joel Rifkin—were raised by adoptive parents. In the "adopted child syndrome," an individual displaces his anger for birth parents onto adoptive parents as well as other authority figures. According to Kirschner, the syndrome is often expressed, early in life, in "provocative antisocial behavior" including firesetting, truancy, promiscuity, pathological lying, and stealing.[24] The deeply troubled adopted child may, in fantasy, create an imaginary playmate who represents his antisocial impulses. Later, he may experience a dissociative disorder or even the development of an alter personality in which his murderous tendencies become situated.

The apparent overrepresentation of adoption in the biographies of serial killers has been exploited by those who are looking for simple explanations for heinous and senseless crimes. In reality, the way in which this link operates has not been completely explained. That is, possible triggering mechanisms might include the effects of rejection by birth parents, maternal deprivation during the critical first few months of life, poor prenatal care by the birth mother, or genetic deficiencies passed on from both biological parents.

Some neurologists and psychiatrists have suggested that many killers—especially killers who commit senseless acts of brutality—have incurred severe injury to the limbic region of the brain as a result of profound or repeated head trauma, generally during childhood. Dorothy Otnow Lewis and Jonathan Pincus and colleagues, for example, examined 15 murderers on Florida's death row and found that all showed signs of neurological irregularities.[25] In addition, Joel Norris reported that excessive spinal fluid was found in the brain scan of serial killer Henry Lee Lucas; Norris argued that this abnormality was caused by an earlier series of blows to Lucas's head.[26]

There is compelling reason to believe that severe head trauma and resulting injuries to the brain can potentially have dire effects on behavior, including violent outbursts, learning disabilities, and epilepsy. Henry Lee Lucas was reportedly beaten by his mother with lumber and broom handles. He later claimed to have experienced frequent dizzy spells and blackouts. Bobby Joe Long, who was convicted by the state of Florida in 1986 and 1994 of a total of nine counts of murder, also appears to have received several severe head injuries. In three different episodes, at the age of five or six, Long fell off a swing, from a horse, and off his bicycle, suffering repeated brain concussions in the process.

There are important possible causal order problems with theories about brain damage and violent behavior. If the individual is a thrill-seeker, then the same set of personality factors may lead to head injuries (e.g., horseback riding, motorcycles, bicycles, and playground equipment). In the presence of other negative social contexts (e.g., physical and sexual abuse, substance use and abuse), the same thrill-seeking need may also act as a predisposing factor to violence. Thus, head injuries may be a result of aggressive and violent behavior rather than their cause.

It is often said that "hindsight is 20/20." This is definitely true in terms of explaining serial murder. Following the apprehension of a serial killer, we generally hear mixed reports that "he seemed like a nice guy, but there was something about him that wasn't quite right." Of course, there is something about most people that "isn't quite right." However, when such a person is exposed to be a serial murderer, we tend to focus on the red flags in his character and biography that were ignored. Even the stench emanating from Jeffrey Dahmer's apartment, which he explained to the neighbors as the odor of spoiled meat from his broken freezer, was unexceptional until after the fact.

The methodological problems in predicting violence in advance are well known. For a category of violence as rare as serial murder, the low base rate and consequent false-positive dilemma are overwhelming. Simply put, there are thousands of white males in their late 20s or 30s who are sadistic, thirst for power, lack strong internal controls, tortured animals as children, and were adopted or abused—but the vast majority of them will never kill anyone.

Victim Selection

Although some serial killers have targeted co-eds, they are much more likely to target particularly vulnerable individuals—runaways, prostitutes, homeless people, or patients in nursing homes and hospitals. Serial killers rarely choose professional athletes, bodybuilders, or NRA conventioneers as their victims. Some research in serial murder has suggested that the victim actually has a symbolic value for the killer; for example, Ted Bundy selected women who physically resembled a girlfriend who had dumped him.[27] The problem with this line of reasoning is that so many of the women in high schools and colleges in the 1970s looked the same. It was popular to wear long, straight hair, parted down the middle. Rather than a Norman Bates-like complex regarding their mothers or their girlfriends, serial killers more likely choose women in general because of their heterosexuality and the inability of most women to defend themselves.

Moreover, the marginality of prostitutes, drug addicts, and runaways gives the killer a special advantage. It generally takes considerable time for a missing person's report to be filed, even longer to recognize that a woman has become a victim of homicide. By the time the police locate a body, they are typically left with skeletal remains—no DNA, fingerprints, fiber, or hair. Indeed, they are lucky to be able to identify the victim, let alone the killer. In November 2003, Gary Leon Ridgway, the Green River Killer, in a plea bargain to avoid the death penalty, admitted to killing more than 48 prostitutes in the Seattle area over a 16-year period. In his statement, Ridgway said he targeted prostitutes "because I thought I could kill as many as I wanted without getting caught." According to the serial killer, "they were easy to pick up without being noticed" and "they would not be reported missing right away, and might never be reported missing." Additionally, the psychological process of victim dehumanization, described earlier, enabled Ridgway to kill prostitutes without remorse.

He recalled this thought while strangling one of his victims: "You made me do it, you bitch, you whore, you worthless piece of garbage."

Finally, there is little pressure on the police to solve a string of prostitute killings or those of certain other marginalized groups like homeless drug addicts. Most middle-class individuals don't feel personally threatened. After all, it's only criminals killing criminals!

ENDNOTES

1. Robert K. Ressler, John E. Douglas, Ann W. Burgess, and Allen G. Burgess, *Crime Classification Manual.* Lexington, MA: Lexington Books, 1992.

2. James Alan Fox and Jack Levin, *Extreme Killing: Understanding Serial and Mass Murder.* Thousand Oaks, CA: Sage, 2006.

3. Janet Warren, Roy R. Hazelwood, and Park E. Dietz, "The Sexually Sadistic Serial Killer," in Thomas O'Reilly-Fleming, ed., *Serial and Mass Murder: Theory, Research and Policy.* Toronto: Canadian Scholars' Press, 1996.

4. James Alan Fox and Jack Levin, "Serial Murder: Myth and Reality," in Dwayne Smith and Margaret Zahn, eds., *Homicide Studies: A Sourcebook of Social Research.* Thousand Oaks, CA: Sage Publications, 1998.

5. Grover Maurice Godwin, *Hunting Serial Predators: A Multivariate Classification Approach to Profiling Violent Behavior.* Boca Raton, FL: CRC Press, 1999.

6. Patricia Pearson, *When She Was Bad.* New York: Penguin Books, 1998.

7. David Abrahamsen. *The Murdering Mind.* New York: Harper & Row, 1973.

8. Donald T. Lunde, *Murder and Madness.* San Francisco, CA: San Francisco Book Co., 1976.

9. Robert D. Hare, *Psychopathy: Theory and Research.* New York: Wiley, 1970.

10. Brad J. Bushman and Roy F. Baumeister, "Threatened Egotism, Narcissism, Self-Esteem, and Direct and Displaced Aggression: Does Self-Love or Self-Hate lead to Violence?" *Journal of Personality and Social Psychology,* 75 (1998): 219–229.

11. Godwin, op. cit.

12. R. A. Prentky, A. W. Burgess, F. Rokous, A. Lee, C. Hartman, R. Ressler, and J. Douglas, "The Presumptive Role of Fantasy in Serial Sexual Homicide," *The American Journal of Psychiatry* 146 (1989): 887–891.

13. Stephen J. Giannangelo, *The Psychopathology of Serial Murder: A Theory of Violence.* Westport, CT: Greenwood Publishing Group, 1996.

14. O. Fedora, J. R. Reddon, and J. W. Morrison, "Sadism and Other Paraphilias in Normal Controls and Aggressive and Nonaggresive Sex Offenders," *Archives of Sexual Behavior* 21 (1992): 1–15.

15. R. A. Prentky, A. W. Burgess, F. Rokous, A. Lee, C. Hartman, R. Ressler, and J. Douglas, "The Presumptive Role of Fantasy in Serial Sexual Homicide," *American Journal of Psychiatry* 146 (1989): 887–891.

16. T. F. Moffit and B. Henry, "Neuropsychological Studies of Juvenile Delinquency and Juvenile Violence," in J. S. Miller, ed., *Neuropsychology of Aggression.* Boston: Kluwer, 1991.

17. John M. Macdonald, "The Threat to Kill," *American Journal of Psychiatry* 120 (1963): 125–130; Daniel S. Hellman and Nathan Blackman, "Enuresis, Firesetting, and Cruelty to Animals," *American Journal of Psychiatry* 122 (1966): 1431–1435.

18. Alan R. Felthous, "Childhood Cruelty to Cats, Dogs and Other Animals," *Bulletin of the American Academy of Psychiatry and the Law* 9 (1981): 48–53.

19. S. Kellert and Alan R. Felthous, "Childhood Cruelty Toward Animals Among Criminals and Non-Criminals," *Human Relations* 18 (1985): 1113–1139.

20. Arnold Arluke, Jack Levin, Carter Luke, and Frank Ascione, "The Relationship of Animal Abuse to Violence and Other Forms of Antisocial Behavior," *Journal of Interpersonal Violence* 14 (1999): 963–975.

21. Steven A. Egger, *The Killers Among Us: An Examination of Serial Murder and Its Investigation.* Upper Saddle River, NJ: Prentice-Hall, 1998.

22. Robert K. Ressler, Ann W. Burgess, and John E. Douglas, *Sexual Homicide: Patterns and Motives.* Lexington, MA: Lexington Books, 1988.

23. Eric W. Hickey, *Serial Murderers and Their Victims.* Belmont, CA: Wadsworth, 1997.

24. David Kirschner, "Understanding Adoptees Who Kill: Dissociation, Patricide, and the Psychodynamics of Adoption," *International Journal of Offender Therapy and Comparative Criminology* 36 (1992): 323–333.

25. Dorothy Otnow Lewis, Jonathan H. Pincus, M. Feldman, L. Jackson, and B. Bard, "Psychiatric, Neurological and Psycho-Educational Characteristics of 15 Death Row Inmates in the United States," *American Journal of Psychiatry* 143 (1986): 838–845.

26. Joel Norris, *Serial Killers: The Growing Menace.* New York: Doubleday, 1988.

27. Hickey, op. cit.

8 Medical Murder

It is a sad fact of life that hospitals, clinics, and nursing homes are places where some people go to die. More tragically, they are also places where some go to be murdered. Several different forms of homicide, serial in nature, can be grouped together because they occur in health care settings. It has become increasingly common to find medical professionals charged with homicides committed in the line of duty.

For our purposes, medical murder includes nurses, doctors, nurse's aides, emergency medical technicians, nursing home aides, and other medical professionals who intentionally kill their patients to satisfy a variety of personal desires and psychological needs. Excluded from this classification, however, are domestic and other homicides committed by people who just happen to be employed as doctors, nurses or other health care workers. There are, without a doubt, many cases of doctors and nurses killing a family member for profit or murdering their spouse during a nasty separation or divorce. Dr. Bill Sybers was accused of murdering his wife in 1991 with a deadly injection. Sybers was convicted of the crime and was sentenced to prison, although the conviction was overturned due to questions about the validity of scientific evidence used at the trial. Sybers, now in his 70s and stricken with cancer, pled guilty to manslaughter in order to avoid more prison time. His son, haunted by the knowledge that his father killed his mother, committed suicide in 1993. Sybers' other two children and his second wife (who was his mistress when his wife was murdered) have all stood by him.

As defined here, however, medical murder does not include these types of cases that are unrelated to the perpetrator's health care role. In addition, our definition of medical murder does not include the tens of thousands of patients who may die each year because of medical incompetence, malpractice, or error. By "medical murder," we mean murders that are intentionally committed by medical staff against patients under their care.

Medical murderers have often been called Angels of Mercy and Angels of Death, but there is nothing angelic or merciful about their crimes. While euthanasia and physician- or other-assisted suicides (e.g., Kevorkian style "medicides") are by law a form of criminal homicide in almost all areas of the United States, assisted-suicide implies willing participation by the patient—a wish to die. But the victims of medical murders are patients who not only had no wish to die, but in most cases, had expected the medical staff to help them get well.

Medical murder is certainly not a new phenomenon. From 1907 to 1912, for example, Amy Archer-Gilligan ran a home for the aged in Connecticut where she poisoned as many as 40 people. Jane Toppan, a nurse's aide in turn-of-the-twentieth century New England, confessed to killing at least 30, but is suspected of poisoning as many as 100 people.

The Medical Murderer by Rupert Furneaux and *One Hundred Years of Medical Murder* by John Camp provide details of several cases of nurses and doctors who murdered patients during the nineteenth and early twentieth centuries.[1] Moreover, the first serial killer to be hanged in the United States was Dr. H.H. Holmes (aka Herman Webster Mudgett) who may have slain as many as 200 women in Chicago from 1892 to 1896. In many of these early medical murder cases, the motive was profit. Thus, although there is a long history of certain medical professionals and nursing home staff members murdering patients in their care, it is only fairly recently (in the last 30 years or so) that medical murderers with motives other than financial gain have been identified and reported. Like the definition for serial murder in general, our focus on medical murder does not include medical professionals who have killed "only" one patient and, thanks to diligent staff, were stopped before they could repeat the crime.

Finally, also not included in our scope of medical murder are mass killings in medical settings. For example, in April 2003, a female doctor went berserk in a hospital in Madrid, Spain, killing two and wounding six people with a knife. Her attack was aimed at colleagues and patients, and, according to co-workers, she was clearly suffering from mental illness in the time frame before the attack—but no one removed her from her position.

Most everyone is familiar with the names of serial killers Theodore Bundy, John Wayne Gacy, and David Berkowitz. But few can name notorious medical killers who were responsible for even higher victim counts over longer periods of time. For example, few people recognize the name Efren Salvidar, a respiratory therapist in California who may have murdered as many as 200 patients between 1989 and 1998, or Donald Harvey, a nurse's aide who may have killed as many as 80 people in Kentucky and Ohio between 1970 and 1987.

Also relatively obscure is Charles Cullen, a nurse who likely killed 35 to 45 patients, ranging from 22 to 80 years of age, in New Jersey and Pennsylvania during a 16-year murderous career. Before being convicted and given 11 consecutive life sentences, Cullen was an institutional drifter, committing murder in at least 10 different facilities. He was fired from five nursing jobs and resigned from two others. Although rumors and accusations about Cullen frequently surfaced, hospital administrators did not share their suspicions with other employers (in most states, hospitals can be sued for negative comments about current or former employees).

Cullen's body count makes him New Jersey's most prolific killer. He has showed no remorse for his crimes, explaining that depression led him to kill. Cullen, now age 47, claims to have attempted suicide more than 20 times during his life—an amazing failure since he clearly knew how to cause death.

Counting Medical Murders

Unlike school shootings, family massacres, and workplace shootings, it is often years before a medical murderer's crimes are discovered. Occurring in a setting where death is commonplace and generally assumed to be a result of the initial reason for admission to the hospital or nursing home, death does not ordinarily raise suspicions. Even when suspicious circumstances do exist—either because of the nature of the patient's death or a curiously large number of deaths, hospital staff are extremely reluctant to admit what may be happening (perhaps in part because insurance coverage often does not include intentional homicides committed by staff members).

As a result, it is difficult to derive an accurate assessment of the number of medical murders that have occurred over time. Since media interest in medical murders has grown in the last 30 years, many observers assume that this type of murder has increased. Yet, we have no way of knowing for certain whether there has been a real increase in the occurrence of medical murder or just improved reporting and detection. In the United States, two cases of medical murder were reported during the 1970s, nine in the 1980s, and nine additional cases in the 1990s.[2] There have been at least six reported cases since 2000.

It is also noteworthy that most of the known medical murder cases overall from 1970 to 2000 were in the United States, although this may be related to the higher surveillance levels in medical care settings here compared to other countries. More recently, however, a number of medical murder cases have come to light in other parts of the world, especially in Great Britain, which may also be a reflection of high-quality surveillance systems.

Colin Norris, 29, of Scotland, is out on bail pending his trial for murdering four elderly patients in 2002. In another Scottish case, Dr. Howard Martin, 71, is accused of murdering three of his patients with morphine overdoses during house calls he made in 2003 and 2004. Benjamin Geen, 25, of Oxfordshire, England, was a thrill-killing nurse who engaged in a three-month spree during 2004 and 2005. Geen killed two people, but was also charged with harming 15 others (bringing his average to as many as five victims per month). Geen injected the patients with muscle relaxants, and has admitted that he loved the attention and the excitement of attempted resuscitations. Geen, who is suspected of being involved in others cases as well, was convicted and sentenced to a minimum of 30 years in prison, where hopefully he won't be permitted near the prison infirmary.

In 2004, a Dutch court sentenced nurse Lucy de Berk, 42, to life in prison for four murders, although she is suspected of at least 13 murders and five attempted murders from 1997 to 2001. De Berk, a former Canadian prostitute, chose victims ranging from infants and children to the elderly, claiming only that she had a strange compulsion to kill.

Sonia Caleffi, 34, an anorexic nurse in Milan, Italy, has been arrested and admitted that she killed her patients to feel powerful and important, even keeping a diary about her victims. Many other deaths at the same hospital are also under investigation. Caleffi injected air into the veins of patients, causing embolisms, respiratory failures, and ultimately death. Caleffi had a history of depression and had worked at a number of different hospitals. It appears that she may have only been trying to create situations in which she could provide life-saving resuscitation, but still the patients died. For the medical murderer, nothing feels better—more invigorating and exhilarating—than the chance to play God.

Stephan Letter, 27, was recently sentenced to life in prison as Germany's worst serial killer, at least since World War II. Letter killed at least 29 patients in 2003 and 2004, with injections of tranquilizers and muscle relaxants. Many other patient deaths were investigated. Over 40 bodies were exhumed, yet many other suspected victims had been cremated, making it impossible to follow through with the investigation. Letter had originally wanted to be a doctor and claimed that he was only trying to help some of his victims by freeing them from pain and suffering. However, he also admitted that he may have acted hastily in some cases when he injected people who had suffered only minor injuries.

Like other serial killers, medical murderers rarely kill themselves. A recent exception may have been the case of Anne Grigg-Booth, 52, of Lancashire, England. Grigg-Booth, like many medical murderers, worked the night shift, when staffing levels are lower. She was charged with three morphine-overdose deaths and may have killed many more during her 25-year nursing career. In 2005, before she could be tried, Grigg-Booth overdosed on antidepressants and alcohol. Her death was ruled an accidental overdose, but she may indeed have overdosed intentionally. Grigg-Booth, known for her domineering personality, was estranged from her family. She had recently gone through a divorce and left behind a houseful of animals. Despite her approach to humans, Grigg-Booth was a rescuer of strays.

A review of known cases over the last 30 years indicates that many perpetrators killed several victims per month during their active phases. We can only assume that there are many more medical murders that go undetected, particularly when these institutional drifters work and kill in several medical settings over the course of their careers.

As illustrated by the long active periods of many of the offenders, medical murders are generally not revealed as homicides until long after the fact. As a result, official crime reporting sources, such as the FBI's *Uniform Crime Reports,* do not count these deaths in statistical tallies. Also, a number of hospitals have conducted investigations into suspicious deaths although no suspect was ever charged with murder. For example, an investigation of Springfield Community Hospital in Dayton, Ohio, which was launched in 1985 (but was halted and then resumed in 1993) discovered that as many as 30 patients may have been murdered. Empty bottles of Pavulon were found in various places around the hospital. Although there was a primary suspect, again no one was arrested.

An attempt to estimate the frequency of medical murder can employ cases over the past couple decades as a starting point. During the 1980s, as many as six to eight cases were detected during any given year. If these offenders followed the pattern of one or two murders per month (as appears to be the average for Orville Lynn Majors, Harold Shipman, and others), then 16 deaths a month would result in nearly 200 deaths per year—and these only include the six to eight offenders who were identified. If only a small proportion of these murders are uncovered, or if the monthly average death toll per offender was as high as four (as in the Springfield, Ohio, case), then the number of medical murders each year could easily reach 500 to 1,000. As our surveillance systems improve, time will tell how many of these murderers have been on decades-long killing sprees in our hospitals, nursing homes, and hospice centers—not to mention the home health care industry where detection of foul play is even more challenging.

Although medical murderers to date were more likely to have been nurses and nurse's aides than other types of medical workers, this may be somewhat artifactual. It seems likely that because nurses have formal ties to patients, their connections are more easily discovered and investigated. However, any number of aides or other medical staff members may be in and out of patient rooms at various and unrecorded times of day. Combined with less easily traceable methods of killings often used in these settings (e.g., suffocation with a pillow or pinching off an oxygen flow), the number of cases of medical murder committed by ancillary medical staff may be especially undercounted.

Motives and Types of Medical Murderers

Medical murderers are similar to other serial killers in that they often choose vulnerable populations as their victims—the sick, the elderly, and children. There are, however, some unique gender ratios for medical murderers. Criminologists have discovered relatively few females among serial killers generally. Eric Hickey's research, for example, found only 16 percent of serial murderers to be female, while Godwin found only 5 percent. Thus, the fact that at least 60 percent of medical murderers are female makes this type of murder quite different from most other serial homicides.[3]

On the other hand, while less than 10 percent of nurses and nurse's aides are male, almost 40 percent of known medical murderers are males.[4] Thus, although females make up a greater proportion of medical murderers than other types of killers, men are still overrepresented among them.

We know that medical murders are more likely than most other types of homicides to be committed by females—in part because they are overrepresented in these professions. We also know that the typical murder weapon—poison—is most likely to be the method chosen by female serial killers (suffocation is the second most common method chosen by female medical murderers).[5] Thus, access to poisons and vulnerable populations creates more of the situational components needed to carry out these crimes.

Most female serial killers select victims with whom they have a relationship—husbands, children, and the like. In medical murder, however, this is generally not the case. More typically, the victim was only a patient for a few hours, but was totally dependent on the caretaker.

Although personal motives—power, control, or attention—predominate in medical murders, some recent cases appear to have been inspired by profit. Harold Shipman, a British physician, was convicted of killing 15 patients over a period of decades, but he may have poisoned to death as many as 400, if not double that. He was detected after forging the will of one of his patients, so there was a clear financial component to some of his killings. However, his motives may have been more complex. He had been overheard complaining about the space that the elderly were taking up in hospitals, and, even though he killed both male and female patients, an overwhelming number of his victims were elderly women. As is the case with many murderers, there may be more than one motive. And rather than an instrumental motive such as financial gain, medical murderers, like other serial killers, may be motivated by more expressive, intrinsic needs for power, control, and glory.

An analysis of the methods used in medical murders as well as the context in which they are committed suggests at least two primary types of medical murderers. One type, the *power killer,* murders in silence, often works the night shift, and seems able to continue killing over a relatively long period of time. The opportunity to determine who lives and who dies provides the power and control that this offender craves. Although some medical murderers boast about their crimes, the power type often kills in relative silence. These nurses and nurse's aides bask in the power of having taken a life and seem to take pleasure in baffling physicians. They tend to prefer a subtle approach such as morphine injection, rather than the "code blue"-inducing Pavulon (which paralyzes the respiratory system while the patient remains conscious) or "heart-stopping" substances such as Digoxin.

Since the power killers' activities take place under quieter circumstances, it may take years before anyone detects or responds to the extraordinarily high number of deaths occurring during their shifts. As is noted in Table 8.1, several of the more recent medical

TABLE 8.1 Selected Cases of Medical Murder

Name and Age of Offender(s)	Location	Years of Activity	Suspected Victim Count	Number of Convictions	Sentence	Method	Motive	Other
Joseph Dewey Akin, 32, Nurse	Georgia, Alabama	1983–1990	Over 100	1	15 years plea agreement manslaughter	Lidocaine or epinephrine	Hero	Fired for false credentials, difficulty getting along with others
Richard Angelo, 26, Nurse	New York	1987–1989	At least 10	4	61 years to life in prison	Pavulon or Anectine	Hero	Former fireman and EMT
Charles Cullen, 43, Nurse	New Jersey, Pennsylvania	1987–2003	35–45	22	11 consecutive life terms in NJ, pled guilty to avoid death penalty, PA charges pending	Digoxin, insulin and others	Power	Works with authorities to offer tips of how to catch others; donated kidney to a friend in August 2006
Roberto Diaz, 46, Nurse	California	1971–1981	12–60 Elderly	12	Death (has been on death row for 21 years)	Lidocaine	Power	Would predict patients' deaths
Jeffrey Feltner, 26, Nurse's Aide	Florida	1990	7 Elderly	1	Life in prison, pled guilty	Smothered	Hero	Police received anonymous tips about unnatural deaths
Kristen Gilbert, 33, Nurse	Massachusetts	1996	4	4	4 life sentences without parole	Epinephrine Ketamine, Acepromazine	Hero	Trying to impress boyfriend, a security guard at hospital; hospital staff nicknamed her "Angel of Death"

Name	Location	Years	Victims	Convictions	Sentence	Method	Motive	Notes
Gwendolyn Graham, 23, and Catherine May Wood, 24, Nurse's Aides	Michigan	1987	10	5	6 life sentences without parole	Smothered	Power/Sex	Took trophies. Wood never actually killed, confessed when Graham began threatening babies
Jeanine Hannah, 55, Nurse	Wisconsin, California, Oregon	2000–2002	2	1 criminal, another civil	99 year prison sentence	Insulin overdose	Money	History of fraud in home healthcare, killed to cover up theft
Donald Harvey, 35, Nurse's Aide	Kentucky, Ohio	1970–1986	32–80	24	4 life sentences	Smothered or hooked patients up to empty oxygen tanks, killed neighbor with cyanide.	Power/Sex	Suicide attempts, mental hospital commitments, 21 electroshock therapies 1983–1986, burglary history
Vicki Dawn Jackson, 36, Nurse	Texas	2000–2001	20–24	Pled no contest to 10 murders	Life in prison	Inject muscle relaxant, mivacurium chloride	Power	Killed demanding patients, including third husband's grandfather
Genene Jones, 33, Licensed Vocational Nurse	Texas	1978–1982	47 Children	1, plus convicted of injuring child	Both sentences total 159 years, eligible for parole in 2009	Anectine, Heparin	Hero	Unattractive, needy, liar, sexually promiscuous
Orville Lynn Majors, 38, Licensed Practical Nurse	Indiana	1993–1995	60–130 Elderly	6	Life in prison	Epinephrine and Potassium Chloride	Power	Hated the elderly

(continued)

TABLE 8.1 Continued

Name and Age of Offender(s)	Location	Years of Activity	Suspected Victim Count	Number of Convictions	Sentence	Method	Motive	Other
Randy Powers, 31, Nurse's Aide	California	1984	12	Convicted of assault on a baby	5 years, released December 1987	Lidocaine	Hero	After release, enrolled in EMT program under false name, rejected for lying when identity discovered
Brian Rosenfeld, 32, Nurse Efren	Florida	1990	23–25	Convicted, no other info located		Not located	Power	Targeted victims in geriatrics ward
Salvidar, 28, Respiratory Therapist	California	1989–1998	100–200	6 Elderly	Life in prison without parole, pled guilty	Pavulon, Anectine, or oxygen deprivation	Power	Claimed other nurses were doing the same thing
Bobbie Sue Terrell, 29, Nurse	Florida	1984	18	4 Elderly	Life in prison, pled guilty	Insulin, asphyxiation, or strangulation	Hero	Schizophrenic, overweight, and shy
Michael Swango, 44, Doctor	U.S. Zimabawe	1983–1997	35–60	4	Life in prison, pled guilty	Potassium Chloride, Epinephrine, Anectine, Cyanide	Power	Suspected of poisoning co-workers' food

murderers have been power killers. Their offenses may also have a sexual component, but interviews with these killers have shed relatively little light on this dimension.

Donald Harvey, a nurse's aide and autopsy assistant, appears to fit the profile of a power killer. He poisoned or smothered patients, neighbors, family, and friends over a 17-year time period in and around Cincinnati. He also had a history of suicide attempts, burglary, and other thefts, as well as institutionalization for mental problems that included repeated electroshock therapies. Like many other criminals, these killers often have multiple levels of problems and dysfunctional histories.

The other major type of medical murderer is the *hero killer,* typically a nurse who craves attention. Hero killers attempt to create a life or death emergency with the goal of either watching others scramble to save the life of the victim or, more usually, of thrusting themselves into the center of the dramatic crisis. Several of these murderers became known as nurses who functioned very well in code blue situations. It is unclear how many of the victims were intended to die. By definition, the nurse takes the victim to the edge of death and, in some cases, may have intended to save the patient's life skillfully and spectacularly rather than to take it.

Even when the patient dies, the murderer has still experienced the excitement of the emergency situation and of baffling other medical professionals as to why the patient died. They may even be praised by co-workers and the victim's family for their vigilant attempts to save the life. For example, Genene Jones, convicted of one murder (and suspected in as many as 47 deaths) in Texas during the late 1970s and early 1980s, worked primarily with sick children. She reveled in the attention and glory of bringing dying young patients back to life in front of their terrified parents. One family was so thankful for her seemingly heroic efforts to save their baby daughter (whose twin had already been murdered by Jones) that they made her the baby's godmother after she rescued the child.

Another medical murderer, Joseph Dewey Akin, was directly linked to 17 suspicious deaths, but suspected of as many as 100. His killing marathon likely began in Georgia in 1983 and ended in North Fulton Regional Hospital in Alabama in 1990. Akin had falsely claimed to have earned a four-year nursing degree when he actually had only two years of training. He was also cited for his difficulty in getting along with others on the job. Exaggerated credentials, braggadocio, and difficulty with interpersonal relationships are characteristic of many of the "hero" medical murderers. Nurse Akin chose drugs that induced cardiac arrest, setting the stage for his grand performance as the heroic lifesaving "super nurse."

Medical murderers who stage emergency situations in the hope of becoming heroes, or at least having the chance to be part of the emergency response, appear similar in many respects to firefighters who intentionally set blazes. John Orr, an arson investigator in Glendale, California, who may have set as many as 2,000 fires (in which at least four people died), is serving a life sentence for murder by arson. Orr's motives included a desire to be at the scene of an exhilarating event (providing sexual excitement for him as well) and to be held up by his peers as an expert who had special talents for identifying arson fires.[6]

In addition to excitement and hero aspirations, some firefighters have set fires for financial reasons, primarily the overtime they can claim from their job. However, in many instances, the arsonist is an unpaid volunteer. In a few cases, it appeared to be an employment grievance against a fire department and/or supervisor that prompted the crime. As is the case with the medical community, firefighters are engaged in a respected helping profession, and there may be strong incentives for a department not to disclose the fact that they have an arsonist in their midst.

Interviews with medical murderers suggest that, in addition to the primary motives of power, control, or attention, these killers may also be motivated in a secondary way by dependent or demanding patients, heavy patient case-loads, and attempts to cover up for other crimes on the job. They may be stealing drugs, money, or belongings from patients. Or, they may be inspired by pure hatred, as was Orville Lynn Majors of Indiana, who poisoned to death at least six patients. Majors stated that he simply "hated old people" and thought "they should all be gassed."[7]

Medical murderers typically suffer from a variety of personality disorders. Those who kill while attempting to achieve heroism are characteristically narcissistic, a personality type that includes a grandiose sense of self and a belief that the world needs to recognize their greatness. It is when their inflated sense of self is questioned by others that they become aggressive.[8]

Power killers, despite an arrogant veneer, may have an overwhelming feeling of worthlessness and lack of control. As with serial murderers in general, many medical killers suffer childhoods filled with trauma, abuse, and/or neglect. Interestingly, neglect appears to be more common than outright abuse, explaining perhaps why they go to such great lengths in order to be noticed.

Being different, feeling like an outsider, and suffering humiliation can also lead to feelings of powerlessness and rage. Robert Hale, focusing on the internal motives of offenders, suggests that serial killers have experienced some form of torment and humiliation early in life.[9] This humiliation turns to rage, and that rage becomes targeted at others—in many cases others who may remind the killer of someone who embarrassed them earlier in life. As described in Chapter 2, Erich Fromm viewed destructive aggression as a response to feelings of powerlessness. For the medical murderer, particularly the hero killers, their not always death-defying acts of endangerment and attempted rescue place them at the center of attention and make them feel important and dominant.

In the medical setting, staff members can be humiliated or embarrassed by others—demanding doctors may snap at overworked nurses or an incompetent nurse may be marginalized by co-workers. Some medical staff may even find the work itself to be humiliating (e.g., bathing the elderly in a nursing home or changing too many bed pans), and so they purposely target their workplace and its captive pool of potential victims in order to seek revenge for perceived mistreatment. Obviously, not everyone who has suffered humiliation and embarrassment turns their feelings into murderous rage, so we must also consider the contextual factors that help explain killings by medical staff.

Munchausen Syndrome by Proxy

One particularly heinous form of behavior involving the medical community is exhibited by the parents, typically mothers, who fabricate symptoms in their children (e.g., apnea, seizures, and convulsions), fake illnesses by manipulating medical tests (e.g., adding blood in urine samples), and induce sickness or death by suffocating their children or exposing them to drugs and other toxic substances. In one case, a mother picked her child's wounds to the bones and filled them with animal feces and pet hair. She became known as a "Munchausen mom."

Munchausen Syndrome, in general, involves making oneself sick or faking various illnesses, usually in order to attract attention or sympathy. For example, veterinary nurse Penelope Angliss of Gloucester, England, started harming herself, first by purposely overdosing on an anesthetic. Three years later, she plunged a pair of scissors deep into her own liver in a desperate ploy to gain attention from the medical practitioners. Then in March 2006, after years of self-inflicted illness and injury, she fatally overdosed on a drug designed to produce an irregular heartbeat; her death was ruled an accident.

A variant of this disorder, Munchausen syndrome by proxy (MSBP), involves inducing or faking illness in someone else, typically a child. MSBP includes a mother who induces illness by poisoning her child or who falsely claims she witnessed the child having a seizure. Whereas faking or inducing an illness can be a powerful way to manipulate others or to shirk responsibilities, MSBP moms harm their children—sometimes fatally—just for attention.

In *Patient or Pretender: Inside the World of Factitious Disorders,* Feldman and colleagues contend that many deaths initially diagnosed as Sudden Infant Death Syndrome (SIDS) may have actually been cases of MSBP.[10] At times, a parent's attempt to use illness for the sake of attention can inadvertently result in death of the victim. Although most Munchausen by proxy cases involve mothers who hurt (or kill) their children, some people attempt to gain similar attention by poisoning or otherwise hurting their pets.[11]

MSBP moms are similar to the hero-aspiring medical killers described earlier—both seek attention through jeopardizing the lives of others, even if subsequent deaths are not specifically part of the plan. A Nebraska case from 2004 illustrates the tragedy that can result from MSBP. Andrea Yager, a 17-month-old girl, died in 2004 after being intentionally smothered by her mother.

On no less than five separate occasions, Jodi Yager, 22, had rushed her baby daughter Andrea to the emergency room. One time Andrea had reportedly swallowed oil from a lantern, and on others she apparently had suffered unexplained bouts of unconsciousness or seizures, episodes that took place only when the child was alone with her mother. Sadly, baby Andrea never made it to her second birthday. Given the suspicious circumstances, Yager was prosecuted for murder, pleading no contest for intentional child abuse resulting in death, in exchange for a 46 year prison sentence.

Due to increased awareness (and hidden video surveillance) by the medical community, there have been a sizable number of MSBP cases reported in recent years. In fact, there are more individual cases of homicide implicating MSBP than of medical murder, although the death toll of each medical murder case is much higher. Tracie Fleck, 34, of Indiana was detected by staff at the Riley Children's Hospital in Indianapolis as she tampered with her 21-month-old daughter's IV. Fleck was attempting to inject her daughter with fecal matter. Authorities became suspicious after Fleck had brought her daughter to the hospital 11 times and the child appeared to become sick after visits from the mother. Fleck pled guilty to two counts of battery in February 2005 and was sentenced to six years of prison followed by two years of probation and is forbidden to have any contact with children, including her own. A Missouri mom, Tammy Sweeden, 31, was charged with child endangerment against her year-old son. Evidence suggests that she began harming him soon after his birth, and further investigation found that she had earlier been diagnosed with MSBP when living in Maine and, as a result, had lost custody of two other children. As is often the case, the child's health dramatically improved when removed from contact with the mother.

Sentences in MSBP cases vary wildly—some receive only probation and counseling, while others are sentenced to relatively short prison stays. One recent Munchausen mom, however, had the book thrown at her. Kimberly Austin, 37, of Houston, Texas, received a 99-year sentence in 2005 for injecting one of her children with a fatal dose of insulin. Austin's four children had been to a doctor or hospital a stunning 235 times. Her techniques included smothering, poison, starvation, injections, unnecessary surgeries, and gagging her children with her fingers.

Women accused of MSBP often have nursing backgrounds. Stephanie McMullen, 30, a former pediatric oncology nurse, was accused of poisoning her son with injections of feces. Her trial resulted in a mistrial, as the jury could not come to a unanimous decision. Her defense attorney claimed that any number of people could have been responsible for the boy's poisonings, including hospital staff. The prosecutor has claimed he will retry McMullen. McMullen's home computer showed that she had been researching child poisonings. The boy's health has improved since being put in foster care.

Like medical murder, the frequency of MSBP is impossible to determine. Often these children are diagnosed with a fairly obscure "failure to thrive." It is usually only the most extreme cases that come to the attention of hospital staff. Schreier and Libow, in *Hurting for Love: Munchausen Syndrome by Proxy,* discovered several cases in one year in the same hospital. They found that approximately 10 percent of the victims of MSBP fail to survive, although others have suggested a death rate may be as high as 25 percent. Finally, there are no reliable estimates of the frequency of MSBP, yet estimates have ranged from 200 to 1,200 cases annually in the United States.[12]

MSBP offenders, again typically mothers, may behave like serial killers, with cooling-off periods during which they are not making their child sick but still basking in the martyrdom of caring for a sick child.[13] These same types of offenders, both mothers who make their child sick and nurses who poison patients and cause code-blue situations, may be similar to people who falsely report crimes in order to gain the attention of others. One recent case was an exception to the mothers-only typical case. A Massachusetts physician, Joseph W. Dullea, 42, and his wife Kristene, 42, were recently accused of assault charges as a result of acts against their two children. Over a period of six years the two boys had broken bones, had been given drugs to induce vomiting, and had unnecessary IVs and other medical procedures, including spinal taps. The doctor's medical license has been suspended and criminal proceedings against him and his wife are pending. They have claimed that they do suffer from MSBP. The boys have been healthy since being removed from the home.

Yorker notes that in most cases, nurses who kill patients do not have previous criminal histories, but some do have previous histories of Munchausen or MSBP—an earlier sign of their desperate need for attention and power.[14] As noted by Rosenberg, however, most people who have MSBP do not also have Munchausen Syndrome, and many researchers agree that rather than just versions of the same disorder, they are, in fact, different syndromes.[15] As is the case with other aggressive and sometimes homicidal offenders (e.g., school shooters), it is unclear whether the source of this desperate need for attention is rooted in extremely low self-esteem or narcissism. Some research has been conducted into the backgrounds of Munchausen moms, and a common theme that often emerges is their profound feelings of being ignored as children.[16] More specifically, many report a physically or emotionally distant father (or husband). Some research has suggested that the doctor may actually represent a father figure to the Munchausen offender. Thus, although these offenders may not have suffered horrendous and overt child abuse, the experience of child neglect may have had dire consequences.

In her book, *Sickened,* Julie Gregory describes her own experiences as a victim of a Munchausen mom. Gregory grew up in rural Ohio with a mother who starved her (so that she would appear sick), beat her, and fed her matches (instead of lollipops), gave her medications that caused migraines, and dragged her from doctor to doctor demanding attention and painful tests. As a child, Gregory unsuccessfully tried to get help from school nurses and her father. Gregory's mother continued to do the same to foster children and has never admitted her deeds.

While in the past society may have been relatively ignorant about MSBP, arguably today's greater awareness may cause some parents to be unjustly accused of wrongdoing as possible sufferers of MSBP. Professor Roy Meadow, a pioneer in the field of MSBP, has recently fallen under criticism for his expert testimony in cases of MSBP. Experts, including Meadow, have been accused of reporting inaccurate statistics about the likelihood of more than one cot death (SIDS) in a single family (Meadows claimed that the likelihood of two SIDS deaths in one family was 1 in 73 million when it was actually as low as 1 in 77). Babies that were thought to be cases of MSBP may have died as a result of other causes, such a neurological problems or reactions to prescribed medications (e.g., Cisapride). For several years, Meadow was not allowed to offer medical testimony as an expert witness, and previous guilty verdicts against accused MSBP moms were overturned. A 2006 decision cleared Meadow of professional misconduct and he is again eligible to offer testimony.

There are risk factors and warning sign for MSBP but, as is often the case, they are vague enough that we must beware of false positives. A review of several cases suggests that these factors include inexplicable illnesses, discrepancies in the medical history as given by parent, events that only occur in the mother's presence (and cease when separated from the mother), a mother who is not appropriately worried about the child and is more interested in interacting with medical staff, and a mom with a medical background and an extensive history of her own illnesses. Again, many of these factors involve subjective value judgments and the medical community would need more evidence before they could suspect MSBP.

The nurse or other caregiver who makes victims sick (and sometimes kills them) may manifest motives similar to people with MSBP—they do it to attract attention from parents, coworkers, doctors, friends, and family members. Unfortunately, these killers continue to get attention after they are apprehended, as some of them have been featured on news programs such as *Dateline NBC, 48 Hours,* and *60 Minutes II.*

Administrative Facilitators

While factors that may promote murderous impulses for those operating in medical facilities are similar to those for other serial killers—childhood neglect, abuse, and/or trauma—some special situational circumstances serve as facilitators for medical homicides. Most obvious is the easy access to drugs that are capable of killing patients. Nurses routinely administer medications and narcotics, so they have access not only to the weapon but also to the patients as potential victims. Medical murders committed by nurse's aides who do not have access to drugs more often use other means such as suffocation or poisoning, but not necessarily with controlled substances. Interestingly, the vast majority of the drugs used as murder weapons by medical murderers are not controlled narcotics, and thus are relatively easy to secure and poorly monitored. However, they can be just as deadly as controlled substances like morphine.

In addition to providing access to the murder weapon and the mode of delivery, hospitals and nursing homes may also more directly facilitate murders due to lack of surveillance, or even more directly through actual cover-ups. Only fairly recently have hospitals begun any sort of "mortality analysis" that might indicate an excessive number of deaths in a particular unit and/or shift. In some cases, there may have been a code of silence similar to the code of silence common in policing, in part because what the murderer did was done occasionally by other nurses on the ward.

Co-workers had joked and gossiped about the deaths of patients under the care of Efren Salvidar, but most did not complain to administrators. According to Salvidar, many other people were doing what he did. Interestingly, not only was Salvidar fired, but four other respiratory therapists were also fired and two management personnel resigned. Particularly troubling is that Salvidar even referred to himself as an Angel of Death before being apprehended by police. Other medical murderers had talked about the patients they killed, and some even kept souvenirs that they showed to fellow staff members.

Even when suspicions arise that there may be a serial killer working in a hospital, staff may be reticent to contact the police. Investigations may be conducted in-house before the police are contacted. When mysterious deaths occur in a hospital or nursing home, there may be some period of time when administrators are attempting to determine if the deaths are due to incompetence or impairment, or if they are intentional. There are obvious litigation issues for medical institutions in the event that a caregiver is killing patients. Given the documented cases of hospitals refusing to acknowledge nurse and physician impairment (e.g., drug and alcohol addiction) and many cases of hospitals enforcing little or no disciplinary action against incompetent doctors and nurses, it is easy to imagine similar sorts of cover-ups for intentional medical killings.

Another contributing factor may be the reluctance of medical professionals to admit that they do not know why a particular patient died. Rather, they may feel pressured to produce a cause of death, however inaccurate or incomplete. In the case of Munchausen moms, the doctors, nurses, and other medical staff are naturally inclined to believe that parents love their children and have a tendency to be sympathetic rather than suspicious of the parents of sick children. Even when suspicions arise, staff may be afraid to verbalize them, much less take action, for fear of lawsuits against them and the hospital. Given the difficulty in proving Munchausen cases, these fears seem reasonable.

A recent study by the Institute of Medicine found that as many as 98,000 hospital deaths a year may result from error.[17] Even unintentional incompetence on the part of a single doctor can result in the deaths of a significant number of people. Dr. Jayant Patel of Portland, Oregon, had been banned from surgery in Oregon and New York by 2001, so he took his skills to a foreign hospital in Australia, where it is alleged that his incompetence led to the deaths of at least 87 patients. As is often the case in the United States, the disciplinary actions against him were not disclosed by any of his references when he applied to the Australian hospital, resulting in institutional blindness to his trail of bodies.

Although medical killers can be very successful in taking the lives of others, they seem to fail in taking their own lives—many of them attempt suicide unsuccessfully multiple times during their very successful murder sprees. It is likely their suicide attempts are not intended to be successful (as they clearly know how to kill people), but are rather yet another cry for attention.

There are still other institutional facilitators that make lengthy medical killing sprees possible. Dr. Michael Swango was glaringly incompetent in medical school, but he managed to graduate, albeit behind his classmates. It was his sinister motivation, not his lack of medical skill, that ultimately placed patients in grave danger. Swango killed an untold number of patients over a period of almost 20 years as he worked in seven different hospitals. Early on, he also worked as an EMT, when he poisoned a number of his co-workers. At a minimum, Swango's killings began during his Ohio State University Hospital internship, from which he was dismissed amidst a frenzy of speculation about the deaths of a number of patients. When Swango applied for jobs, almost no one called to check his references or background. Investigations took place in nearly every hospital where he worked, but in most cases, no charges were ever filed. Finally, several different investigators and school administrators spread the word about Swango, but not before he had killed at least 35 people, and probably many more. As illustrated by the Swango case, the disciplinary records of nurses and other medical professionals are confidential. Thus, it can be very difficult to track incompetent medical staff or even worse, predators who switch hospitals or nursing homes and move from state to state.

Prevention and Intervention

Monitoring all of the activities in hospitals and nursing homes, much less in the home health care industry, would seem an impossible task. At a minimum, hospitals should initiate surveillance and mortality analysis systems. These can include data systems that document drug use, patient deaths, and so forth, by shift, staff, and unit. Obviously, by the time these systems could alert the hospital to an unusual number of deaths, a serial killer would already have enjoyed a significant period of activity at the deadly expense of several patients. Video surveillance may also be an asset for the prevention of both medical murder and MSBP, as many mothers continue to poison or suffocate their children even while they are in the hospital.

In addition, to the extent that nursing shortages and burdensome working conditions contribute to caregivers' desires to end a patient's life, hospitals should be required to maintain suitable staff–patient ratios. More reasonable staffing levels would also allow supervisors to monitor staff activities. In the event that hospitals and nursing homes mandate limits on staff hirings, patients may need to be prepared to be turned away when there are staffing shortages. Obviously, greater attention should be paid to investigating the credentials and previous work histories of applicants for positions in medical facilities; unfortunately, state regulations related to hiring practices and background checks vary considerably across the country. Recently, because of the Cullen case, New Jersey became one of the first states to allow healthcare facilities to report to other facilities when an employee has been disciplined. No longer will professional misconduct or incompetence be hidden for fear of lawsuits from the offender. In addition, criminal history background checks are now required for all healthcare personnel, as a condition of professional license renewal. There is a federal National Practitioner Database that can be used by all states to document incompetence and malfeasance.

Prevention and intervention strategies should include closer monitoring of narcotics and other drugs (even those that, although not controlled substances, can be lethal nonetheless) and significant penalties for hospital administrators who attempt to cover-up suspicious circumstances. To track cases of MSBP, hospital registries for both patients and staff members (much like criminal history data bases) may have merit in response to the mobility of perpetrators. Some MSBP parents take their children to different doctors or different hospitals when suspicions arise. Similarly, nurses and other health workers sometimes change jobs when rumors start to spread, only to resume their deadly treatments at a new location.

As is often true when female perpetrators are at work, the law underplays the seriousness of MSBP. In almost all states, mothers caught poisoning and otherwise intentionally harming their child in a Munchausen scenario are typically charged with low-level misdemeanors. Until endangering the life and health of a child is handled more harshly, these offenders will continue to play out their selfish schemes with relative impunity.

Since the deaths of patients in hospitals and nursing homes is to some extent "expected," closer inspection of these deaths by medical examiners and/or coroners is warranted. Many states have created death review teams for the investigation of any child's death, and similar types of oversight may be needed in nursing homes.

Now that hospitals and nursing homes have become sensitized to these types of killers in their midst (and have been sued on a few occasions), we may see both an increase and a decrease in these crimes. At least initially, as enhanced surveillance and tracking systems are put in place, a significant number of killers who have been active in the past may come to light. In the long term, these surveillance systems should prevent any one individual from claiming large victim counts. However, since crime is in part a function of opportunity, it is clearly possible that as our population ages and more and more people reside in nursing homes and are treated in some type of medical setting (including in-home care and hospice), these and other related crimes may increase. New death surveillance systems may help to track suspicious deaths in hospitals and nursing homes, but one of the most notorious killers, Dr. Harold Shipman, did most of his work in patient's homes, murdering hundreds of people for financial gain. Even protocols for multiple physician signatures on death certificates did not stop Shipman—he had no trouble finding colleagues to sign the death certificates even though they knew his patient death toll was much higher than their own. Sadly, Shipman started his medical career with convictions for drug-related offenses as far back as 1976, but he was able to gain recertification. Prevention of medical murder should include a system for monitoring mortality in general practice and home healthcare.

One recent analysis of medical murderers finds several common threads and makes important recommendations. Furbee, a doctor at Indiana University Medical Center in Indianapolis, found that offenders often kill around mealtimes when other staff members are absent, have patients whose deaths are abrupt rather than gradual, have patients who are less likely to survive code blue situations, and engage in uncharted injections. Furbee also noted a pattern of ignoring patient and staff complaints about the perpetrator and poor communication between hospitals.[18]

This chapter has discussed nurses and doctors who intentionally kill patients. But what about the caregiver who intentionally neglects a patient's bedsores, resulting in death? At what point is neglect of a patient's needs for food, water, medication, or basic personal hygiene actually a form of slow murder?

A significant number of medical murderers have not been charged with homicide at all. For a number of reasons—including difficulty proving intent and a lack of proper medical documentation, forensic deficiencies, and a lack of hospital cooperation—many of these killers are convicted of some level of assault, neglect, or even something as trivial as distribution of a controlled substance.

In August 2003, the criminal complaint against Richard Williams was dismissed, surprising many observers close to the case. Williams had been charged with 10 counts of first-degree murder of patients in a Missouri Veteran's hospital. The prosecutor was forced to dismiss the charges due to lack of hospital cooperation and incompetent procedures at the private crime laboratory that had handled the forensic evidence from the case. Williams, who was originally suspected in over 40 deaths, sued the lab for negligence but the Eighth Court of Appeals recently dismissed that suit.

Hell hath no fury, and just when we think we have thought of all of the possible motives for a medical murder, a new twist arrives. Sally Jordan Hill, 45, a nurse anesthetist, has been accused of murdering a female patient in order to carry out a 30-year grudge. Sandra Joyner went in for a facelift in 2001 and, while in the recovery room, was given a lethal unscheduled dose of Fentanyl by Hill, causing respiratory arrest and eventually death. Joyner's death was at first thought to be a result of medical error, but then more sinister motives surfaced during civil proceedings. When Joyner first visited the doctor's office to begin her cosmetic surgery, Hill mentioned to her colleagues that Joyner had stolen her boyfriend 30 years ago in high school. Hill lost her nursing license for being grossly negligent in administering the drug and delaying notification of the doctor when Joyner was dying. Hill has been jailed without bail and is awaiting trial on charges of first-degree murder.

Just as the population of prostitutes, the homeless, and runaway kids has provided hunting grounds for the sexual serial killer, hospitals and nursing homes are the hunting grounds of the medical murderer. Looking ahead, the next hunting ground may be our nation's jails and prisons. It has been recently publicized that physicians who have been convicted of crimes and/or lost their medical licenses because of various forms of misconduct are being hired by some states faced with increasing jail/prison populations and growing heath care demands.[19] Physicians who drugged and sexually assaulted former patients are now serving the inmate population. Who will believe the incarcerated felon over the word of a doctor when some form of medical misconduct occurs? Will anyone care about or investigate the unexpected death of a violent prison inmate?

The crime of medical murder has recently surfaced in the war in Iraq. In March of 2006, a doctor who was sympathetic to the radical Sunni Arab insurgents confessed to killing at least 35 Iraqi soldiers and police officers either by lethal injection, stopping breathing machines or other equipment, or tampering with their wounds. The doctor was paid up to $100 for each murder, and he reportedly said that he also hates Americans and resents their presence in Iraq. Another recent case in Russia uncovered a group of four doctors who have been murdering patients to steal their organs for transplants. And in Poland, two doctors and ambulance workers were recently charged in as many as 19 deaths (but thousands of other deaths are now being investigated) for killing patients to receive kickbacks from funeral homes. Clearly, emotional, political, and financial motives for murder plague hospitals throughout the world, not just in the United States.

ENDNOTES

1. John Camp, *One Hundred Years of Medical Murder.* London: The Bodley Head LTD, 1982; Rupert Furneaux, *The Medical Murderer.* New York: Abeelard-Schuman Limited, 1957.

2. Beatrice Crofts Yorker, "Serial Murder in Hospitals," Presentation at the Forensic Nursing Clinical Update, Phoenix, AZ, 2001.

3. Eric W. Hickey, *Serial Murders and Their Victims.* Belmont, CA: Wadsworth, 2002.

4. Yorker, op. cit.

5. Hickey, op. cit.

6. Joseph Wambaugh, *Fire Lover: A True Story.* New York: Harper Collins, 2002.

7. Indiana v. Orville Lynn Majors Jr., "Probable Cause Affidavit," December 29, 1997.

8. Brad J. Bushman and Roy F. Baumeister, "Threatened Egotism, Narcissism, Self-Esteem, and Direct and Displaced Aggression: Does Self-Love or Self-Hate Lead to Violence?" *Journal of Personality and Social Psychology* 75 (1998): 219–229.

9. Robert Hale, "The Role of Humiliation and Embarrassment in Serial Murder," *Psychology, A Journal of Human Behavior* 31 (1994): 17–23.

10. Marc Feldman, M.D., Charles Ford, M.D., and Toni Reinhold, *Patient or Pretender: Inside the Strange World of Factitious Disorders.* Toronto: John Wiley and Sons, Inc., 1994.

11. *Reuters Health,* September 6, 2002.

12. Herbert Schreier, "Munchausen by Proxy Defined," *Pediatrics* 110 (2002): 985–988; B. Vennemann, T. Bananowski, B. Karger, H. Pfeiffer, H. Kohler, and B. Brinkmann, "Suffocation and Poisoning—The Hard-Hitting Side of Munchausen Syndrome by Proxy," *International Journal of Legal Medicine* 119 (2005): 98–102; Herbert Schreier, "Munchausen by Proxy," *Current Problems in Pediatric Adolescent Healthcare* 34 (2004): 126–143; H. Schreier, "Error in Munchausen by Proxy Defined," *Pediatrics* 113 (2004): 1851–1852; and Guy E. Brannon, "Munchausen Syndrome by Proxy," *e-medicine specialties,* on-line document, updated April 4, 2006.

13. Herbert A. Schreier and Judith A. Libow, *Hurting for Love: Munchausen Syndrome by Proxy.* New York: Guilford Press, 1993.

14. Fred Bayles, "Nurse Gets Life In Prison for Killing 4: Veteran's Experts Explore Motives of Medical Murderers," *USA Today,* March 27, 2001.

15. Donna A. Rosenberg, "Web of Deceit: A Literature Review of Munchausen Syndrome by Proxy," *Child Abuse and Neglect* 11 (1987): 547–563.

16. Schreier and Libow, op. cit.

17. Institute of Medicine, *To Err Is Human: Building a Safer Health System,* September, 1999.

18. R. Brent Furbee, "Criminal Poisoning: Medical Murderers," *Clinics in Laboratory Medicine* 26 (2006) 255–273.

19. Andrew A. Skolnick, "Critics Denounce Staffing Jails and Prisons with Physicians Convicted of Misconduct," *Journal of the American Medical Association* 280 (1988): 1391–1392.

9

Rampage

Interestingly enough, most middle-class people probably think more of the possible serial killer in their midst, when, in reality, the risk of mass murder is much greater. As we suggested in Chapter 7, the victims of the typical serial killer are female prostitutes. By contrast, the victims of the mass murderer tend to be students, teachers, co-workers, friends, and family. Whether a disgruntled former employee or a spouse, an unhappy customer, a client or student, we all bear some risk of becoming a mass murder victim, whether at work and school, eating out, or running errands—not to mention the risk we face when we get home. A significant number of mass killers have annihilated their families.

While the terms mass and serial murder were used interchangeably when research into these phenomena began some 25 years ago, much research has more recently been directed at defining the mass killer as a distinct and separate type. Yet, much confusion remains.

Were the September 11, 2001, deaths a mass murder? If so, then three thousand people died in a massacre, where the weapon was an airplane. Clearly, we have to make some decisions when creating our mass murder typologies, as there are very different prevention and intervention implications for the workplace shooter, the family annihilator, and the terrorist with an airplane. We have chosen to discuss mass school shootings, hate crimes, and terrorism in separate chapters due in part to their possibly different causal factors and policy implications. In this chapter, we focus on mass killers who target family, former and current co-workers, and total strangers, without a political motive.

Methodical and Selective

Mark Barton's exit line dripped with evil sarcasm. "I hope this won't ruin your trading day," said the 44-year-old stock investor as he wrapped up his July 29, 1999, bloody rampage in Atlanta's financial district. Armed with two semiautomatic pistols, a Colt .45-caliber and a Glock 9 mm, the gunman had navigated deliberately through two Atlanta investment offices, All-Tech and Momentum Securities, located just across Piedmont Road from each other. The afternoon shooting spree left nine dead and a dozen others wounded. By sundown later that evening, Barton had turned his gun on himself when cornered by police at a gas station several miles northwest of the scene of the crime.

What was it that caused Mark Barton to snap? And, did he in fact snap? The widespread notion that mass gunmen like Barton erupt suddenly into an uncontrollable, murderous rage is deeply rooted in the popular vernacular frequently used to describe these events: expressions such as "going berserk," "going ballistic," or even "going postal" (a code word for workplace massacres coined after a string of post office shootings in the mid 1980s and early 1990s). Psychiatric research has also generally supported the idea that mass murderers "run amok"—they are totally out of touch with reality (i.e., psychotic) and select victims at random who happen to be "in the wrong place at the wrong time."[1]

A more careful examination reveals quite a different picture. On the contrary, most mass killers do not just snap and start shooting anything that moves. Typically, these murderers generally act with calm deliberation, often planning their assault days, if not months, in advance. Their preparations often involve assembling the arsenal of weaponry as well as the most effective means of ambush. In addition, mass murderers tend to be quite selective in targeting their victims. They aim to kill those individuals they are convinced are responsible for their miseries, frequently ignoring anyone not implicated in the plot against them.

Mark Barton surely didn't just wake up on that warm July day and spontaneously decide to perpetrate a bloodbath. His crime spree was hardly sudden and episodic. Two days earlier, Barton had rammed a claw hammer into the skull of Leigh Ann, his 27-year-old second wife, stuffing her body into a closet at their home in the Atlanta suburb of Stockbridge. The next morning, he took his two children, 12-year-old Matthew and 8-year-old Mychelle, to get haircuts. Later that night—the eve of his downtown shooting spree—Barton bludgeoned his son and daughter as they slept in their beds. He then held each child face down in the bathtub to ensure they would not wake up in pain. Once he was certain they were dead, he tucked them both into their beds and placed a favorite toy next to each of them—a Game Boy for his son and a stuffed animal for his daughter.

Barton was so deliberate in his actions that he left a note at his home explaining his motives. "I killed Leigh Ann because she was one of the main reasons for my demise," Barton wrote. "I killed the children to exchange them for five minutes of pain for a lifetime of pain. I forced myself to do it to keep them from suffering so much later. No mother, no father, no relatives." He also left several other notes around the house relaying whatever sentiments came to mind. Next to his son's body, Barton placed a brief message to God: "I give you Matthew David Barton—my son, my buddy, my life. Please take care of him."

There is considerable evidence, moreover, that Barton's murder string may have actually started six years earlier. He was a suspect in the untimely death of his first wife and her mother at his in-law's home in Alabama. Not only did this clear the way for him to be with his 21-year-old girlfriend/mistress, Leigh Ann (who later became his second wife and next victim), but the life insurance proceeds became invaluable for him to get a fresh start on his slumping career.

The popular image of a killer who shoots randomly at human targets without rhyme or reason would hardly characterize Barton's crimes or, for that matter, the actions of most mass killers. It was no accident or random choice that Barton selected the location for his vengeful shooting spree. The two day-trading centers were the very places where he had been ruined financially. He had failed miserably in the high-stakes, high-pressure occupation of day-trading in volatile technology stocks.

Barton lost $153,000 in a single day, forcing Momentum Securities to call in his credit. He turned next to All-Tech and pushed his losses to almost a half-million dollars. He also resented those around him who had profited so handsomely on trades of shares of

Internet stocks like Amazon and Yahoo. As he wrote in his suicide letter, "I don't plan to live very much longer. Just long enough to kill as many of the people that greedily sought my destruction."

There are, of course, cases of mass murderers who do kill more or less indiscriminately. On October 16, 1991, George Hennard, Jr., rammed his pickup truck through the plate-glass window of the Luby's Cafeteria in Killeen, Texas, and then randomly opened fire on customers as they ate their lunch, killing 23. On April 23, 1987, William Cruse, a 59-year-old retired librarian, went on a bloody rampage in a Palm Bay, Florida, shopping center, killing six and injuring another 12. Neither Hennard nor Cruse knew any of the victims nor had anything more than a casual connection to their respective murder sites.

Yet more often, the location and even the particular victims are chosen because the killer sees them as responsible for his misfortunes. In 1989, for example, Marc Lepine burst into a lecture hall at the University of Montreal, commanded the men to leave, and started executing the remaining female students, killing 14. Lepine despised women—especially feminists—and blamed them for all of his problems.

Lepine didn't just pick any place for his vengeful rampage. He didn't choose the nursing program where far more women would literally be under his gun. Instead, he purposely chose the Engineering School, where he saw women pursuing "man's work." In fact, Lepine had been denied admission to the Engineering School and was punishing those who had taken his seat in the class.

There are many mass killers who target an entire category of victims, often expressing in the most extreme violence their disdain for one group or another. Twenty-five-year-old Patrick Purdy was a young man filled with resentment. In the end, however, he singled out a particular group—Southeast Asians—as being especially blameworthy. On January 17, 1989, Purdy visited his former elementary school in what had become a predominantly Southeast Asian section of Stockton, California. Purdy killed five children and wounded dozens more, before committing suicide just as the police arrived.

Lepine hated women; Purdy despised Southeast Asians. Twenty-eight-year-old Kyle Huff was intensely hostile toward members of Seattle's rave community, blaming them for what he saw as rampant sexual immorality in U.S. society. Huff had been virtually unable to maintain a long-term intimate relationship, whereas the ravers flaunted their promiscuity. Moreover, ever since arriving in Seattle from his home in Whitefish, Montana, Huff was essentially without friends and unable to hold even a menial job; by contrast, the ravers were extremely sociable, holding parties for hundreds of young people on the weekends.

Hoping to make a friend or two, Huff had attended rave parties, but from the beginning felt like an outsider. He was older and more conventional than the ravers; they listened to different kinds of music, took different sorts of drugs, and were openly sexual. While the Ecstasy-inspired dancing proceeded, Huff would stand off to the side of the room near the bar by himself, drinking a beer and feeling like an outcast.

During the early morning hours of Saturday, March 25, 2006, Huff decided it was time to take action. Following an all-night rave with the theme Better Off Undead, Huff drove to an after-party at a home in the Capitol Hill section of the city. He had been invited by a group of ravers who apparently felt sorry for the stranger. But Huff failed to recognize that his hosts at the party were sympathetic. In his mind, they were flaunting their sexuality and laughing at him behind his back. They were destroying the traditional American way of life and deserved to be eliminated. In his warped way of thinking, he was a victim of injustice, a misunderstood hero of sorts who was willing to sacrifice himself for the greater good; he would not stand idly by and let these degenerate and promiscuous young people completely obliterate every decent and virtuous American tradition.

Huff had brought with him an arsenal of weapons. At about 7 A.M., he left the party and walked to his pickup truck, parked nearby, where he retrieved a shotgun and semiautomatic handgun as well as three hundred rounds of ammunition. Then, as though announcing the imminence of his attack, Huff spray-painted the word NOW on the sidewalk and returned to the house where he calmly opened fire.

Almost immediately, the emergency 9-1-1 center was flooded with calls about the attack. Some of the reports were from terrorized ravers who whispered frantically into their cell phones while attempting to hide from the gunman.

A police officer arrived promptly at the scene, and ordered Huff to drop his weapon. But without any hesitation, Huff raised his shotgun, inserted the barrel into his mouth, and pulled the trigger. It took just a few minutes for the horrific rampage to end, leaving six ravers dead (including a 14-year-old girl) and two others wounded. It took weeks, however, to determine the motive for the assault.

A month after the massacre, the Seattle police recovered a suicide letter from a garbage bin not far from Huff's apartment. The note had been written by Huff to his twin brother and was dated two days before the attack. Huff suggested that the behavior of ravers—especially their sexually explicit lifestyle—was too disturbing to tolerate. "I hate this world of sex that they are striving to make," he explained, "this is a revolution brother." Apparently, Huff's mind was made up: someone—meaning him—had to act fast and furiously to quash the threat.[2]

Many rampages are much more selective than indiscriminate, occurring at the killer's workplace or residence where relationships that turn sour can have a profound impact on his self-esteem and hope for the future. Michael McDermott, in December 2000, killed seven of his co-workers at Edgewater Technology in Wakefield, Massachusetts, but he hardly shot indiscriminately at anything that moved. Blaming his dire financial position on certain offices of the company, McDermott selectively targeted his fellow employees only in payroll and human resources. Moreover, McDermott's rampage was anything but spontaneous. A day earlier, he had left a cache of weapons and ammunition under his desk, so as to be fully prepared for his murderous onslaught. In court, McDermott tried to convince the jury that he was a victim of severe mental illness—that he had been convinced that he was killing not co-workers but Hitler and six of Hitler's henchmen. Not believing the defendant, the jury gave McDermott a life sentence without parole eligibility.

More often than not, mass killers select particular victims to kill in order to avenge perceived injustices. After Ronald Gene Simmons executed 14 family members for insult and insubordination, he then launched a 45-minute shooting spree through the town of Russellville, Arkansas, killing a woman who had spurned his romantic advances and a former boss, and wounding several others at former worksites. As he surrendered, Simmons remarked, "I've gotten everybody who hurt me."

Despite the killer's selectivity, even in the most focused rampage many innocent victims die in the crossfire or because they stand in the way of the killer's murderous swath. Frequently, however, they are killed because the gunman associates them with the primary target. The notion of murder by proxy (described earlier in Chapter 4) explains the carnage at many worksites. On August 20, 1986, the morning after being reprimanded for poor job performance, 44-year-old Patrick Henry Sherrill arrived early at the Edmond, Oklahoma, post office with his mail bag full of guns and ammunition. Sherrill's first victim was a supervisor who had threatened his job. He then opened fire on his co-workers, all associated in his mind with the more amorphous enemy, the unfair postal service.

Losses and Frustrations

Even though mass slaughters may not be sudden, there generally are still clear-cut events that precipitate the bloodshed. The most random crimes are often inspired by small and seemingly insignificant matters, but which in the killer's paranoid and sometimes psychotic view of the world are important concerns. Hennard, for example, was especially irate about the Senate confirmation hearings for Supreme Court Justice Clarence Thomas, during which Anita Hill alleged she had been sexually harassed by Thomas, her former supervisor at the EEOC. Hennard watched the televised proceeding in a local bar, yelling and throwing food at the TV.

In more typical cases, the gunman seeks to redress a personal slight, often real, usually involving a catastrophic loss—the loss of a relationship, of a job, or even of honor. Earlier in Chapter 4, we examined certain cases of mass murder within the family. One of the more common forms of mass killing involves a head of household who either decides to punish his wife and children for some transgression or, alternatively, to protect them from the misery of living in a cold, cruel world. However, one of the most common forms of mass murder, particularly in recent years, surrounds employment disputes—a firing, layoff, warning, or losing out on a promotion or award.

One-third of the mass murders in the United States are in the family, as opposed to the random shootings of strangers at a fast-food restaurant or a shopping mall or the targeting of a category of people. There have been nearly 250 mass slayings from 1976 to 2005 in which four or more family members were killed. In most of these cases, the father murdered his wife (or ex-wife), children/stepchildren, and often times even the family pet. Chapter 4 described the most common types of family slaughter—illustrated by Ronald Gene Simmons's massacre of his wife, children, and grandchildren as punishment for disobedience and disloyalty and John DeLisle's only semisuccessful attempt at family murder-suicide to put an end to his personal and financial problems.

While these two prototypes of family mass murder clearly predominate, certainly other motivations arise as well. Using a broad definition of family, in February 1998, Christopher Churchill of Noble, Illinois, a town of about 300 people, bludgeoned to death five people including his half-brother (age 17), his brother's girlfriend (age 35), and her three children (ages 12, 10, and 6). Now serving a sentence of life imprisonment, Churchill was not eligible for the death penalty due to his age at the time of the crimes—16. After the brutal mass slaying, Churchill sexually molested the bodies of the male and female children as well as their mother, both as they were dying and after they were dead. He later said he just "felt like being sick." It was later learned that Churchill had fantasized about the murders for over a year. He was supposedly envious of the relationship his brother had had with his older girlfriend, and was furious when one of the children had broken one of his CDs. Churchill went in and out of the murder scene for days after the killings—showering, molesting the bodies, and taking cash and cigarettes. Teachers finally started asking questions because the slain children had not been to school and neighbors noticed that the house was too quiet.

Following family annihilations, the second most prevalent form of mass killing involves employment disputes. Thirty-three-year-old Paul Calden said that he'd be back, and regrettably for the employees of the Fireman's Fund Insurance Company in Tampa, Florida, he was true to his word. On January 27, 1993, eight months after being fired from his job, he returned to get his revenge. This time, however, he'd be the one to do the firing. Calden sat in the company cafeteria. He was as cool as the ice in the Diet Coke that he sipped while waiting patiently for his victims to arrive for lunch. Calden approached three of his former supervisors as they were seated together at the back of the lunchroom. Standing over the table and taking aim with his 9 mm semiautomatic pistol, Calden announced, "This is what you get for firing me," and calmly started shooting, methodically encircling the table with gunfire. By the time it was all over, Calden had killed his three former managers and had wounded two other employees. His next and final victim was himself.

Paul Calden was the quintessential disgruntled employee—the so-called Co-worker from Hell. He had drifted from job to job, causing trouble wherever he worked. Just prior to his employment at Fireman's Fund, Calden had worked at Allstate Insurance, where he threatened his supervisor by deliberately displaying the butt of a gun inside his briefcase. This manager was so frightened by Calden that he offered him a severance package that he couldn't refuse.

During his two-year employment at Fireman's, Calden had developed a reputation for being a belligerent hothead. He constantly challenged his supervisors' authority, at one point nearly coming to blows because of a reprimand. He threatened to sue the company for denying him a raise that he felt he deserved. He shouted obscenities at a female co-worker who had taken his favorite parking place. He even filed a harassment complaint because a fellow employee displayed a bumper sticker on her car that offended him.

In contrast to Calden's spotty work record, other vengeful employees come to feel invulnerable to job loss because of their long-term employment with the same company. From their perspective, they have given their best years to the boss, have unselfishly dedicated their careers to the organization, and resent that their hard work and loyalty are not being returned in kind by the company.

Forty-seven-year-old Joseph Wesbecker, for example, was furious about perceived mistreatment by management at the Standard Gravure Printing Company. The Louisville, Kentucky, plant had recently been sold to a new owner, and Wesbecker felt strongly that the new management team didn't appreciate his over twenty years of hard work. By all accounts, he was an excellent pressman, and he always put in long hours of overtime and extra shifts, which had earned him the nickname "overtime hog."

Suffering from depression, Wesbecker sought an exemption from a certain job task that was particularly stressful to him, a request that was endorsed by a government employment arbitrator but resisted by management. Wesbecker was so resentful that he told a co-worker that he was going to get even with the company and even showed him the gun in his lunch bag with which he intended to carry out his plan of action. He also talked about his "hit list" of intended victims.

Months later, on September 14, 1989, while out of work on long-term disability for depression, Wesbecker made an unscheduled visit to work—he had a job to do. Roaming the corridors with an AK-47, Wesbecker systematically sought out his intended targets, killing eight and wounding a dozen others. He was so methodical in his assault that he purposely spared a friend: "Not you, John," Wesbecker said to the fortunate co-worker who cowered in front of him, and sauntered on by.

Not unlike their dominance in committing family annihilations, most mass murderers in the workplace are men. One recent exception to this rule is the case of former postal worker Jennifer Sanmarco, a 44-year-old woman who, on January 31, 2006, fatally shot five employees of the Goleta Postal facility in Santa Barbara County, California. In the parking lot of the mail sorting facility, Sanmarco first opened fire with a semiautomatic 9-millimeter pistol on two employees, killing both of them. She then used a stolen key-card to enter the building. Once inside, she fatally shot three more workers before taking her own life.

The police were never able definitively to identify Sanmarco's motive for perpetrating mass murder. Her neighbors seemed to believe that she suffered from a major mental illness, claiming that she was "difficult and inflexible" and was often seen talking to herself. While an employee at the facility, Sanmarco had been placed on medical leave because of depression so severe that her co-workers became concerned that she might become self-destructive. Little did they know at the time that Sanmarco's self-destructive behavior would also be directed outward toward them.

Profile of the Workplace Avenger

According to the offender age patterns presented in Chapter 3, teens and young adults are overrepresented among all murderers, with a mean age of 29 years old. Workplace murder is a notable exception to the rule of youth, with workplace avengers averaging 38 years of age. As shown in Table 9.1, moreover, well over half are at least 35 years old. Also as shown, whites represent nearly three-quarters of vengeful workplace killers, compared to the more even racial split for homicide offenders generally. In fatal workplace disputes, finally, the gender ratio is very close to that for murder in general, with more than 90 percent male perpetrators.

The overall profile of the typical workplace murderer is a middle-aged white male, who feels that his employment problems signal the end of the world as he knows it. Despite changing gender roles, men—much more than women—still tend to judge their self-worth by what they do, rather than who they are. If they aren't doing anything, then what good are they? Furthermore, men tend to regard violence as a means for establishing control, as an offensive move, whereas women see it as a last resort, as a defensive move.[3] Thus, men who suffer psychologically because of the loss of a job are more likely to respond violently in order to "show them who's boss." Or perhaps, women are more content to exact their revenge in quieter ways, for example, by means of poisoning, assassinating someone's character, gossiping, or getting others to do their dirty work.

There are relatively few female workplace avengers. While women have been offenders in a number of mass murders, they typically massacre their families. Other women have gone on rampages but have shot to death only one or two victims and thus don't fit the

TABLE 9.1   **Characteristics of Workplace Murderers, 1976–2005, Combined (Non-felony related with at least one victim)**

Characteristics	Category	Percentage
Age of Offender		
	Under 25	22.2
	25–34	28.7
	35–44	23.0
	45–54	14.8
	55+	11.3
Race of Offender		
	White	73.5
	Black	23.7
	Other	2.8
Sex of Offender		
	Male	90.5
	Female	9.5
Weapon		
	Firearm	65.8
	Knife	15.7
	Blunt object	8.3
	Brute force	6.1
	Other	4.0

widely accepted definition of a mass murderer. In a rare case of a woman targeting a number of strangers, Sylvia Segrist in 1986 randomly shot to death three people outside a shopping mall in Springfield, Pennsylvania. As women begin to focus on their careers in the way that men have traditionally done they can be expected to face similar disappointments and to become more skilled in the use of firearms. If so, we might reasonably expect to see more female mass killers.

Some workplace murders involve youthful perpetrators, but most do not. To a younger employee, a job is often just a job, certainly not a career, and there is always another opportunity down the road. The middle-aged employee, however, views termination or the threat of termination as truly the end of the road. He sees few opportunities for alternative employment at the same wage, benefit, or status level to which he has grown accustomed. At this juncture, the middle-aged man expects to be at the top of his career, not hitting rock-bottom.

In part, the middle-aged worker responds desperately and violently, not just because of limited opportunities in the future but because of what has transpired in the past. The road to mass murder, particularly at the job site, is a long one, involving a good number of bumps along the way.

Mark Barton, for example, had experienced years of disappointment, which likely eroded his ability to cope and intensified his feelings of persecution. After graduating from the University of South Carolina with a degree in chemistry, he seemed to fail at each and every turn. He was pushed out of an executive position at TLC Manufacturing in Texarkana, Texas, a company he helped to form. Moving next to Georgia, he tried his hand at chemical sales, another dead end financially. Finally, he used the profits from the insurance settlement from his first wife's death to invest in the stock market, a move that ultimately bankrupted him.

Of course, most disgruntled employees and ex-employees don't take out their anger on the company. Some may blame themselves, become depressed, and consider suicide as their only option. Others may take out their frustrations on their family. But for the one who typically externalizes blame, responsibility always lies elsewhere. When fired from his job as a public parks worker in Ft. Lauderdale, Clifton McCree, a 41-year-old African American, was unequivocal in his view of whom to blame. In a suicide note written just prior to his February 9, 1996, killing spree that claimed the lives of five former co-workers at the Department of Parks and Recreation, McCree alleged racism to be at the core of his unfair termination by the city over a year earlier:

> None of this would have happened. All the hope, effort, and opportunity at employment only prove to be futile after [being] terminated by the city of Ft. Lauderdale. I felt I was treated very unfairly by the city after 17 years. The malicious and racist nature of how my situation was "set up" and handled. The economic lynching without regard or recourse was something very evil. Since I couldn't continue to support my family, life became nothing. I no longer wanted to live in this kind of world. I also wanted to punish some of the cowardly, racist devils that helped bring this about, along with the system. I'm glad illness did it. It became war. There should have been a more humane system. But NO . . .

On July 8, 2003, a workplace shooting at a Lockheed Martin plant in Meridian, Mississippi, took the lives of five employees and injured 11 others. The death toll was actually six, if one includes Doug Williams, the shooter who ended his rampage by killing himself. Whether we count the offenders in the body count may be another basis for deciding who makes the mass killer list. Technically the death of the offender is usually either a suicide or a justifiable homicide by police, so their death should not be counted in the mass murder death toll. Ironically, the Mississippi shooter left an ethics and sensitivity training session, went home and armed himself with a shotgun, a Ruger, a derringer, a rifle and scope, an automatic pistol, and lots of ammo.

Many workplace avengers commit suicide, but not until exacting revenge for the wrongs they perceive have been committed against them. Almost without exception, workplace murderers feel as though they are the victim, and that others, especially the boss, have treated them unfairly. Were they to trace the job disappointments to their own inadequacies, they might turn aggression inward. Seeing everyone else to blame, however, they choose to execute those responsible, before taking their own life.

On February 25, 1998, 35-year-old Matthew Beck, back to work at the Connecticut State Lottery following a stress-related leave, went on a deadly rampage, killing four of his superiors before turning the gun on himself. Beck had complained to co-workers that his supervisors were stalling on negotiations to pay him back wages and that he was not being assigned any work to do. Months earlier, he had filed a grievance contending that he was being assigned jobs outside of his work classification and that he deserved a raise of $2 an hour. Just a few days before going on his rampage, the gunman spoke angrily of suing the Lottery for job discrimination.

Many Americans, of course, suffer the kinds of catastrophic losses and letdowns endured by Beck, Barton, and Wesbecker, yet they are able to lean on close friends and family to help them deal with life's disappointments. Most of the workplace avengers, however, are socially isolated. Either they are like Paul Calden and live in seclusion or like Barton and don't feel sufficiently connected to family. Socially and psychologically alone, they regard work as the only meaningful part of their lives. When they lose their job, they lose everything. They lack not only the emotional support for their problems but the healthy reality check as their feelings of paranoia and persecution build.

This is exactly how it was for Joseph Wesbecker. He was divorced for the second time, and his relationships with his children were badly strained. His job was the only thing in his life that was going well and that gave him some sense of purpose and satisfaction—a reason to get up in the morning. But that was taken away when management forced him to take long-term disability rather than to make a reasonable accommodation for his psychological disability, which was to be exempted from performing a particularly stressful job function.

For the lonely employee, like Wesbecker, termination from a job means not just a loss of self-esteem, and not just the loss of income. It also means the loss of his only source of companionship—his co-workers. Therefore, job loss carries a double burden: frustration and anger, on the one hand, and a severance of important social anchors, on the other.

Here, too, there is a trend in society that places more and more middle-aged men at risk. An increased rate of divorce, greater residential mobility, and a general lack of community and neighborliness mean that, for many Americans, work is their only source of stability and companionship. And men, much more than women, often center all of their friendships on the job.

Finally, a worker may be frustrated and angry, lonely and isolated; he may blame the boss and feel that management is corrupt and unfair. But if he doesn't have access to a powerful weapon or know how to use it, the disgruntled employee may not be able to exact the kind of revenge that he seeks.

Firearms play a key role in several respects. Most important, the gun corrects the perceived power imbalance between the employee and his superior—it's The Great Equalizer, as 28-year-old Gang Lu put it in a letter to the press just before his 1991 rampage at the University of Iowa in which he sought out and executed three professors who had overlooked him for an important dissertation prize. Actually, over a 12-minute period, the graduate student in physics shot to death five members of the university community. If he had had a knife or had used his hands, there is little chance that Gang Lu would have amassed such a large body count.

The gun, of course, is simply far more lethal, particularly if the avenger seeks to execute large numbers. Table 9.2, which lists the ten largest mass shootings in the United States, illustrates the extent of carnage literally triggered with firearms.

The gun also psychologically distances the attacker from his victims. Although full of rage, he might be deterred were it necessary to kill with his hands. By contrast, a gun makes it very easy psychologically . . . and U.S. gun laws make it very easy for him to acquire what he needs to carry out his act of vengeance. Louisville's Joseph Wesbecker went into a gun shop, pointed to a semiautomatic weapon displayed under the counter, and asked "How much?" Surprised at the price, he responded, "That's all? I'll take two!"

TABLE 9.2   Ten Largest Mass Shootings in the United States

Mass Shooter(s)	Victim Count	Date/Location
Seung-Hui Cho	32	April 16, 2007 Blacksburg, Virginia
George Hennard	23	October 16, 1991 Killeen, Texas
James Huberty	21	July 18, 1984 San Ysidro, California
Charles Whitman	14 plus wife and mother on the day before	August 1, 1966 Austin, Texas
Patrick Sherrill	14	August 20, 1986 Edmund, Oklahoma
Willie Mak Benjamin Ng Tony Ng	13	February 18, 1983 Seattle, Washington
Dylan Klebold Eric Harris	13	April 20, 1999 Littleton, Colorado
George Banks	13	September 25, 1982 Wilkes-Barre, Pennsylvania
Howard Unruh	13	September 6, 1949 Camden, New Jersey
James Ruppert	11	March 30, 1975 Hamilton, Ohio

Curiously, most disgruntled workers and other mass killers would not even consider buying a weapon through illegal means. After all, they see themselves as law-abiding citizens, not criminals. They are just looking for some justice. To them, the murder is not a crime; it's simply just desserts. For example, 35-year-old Colin Ferguson, who on December 7, 1993, transformed the Long Island Railroad into a shooting gallery, purchased his gun legally in California. Nine months before going on his killing spree, he checked into a cheap hotel and waited more than the necessary two weeks to qualify for a legal gun purchase.

Nationally, as many as six people are murdered every month at the hands of a co-worker or former co-worker.[4] And for every tragic incident of workplace homicide, thousands of workers are assaulted or threatened by an associate on the job. Even less conspicuous are the countless numbers of angry workers who seek to sabotage their company's bottom line. They may spread ugly rumors to discourage sales or surreptitiously subvert the manufacturing process. In one recent case, an angry worker was caught on videotape as he secretly urinated into the company office coffee pot.

In response to rising levels of violence in the U.S. workplace, a wide range of books and pamphlets, seminars and consultants have surfaced to help companies, large and small, cope with the growing threat of violence on the job. Some experts focus on security concerns, others on promoting effective Employee Assistance Programs (EAPs). Still others recommend processes to enhance employment screening techniques or channels of communication to alert management about troublesome workers before they explode.[5]

While all these approaches may be useful, the overriding goal should be to make civility and decency in the workplace as critical a goal as profit. Companies need to upgrade and humanize the way in which they deal with all employees every day rather than just to focus narrowly on how to respond to the occasional worker who has made threats.[6] Long-term planning to improve employee morale pays off in human terms. A study conducted for Northwestern National Life Insurance concluded that companies with effective grievance, harassment, and security procedures also reported lower rates of workplace violence.[7]

Twenty or thirty years ago, the bond between management and worker was far stronger. Most Americans believed that bosses had the best interests of workers in mind; managers felt that their workforce was loyal to the company. But the expectation of loyalty between worker and boss has gone the way of the dinosaur and has been replaced with an adversarial perspective on both sides. In an era of corporate takeovers, mega-mergers, and corporate CEO scandals, workers often feel that they are left with nothing while the corporate fat cats have multimillion-dollar homes and enormous savings accounts. This represents a lethal mix for disenfranchised, marginalized, mentally ill workers who have been demoted, passed over for promotion, or fired.

Murderous Customers and Clients

It isn't only workers and ex-workers who blame their problems on the company. Disgruntled customers, clients, and even patients sometimes seek to avenge perceived mistreatment by banks, loan offices, law firms, hospitals and clinics, schools and colleges, unemployment offices, courthouses—in short, "the system"—through violence and murder. Each year, several dozen workers are killed at the hands of customers or clients.[8]

Mental health and medical workers are at particular risk of being attacked by the people they serve. On occasion, a violent incident with a disgruntled patient results in the murder of a practitioner who works in a clinic, a hospital, or at a client's residence. In August 2004, for example, 26-year-old Teri Zenner, a social worker and graduate student at the University of Kansas, made a home visit to her 17-year-old mentally ill client. Without warning, he became irate and pulled out a knife, stabbing the social worker to death. Since his wife's murder, Matt Zenner has worked tirelessly to bring to public attention the dangers faced by social workers. He established a scholarship in Teri's memory and has testified before Congress on the problem of violence perpetrated by clients.

In some cases, getting even with the system means targeting a number of individuals. For example, 45-year-old George Lott opened fire with a concealed 9 mm semiautomatic handgun during an appellate court proceeding in Ft. Worth, Texas, on the morning of July 1, 1992. It appeared to those present in the crowded fourth-floor courtroom that Lott was shooting wildly at anything that moved. The two attorneys who were slain and a third attorney and two judges who were wounded just happened to be at the wrong place at the wrong time. Lott escaped through the mass confusion, only to show up six hours later at a local television station to tell his side of the story. Speaking on-air with the news anchor, Lott detailed his deep-seated grudge against the judicial system that he believed had been unfair to him.

Similarly, in July 1993, eight people were slaughtered at a San Francisco law firm by a former client; eight others were shot to death at a Jacksonville GMAC office in June 1990 by an embittered customer whose car had been repossessed. Four public employees were gunned down at the Schuyler County Courthouse in October 1992 by a "deadbeat dad" who questioned the legitimacy of the child support demands. And in 1993, three doctors at the Los Angeles County Medical Center were shot by a patient who believed that the doctors weren't taking his chronic illness seriously enough.

Fifteen years ago, it was virtually unheard of for a dissatisfied customer or client to seek revenge through murderous means. Times have changed, however. "Fighting city hall" has taken a new and ominous meaning. Economic resentment can be felt not only by vengeful employees but also by disgruntled clients and customers who seek to get even with the system—to win one for the little guy.

In a complex, bureaucratic society, more and more citizens are feeling powerless against the red tape and unresponsiveness of big business and government. Most, of course, will do little more than complain loudly about the injustice. But increasing numbers simply refuse to sit back and take it.

Like the disgruntled employee, the vengeful customer/client is typically an isolated, middle-aged man who, after a prolonged period of frustration suffers a major financial or personal setback that he views as catastrophic. With no one to turn to for assistance or support, he deliberately decides to punish the institution that has caused him so much grief. Tending to externalize blame, he sees himself as a victim, not a criminal, who seeks justice through killing.

Part of the problem lies in the impersonal or ineffective response of customer relations in both public and private sectors. Increasingly, consumers are frustrated by automated phone systems with endless button-pushes and lengthy holding queues, by poorly trained or overburdened customer relations representatives, and, of course, by computer glitches. In many companies, customer service has become customer disservice.

And now, with virtually every company having an Internet site, getting help is even harder. They may have Web pages with Frequently Asked Questions, but they rarely seem to be the questions that the frustrated customer has in mind. For that, he might just have to connect to www.customerservice.com/dont-hold-your-breath.

When customers or clients deal with a small company, they can easily identify the right person to see in order to resolve a complaint. In large, impersonal bureaucracies, however, finding a responsible party is all but impossible. Some customers get mad, yet give up in frustration; a few decide to get even through sabotage or, worse, through murder.

Murder by dissatisfied customers or clients will likely never reach epidemic proportions, but these incidents reflect, albeit in the extreme, a more general problem in the United States today. In the face of growing alienation and cynicism, large companies and agencies must upgrade and humanize their customer relations efforts. They must always remember the adage: "The customer is always right, especially when he's holding a gun!"

ENDNOTES

1. See Joseph Westermeyer, "Amok," in Claude T. H. Friedmann and Robert A. Faguet, eds., *Extraordinary Disorders of Human Behavior.* New York: Plenum Press, 1982.

2. James Alan Fox, Ann W. Burgess, Jack Levin, and Marleen Wong, "Panel Report on the March 25, 2006 Capitol Hill Shooting." Seattle Police Department, July 17, 2006.

3. Anne Campbell, *Men, Women, and Aggression.* New York: Basic Books, 1993.

4. U.S. Department of Labor, Bureau of Labor Statistics, *Census of Fatal Occupational Injuries.* Washington, DC, 1996.

5. Sandra L. Haskett, *Workplace Violence: Before, During and After.* Boston: Butterworth-Heinemann, 1996.

6. Mark Braverman and Richard V. Denenberg, *The Violence Prone Workplace: A New Approach to Dealing with Hostile, Threatening, and Uncivil Behavior.* Ithaca, NY: Cornell University Press, 1999.

7. Northwestern National Life, "Fear and Violence in the Workplace." Minneapolis, MN, 1993.

8. U.S. Department of Labor, op. cit.

10 Hate Homicides

According to the FBI, hate or bias crimes, including homicides, involve "criminal offenses committed against persons, property, or society that are motivated, in whole or in part, by the offender's bias against a race, religion, disability, sexual-orientation, or ethnicity/ national origin."[1] Thus, the FBI definition specifies the motivation for committing the offense; it requires that a racial, religious, ethnic, or some other identified difference between victim and offender play at least some role in inspiring the criminal act (28 states also include gender as a basis for bias). For example, an individual who illegally takes money to buy illicit drugs may decide to rob only Asians because of some stereotype he holds regarding this group of people. If part of the motivation for the robbery involves the victim's Asian identity, then the offense can be regarded as a hate crime.[2]

The term *hate crime* was coined in the late 1980s in response to a racial incident in the Howard Beach section of New York City, in which a black man was killed while attempting to evade a violent mob of white teenagers, shouting racial epithets. Although widely used by the federal government, the mass media, and researchers in the field, the term is somewhat misleading because it suggests incorrectly that hatred is invariably a distinguishing characteristic of this type of offense. While it is true that many hate crimes involve intense animosity toward the victim, many others do not. Conversely, many crimes involving hatred between an offender and a victim are not "hate crimes" in the sense intended here. For example, an assault that arises out of a dispute between two co-workers who compete for a promotion might involve intense hatred, even though it is not based on any racial or religious differences between them. Similarly, a love-triangle may provoke intense emotions, having nothing at all to do with race or religion.

Characteristics of Hate Homicide

Estimates of the prevalence of hate crimes vary widely. According to the FBI, there were some 7,163 bias incidents in 2005, including 5,190 involving some form of personal violence. Among the victims of hate-motivated violence, 48.9 percent were intimidated, and 50.7 percent were assaulted. Six murders and three forcible rapes were reported as hate crimes.[3] Of course, the FBI count is based on a voluntary reporting system to which many local jurisdictions refuse to contribute, causing hate offenses of all kinds to be underreported. In 2005, almost 12,417 law enforcement agencies representing more than 245 million people, or 82 percent of the country's population, reported hate crimes to the FBI. Some notable nonparticipants included the state of Hawaii, as well as the states of Alabama and Mississippi, where no hate crimes were reported. Wyoming reported only three.

Moreover, an offense may not be recorded as a hate crime because of lack of evidence that it was motivated by bias. The perpetrators might not have used a racial slur or written hate graffiti, might never have confided their intent to the police or an acquaintance, or might remain unknown to law enforcement. In October, 2006, for example, a mother of six, wearing a *hijab* (the head scarf of a devout Muslim woman), was gunned down while walking on an affluent residential street in Fremont, California. Because her assailant has not yet been apprehended and did not leave any indication of his intent at the crime scene, the motivation for this murder cannot be definitively identified. Yet relatives of the victim as well as local Muslim leaders who have been able to rule out such other possibilities as robbery and revenge are convinced that the motive was hate. But even if the motivation for such violent crimes is unclear and the FBI statistics vastly underestimate hate homicides, it is still hard to imagine—using the federal criteria—any more than thirty or so committed in the United States in any given year.

National data on hate homicides collected by the Southern Poverty Law Center (SPLC) in Montgomery, Alabama, and published in its *Intelligence Report* suggest a much larger number of hate attacks committed in the United States.[4] Based on newspaper accounts, law enforcement reports, and interviews, the SPLC estimates that in the year 2001, as many as 50,000 hate crimes, including 21 homicides, were committed. During this period, gay or transgendered individuals (or perceived to be gay or transgendered) were murdered more often than any other of the groups studied. Specifically, out of the 21 hate homicide victims killed, 11 were gay or lesbian, six were (or perceived to be) Muslims or Arabs, two were Asian, one was black, and one was Latino. These hate killings occurred in 12 states, including four victims each in California and Florida. The victims ranged in age from 16 to 76.

Though vastly higher than police reports, even the SPLC estimate of the number of hate crimes annually may be too low. When victims are asked, the number of hate crimes is much larger. For example, a recent Justice Department study based on police reports *and* victim accounts suggests there may be not 7,000 as indicated by law enforcement, not 50,000 as the Southern Poverty Law Center estimates, but almost 200,000 hate crimes yearly in the United States.[5] Still, even victim reports probably underestimate the actual prevalence of hate offenses. It isn't only law enforcement personnel who are reluctant to report hate attacks. There are apparently numerous victims who also prefer not to inform anyone—and especially not the police—that they have been targeted.

According to a recent study by criminologist Jack McDevitt, many high school students refuse to report hate crimes to the police, a parent, or a teacher.[6] If they inform at all, it is more likely to a friend—which means that their report never gets official attention. Only 3 percent of the youthful victims of hate crimes reported their offense to the police. Moreover, immigrants may come from states where the police are seen as part of a repressive regime and not trusted. Racial minorities may feel the police are the "enemy of occupation." Such victims never report hate crimes against them. A recent survey found that almost 80 percent of Shiite Muslims in the United States who were victims of "post 9/11 discrimination" failed to report the incidents to the police.[7]

Judging by the amount of media attention that they typically receive, the influence of hate homicides seems much greater than their relatively small numbers might indicate. Not unlike less serious hate offenses, they impact not just a particular individual, but every member of a victim's group. In June 1998, three white men dragged James Byrd, a black man, to his death behind their pickup truck down a rocky country road in Jasper, Texas. Whether intended or not, the killers sent an unmistakable message to every black person in town regarding their vulnerability.

Similarly, the vicious murder in October 1998 of 21-year-old gay college student Matthew Shepard by two young men in Laramie, Wyoming, was a warning to every gay person not to exercise their constitutionally guaranteed rights. For his "sin," Shepard was beaten into a coma and left tied to a fence in the desert. He died five days later.

After 9/11, hate crimes targeting Muslims (and anyone who might possibly have been a Muslim) increased some 1,600 percent from the year 2000, making them the second-most likely religious group (behind Jews) to be victimized. Many were victims of arson, vandalism, or assault. A few were murdered not to rob them, but simply because they wore a turban or spoke with an accent. In Mesa, Arizona, a 49-year-old Sikh Indian wearing a turban was shot down in front of his gas station. In Dallas, a Pakistani Muslim was found shot to death in his convenience store. In San Gabriel, California, an Egyptian Christian was killed in his grocery store.

Perhaps because they target a group of people rather than an individual, hate-motivated murders generally attract tremendous amounts of media publicity. This was certainly true during the summer of 1999, when national attention was given to several hate homicides. In July, a former student at Indiana University, Benjamin Smith, went on a two-state shooting spree resulting in the death of a graduate student from Korea who was studying at Indiana University and a black man who was formerly the basketball coach at Northwestern University. Driving his blue Ford Taurus through a Jewish neighborhood in Chicago's far north side, 21-year-old Smith then opened fire on a group of Orthodox Jews, but managed only to injure six of them. Then, he took his own life.

Just weeks later, a 37-year-old white supremacist, Buford Furrow, walked into the North Valley Jewish Community Center in Los Angeles with a semiautomatic, where he fired more than 70 bullets, wounding six people. While attempting to avoid the law, he then approached an Asian American letter carrier and asked him to mail a letter. Before the postal worker could reply, Furrow shot him to death. In March 2001, in a Los Angeles courtroom, U.S. District Judge Nora Manella imposed a life sentence without the possibility of parole. "Your actions were a reminder that bigotry is alive," the judge told Furrow. "If you've sent a message, it is that even the most violent crimes can strengthen a community."[8]

Another characteristic of hate homicides is that their perpetrators are more likely than in other bias crimes to be linked with an organized hate group. The three killers of James Byrd had met behind bars where they joined the Aryan Brotherhood, a penitentiary hate group for white inmates who, after serving their time, are frequently recruited by white supremacist groups on the outside. The three perpetrators also had connections to the Ku Klux Klan. Indeed, they had planned to start a local chapter in the Jasper community.

Similarly, Benjamin Smith was a member of the World Church of the Creator (now known as the Creativity Movement), a relatively obscure white supremacist group whose members preach an anti-Christian, anti-Semitic, and racist set of doctrines. Operating out of

East Peoria, their inspirational leader and father-figure, 27-year-old Matthew Hale, was denied the ability to practice law by the state board's Committee on Character and Fitness, whose members argued that he had flunked their test of ethics and character. Indeed, there is reason to believe that Hale's rejection by the Illinois bar may have angered his protege, Benjamin Smith, enough to precipitate his killing spree. We can only conjecture just how angry Smith would have been had he lived to see his mentor serving a lengthy prison sentence for conspiring to murder a federal judge in Chicago. Buford Furrow also had connections to organized hate groups. He held membership in Aryan Nations, a white supremacist organization, and practiced the bigoted pronouncements of Christian Identity, the theological arm of a number of different hate groups around the country whose members believe that blacks and Latinos are subhuman "mud people" and that Jews are the children of the Devil.

The influence of group membership can hardly be exaggerated in the case of murders inspired by hate. As a cultural phenomenon, there may be literally millions of Americans who have adopted ethnocentric attitudes. They may tell racist jokes, use racial epithets, and verbalize their dislike of immigrants, gays, Jews, or people of color. Most Americans, however—notwithstanding their bigoted beliefs—would never dream of translating their hate into the commission of a crime, especially not murder.

But for someone who is angry and hate-filled, membership in an organized group can make all the difference. For one thing, the hatemonger's group teaches him that he is not alone in his bigotry. He knows, perhaps for the first time, that other people share the depths of his concern and his revulsion about the state of the nation and the decline of his "heritage" or race. Joining up gives him the inspiration needed to translate his attitudes into activism, to risk his personal safety in order to take a strong stand against race mixing, communism, or the so-called Zionist conspiracy. Second, if a hatemonger works together with other members of a group, then there often is some sharing of tasks that weakens his feeling of personal responsibility. He has only driven the car or gone along for the ride; he only kicked or hit the victim, but never delivered the fatal blow. Moreover, owing to what social psychologists call a group effect, he may also be able to take risks with his personal safety that he would have regarded as unthinkable before taking membership in a group of like-minded comrades. Finally, white supremacist organizations tend to be apocalyptic, preaching to their members that global racial war is inevitable. The battle cry of the World Church of the Creator, for example, is "Rahowa"—standing for racial holy war. The bible for many hate groups is Andrew Macdonald's novel, *The Turner Diaries,* a fictionalized account, written by a white supremacist (the late William Pierce) under a pseudonym, in which a bloody racial war is waged and won by the Aryan good guys. The FBI has suggested that *The Turner Diaries* provided the blueprint for the tragic Oklahoma City bombing episode in which 168 innocent people lost their lives.

Types of Hate Homicide

Hate homicides, not unlike hate crimes, generally seem to fall into one of four categories in terms of their perpetrators' motivations: thrill, defense, retaliation, and mission.

Thrill hate crimes are typically perpetrated by groups of teenagers or young adults who, bored and idle, decide to go out together looking for someone to attack. The sadism and excessive brutality involved in many thrill homicides suggest that at least some of the killers—perhaps the leaders of the group—have an excessive need to feel powerful at the expense of their victim. It takes only one sadistic bigot with power to exercise his will in a group of young people who are eager to please their peers and be accepted. Most thrill offenders might easily fit the label, offered by political scientist Meredith Watts, as "fellow travelers."[9] They may not harbor intense hatred toward their victim, but they also cannot bear the idea of being rejected by their friends. These are typically marginalized and alienated youngsters, whose thrill attack gets them little more than bragging rights and a vague sense of their own importance. And that is apparently enough to provide the inspiration for singling out a vulnerable victim. Almost half of all hate attacks can be regarded as thrill hate crimes.[10]

Most thrill attacks take the form of vandalism, desecration, and assault. Occasionally, however, a group of young people looking for some excitement will attack their victim with lethal force. Twenty-year-old James Burmeister and his two buddies were soldiers stationed at the Ft. Bragg army base outside of Fayetteville, North Carolina. They were also racist skinheads who hated blacks, Latinos, and Jews. The three friends didn't belong to any nationally organized hate group. By day, they completely immersed themselves in the disciplined military training required of all recruits on base. But, at night, they shed their military uniforms in favor of the steel-toed boots and green jackets associated with the Nazi movement.

During the early morning hours of December 7, 1995, the three soldiers drove their Chevrolet Cavalier into a black neighborhood located in the heart of town. They had spent the night drinking, playing pool, and watching topless dancers at a local sports bar.

All the while, Burmeister had made his intentions clear enough—he talked incessantly to his friends about wanting to find the enemy and have a little fun, about wanting to earn a badge of honor in the form of a spider web tattoo worn only by those members of the movement who had killed in order to further the Nazi cause. He liked the excitement, the thrill, and the bragging rights.

Shortly after midnight, the three spotted the victims, Michael James, 36, and Jackie Burden, 27, who were walking together along a dirt road, totally unaware of the danger lurking just ahead. Burmeister jumped out of the car and, without warning, immediately opened fire on the black couple with his 9 mm Ruger handgun, killing them both. The three then sped away from the scene of the crime, leaving the bodies of their two victims to be discovered by passersby.

In contrast to thrill offenses motivated by a need to be accepted and feel important, defensive hate crimes are, from the perpetrators' viewpoint, designed to protect their turf, territory, neighborhood, women, job, reputation, school, or campus—in general, their birthright. In some precipitating episode, the victims are perceived to threaten what the offender regards as belonging to him: members of a black family moving onto a previously all-white block, the first Asian student in a college dormitory, a gay man attending a party. The attack is typically aimed at particular victims, those who dare challenge or threaten the security or well-being of the offender. When the threat subsides, so does the attack.

Defensive hate crimes may begin with relatively harmless acts designed to alert the victim that he is trespassing on private property. If, however, the original message is disregarded—if the black family remains on the block, if the Asian student fails to change residence halls, if the gay man refuses to leave the party—then the offense may escalate into violence, until the desired result has been achieved.

Defensive hate crimes are occasionally provoked by a highly personalized threat, especially when it involves a challenge to a perpetrator's sexual orientation. In February 1999, 25-year-old Steven Eric Mullins lured Billy Jack Gaither, a 39-year-old gay man, to a remote area in a small Alabama town for the purpose of taking his life. When Gaither showed up, the 25-year-old Mullins approached his victim from behind, slashing his throat with a long-bladed knife, and cracking open his head with an ax handle. Along with his 21-year-old companion, Charles Butler, Mullins then burned Gaither's body and car in order to destroy the evidence.

The defensive motivation underlying Mullins's attack became clear in court. He had decided to eliminate Gaither in order to cover up his own homosexual tendencies, if not the relationship he had had with his victim. According to the testimony of eyewitnesses, the defendant had recently attended a party of gay men and had been observed dancing with his victim. Mullins testified in his own defense that he and Gaither had been drinking partners until Gaither propositioned him. That's when the defendant decided it was necessary to defend his reputation from irreparable damage.

A single hate crime is often followed by a number of retaliatory follow-up attacks by members of the victimized group. The month with the most hate offenses in New York City's history, for example, followed the brutal murder of a young black man, Yusuf Hawkins, in the white community of Bensonhurst. Believing that someone should pay, those in the black community who attacked in the aftermath of Hawkins's death were looking for revenge.

Retaliatory attacks tend to have the greatest potential for fueling additional hate crimes on both sides. Unlike defensive hate crimes designed to eliminate a particular "outsider" from a neighborhood, a workplace, or a school, retaliatory offenses often target not the original offender but anyone from the offender's group. Thus, the victim of a retaliatory crime is selected at random, so long as he is perceived to belong to the perpetrator's group.

An important example of how the desire for general revenge can lead to an escalation of violence between groups can be found in an incident that occurred in the Crown Heights section of New York City in August 1991. Seven-year-old Gavin Cato, a black child who lived in the Crown Heights section, was accidentally killed when the car driven by an Orthodox Jewish motorist jumped the curb.

In retaliation, a 29-year-old rabbinical student from Australia who was totally unconnected to the accident, was stabbed to death. For almost a week, blacks and Jews exchanged insulting remarks, hurled rocks and bottles at one another, and broke windows in homes and cars. Dozens more were injured.[11]

In Crown Heights, mistrust and suspicion were palpable between blacks and Jews. Many black residents believed that the motorist who hit the black child would get special treatment from city officials and get off scot free. At the same time, many Jewish residents of Crown Heights were convinced that the black mayor of New York City would rather look the other way than to bring the black murderer of the Australian rabbinical student to justice.

Mission hate crimes are the rarest and also the most dangerous category of offenses. They are the most likely to involve the members of an organized hate group as well as severe mental illness on the part of the perpetrator. They are also the most likely to result in a murder. Mission hate offenses represent no more than 5 percent of all hate crimes but probably a much larger proportion of hate homicides.[12]

Unlike thrill, defensive, and retaliatory attacks, mission hate crimes tend to be broad in scope and extend over time. Their perpetrators generally have no particular person or persons in mind to victimize; instead, they seek to destroy each and every member of a particular group. As a result, they may kill indiscriminately within a category, targeting a number of people simultaneously or going on a killing spree in a number of venues. For those who have made a career of bigotry, they might continue their killing spree until such time that they are finally apprehended by law enforcement.

In November 1995, four young men affiliated with the Nazi Lowriders of Lancaster, California, brutally murdered Milton Walker, a 43-year-old black homeless man in a vacant lot behind a fast-food restaurant. While shouting racial slurs at their victim, the young, white attackers repeatedly bludgeoned him with a wooden board, kicked him, and then smashed him in the face with a pipe. The assailants were at least partially inspired by a desire to impress other members of their group. But their motivation went far beyond the bragging rights bestowed on those who kill. All of the perpetrators were devoted to the cause of eliminating minorities from their town.

Indeed, the attack resulting in the slaying of Milton Walker was no isolated incident committed by dabblers, but one episode in a much larger series of offenses carried out by the Lancaster Nazi Lowriders, whose members had sought for years to eliminate minorities and create an all-white community. Their group had a long record of intimidating and attacking minorities for the purpose of leaving the impression that Lancaster was not safe for blacks, Latinos, and Asians. Members had taken part in a number of racially motivated beatings, stabbings, and threats.

Not every mission killer is connected, of course, with some organized hate group. Included in the mission category are also the relatively rare individuals who, acting out of severe mental illness, go gunning for victims representative of a group they despise. In 1989, for example, Patrick Purdy murdered five Southeast Asian children as they congregated on the playground at the Cleveland Elementary School in Stockton, California. Having drifted from place to place and unable to hold a steady job, his mental health deteriorated rapidly. In his distorted thinking, Purdy came to blame the immigrants who had recently moved into his community for all of his personal problems.

Another example of a mission killer operating on his own took place more recently in a Pittsburgh suburb, when Ronald Taylor, a 39-year-old black resident of Wilkinsburg, Pennsylvania, decided to settle the score with all those bigoted white people he held responsible for his miseries. On March 1, 2000, disturbed that the superintendent of his apartment building had not yet repaired his broken front door, Taylor reportedly first set his apartment on fire and then shot five people, three of whom died. According to investigators, Taylor targeted only whites. At one point in his rampage, while waving his gun and making threatening gestures toward a group of people, he yelled at a black woman, "Not you, sister." In his apartment, the police found letters written by Taylor, in which he expressed anger toward whites, Jews, Asians, Italians, and law enforcement officers.

The extent of human destruction perpetrated by someone on a mission depends on his or her ability to avoid apprehension. Shortly after midnight on February 2, 2006, 18-year-old Jacob Robida walked into Puzzles Lounge, a popular gay gathering place in the city of New Bedford, Massachusetts, 50 miles south of Boston, and ordered a drink at the bar. Then, after having one more shot of whiskey, he walked to the back of the room near a pool table and removed a hatchet from his black trenchcoat. Two men were able to grab the hatchet from the assailant's hands, but not before Robida had slashed both of them in the face. He then pulled out a 9 mm pistol and shot a third man in the stomach. Next, he put the gun to his own head and squeezed the trigger; but when it failed to fire, Robida ran out the front door of Puzzles Lounge and into the night.

Robida's rampage had just begun. After escaping from the gay bar where he left three men seriously wounded, he drove to Charleston, West Virginia, and picked up 33-year-old Jennifer Bailey, a woman with whom he had previously lived. The couple drove to Gassville, Arkansas, where Robida confronted police officer James Sell, who asked him to pull over to the side of the road in a routine traffic stop. Robida first gunned down Sell, then shot to death his female companion, and finally turned the gun on himself, taking his own life as the police closed in on him.

It was no coincidence that Robida had initiated his rampage targeting gays. The first thing he had asked the bartender before slashing and shooting patrons was "Is this a gay bar?" According to those who knew him well, he hated gays and lesbians, but he also despised blacks and Jews. His Website on MySpace.com contained a photograph of Robida wielding a firearm with a swastika in the background. His bedroom walls were covered with anti-Semitic writings and swastikas. Robida had an extensive collection of Nazi memorabilia, including books about the Third Reich, Nazi flags, and a sword. Among his books was a copy of *The Turner Diaries,* a neo-Nazi novel which many believe had inspired Timothy McVeigh's 1995 massacre in Oklahoma City.

Murderous mission hate crimes are planned, sometimes far in advance. Typically, they are intended to maximize the loss of human life and to generate widespread publicity among a population. The killer has a message to send. He is angry and frustrated; he blames the members of a certain group; and he is willing to sacrifice his personal well-being for the sake of a larger cause.

In July 2006, a 30-year-old Muslim American who had developed an intense anger toward Jews forced his way through the front door of the Jewish Federation in Seattle and opened fire with two semiautomatic handguns, killing a 58-year-old woman and injuring five others. The intruder blamed Jews for the war in Iraq and U.S. cooperation with the state of Israel. He had bought his weapons and ammunition days earlier, and searched the Internet for Jewish organizations before settling on the Jewish Federation as a target. Ending his rampage, the perpetrator was convinced by one of his wounded victims to phone 9-1-1. He told the operator that he had a gun to the head of a hostage and asked her to contact the media. Within minutes, the police arrive on the scene to apprehend the gunman, bringing an end to his deadly mission of hate.

Organized Hate Groups

Most Americans are at least somewhat acquainted with the objectives of white hate groups like the Ku Klux Klan and neo-Nazis. Those who are familiar with U.S. history know that the Klan has risen and fallen time and time again in response to challenges to the advantaged position of the white majority. During a short period of post-Civil War Reconstruction, for example, many whites were challenged by newly freed slaves who sought some measure of political power and began to compete for jobs with white working-class southerners. As a result, the Klan, responding with a campaign of terror and violence, lynched thousands of blacks. Klan-initiated violence increased again during the 1920s, as some Americans sought "protection" from an unprecedented influx of immigrants from Eastern and Southern Europe. During the 1950s and 1960s, uniformed members of George Lincoln Rockwell's American Nazi Party gave the Nazi salute and shouted "Heil Hitler." Over the same period, Klansmen in their sheets and hoods marched in opposition to racial desegregation in schools and public facilities.

By contrast, the newer organized hate groups operating since 1980 aren't necessarily known for bizarre uniforms or strange rituals. Followers of such white supremacist groups as John and Tom Metzger's White Aryan Resistance (WAR) have shed their sheets and burning crosses in favor of more conventional attire. They often disavow the Klan and the neo-Nazi movement in favor of a brand of "American patriotism" that plays better among the working people of America.[13]

Tom and John Metzger's suspicion about the declining appeal of the Klan seems justified. They now wear shirts and ties, not sheets or hoods. Some of their most influential followers are former KKK members who recognize the futility of looking deviant, perhaps even anti-American. The new groups talk in code words and phrases about the very issues that concern middle America. They preach that the heritage (meaning race) of white Christians is being eroded by foreign (meaning Jewish/communist) influence; they lament the rise of government interference (meaning Jews in high places who supposedly force racial integration down the throats of white Americans) in the lives of average citizens (meaning white Christians); and they condemn welfare cheating (meaning blacks and Latinos), which they incorrectly perceive as being rampant. In addition to wearing business suits, some get face-lifts (like former Klan leader David Duke did) or don hairpieces (for a while Tom Metzger had one). Several have run for public office. For example, Duke once ran for governor of Louisiana; Christian Identity's Richard Butler entered the race for mayor of Hayden, Idaho. Even in their support of bizarre-looking skinhead youth, they themselves are more concerned with projecting a respectable public image. They realize that younger people often reject the robes and ritual in favor of paramilitary dress. Concerned with the reaction of both the public and the police, some skinhead groups have recently taken a cue from their mentors by wearing their hair longer and getting rid of their black leather jackets.

Even some Klan leaders have changed their tune, at least in the way it is played for recruiting purposes. The leader of the Knights of the Ku Klux Klan in North Carolina, for example, actually barred violent neo-Nazis from its meetings. The head of the Klan in Florida urged its members to become a group "known for hating evil, instead of being a group known for hating Negroes." He has repeatedly suggested that his group does not hate anyone, but "loves the white race."

In 1978, after leaving his position as national director of the KKK, David Duke launched the National Association for the Advancement of White People. More recently, after spending a term of office in Louisiana's House of Representatives, Duke inaugurated a "civil rights group" for the purpose of fighting the "massive discrimination" against "European Americans" and in favor of blacks, Latinos, Jews, and gays. But, according to Ken Jacobson of the Anti-Defamation League, Duke's organization represents nothing more than an obvious attempt on the part of a "leading racist" to pitch himself in a more socially acceptable manner as a civil rights leader. Then, on March 29, 2004, more than 300 white supremacists came together in New Orleans to celebrate the return of Duke, who was released from federal prison after serving time for fraud. Almost two years later, on December 11, 2006, Duke attended the Holocaust Denial Conference in Tehran, sponsored by the Iranian Foreign Ministry.

According to the Southern Poverty Law Center's Klanwatch project, there may be 20,000—and almost certainly no more than 50,000—members of white supremacist groups across the nation. Considering that the United States is a country whose residents number some 300 million, this is a relatively small total.[14] To place this figure in historical perspective, consider that during the 1920s four million Americans were members of the Ku Klux Klan.

Still, the SPLC estimates that hate groups are on the rise. In 2005, there were more than 800 white supremacist organizations in the United States, an increase of more than five percent from 2004 and more than 30 percent since the year 2000. The greatest growth in the hate movement seems to have occurred in its most violent sectors—among racist skinheads who have moved into the hate music business and proponents of Christian Identity. At the same time, thanks to a vacuum of leadership, the influence of certain neo-Nazi organizations seems during the last few years to have declined. Several of the leading organizations in the hate movement—the National Alliance, David Duke's European-American Unity Organization, Matt Hale's World Church of the Creator, and Aryan Nations—all suffered setbacks of major proportions.

In the wake of the death of its leader William Pierce in 2002, the National Alliance's major source of revenue, Resistance Records, a distributor of racist and anti-Semitic white power CDs, took a serious hit. Visits to Resistance Records's Website declined substantially. Sales of Resistance Records's CDs plummeted. Many of its younger associates withdrew their memberships in the organization, as followers of Pierce sought to abandon what they saw as a "sinking ship."

In December 2002, after two years in Europe, David Duke was incarcerated for embezzling money from his followers in order to support a gambling addiction. Matthew Hale, leader of the World Church of the Creator, was charged with soliciting the murder of a federal judge. And Aryan Nations, formerly one of the most important neo-Nazi groups, was successfully sued by the Southern Poverty Law Center.[15] Although these demagogues of hate may have fallen from grace, surely other hatemongers are waiting in the wings to exploit the irrational fears of certain Americans in order to catapult themselves into positions of power.

Current State of Hate Crime Laws

In 1990, the Congress of the United States passed the Hate Crime Statistics Act, which requires the reporting of statistics on hate crimes nationally. When it comes to formulating hate crime legislation, however, the task has been mostly left up to the states. While 49 states (absent Wyoming) presently have some form of hate crime statute, there exists a wide variation among states in the specifics of their laws. For example, in the area of protected groups (i.e., particular groups are designated as protected in the statute), most states list crimes targeted toward individuals because of their race, religion, or ethnicity as prohibited. However, a number of states also include sexual orientation, disability, and age. The implication of this lack of uniformity is that members of a particular group may be protected by a hate crime statute in one community but not protected in a neighboring community in an adjacent state.[16]

Hate crime laws have been recently challenged by legal scholars and social scientists who suggest that by punishing speech, the statutes violate the First Amendment. Yet hate crime laws do not punish constitutionally protected hate speech. Most of these statutes only increase the penalty for behaviors that are already illegal—vandalism, harassment, murder, and the like. Moreover, using the words of a perpetrator who utters racial slurs or ethnic epithets to establish motivation is nothing new or unusual in criminal law. For example, the difference between killing someone in self-defense versus committing first-degree murder may rest largely on what a defendant has said. Criminal law has always taken into consideration the motivation and intent of the offender.[17]

The United States has chosen not to follow the lead of many European countries, where anti-hate speech legislation has been passed. Countries including Canada, France, Great Britain, and Germany have all passed laws prohibiting at least some forms of hate speech. In Germany, these forms of prohibition have been applied most broadly, particularly in the area of Nazi propaganda and symbols that are illegal to own or display. Consistent with its long tradition of free speech protections, the United States has, except on college campuses, decided not to develop similar legislation. Even in the area of campus speech codes, moreover, efforts in the United States to control offensive speech have been met with significant resistance and debate.[18]

Another argument often espoused in opposition to hate crime laws is that they apply only to "special groups." In reality, however, each and every American potentially receives protection from hate crime statutes that criminalize acts motivated by a characteristic of the victim. Thus, Christians who are targeted are as likely as Jews and Muslims to be protected by the law. Whites are as likely to be protected as blacks, Asians, and Latinos. Straights are as likely as gays and lesbians. In fact, some 20 percent of all racially motivated incidents reported to the FBI involve white victims targeted by members of another racial group.

When a bias crime results in murder, opponents of hate crime laws take the opportunity to emphasize that enhanced penalties are meaningless when applied to a crime for which a life sentence or the death penalty is already the only option. How is it possible, some argue, for hate crime legislation to have deterred the killers of Matthew Shepard or James Byrd?

Actually, the arguments surrounding hate crime legislation are much more complex than some have suggested. First, as noted earlier, most hate crimes do not rise to the level of murder—they are intimidations, vandalisms, and assaults. Second, bias-motivated murders may be committed by several individuals—a leader who possesses sadistic tendencies and fellow travelers who join in because they fear being rejected by their friends. While, hate crime laws may not discourage a sadist who plays a leadership position in a group, they might very well dissuade those who are on the fence about going along for the ride and helping out. In the beating death of Matthew Shepard, for example, the two perpetrators were accompanied by their girlfriends, who were accused of serving as accomplices by, among other things, helping to dispose of the killers' bloody clothes.

Finally, even if they fail to deter a single homicide, hate crime laws send a symbolic message of some importance, first, to members of vulnerable groups who are eager to know that not every American is a hatemonger and, second, to good people everywhere who disavow hate and intolerance but are not always so sure that they have company. In sum, from the perspective suggested decades ago by French sociologist Émile Durkheim, hate crime legislation plays a symbolic function by reflecting and reinforcing the values—tolerance and respect for diversity—that Americans claim to cherish.

ENDNOTES

1. Federal Bureau of Investigation, *Crime in the United States–2005.* Washington, DC: U.S. Government Printing Office, 2006.

2. Jack Levin and Jack McDevitt, *Hate Crimes Revisited.* Boulder, CO: Westview Press, 2002.

3. Federal Bureau of Investigation, *Hate Crime Statistics–2005.* Washington, DC: U.S. Government Printing Office, 2006.

4. Southern Poverty Law Center, "Tolerance in the News," *Intelligence Report,* May 23, 2002; Jack Levin, *The Violence of Hate.* Boston: Allyn and Bacon, 2007.

5. Caroline Wolf Harlow, *Hate Crime Reported by Victims and Police. Bureau of Justice Statistics Special Report.* Washington, DC: Bureau of Justice Statistics, 2005.

6. Michael Rosenwald, "Many Teens Silent on Hate Crimes, Study Finds," *The Boston Globe,* January 28, 2002, p. B2.

7. Religion News Service, "In Brief," *The Washington Post,* November 19, 2005, p. B9.

8. Associated Press, "Man Gets Life for California Hate Crime," March 27, 2001.

9. Meredith W. Watts, *Cross-Cultural Perspectives on Youth and Violence.* Stamford, CT: JAI Press, 1998.

10. Jack Levin and Jack McDevitt, op. cit.

11. Jack Levin and Gordana Rabrenovic, *Why We Hate.* New York: Prometheus Books, 2004.

12. Jack Levin and Jack McDevitt, *Hate Crimes: The Rising Tide of Bigotry and Bloodshed.* New York: Plenum Press, 1993.

13. Mark Potok, "The Year in Hate," *Intelligence Report,* 2003.

14. Ibid.

15. Ibid.

16. Jack Levin and Jack McDevitt, *Hate Crimes Revisited, o*p. cit.

17. James B. Jacobs and Kimberly A. Potter, "Hate Crimes: A Critical Perspective," in Michael Tonry, ed., *Crime and Justice: A Review of Research.* Chicago: University of Chicago Press, 1997.

18. Samuel Walker, *Hate Speech: The History of an American Controversy.* Lincoln: University of Nebraska Press, 1994.

11 Murderous Terror

Some mission-oriented hate homicides can be regarded as acts of terrorism. Using the FBI's definition, these crimes involve "the unlawful use of force or violence against persons or property to intimidate or coerce a government, the civilian population, or any segment thereof, in furtherance of political or social goals."[1] Clearly, there are violent mission hate offenses whose purpose is to send a message of coercion and intimidation. As noted earlier, for example, the Lancaster Nazi Lowriders had sought for years to eliminate minorities from their town and create an all-white Lancaster.

According to specialists on the topic, terrorism is a premeditated act of violence which aims to produce a climate of fear and anxiety. It is aimed, then, not just at a set of immediate victims, but at a much wider audience. The terrorist attacks are typically random and symbolic, targeting civilians and government officials. Because terrorism is widely regarded by society's members as a deviant act, it causes a general sense of outrage.[2]

The September 11th Attack on America has all of the elements associated with an act of murderous terror. Its perpetrators, the 19 suicide bombers who flew planes into the World Trade Center and the Pentagon, had planned their attack for years, hoping to optimize its impact in spreading anxiety across the United States. Thousands lost their lives in the assault, but almost every American was impacted as secondary or tertiary victims. Afterwards, millions refused to take a plane or travel abroad; for a period of time, they wished to stay close to home. Flag-waving became a national pastime. Almost everyone felt profoundly threatened.

Hate Homicide and Domestic Terrorism

Not every terrorist act is a hate crime; not every hate attack is an act of terror; but the line between hate crime and terrorism is not always clearly drawn. At the Los Angeles International airport (LAX) on the morning of July 4, 2002, Hesham Mohamed Ali Hadayet waited patiently in line at the El Al airlines second-floor ticket counter, and then, without uttering a word, opened fire with his .45 Glock semiautomatic handgun. Before security guards could wrestle him to the ground, the Egyptian immigrant had managed to spray a dozen bullets into a crowd of people, fatally gunning down two innocent victims, both Israeli citizens.

The 41-year-old assailant was a Cairo-born accountant who had migrated to the United States some 10 years earlier. Unfortunately, his personal life had recently fallen apart. The small limousine service he had been running out of his apartment in Irvine had become mired in debt. And a few days before his deadly rampage at LAX, Hadayet's wife and two sons had left him to return to Egypt. Hadayet's grievances were political as well as personal. He was outraged by the policies of the United States toward Palestinians and had long argued that the government of his Egyptian homeland be overthrown. He had told an ex-employee that he despised all Israelis. And he had vented his anger at a neighbor for flying an American flag after September 11, 2001. Somehow, Hadayet's political views and personal problems intersected in his mind, as he searched in vain for some reasonable resolution to the circumstances that had left his life in shambles. In the end, however, he solved his problems by committing murder.

From the standpoint of the Israeli government, there was no doubt from the beginning that Hadayet had committed an act of terrorism. Rather than target Aer Lingus, Air Canada, or Alitalia, he had directly and exclusively attacked the Israeli national airline. And Hadayet was an Egyptian who despised Israelis. From the FBI's viewpoint, however, the assailant had more likely committed a hate crime. He had personal problems: his wife and children were gone; he had recently suffered financial disaster; and he hated Jews. What is more, there was no evidence that Hadayet was a member of any organized terrorist group. Almost one year after the assault at LAX, however, the FBI admitted that Hadayet's crime was an act of terrorism, even if it was also a hate crime. The two types of attacks are not mutually exclusive. An individual who for personal reasons incites terror among a civilian population can still be regarded as a terrorist, based on the consequences of his behavior. Moreover, even if he is not a member of al Qaeda, someone who hates Jews, Americans, Muslims, or any other group of people can be regarded as committing a terrorist act. Attacking as an individual rather than a group simply does not disqualify him from fitting the FBI's definition.

International Terrorism

The worst act of international terrorism ever committed occurred in the United States on September 11, 2001. Coordinated by the al Qaeda terrorist network, the attack involved four jet hijackings by 19 terrorists: an American Airlines flight from Boston to Los Angeles that was instead crashed into the North Tower of the World Trade Center in New York City, a United Airlines flight from Boston to Los Angeles that was deliberately flown into the South Tower of the World Trade Center, a United Airlines flight from Newark to San Francisco that crashed in Stony Creek Township, Pennsylvania, and an American Airlines flight from Washington's Dulles Airport to Los Angeles that was guided into the Pentagon in Arlington, Virginia. Some 3,000 people—citizens of 78 nations—lost their lives in these four terrorist attacks.

In response, President Bush sought to eliminate the base of operations and training facilities for worldwide terrorism. On October 7, 2001, he initiated Operation Enduring Freedom, a military maneuver designed to destroy the al Qaeda training camps and Taliban military installations in Afghanistan, where—according to intelligence sources—Islamic extremists from around the globe had assembled. As a result, the Taliban governing body was forced from power and some 1,000 members of al Qaeda were arrested. To this day, United States armed forces remain in Afghanistan in order to protect the viability of its friendly government and secular institutions.

Also following September 11, the Bush administration moved to expand the power of federal law enforcement to detain, investigate, interrogate, and prosecute suspicious individuals in this country. Congress, in immediately passing the Patriot Act, made it easier to conduct searches, wiretap telephones, and secure electronic records. Attorney General John Ashcroft approved of giving FBI agents increased powers to monitor the Internet, political rallies and demonstrations, and mosques. Almost 80 percent of Americans expressed their willingness to forfeit certain freedoms for the sake of security. More than five years after its enactment, a modified version of the Patriot Act remained in force.

Hundreds of civilians and government officials around the world are killed each year by terrorists. In January, 2002, for example, Daniel Pearl, a reporter with the *Wall Street Journal,* was kidnapped and murdered in Karachi, Pakistan. In October of the same year, a car bomb detonated in a crowded resort area of Bali, Indonesia, killing more than 200 people from 24 countries. On March 11, 2004, 191 commuters lost their lives when terrorist bombs ripped through Madrid's train station during morning rush hour. In July 2005, 54 people were killed by explosives planted aboard London's underground commuter trains. Some of the terrorists turned out to be British citizens; others claimed allegiance to other nations.[3]

Homegrown Terrorism

Largely as a result of the September 11th attack, most Americans, when they envision terrorism, understandably conjure up the name of Osama Bin Laden and fixate on al Qaeda, Hezbollah, and Hamas. To most Americans, terrorist murder arises not out of the warped and perverted psyches of their deranged, vengeful, or sociopathic friends and neighbors, but in the plotting and planning of blood-thirsty groups originating in the Middle East.

Yet in October 2002, 10 innocent people lost their lives when John Allen Muhammad and Lee Boyd Malvo, two down-and-out criminals—one a U.S. citizen, the other a teenager originally from Jamaica—conspired to hold the Washington, D.C. area hostage to their demand for $10 million. Their three-week killing spree was meant to intimidate or coerce government officials. Their targets were not soldiers but civilians. Their motivation was apparently mixed: to extort a fortune from authorities, but perhaps also to get even with Americans for their treatment of immigrants and Muslims after 9/11, and to gain a sense of power by taunting the police and becoming celebrities. The DC sniper episode reminds us, in a particularly chilling manner, that much of the terrorism in the United States is home grown, originating as much in the psychopathology of the perpetrators as in their politics.

According to the FBI, only slightly more than one-third of all terrorist acts in the United States are international in origin.[4] Most are instead perpetrated by U.S. citizens who hold a deadly grudge against the federal government, a particular category of people, or all humankind. The terrorists see social and political issues in black-and-white terms and feel frustrated in their attempts to change society. They are self-righteous and utopian in their beliefs about the world. They are socially isolated, having no place to turn when they seek to confirm the validity of their ideas. Finally, they possess a cold-blooded willingness to kill, in order to secure a measure of sweet revenge through the barrel of a gun or a bomb and perhaps also a sense of their own power and importance.[5]

The terrorists may elect to play a cat and mouse game with law enforcement, which they are convinced they will ultimately win. They may hope to terrify the community. They may seek to become celebrities, reading about their crimes in the headlines, on the 11 o'clock news, and on the cover of *People* magazine. Or, they may attempt to play God by deciding whether, and in what manner, their victims live or die. The terrorists might choose to strangle and mangle, torture and rape, bomb, or spray bullets at random targets. And, in the process, they get even with those they hold responsible for their miseries and wreak havoc throughout a community, a region, or an entire nation.

Since 9/11, citizens have felt very vulnerable. But many Americans are completely unaware that they were just as unsafe, perhaps more so, long before Middle Eastern terrorists decimated the Twin Towers in September 2001. FBI data indicate that almost 500 acts of terrorism occurred in the United States between 1980 and 2001. The unprecedented carnage of 9/11 can obviously never be ignored, but there have been numerous acts of terror committed against U.S. citizens long before al Qaeda became a household name. Indeed, the 1993 bombing of the World Trade Center in New York City took the lives of six people, a number that was apparently too small to make Americans pay attention.[6]

Since 9/11 and through January of 2006, there have been 64 incidents of terrorism in the U.S., causing death or injury to 54 victims. The post-9/11 terrorism-related deaths were the result of anthrax poisonings (of employees at the *National Enquirer,* of postal workers, of a hospital worker, and of a 94-year-old woman whose source of exposure is undetemined), and also of the Hadayet shooting at LAX airport in July of 2002.

Acts of domestic terror have been attempted by persons operating on their own, small groups of individuals, as well as the members of highly organized groups. In June 2006, seven men were charged with concocting a plot to blow up Chicago's Sears Tower and "kill all the devils we can." Most of the suspects were U.S. citizens who, it was alleged by undercover FBI agents, had been organizing an Islamic army to wage a jihad in the United States. Prior to being arrested, their final act was to give an FBI informant a list of equipment they needed—boots, uniforms, machine guns, radios, vehicles, bullet-proof vests, and $50,000 in cash. Another recent attempt at domestic terrorism to be thwarted by the intervention of federal officials occurred in December 2006. Derrick Shareef, a 22-year-old resident of Rockford, Illinois, had allegedly planned to set off hand grenades at a crowded suburban shopping mall, some 90 miles northwest of Chicago. The would-be terrorist was arrested when he attempted to buy four grenades and a handgun from an undercover federal agent.

The bombing offensive committed by the Unabomber, Theodore Kaczynski, represents one of the most deadly examples of domestic terrorism committed by a single individual. Not only was the Harvard educated mathematician alone when he perpetrated his 18-year killing spree, but he was also a loner who despised high-tech society and, in order to communicate his message of destruction, decided literally to blow it up through the mail. Injuring 23 and killing three was as close as he came.

The Unabomber had spent his days in an out-of-the-way Montana cabin, constructing bombs to be sent to his enemies and typing his manifesto, in which he railed against the evils of post-modern, technology-dependent America. Kaczynski's manifesto was printed in its entirety—just as he had demanded—in the *Washington Post,* where it accomplished its twofold purpose. First, from the point of view of the killer, it made the Unabomber into some kind of folk hero—a high-tech Robin Hood, the image of a well-meaning if misguided humanitarian who had dedicated his life to saving us from ourselves. From the viewpoint of the FBI, however, printing the manifesto had a different result—it provided people with a set of clues that could be identified with the Unabomber's background and ultimately contribute to his apprehension. In the end, both objectives may have been realized: Americans organized Unabomber fan clubs and defense funds; they wore Unabomber T-shirts and watched as Jay Leno participated in Unabomber skits on his nightly TV show. At the same time, the Unabomber's brother, David Kaczynski, easily recognized certain idiosyncrasies in the syntax and substance of the Unabomber's manifesto which, according to the FBI, led to Theodore's arrest. Thanks to a family that turned in one of its own in order to save the lives of people they didn't know, Kaczynski is presently serving a life sentence in a California prison.

In carrying out murderous terrorist acts, the number of perpetrators does not always come close to matching the number of victims. It is ironic indeed that an act of domestic terrorism resulting in a record-setting body count—168—would have been committed by perhaps only two or three individuals who together concocted a plan to retaliate against the United States Government for failing to respect the constitutional rights of citizens by blowing up a federal building and killing large numbers of government workers. But this is precisely what occurred in Oklahoma City in 1995, when Timothy McVeigh and his buddy got even with Uncle Sam.

In a very real sense, students who seek to destroy their schools with gunfire or bombs can be considered homegrown terrorists. Many of the distinguishing features of terrorism (e.g., premeditation, creation of fear and anxiety, victimization of a civilian population larger than the death toll, and outrage) can be seen in episodes of school slaughter like those discussed in Chapter 7. In an odd but telling twist, the diary of Eric Harris, who teamed with his buddy Dylan Klebold to perpetrate the April 1999, Columbine massacre, described their plans to crash a hijacked plane into the New York City skyline. What for millions of Americans seemed after September 11, 2001, to be absolutely unthinkable—intentionally to fly a jet into a skyscraper—had been conceived by a pair of Colorado teenagers more than two years prior to the Attack on America.

Left-Wing vs. Right-Wing Terrorists

Domestic terrorism can also be linked to the operation of organized groups whose members plot and conspire to carry out the objectives of some violent master plan. For much of the 20th century, and especially between 1960 and the mid-1980s, murderous domestic terrorism came for the most part from political extremists on the left—from Marxist-communists, socialists, militant minority groups, and Puerto Rican nationalists. Left-wing terrorists tended to be young, well-educated, upper-middle class, and from urban areas. Many were African- and Latino-Americans; almost one-third were women.

In 1970, a group known as the Weather Underground declared war against the government of the United States. While preparing a bomb in a New York City safe house, three Underground members were accidentally killed. They later bombed the U.S. Capitol building, the Pentagon, police stations, and prisons.

Weather Underground members committed a number of murders in a series of bank robberies. In September 1970, campus revolutionary Katherine Ann Powers and three companions set fire to a National Guard Armory in Massachusetts, stealing a truck and ammunition, which they supplied to the Black Panthers, a group of black militants. Three days later, the same Underground members robbed the Brighton bank in Boston, taking $26,000 with which they hoped to fund their revolutionary army. In the process, they murdered Walter Schroeder, a 42-year-old police officer who had responded to the bank's call for help. Although her four accomplices had long ago been apprehended and convicted, Powers remained a fugitive for 23 years before she surrendered to authorities. For her conviction of armed robbery and manslaughter, she was paroled in 1999 after serving 6 years in prison.

Another member of the Weather Underground, Kathy Boudin, participated in the 1981 robbery of an armored Brinks truck in suburban Nanuet, New York. During the holdup, Boudin and her friends shot and killed a security guard and two police officers. They made off with $1.6 million. For her part in the crime, Boudin was convicted of second-degree murder and served 22 years in prison. She was freed on parole in September 2003.

Left-wing terrorism has also come from the ranks of organizations dedicated to the cause of gaining independence for the Commonwealth of Puerto Rico. A small but obtrusive minority of Puerto Ricans have sought, through violent means, full and complete independence from the United States. In the 1970s and early 1980s, for example, the Armed Forces of National Liberation (FALN, after its Spanish name) was responsible for more than 100 bombings in New York City and Chicago, resulting in at least five deaths, 83 injuries, and more than $3 million in property damage.

The most spectacular and deadly attack perpetrated by FALN occurred in New York City's crowded financial district on January 24, 1975, when a terrorist bomb ripped through Fraunces Tavern. Inside, dozens of Wall Street workers having lunch in the packed dining room were badly injured. Four died in the bombing; one was decapitated by flying debris. An hour later, wire service reporters received a phone call from an FALN representative, claiming responsibility for the terrorist attack. The caller explained the rationale for the deadly bombing: to retaliate for the CIA's killing of supporters of the Puerto Rican independence movement and to convince the United States government to abandon its "occupation" of the Island of Puerto Rico.

Most of the terrorist murders committed from 1960 through the early 1980s involved left-wing revolutionaries in groups like the Weather Underground and the FALN. By contrast, Americans committing murderous acts of organized domestic terrorism since the mid-1980s have tended to represent right-wing extremist causes, often involving white supremacy and/or hatred toward what they regard as a communist-controlled federal government. Typically, those Americans reputedly involved in right-wing terrorism are middle-aged, mostly white males who lack college degrees, and are likely to be unemployed or impoverished. In the mid-1980s, a white supremacist militia group known as The Order sought to make good on its promise to spark revolution and to rid the nation of Jews, people of color, and liberals. In 1985, the novel by William Pierce (aka Andrew Macdonald) about the inevitability of a global race war came to the attention of the U.S. Department of Justice, when members of The Order committed a number of robberies and murders in an effort to ignite the same kind of bloody war depicted in *The Turner Diaries*. The group committed crimes ranging from robbing armored cars and counterfeiting to gunning down a Jewish talk show host in the driveway of his Denver home.

More recently, Eric Rudolph caused the deadly pipe bomb explosion, on July 27, 1996, that ripped through crowded Centennial Olympic Park in Atlanta, Georgia, killing 44-year-old Alice Hawthorne of Albany, Georgia, and injuring more than 100. To maximize the damage, Rudolph had packed his 40-pound pipe bomb in a knapsack along with screws and nails.

Hiding in the hills of North Carolina, Rudolph was able to stay on the loose for five years until he was finally apprehended in 2003, while rummaging through a dumpster to find food behind a restaurant. Though typical of "lone wolf" terrorists who operate, for the most part, on their own, Rudolph was suspected by the FBI of having been assisted in securing food and shelter by local individuals who were ideologically friendly to the fugitive.

During his appearance in federal court in April, 2005, Rudolph admitted committing the Olympic Park bombing as well as three others. During his two-year series of attacks in the Deep South, he also injured four people in an explosion at the Otherside Lounge, a lesbian nightclub located on the northeast side of Atlanta, and killed 35-year-old Robert Sanderson at a women's health clinic in Birmingham. Rudolph also confessed to bombing a women's clinic that performed abortions in Sandy Springs, Georgia.

Having murdered two innocent people, Rudolph was definitely eligible to be executed by the federal government. Instead, he was sentenced in a plea bargain to four life sentences without parole, escaping death by, in return, confessing to his crimes and divulging to authorities the location of hundreds of pounds of dynamite he had stockpiled while hiding in the hills of North Carolina. Rudolph's motive? To anger and embarrass the federal government in the eyes of the world.

Allen Sapp has identified three trends in the right-wing movement beginning in the mid-1980s.[7] The first involves Americans having group affiliations which read like a "Who's Who" of organizations promoting white supremacy—Aryan Nations, Arizona Patriots, Ku Klux Klan, The Order, and Posse Comitatus. Their main objective in perpetrating terrorist acts is to prevent minority Americans from exercising their constitutional rights, by sending them a message of fear and terror. The second trend noted by Sapp consists of survivalists who withdraw from conventional society in order to construct armed compounds in rural areas. They build bunkers, in which they can stockpile weapons and food, and await the demise of the federal government. The third and final trend in right-wing extremism, according to Sapp, involves the growth of Christian Identity, a set of religious tenets that provides a theological basis for believing that white Christians are intellectually and morally superior to people of color and Jews. White supremacist organizations often cloak their hatred in the aura and dogma of religion. Followers of the Identity Church are only "doing the work of God." At Sunday services, they preach that white Anglo-Saxons are the true Israelites depicted in the Old Testament, God's chosen people, while Jews are actually the children of Satan. They maintain that Jesus was not a Jew, but an ancestor of the white, northern European peoples. In their view, blacks are "pre-Adamic," pre-Old Testament, a species lower than whites. In fact, they claim that blacks and other nonwhite groups are at the same spiritual level as animals and therefore have no souls.

Members of this movement also believe in the inevitability of a global war between the races that only white people will ultimately survive. The survivalists among Christian Identity followers prepare for war by moving to communes where they can stockpile weapons, provide paramilitary training, and pray. According to a recent Identity directory, there are Identity churches in 33 states, Canada, England, South Africa, and Australia.

Author Kenneth Stern has noted three important events and issues which were responsible for reinvigorating the extremist right beginning in the closing decade of the 20th century.[8] First, federal gun control legislation (especially the waiting period initially included in the Brady law) caused white supremacist organizations to downplay their racist rhetoric in favor of espousing the belief—much more appealing to mainstream America— that the federal government was out to eliminate gun ownership. Second, the mishandled attempt on the part of ATF undercover agents in 1992 to arrest white supremacist Randy Weaver on firearm charges galvanized right-wing forces already convinced that the federal government was their enemy. During a prolonged standoff outside of Weaver's mountain cabin at Ruby Ridge, Idaho, federal snipers killed the white supremacist's pregnant wife and young son. Third, distrust of the federal government was further reinforced by the 1993 FBI siege of the Branch Davidian compound outside of Waco, Texas, which ended in a tremendous conflagration killing some 80 people, including two dozen children. Botched attempts on the part of federal agents to arrest extremists on weapons charges—episodes such as those at Ruby Ridge and Waco—added fuel to the fire of discontent among Americans who already doubted the competence and trustworthiness of the government. For a relatively few extremists, such incidents inspired organized efforts to "defend the Constitution" and served to justify their acts of murderous terrorism. Membership in right-wing citizens' militias and survivalist groups together comprising the so-called Patriot movement has been estimated at between 15,000 and 100,000.[9]

The Southern Poverty Law Center suggests that these militia groups have declined every year since 1996, when the militia movement reached its peak with 858 groups. Evidence that Timothy McVeigh, just prior to his bombing of the federal building in Oklahoma City, had visited an Arizona chapter of the Patriot movement and had phoned a white supremacist compound in Oklahoma caused many Americans to turn away from right-wing extremist groups. The enormity of McVeigh's attack—taking the lives of so many men, women, and children—apparently disgusted potential members of the Patriot movement. By 2002, the number of groups in the Patriot movement had dropped to only 143. According to the Southern Poverty Law Center, many Patriot groups simply disappeared. Not unlike international terrorists around the world, Patriots have now organized themselves into small "cells" with no centralized leadership.[10] Though possibly limiting the ability of right-wing groups to amass resources, this lack of structure also restricts the effectiveness of any surveillance efforts on the part of federal security forces in their efforts to track political extremists.

Many members of the Patriot movement are residents of rural and small-town America who experienced financial disaster beginning with the deep recession of the early 1980s, when ranchers, farmers, miners, and timber workers suffered profoundly. They were joined by blue-collar workers from major cities, who lost their jobs when the automobile industry went into severe decline.

It should also be pointed out that the militia movement in the United States is diverse. Some members are clearly bigoted in their beliefs and despise Jews and blacks, but there are also Jewish and black militia members.[11] The constitutionality of militia activities has, however, been challenged by observers who regard them as illegal private armies.[12] In addition, there seems to be some degree of overlap in the memberships of white supremacy groups and militias, perhaps accounted for by the fact of their shared conspiratorial thinking and their hatred for the federal government. Following McVeigh's 1995 rampage, some disillusioned militia members withdrew from the movement, abandoning any organized effort or joining a white supremacist organization instead.[13]

Single-Issue Terrorism

Acts of single-issue terror—for example, against environmental pollution, animal abuse, genetic engineering, abortion, company policies, or the like—may not be derived from some broad ideological position on the political left or right. Instead, single-issue terrorists are typically perpetrated by persons operating on their own or in groups who argue that the particular "evil" they hope to undermine has received the protection of society's legal system. They are therefore left having to go outside of the law.

The Earth Liberation Front (ELF) and the Animal Liberation Front (ALF) are the major organizations that have served to unite individuals in the United States who are willing to take illegal measures against environmental destruction or animal cruelty. Until recently, ELF and ALF were widely regarded as misguided but essentially benign organizations whose idealistic members had worked toward honorable goals—a cleaner environment and the humane treatment of animals. Representatives of ELF and ALF point out that their members have not injured or killed anyone in the United States. They would, however, break into a mink farm and free thousands of animals. Or, they would set fire to dozens of SUVs in the lots of automobile dealerships. In addition, the potential for injury and death seems to have increased, as the use of such tactics as firebombing property and spiking trees has been on the rise.

During the last decade, ELF and ALF seem to have escalated their unlawful tactics. The FBI estimates that since 1996, so-called eco-terrorists from these two groups have committed more than 600 criminal acts, resulting in damages of more than $43 million. The targets of such terrorist acts have also broadened considerably, now including laboratories in which genetic engineering research is conducted. In 2004 alone, the FBI reported ecological extremism as the number-one threat of domestic terrorism. Moreover, the illegal activities of such groups have indirectly caused injuries to human beings. In 1998, for example, a firefighter was treated for injuries incurred in a Vail, Colorado, resort fire set by ELF. Outside of the United States, eco-terrorism has taken a more dangerous tact. In 2003, less than two weeks before voters in the Netherlands went to the polls to elect a new government, animal-rights activist Volkert van der Graaf shot to death a right-wing candidate for prime minister who had supported pig farmers in their battle against the animal rights movement.[14]

The Impact of Murderous Terror

To the extent that a sizable number of Americans remain alienated and marginalized, murderous acts of domestic terrorism cannot be expected to disappear entirely from the societal landscape. Depending on the state of our economy, the effectiveness of our government's foreign policy, and the ability of our society to reach residents who feel angry and ignored, there are bound to be violent and explosive outbursts from time to time, aimed at terrifying citizens or eliminating government officials.

International terrorism can similarly be expected to continue having an impact not only in the United States but around the world. Wherever the peace process moves forward, extremist groups will predictably turn to violence. So long as terrorists believe that peace only robs them of their political and military clout, they will increase their efforts to destroy prospects for ending armed conflict. This is precisely what has recently occurred between Israelis and Palestinians in the Middle East, and during an earlier period, between Catholics and Protestants in Northern Ireland, as well as between Muslims and Hindus in India. As of this writing, terrorist attacks have continued to erupt in Iraqi cities, where local leaders have cooperated with the U.S. occupation or have sought to restore some semblance of normalcy to everyday life. The sectarian violence is often fueled by militant insurgents who are convinced that a large-scale civil war would promote their political and religious objectives.

Years have passed since the September 11th Attack on America, but we are only now beginning to assess the full impact of this tragic event on our way of life. Thousands lost their lives, including 60 police officers and 343 firefighters. And the Twin Towers were crushed into nearly two million tons of burning concrete and steel.

Most Americans have not put completely out of their minds the pain and suffering experienced by thousands of primary victims at the Twin Towers, the Pentagon, or in a doomed airliner over Pennsylvania, as well as tens of thousands of family members and friends and hundreds of thousands who knew a friend or the relative of a victim. In addition, there were millions of Americans in places like California, Arkansas, Michigan, and Massachusetts, who never had the opportunity of knowing the victims of 9/11, but nevertheless felt as though they had been robbed of a family member or a good friend. Some Americans responded to the 9/11 attacks by directing their anger toward the six million Muslims in the United States. After 9/11, there was a 1300 percent increase in hate crimes perpetrated against America's Muslim population. Most were acts of intimidation, but there were also numerous aggravated and simple assaults. Even in 2006, four in 10 Americans admit feeling some prejudice against Muslims.

Notwithstanding its horrific carnage, not all of the news about 9/11 has been bad. In fact, only about 15 percent of all Americans still suffer psychologically—depression, anxiety, trauma, and stress. Nearly 60 percent claim that the Attack on America has not made them more pessimistic about our nation's future. More than 80 percent are opposed to singling out Arabs or Muslims for questioning without probable cause. And more than a third of all Americans say that they coped with the horrors of September 11, not by purchasing a firearm or hiding in their homes, but by reaching out and establishing a closer relationship, a tighter bond with their families and good friends. Moreover, Americans' naivete concerning the likelihood of being victimized by international terrorism has been replaced by a new collective awareness—vigilance—regarding the possibility of another major attack.[15]

September 11 has given us new heroes—firefighters, police officers, the former mayor of New York City, the President of the United States, the volunteers at Ground Zero, the family members of victims, the passengers on Flight 93 who refused to allow terrorists to fly into the White House or the Capitol, and our military in Afghanistan and Iraq.[16] Rather than focus so much celebrity on the evil people among us, the Attack on America has changed our thinking—90 percent of all Americans continue to rate firefighters as honest and trustworthy. And after much controversy about whether to feature Osama Bin Laden as its "Person of the Year" for 2001, *Time Magazine* decided instead to honor Mayor Giuliani of New York City for his heroic efforts in the aftermath of the Attack on America. Subsequent issues of *Time* continued to feature virtuous individuals—for example, an Enron whistle-blower and our troops in Afghanistan, until the year 2005, when the magazine chose to honor "you"—all Americans who use the Internet.

September 11 has brought out the generosity and compassion of Americans everywhere. In the months after the attack, much of the extreme hostility targeting Arabs and Muslims subsided, and grieving Americans found a more productive and healthier way to mourn our nation's loss—they volunteered at Ground Zero, they donated money, time, or blood, and they prayed for the victims.

Following 9/11, the nation's charities were swamped with checks, cash, clothes, and even frequent flier miles. This was the biggest flood of donations that fund raisers had ever seen. During the first two weeks alone, donations hit $500 million. By August 2002, the 10 largest charities claimed they had collected $2.3 billion. The sources of charity were diverse: race drivers donating their helmets, an all-star rock concert at Madison Square Garden, school bake sales in Wyoming, and a Massachusetts congressman's education fund to help the victims' families.

On September 11, 2001, Americans witnessed the most violent single incident of hate-motivated violence in our country's history. The Attack on America was apparently inspired by an intense hatred of America and a desire to eliminate as many U.S. citizens as possible. This horrendous incident demonstrated the power and devastation that hate is capable of generating. One of the important lessons learned from the Attack on America was that to ignore murderous terrorism is to risk the potential for unimaginable tragedy.

ENDNOTES

1. Brent Smith, *Terrorism in America: Pipe Bombs and Pipe Dreams.* Albany, NY: State University of New York Press, 1994.

2. Paul Wilkinson, "Current and Future Trends in Domestic and International Terrorism," *Violence and Terrorism: Annual Editions.* Guilford, CT: McGraw-Hill/Dushkin, 2004.

3. Federal Bureau of Investigation, *Report on International Terrorism,* www.fbi.gov, 2001.

4. Federal Bureau of Investigation, *Report on Terrorism, 1980–1999,* www.fbi.gov, 2000.

5. Paul Davis, "The Terrorist Mentality," *Violence and Terrorism: Annual Editions.* Guilford, CT: McGraw-Hill/Dushkin, 2004.

6. Federal Bureau of Investigation, 2000, op. cit.

7. Allen Sapp, "Basic Ideologies of Right-Wing Extremist Groups in America," paper presented at the annual meeting of the Academy of Criminal Justice Sciences. Las Vegas, NV: 1985.

8. Kenneth S. Stern, *A Force Upon the Plain: The American Militia Movement and the Politics of Hate.* New York: Simon and Schuster, 1996.

9. Jonathan Karl, *The Right to Bear Arms: The Rise of America's New Militia.* New York: Harper, 1995.

10. Southern Poverty Law Center, "Two Years After: the Patriot Movement Since Oklahoma City," *Intelligence Report,* Spring, 1997, pp. 18–20; John Solomon, "FBI Chided for Oklahoma Bomb Investigation," Associated Press, December 25, 2006.

11. Jack Levin, "Visit to a Patriot Potluck." *USA Today,* March 1, 1997, p. 6A; Jack Levin, *Domestic Terrorism.* Philadelphia: Chelsea Books, 2006.

12. Thomas Halpern and Brian Levin, *The Limits of Dissent: The Constitutional Status of Armed Civilian Militias.* Amherst, MA: Aletheia Press, 1996.

13. Karl, op. cit.; Levin, 1997, op. cit.

14. Heidi Beirich and Bob Moser, "From Push to Shove," *Violence and Terrorism: Annual Editions,* op. cit.

15. Gallup Organization, www.gallup.com, December 2001–January 2002.

16. Gallup Organization, www.gallup.com, February 2001.

12 Cult Killings

In popular culture, almost any bizarre or esoteric group one can imagine has been considered a cult. In this broad view, tens of millions of Americans have been involved for varying periods of time in one cult or another, whether organized around neo-Christian religious beliefs, Hindu and Eastern religion, the occult, witchcraft or Satanism, Zen and other Sino-Japanese philosophical or mystical orientations, race, psychotherapy, politics, or self-improvement. Even broader in scope, the term *cult-like following* has been applied to include the inspired fans of certain rock groups, rap artists, movies, and sports teams, as well as the zealous followers of exercise or diet regimens. Similarly, referring to the cult-like characteristics of a group stretches the scope of inquiry to encompass almost any group—a gang, a fraternity, even a business enterprise—to which members are "slavishly devoted."[1]

In this chapter, we have adopted a more limited view of what constitutes a cult, defining it as a loosely structured and unconventional form of religious group, whose members are held together by a charismatic leader who mobilizes their loyalty around some new religious cause. Typically this cause is at odds with that of more conventional religious institutions. Using this definition, almost any new religious group that hasn't yet become institutionalized or widely accepted—whether benign or dangerous—could be regarded as a cult. From this perspective, then, early Christianity during Roman times was a cult; but so were the Branch Davidians who in 1993 perished in the flames of Waco orchestrated by their leader David Koresh. Our definition would, at the same time, exclude from consideration here a wide range of groups that might have a strong influence on their members, but are essentially secular rather than religious in their objectives.

As a force for social change, the cults or new religious groups of one generation may represent the conventional religious institutions and traditions of another. For example, the Church of Jesus Christ of Latter-day Saints (aka the Mormons) began in 1830 as a small cult in an upstate New York village but now numbers more than 10 million church members around the world. Similarly, recently established cultural ideas and practices such as gender equality on the job, shelters for victims of domestic violence, and healthier diets all began as heretical or pioneering cult concepts (in this case, from the Oneidas, the Holy Order of MANS, and the Seventh-Day-Adventists, respectively).

Dangerous Cults

Of course, many people nowadays restrict the use of the term *cult* to refer only to new religious groups that they regard as destructive or dangerous. And there are many cults that give anticultists plenty of reason to despise them. Some cult members recruit in a deceptive way—they might, for example, lure unsuspecting students by promising them a party or a get-together at some out-of-the-way retreat while they fail to inform the students of their true intent—which is to convert them; other cults are said to use methods of mind control or thought reform. And many groups regarded as cults require their members to become totally dependent on some authoritarian group leader who claims to have a special knowledge, gift, or talent. In extreme cases, the recruit is no longer allowed to make any important personal decisions of his or her own and must give up all relationships with old friends and family. The cult becomes a total and tyrannical institution.

Cult specialist Margaret Singer defines dangerous cults in terms of characteristics of its leaders, its leader–follower relationships, and its programs of persuasion. Based on these dimensions, she suggests that cults exhibit the following characteristics: 1) authoritarian leaders who claim a special mission and/or knowledge; 2) a charismatic, dominant leadership style; 3) leaders' claims to total allegiance; 4) claims to an innovative and exclusive answer to individual and societal problems; 5) an "ends justifies the means" logic that justifies manipulation of outsiders; 6) totalistic ideological and behavioral control over members; and 7) a major transformation of lifestyle.[2]

Most traditional religious organizations don't have a pressing need to use such tactics; established Christian churches may, for example, recruit, but they can also depend on the process of socialization to attract new members—generation after generation of parents who teach their children the religious traditions they were taught at home. The last thing desired by conventional religious groups, in most cases, is to separate family members from one another—they are the most effective recruiters.

But new religious groups typically don't have the luxury of being able to count on their beliefs and rituals being passed from parents to children in their congregations—not unless, of course, they are successful enough to stick around for more than one generation. And most of them don't. So it's either recruit from the ranks of the nonbelievers, or perish as a religious group. As a result, the pressure for deception and unethical tactics of persuasion (also known as brain washing) can become fierce. In addition, the extreme dependency often found among cultists can force members of a cult to abandon their relationships outside—relationships that might otherwise reduce their loyalty to their fellow cultists, to their cause, and to their charismatic leader as well. So, there may be considerable pressure to give up old friends and reduce contact with family members. There are powerful forces within the cult to conform, comply, go along with the program. At the extreme, such forces have occasionally been harvested by a deranged but convincing father-figure who seeks to persuade his flock to follow him like sheep into practicing human sacrifice or committing murder.

It should be noted that the all-encompassing popular culture definition of cults, while too broad for our purposes, also makes an important point. Even though gangs, fraternities, and exercise groups are not cults, their appeal may depend in part on certain of their cultish features—for example, their ability to isolate new members from former friends and relatives and an authoritarian decision-making structure.

Writing about the success of the Microsoft Corporation, reporter Bob Weinstein compared Microsoft with the Branch Davidians:[3]

> Both organizations are cults. No joke. The only difference is one is religious (Davidians), while the other (Microsoft) is corporate. . . . Both are classified as cults because the members

of these organizations are cut off from the real world and are obsessed with achieving the mission of their leaders. . . . Just as religious cults revolve around the lofty mission of their leaders, work cults center around the rules, regulations, and culture of the organization.

Thus, even a major U.S. corporation can have cult-like characteristics. Indeed, the ability of a company to secure the unwavering loyalty of its workforce to corporate goals and leadership may help determine its long-term viability in the marketplace. Microsoft is certainly no cult, applying the narrow definition of the term. It is not a religious organization, nor does it seek to eliminate relationships of workers with old friends and relatives. But Microsoft, just like many other successful corporations, can draw a lesson or two from the operation of those groups in society that have established themselves firmly as the cults in our midst.

The Appeal of Cults

Cults seem to become more attractive to the members of society during periods of rapid social change, at times when individuals are feeling a lack of structure and belongingness in their lives. Such new religious groups reflect tensions in society that make many citizens receptive to ideas originating outside of the conventional culture. In the second quarter of the nineteenth century, for example, as new technologies began having an impact throughout U.S. society, there was a dramatic upsurge in evangelical and communal organizations. During the tumultuous 1960s, as social and cultural change quickened its pace, cult activity once again swept across the country. These were periods during which the credibility of traditional institutions suffered, and that is typical.

The rise of marginal groups such as cults also has at least something to do with the calendar. At the end of every century (not to mention every millennium), organized groups emerge to prophesize the end of the world. This millennial myth can be traced back to ancient Biblical writings that predict that a cosmic cataclysm orchestrated by God will destroy the ruling powers of evil and raise the righteous to a new existence in a messianic kingdom lasting 1,000 years. This is the prophesied millennium.[4]

But not all contemporary millennialists sit back and wait for God to destroy the old system and usher in the new. Their vision of apocalypse goes far beyond any vision of a spiritual New Age metamorphosis. For some of these new apocalyptic thinkers, increasing income inequality since 1970 is the result not of abstract forces such as global competition and automation, but of active behind-the-scenes covert manipulation by human beings with a purpose—international bankers, the United Nations, the federal reserve system, and one-world-order types who benefit at the expense of the average American. Their notion of apocalypse is just as active and just as physical—all-out-war, nothing more, and nothing less.

Some apocalyptic thinkers have given death a helping hand. In April 1999, 39 members of the Heaven's Gate cult committed mass suicide in their rented mansion in Rancho Santa Fe near San Diego. Marshall Applewhite, the cult's leader, had convinced his followers—20 women and 19 men ranging in age from 26 to 72—that a spaceship traveling behind the Hail Bopp comet was coming to pick them all up soon after they had shed their vehicles or containers (also known as bodies). They were totally convinced that civilization on Earth was about to end, but that they could enter a higher life form by getting rid of their bodies and boarding a spaceship to travel to what they called the next level. So they took lethal doses of poison after having positioned themselves in a ritualistic way. Each was dressed in black pants, dark socks, and new Nike sneakers; each was covered by a purple sheet that was neatly folded to resemble a diamond. When the bodies were found, each had a five dollar bill and several quarters in his or her pockets. Applewhite had also demanded that his male followers castrate themselves, and they had all complied.

Not only did the Heaven's Gate suicide victims represent both genders and a wide range of ages, but they also consisted of blacks, Latinos, and whites who had come from all over the country—from New Mexico, California, Texas, Utah, Colorado, Florida, Minnesota, Washington, Ohio, Massachusetts, Arizona, Missouri, Iowa, Wisconsin, New York, Idaho, and Nebraska. And these were not stupid or uneducated people. They were computer-skilled, musically talented, and scholarly—but they were also needy, lonely, and depressed. Many had abandoned their families and friends months or years earlier and were completely on their own.

The Heaven's Gate cultists were hardly the first to commit mass suicide by poison. Over a 15-month period, beginning in October 1994, the bodies of 69 members of the Order of the Solar Temple were discovered in Switzerland, Canada, and France. Most of the charred bodies had been ritualistically positioned in a star formation and burned, with their feet facing the ashes of a campfire. Several handwritten notes found in homes and meeting places used by the cult suggested mass suicide. In one letter, the doomsday cultists explained that they were "leaving this Earth to find a new dimension of truth and absolution, far from the hypocrisies of this world." However, it was determined upon closer inspection that most of the members of the Solar Temple had died methodically planned deaths—by shooting, poisoning, stabbing, or asphyxiation. Even if all of the adult members had consented to be killed, it would be hard to argue that the many children (as young as age 2) were anything more than murder victims. Incredibly, many of the Solar Temple cultists who died were wealthy, well-educated, and respected members of their communities—architects, nurses, and celebrated police officers—who were philanthropic, owned expensive property, or were regarded as intellectuals.

Charismatic Leaders and Their Followers

The body counts amassed by Heaven's Gate and the Solar Temple cultists are bad enough, yet they pale by comparison with the November 1978, mass suicide in Jonestown, Guyana, in which 913 Americans, all members of the People's Temple, perished. The complete domination of the People's Temple leader, 47-year-old Jim Jones, had a great deal to do with the effectiveness of the mass suicide. He had brought his followers from the United States to their new home in an isolated area in the jungle, thousands of miles from the influence of family or friends. Jonestown was located literally in the middle of nowhere.

Indeed, the one and only reality for the followers of Jim Jones was the power of Jones himself, whose charismatic sermons and rantings and ravings were the means by which he exercised control. Jones was convinced that the FBI and the CIA were closing in on him and his flock. He decided to take everyone to a better life in the hereafter.

It is relatively easy to explain why a reportedly psychotic individual like Jim Jones might turn his paranoia and delusional thinking into destructive behavior. It is more difficult to understand how apparently normal, intelligent people can buy into a philosophy promising that they would achieve a better life in the hereafter or even that human sacrifice would miraculously protect them from harm. As illogical and immoral as such beliefs may seem, however, many people could be made to accept these promises given the right set of circumstances.

According to social psychologist Philip Zimbardo, Jones may have acquired his ability to persuade from the classic novel by George Orwell entitled *1984,* in which a courageous individual attempts to resist the institutionalized techniques of mind control employed by government in order to control the masses.[5] Not unlike the procedures of thought reform described by Orwell in his fictional futuristic account, Jones assured the loyalty of his followers by demanding that they spy on one another and by keeping his presence in public consciousness through the messages he broadcast 24 hours daily over powerful loudspeakers. In both the novel and in Jonestown, "big brother" was constantly watching over the activities of community members.

In Orwell's novel, ordinary citizens were urged to kill themselves rather than to give up to the enemy who threatened to wage war on their society. The hundreds of Jonestown cultists were similarly persuaded that suicide would be a far better fate than to be killed by federal officials. Thus, the members of Jonestown were rehearsed in the collective suicide procedure whereby they would take their turn to willingly drink a lethal dose of cyanide-laced Kool Aid. Men, women, and children stood in long lines, awaiting with faith and confidence their chance to sip the Kool Aid and die with their comrades. But those who resisted and tried to escape were instead shot to death by Jones' armed guard. Others knew they had no realistic options, and died taking the path of least resistance. During the mass suicide he had orchestrated, and knowing the end was near anyway, Jim Jones raised a pistol to his head and fired a single bullet through his brain.

Abnormal situations can make normal people do "crazy" things, especially if they perceive a strong self-serving purpose in doing so, such as profit, power, or protection. On April 12, 1989, the Mexican police unearthed a mass grave containing 15 victims of ritualistic human sacrifice—including many Americans—on an isolated ranch some 20 miles west of Matamoros, Mexico, just south of the Texas border. Within 24 hours, police had arrested four young men and sought several others, all members of a major drug ring, who allegedly were involved in the killings.

The police identified the spiritual ringleader of the drug smuggling cult as Adolfo de Jesus Constanzo, a 26-year-old native of Cuba. His loyal followers called their charismatic leader "El Padrino"—the Godfather. Because of his spellbinding influence over his devotees, Constanzo allegedly was able to convince them that their drug activities could never be touched by the law so long as they obeyed his command to, among other things, kill for survival. His band of drug smugglers practiced Palo Mayombe. This black-magic derivative of Santeria ("the way of the Saints"), a Caribbean voodoo belief, was blended with both Satanism and Bruja, a form of witchcraft practiced by sixteenth-century Aztecs. Human and animal sacrifice was thought by the group to bring them immunity from bullets and criminal prosecution while they illegally transported 2,000 pounds of marijuana per week from Mexico into the United States.

Just as the disciplines of Jim Jones and Marshall Applewhite seemed within the range of psychological normality, the followers of Constanzo were hardly the crazed lunatics that many people associate with ritualistic slaughter and human sacrifice. Most of the cult members grew up in relatively affluent families and did not have histories of violence. Believed to be the high priestess or witch of the operation, for example, 24-year-old Sara Maria Aldrete Villareal was an honor student at Texas Southmost College, where she was listed in the college's "Who's Who" directory.

In a sense, Constanzo was the "Hitler" of his cult. Adolf Hitler, as a charismatic leader, had transformed ordinary German citizens into brutal SS (*Schutzstaffel*) killers through constant marches, all-day group singing of the Party's anthem, and required cheering. Hitler capitalized on the promise of turning around Germany's terrible economy to help convince his followers of the urgency of his grand plan. Constanzo similarly capitalized on a powerful economic incentive, as well as on group pressure in order to foster obedience to his command. Like Hitler's marches and chants, Constanzo involved his followers in the elaborate and mysterious rituals—animal sacrifices and demonic incantations—in order to achieve in his flock selfless devotion to the cause. Over time, they came to believe that they had been privy to a secret wisdom revealed only to their leader's disciples.

Constanzo's final command was to perform a death ritual—this time his own death. Several of his followers obediently shot Constanzo to death as police authorities closed in on them in Mexico City. Apparently, the practice of Palo Mayombe couldn't really protect Constanzo from bullets, nor could it immunize Aldrete and other cult members from prosecution for murder.

Part of the influence of a dangerous cult rests with the ability of its leader to convince his followers of his supreme, perhaps supernatural, wisdom. A veneer of religious doctrine and ritual is often employed in order to reinforce and encourage dedication to the cause, regardless of how deadly it may be. In many cases, the leader himself is convinced of his otherworldly talents. He sees himself as all-powerful, as possessing the ability to conquer all enemies.

Thirty-nine-year-old Jeffrey Don Lundgren of Kirkland, Ohio, was determined to do God's work. Having broken from a branch of Mormonism, the Reorganized Church of Jesus Christ of Latter-day Saints, Lundgren was certain that the Creator was sending messages to him directly. It was his sacred duty, then, to carry out God's Will, no matter how distasteful or violent. After all, God's commandments transcend human laws.

Lundgren preached that the armies of Satan were about to strike. To save themselves, he and his flock would have to give up their worldly possessions (donating them to his Church), and come together to live off the land until such time that Christ returned. In the meantime, there would be no electricity or shelter. And his followers would have to protect the temple by whatever means possible. For this purpose, Lundgren purchased semiautomatic rifles and handguns, along with tents, camping supplies, food, and hundreds of rounds of ammunition.

Early in April 1989, Lundgren had a vision in which God suggested that the enemy had already infiltrated his camp and must be eliminated. His victims were Dennis Avery and his family, followers who had given all of their worldly possessions to the divine cause but who also remained somewhat skeptical of the cult leader's legitimacy. On occasion, Dennis Avery had challenged Lundgren's divine authority.

On the evening of April 17, the self-appointed prophet led the members of the Avery family, one by one, into a red barn behind his farmhouse. Lundgren and five of his men had dug a deep pit in the barn's dirt floor. Each victim—Dennis, his wife Cheryl, and their three young daughters—was walked from the farmhouse to the barn, where their hands and legs were bound with duct tape. Then, Lundgren repeatedly shot his victims with hollow-point slugs from a .45 semiautomatic and threw their lifeless bodies into the pit.

On September 21, 1990, Lundgren's trial for first-degree murder came to a conclusion, when he was sentenced to die. Hearing the judge's decision, he told his attorney that everything was going according to God's plan, that his death sentence was predetermined. On October 24, 2006, Jeffrey Lundgren was executed at the Southern Ohio Correctional Facility.

Needs Fulfilled by Cults

Cults have historically had much drawing power with alienated youth. Teenagers who join satanic cults often suffer from mood disorders (e.g., depression and bipolar disorder), post-traumatic stress disorder, and personality disorders (including antisocial personality disorder).[6] Moreover, cults have a long history of recruiting lonely college students. Away from home for the first time and trying to make friends and fit in, they may be particularly vulnerable to psychological manipulation. Colleges across the United States have banned from campus some of the more extreme religious groups known to prey on students (e.g., the International Churches of Christ and their sister group, HOPE Worldwide, University Bible fellowship, Hare Krishnas, and the Boston Church of Christ). Like many of the hate groups discussed in Chapter 10, cults often hide behind a facade of Christianity. Other life stressors—a divorce or break-up, job loss or deterioration in mental health—may all act as risk factors for the charismatic lure of a cult. Like serial killers, cult killers prey on the vulnerable. Although 14-year-old Elizabeth Smart of Salt Lake City was not killed, she fell under the spell of a crazed, cult-like husband and wife who were masters of religious persuasion. There now exists a new hunting ground for cults—the Internet. A perusal of virtually any chat room finds the cult-recruiters proselytizing via instant messages.

Adolescence is a stage of development frequently marked by a profound sense of marginality and powerlessness. Teenagers are neither children nor adults; they are expected, at the same time, to remain submissive to the demands of the older generation and to achieve some sense of independence. For a youngster troubled in his search for belonging and personal meaning, a group that promises to provide both friendship and a sense of importance can be extremely attractive. As a result, cults organized around themes of vampirism and Satanism may be particularly appealing to teenagers who feel thwarted in their quest for power and who are dissatisfied with their conventional peer relations.

In November 1996, a group of youngsters from in and around Murray, Kentucky, all members of a self-described Vampire Clan, traveled to Eustis, Florida, and the home of Richard and Ruth Wendorf, where they bludgeoned the couple to death with a crowbar. The victims were the parents of one of the murderous cult disciples—a 15-year-old girl who claimed to have been a demon in past lives. Along with her four fellow cultists, she fled the bloody scene in her parents' 1994 Ford Explorer, inside of which police later found a credit card belonging to the dead couple, a blood-drenched sheet, and books on ancient spells and vampirism.

The youthful members of the cult all believed they were vampires who possessed supernatural powers and who communicated with spirits while engaging in rituals in which they drank their own blood and that of mutilated animals. According to the 17-year-old leader of the cult, Rod Ferrell, as he gave his confession in court, slaying the Wendorfs was a necessary act that would "open the gates to Hell."

As vulnerable to cult influence as adolescents may be, alienation and marginality are hardly peculiar to the teenage years. Individuals from all age groups may be persuaded to commit even the most evil acts if they are also convinced of the righteousness of their cause. Those cults whose members are intensely hostile to conventional institutions have a potential for espousing and practicing violence.

According to Lifton, this potential for violent behavior has recently taken a much more dangerous turn for the worse.[7] In fact, weapons of mass destruction in the hands of apocalyptic, paranoid cults pose a new—perhaps unprecedented—form of danger for citizens of countries around the world.

The doomsday cult known as Aum Shinrikyo (Supreme Truth) is a case in point. In March 1995, its members killed 12 people and injured 5,500 more in a sarin nerve-gas attack in the Tokyo subway system. The cultists left packets of frozen sarin on the trains, timing their assault so that the nerve-gas thawed just in time to poison the rush-hour commuters.

Orchestrated by its 41-year-old charismatic leader Shoko Asahara, the subway mass murder was part of a vastly larger plot designed to overthrow the Japanese government, establish a kingdom ruled by Asahara, and then ultimately to initiate a worldwide nuclear disaster that only he and his disciples would survive. Along the way, the cultists had committed murder and kidnapping, had smuggled in firearms, and had produced the Nazi-era nerve gas. Their deadly subway attack was designed to divert the attention of the police from an imminent raid on the cult's headquarters in the village of Kamikuishiki near the foot of Mt. Fuji. By the time they perpetrated the subway assault, the cultists were already under suspicion in a wave of violent acts including the murder of a local lawyer and his family, the kidnapping and killing of a notary public, the explosion of a letter bomb in City Hall, and the shooting of the Chief of Police. Their ultimate objective was world annihilation.

Yet many talented and wealthy people were attracted to the cause of Supreme Truth, including physicians and scientists who sincerely believed that Asahara possessed supernatural powers. In total, there were more than 9,000 members of Aum Shinrikyo including 500 who lived in centers around Japan, many of whom donated their entire life savings and personal property to the cult. They were attracted by Asahara's Hindu and yogic teachings and powerful presence and were convinced by his promise to develop their supernatural talents.

First of all, distraught or troubled people have an amazing capacity to rationalize their dangerous behavior. They don't need Satanism or Vampirism or even Heaven's Gate or Jim Jones, although such influences make a difference. At the same time, troubled people can take the most benign, even honorable idea, and twist it into something hideous and evil.

In 1992, for example, five middle-class suburban New Jersey high school students murdered one of their classmates for kicks. The five youngsters ranged from 14 to 18 years of age; one was an altar boy and an Eagle Scout; another was a high school dropout who worshiped the Mafia. The victim, Robert Solimone, Jr., was a perpetual outsider, a young man with a reputation around school as nothing more than a nerd. Then, one night, the victim sat with his buddies in the front seat of a car parked next to their high school. Everybody in the car convinced him to recite Hail Marys and then suddenly, without warning, he was taken from behind and strangled to death with an extension cord. These youngsters had used religious ideas to give their evil deeds an aura of morality. They never constituted a cult in any formal sense, but they practiced a perverted version of mainstream religion that permitted them to commit murder with moral impunity.

As in the murder of Robert Solimone, it is sometimes difficult to conclude that violence is a consequence of participating in a cult. Both cult membership and homicidal (or suicidal) behavior may be a result of another set of factors—personality and mood disorders, sociopathy, and so on. So when cult membership and homicidal behavior occur in the same people, one of the factors is not necessarily a cause of the other.

Normal People in Abnormal Situations

It is all too easy to regard all cultists as crazy or naive. As we have seen, the truth is that normal but vulnerable individuals can do abnormal, even insidious things. In August 1969, a number of young people under the guidance and direction of Charles Manson brutally murdered seven people in Beverly Hills. Manson was a charismatic leader who convinced his followers of his great power. If Manson had killed alone, it would have been understandable; he had grown up in the most horrific circumstances imaginable and had spent most of his life behind bars.

But his followers represented something else. Members of the so-called Manson family sincerely believed that Manson was Jesus Christ. Most of the Manson family members were white and middle-class. Many were well educated; in high school, one had been voted most likely to succeed. Another had a master's degree in social work. You see, Manson's followers were given a cause—they really believed that through the race war they hoped to precipitate that they would assume the leadership of the country. This objective more than justified their staying together.

In fact, being part of the family and serving its cause were seen by the Manson cultists as the ultimate solution to all of their problems. The Manson followers were as active as Manson himself in committing murder. None of them had been brainwashed into joining the family. Each was attracted to Manson by the promise of becoming a very important, extremely special person who was destined to make a mark on the world.

At various times in their lives, many people can fall into vulnerable states—they may be lonely, hurting, having a hard time socially, having academic problems, or feeling overwhelmed or confused. During such temporary periods of misery and loss—for whatever reason—another person can have a great deal of influence—especially another person who promises to point the way out of misery. Vulnerable people tend to be especially suggestible when they are flattered, deceived, lured, enticed, or are feeling very needy.

Under such conditions, many people are more suggestible, more malleable, and more likely to be deceived. After all, when people are miserable, they are looking to change. Conformity and obedience become powerful forces under such conditions.

Psychologist Stanley Milgram long ago demonstrated that ordinary people from a broad range of occupations and social classes, both men and women, are willing to administer a severe—even lethal—electrical shock to a stranger, simply because they have been told to do so by an authoritative leader.[8] We shouldn't be surprised that vulnerable people are especially responsive to the demands of an authority figure—someone who is treated by fellow cultists as possessing special—perhaps even supernatural—knowledge, powers, or talents.

Once an individual joins a group, there are strong pressures to conform to its norms. Few people want to be left out, to be rejected by one's peers, to look different in a negative way. Numerous psychological studies have shown that many otherwise healthy and normal individuals will give an incorrect answer to a simple and obvious question after observing other people give an incorrect response—not because they are confused but because they don't want to look different, even if it means being wrong.[9]

A classic study launched in 1971 by psychologist Philip Zimbardo and his associates at Stanford University may help shed additional light on the phenomenon of normal people doing abnormal, even horrific, things in order to fit in and belong to a group.[10] Zimbardo and his colleagues turned the basement of a building on campus into a mock prison. They created a number of cells by installing bars and locks on each room and then placing a cot in each one. Twenty student volunteers, all chosen for their mature and stable personalities, were selected to participate in the study. On a purely random basis (the flip of a coin), half of the students were assigned to play the role of guards and the other half were assigned to play the role of prisoners.

The experiment actually started at the homes of the 10 student prisoners. To increase the realism of the study, all of them were arrested, put in handcuffs, read their rights, and then driven to "jail" in police cars. They were then completely stripped, sprayed with disinfectants, issued prison uniforms, and placed into locked cells.

Everyone knew that the experiment was artificial and that it was supposed to end in two weeks. Nobody was really a prisoner; nobody was really a guard. It was make-believe; the roles decided purely by chance. Yet after only a few days, both the prisoners and the guards were playing their roles to the hilt.

Guards were told only to keep order. Instead, they began to humiliate and embarrass the prisoners, coercing them to remain silent on command, to sing or laugh in front of the other inmates, and to clean up messes made by the guards. In some cases, the guards verbally and physically threatened and intimidated the prisoners, apparently for the purpose of asserting their authority.

The prisoners became more and more passive and compliant. In accord with the roles to which they had been assigned, the prisoners obeyed orders and accepted commands, no matter how unreasonable. They began to feel totally powerless to fight back. After only six days, four of the prisoners had to be excused from the study, having suffered serious episodes of anxiety, anger, or depression. In fact, the entire experiment was ended in less than a week when it became clear that the guards had become abusive and the prisoners were emotionally at risk.

Interviews conducted after the experiment ended were revealing. Both the prisoners and the guards told Zimbardo and his associates that they were both shocked and ashamed at how they had behaved. None of them would have predicted that they were capable of such cruelty, in the case of the guards, or obedience to authority, in the case of the prisoners.

Remember that all of the student volunteers had been selected for their mature and stable personalities. Yet they all acted according to the roles created by the structure of prison life.

Zimbardo's prison experiment indicates the incredible power of situational factors to influence normal individuals, whatever their psychological makeup, to mistreat other human beings or to obey the cruelest sort of authority. The hopeful implication of Zimbardo's findings is that it is easier to change situations than to change individual predispositions. We can often structure the experiences of society's members in such a way that blind conformity to unhealthy norms of behavior is minimized.

Yet in most live-in cults, just about every detail of everyday life comes under the scrutiny of the group. In many, there are dress codes, restrictions on what the members can eat and drink, and enforced marriages and relationships. Most of the members work for cult-owned businesses. Of course, there are also cults whose members seem to belong on only a part-time basis. For example, they might work outside of the cult. But even when the control of a cult seems less than total, members are often restricted in terms of their friendships, what happens to the money they earn, where they are permitted to live, and whether they are allowed to raise their own children.

Because society romanticizes the teenage years, it may not be obvious that there are probably numerous students who are miserable enough to want to make profound changes in their lives. They hope to feel a sense of power and control; they want very much to be accepted, to have a sense of belonging. Some will lower their level of aspiration; others will change their goals to those that do not require an advanced degree; still others will find a source of satisfaction outside of their jobs, school, or family. A few who cannot adjust and remain miserable in their quest for acceptance and success may even choose an illegal alternative. Others will continue ritualistically to go through the motions of getting an education without knowing why.

Once a student is motivated to accept an alternative approach, however, instructors, advisors, friends, clergy, family members, resident assistants, and counselors have a special opportunity to become agents of change. This is when they ought to intervene to provide structure and support and, in some cases, to avert disaster. Students need inspired mentors and role models. Instead, they may seek peer counseling and involvement and perhaps an alternative point of view. Some will look for tutoring and advice. Others will want support and encouragement. If they find what they need, they may become productive, happy citizens. If not, they may remain miserable, whether or not they join some dangerous cult.

Suicide or Homicide?

Because of the tremendous influence of cult leadership, there can be a fine line between mass homicide and mass suicide. At the very least, the ritualized act of self-destruction of the Heaven's Gate cultists, for example, was encouraged by their charismatic leader. It is reasonable to speculate that most, if not all, of the 39 Heaven's Gate victims would still be alive today, if they hadn't met up with Marshall Applewhite. The same probably applies to members of the Solar Temple. Out of loyalty to their spiritual mentor and to one another, cultists are especially vulnerable to commandments for self-destruction. The last thing they want is to be rejected by their deified leader and their cherished fellow cultists. The strong group processes in a cult—conformity, suggestion, obedience to authority—make it all but impossible for dedicated cultists to defy the collective will of the group and ignore an order, even if it means dying for the cause. This was apparently true of the Heaven's Gate victims.

Suicide bombers in the Middle East have been similarly encouraged to take their own lives. In some extremist Islamic groups, martyrdom is taught as a technique for furthering their religious and political agenda. Dedicated members are urged to strap on an explosive device and become a human bomb, killing as many civilians as possible. Recruits are typically young men and women who have been taught that self-sacrifice in the struggle against the infidels will assure them a place of honor on earth as well as in the hereafter. To encourage suicide, the photographs of bombers are placed on a wall of honor, in the way that the pictures of sports heroes and entertainment celebrities are featured in the Western world. They receive the respect and admiration of the people who mean the most to them—their fellow cultists. Much of the same logic seems to motivate the suicidal attacks perpetrated by a terrorist cult known as al Qaeda. On September 11, 2001, this religious and political group perpetrated the most deadly incident of mass murder in American history, killing some 3,000 people at the World Trade Center in New York City, the Pentagon in Washington, D.C., and a crash-site in rural Pennsylvania.

If we claim that people under duress should not be held to the same level of responsibility for their criminal behavior, then people who have fallen under the "spell" of a tyrannical cult leader can be regarded as incapable of making a decision about taking their own lives. The abduction of 14-year-old Elizabeth Smart by a self-styled cultist and his wife has provided a recent illustration of this point. Smart was snatched from her bed in the middle of the night and held captive for more than a year, during which time she may have had, but didn't take, opportunities to escape her kidnappers. In a sense, she was a "prisoner of war" whose very survival depended on the mercy of her captors. Her life was constantly threatened, as were the lives of her family members. Fear was a powerful motivator. It eventually forced Smart to believe that her abductors had absolute control over her fate and the fate of her loved ones.

Basing his notion of cultic persuasion on the experiences of prisoners of war, Lifton has identified a number of characteristics of a thought reform (aka brainwashing) environment: 1) milieu control, which involves control over all communication and information, to prevent doubt about the omnipotence of the group from arising; 2) mystical manipulation, which involves a claim of higher authority that morally elevates the group's ends, justifies its practices, and undermines the individual independence of its members; 3) demand for purity, which involves a black-and-white worldview that allows leaders to control members through inculcation of guilt; 4) sacred science, which involves defining group ideology as ultimate truth and inhibits individuality of members; 5) loading the language, which involves use of insider jargon that constricts members' capacity for independent thought and feeling; 6) doctrine over persons, which involves denial of any self and reality that is independent of the group; and 7) dispensing of existence, which involves degrading outsiders and creating an us-versus-them mentality.[11]

Lifton's list of persuasive techniques and beliefs operates only to the extent that a recruit is virtually a prisoner whose total environment has been modified and controlled by his cult membership. In most cases of cultic influence, by contrast, it is pure myth to suggest the image of a totally passive recruit who lacks any power to resist while under the spell of a madman. Some social scientists have argued instead that cult recruits possess an element of free will that can only be manipulated so much.[12] They regard affiliation with cultists as fundamentally voluntaristic. Some even refer to the groups not as cults, but as "new religious movements," because they do not conclude that the group structure of recruitment processes undermine individual autonomy and voluntarism.[13]

As suggested by Bromley and Shupe, moreover, what appears to be extreme behavior may not actually represent a personal transformation but rather conformity to expected role behavior.[14] Even extremely vulnerable individuals possess an active self—they are typically not brainwashed into misbehaving, but comply willingly to the requirements imposed on their membership. From this viewpoint, there is a definite limit to the power of a charismatic leader to mold or shape the behavior and beliefs of his disciples. Most cult leaders are not in the category of a Jim Jones or Marshall Applewhite, even if they are extremely persuasive. When they do harm to others, cult followers are therefore responsible for their criminal behavior.

ENDNOTES

1. Nicole Biggart, *Charismatic Capitalism.* Chicago: University of Chicago Press, 1989.

2. Margaret Singer, *Cults in Our Midst.* San Francisco: Jossey-Bass, 1995.

3. Bob Weinstein, "Be Wary of the 'Corporate Cult,'" *Newsday,* March 5, 2000, p. 12B.

4. Philip Lamy, *Millennium Rage.* New York: Plenum Press, 1996.

5. Melissa Dittmann, "Lessons from Jonestown," *Monitor on Psychology* 34, no. 10 (November 2003), p. 36.

6. Margaret Singer and Richard Ofshe, "Thought Reform Programs and the Production of Psychiatric Casualties." *Psychiatric Annals* 20 (1990): 188–193.

7. Robert Jay Lifton, *Destroying the World to Save It.* New York: Metropolitan Books, 1999.

8. Stanley Milgram, "Behavioral Study of Obedience," *Journal of Abnormal and Social Psychology* 66 (1963): 371–378.

9. Solomon Asch, "Effects of Group Pressures upon the Modification and Distortion of Judgement," in George Swanson, Theodore Newcomb, and E. Hartley, eds., *Readings in Social Psychology.* New York: Holt, Rinehart and Winston, 1952.

10. Philip C. Zimbardo, Craig Haney, and William C. Banks, "A Pirandellian Prison," *New York Times Magazine* April 8, 1973, p. 7.

11. Robert Jay Lifton, *Thought Reform and the Psychology of Totalism.* Chapel Hill, NC: University of North Carolina Press, 1989.

12. James D. Tabor and Eugene Gallagher, *Why Waco?* Berkeley, CA: University of California Press, 1995.

13. Eileen Barker, *The Making of a Moonie.* Oxford: Blackwell Press, 1984.

14. David Bromley and Anson Shupe, "Affiliation and Disaffiliation: A Role Theory Approach to Joining and Leaving New Religious Movements," *Thought: A Review of Culture and Ideas* 61 (1986): 197–211.

CHAPTER

13 Catching Killers

If one were to judge solely from television crime dramas like *Law and Order, CSI: Crime Scene Investigation*, and *Crossing Jordan*, crime doesn't pay. Almost without exception, TV criminals, and murderers in particular, are identified, arrested, and convicted, all in under an hour (unless it's a "two-parter," of course). Although these shows may frequently feature real stories that are "ripped from the headlines," the lesson that virtually no one gets away with murder is obviously more than a slight exaggeration. After all, this is television-land, and the good guys usually prevail.

Hollywood distortion aside, the idea that murderers are typically apprehended is actually not so out of line with the facts. Of the seven so-called "index offenses" that comprise the FBI's collection of serious crimes, homicide has the highest clearance rate—that is, the percentage of offenses known to the police that are cleared or solved by law enforcement authorities. As shown in Figure 13.1, violent crimes (murder, forcible rape, robbery, and aggravated assault) have clearance rates that exceed those of the three property offenses (burglary, larceny-theft, and motor vehicle theft), and murder ranks at the top of the clearance rate list. In 2004, over three out of five homicides reported to the police were cleared by an arrest or some other exceptional means (e.g., suspect flees the country or commits suicide).

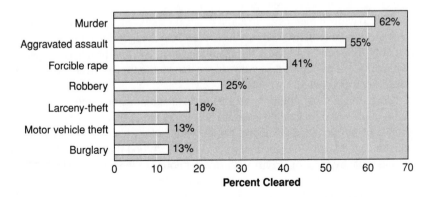

FIGURE 13.1   Offense Clearance Rates, 2005

Science of the Lambs

The greater success that police enjoy in working murder cases may at first appear a bit surprising. After all, the victim isn't able to identify the perpetrator in a police line-up or describe to the detectives exactly what transpired leading up to the attack. Yet, the victim—or at least the corpse—does "speak" in a sense through the wealth of forensic clues left under fingernails, on the skin, or within vital organs, all available to lab experts and medical examiners to exploit in their investigation. Indeed, it is the uniquely violent nature of the homicidal act that tends to produce a large volume of physical evidence for forensic specialists. In addition, many homicides are preceded by a sequence of events—an argument, a challenge, a business dispute, marital infidelity—that often allow the police to identify the perpetrator.

The work of forensics units begins as soon as the homicide (or suspicious death or disappearance) is discovered. The first officer to arrive at the location protects the crime scene, cordoning the area off in yellow police tape and keeping it free of intruders (including other police personnel) until a systematic search and record can be constructed. Photographs and videotapes of the area are taken as soon as possible so that the body can then be sent for an autopsy before certain transient evidence (e.g., stomach contents) becomes compromised.

One of the first objectives for the medical examiner or coroner is to determine the time of death—a window of time when the murder would have occurred that helps ultimately to assess which possible subjects could or could not have had contact with the victim during this time frame. A rough estimate of time of death can be derived from the body temperature. A dead body cools at a rate that can be modeled mathematically, factoring in climate and atmospheric conditions. This process yields an interval of hours when death would likely have occurred. In addition to body temperature, the presence of rigor mortis (stiffness in the muscle tissues) can help narrow down time estimates. Rigor first appears in the small muscles of the hands and jaw within two to four hours, progresses to larger muscle groups within four to six hours, and becomes fully developed in about 12 hours. This stiffness then begins to taper off as the body starts decomposing.

Victims discovered after several days, if not longer, pose greater challenges. For forensic entomologists, the human corpse is viewed as a welcoming host for insect ecosystems or life-cycles that are governed by predictable time patterns. A variety of flies are attracted quickly to moist areas of a cadaver (e.g., open wounds, mouths, nostrils, and eyes) as a place to deposit their eggs. In about a day, the eggs hatch into maggots and begin feeding off the human remains. During this process, the maggots shed their casings (pupae) and eventually transform into flies. By examining the type and progress of insect infestation and the presence of pupae, the entomologist can assess time of death and possibly location (if the body was moved).

Just as critical, if not more so, the medical examiner attempts to isolate the cause of death—to discern if, in fact, the case is a homicide, rather than an accident or a suicide. The presence of lividity (or livor mortis) often yields clues about the final moments prior to death. Once the heart stops functioning to circulate blood throughout the body, blood cells pool and settle by force of gravity to the lowest points of the body as it rests against the floor or other objects. A purplish discoloration of the skin at the low points sets in within thirty minutes and becomes fixed in about eight hours. Furthermore, the shade of discoloration can help to indicate cause of death. For example, carbon monoxide poisoning results in a cherry-red hue to the skin affected by livor mortis. On the other hand, death resulting from heart failure or asphyxia causes a particularly deep purple tinge. In addition, if lividity is at all visible upon discovery of the corpse (that is, if the discoloration of the skin is not face down), then the body would have to have been moved or turned following death. Examination of the skin also reveals much about the assault. The extent of bruising around injuries can suggest whether they were inflicted pre- or post-mortem, because bruising can only occur while the heart is pumping blood to the affected area. Also, some bruising takes time to appear, and therefore may only become evident after the victim is dead.

The medical examiner routinely performs toxicological tests to identify poisonings and drug overdoses. Inspection of knife wounds, blunt trauma, lacerations on bones and organs, as well as gunshot wounds all offer clues, not just to cause of death, but often the exact nature and size of the weapon and possibly the stature and approach of the assailant. Also, the examiner relies on a range of circumstantial evidence, such as the kind of ligature used and the absence or presence of a note, to distinguish a suicidal hanging from an auto-erotic asphyxiation fatality (accidental death while inducing suffocation to enhance sexual arousal). Similarly, a psychological autopsy of an apparent victim of sexual homicide may be needed to rule out an accidental death as the victim was staging his or her sexual bondage fantasy.

In attempting to establish cause of death, recent medical advances help coroners discern purposeful acts of infanticide (e.g., shaken baby, or suffocation) from crib death or accidental falls. Until recently, medical professionals were easily fooled by deceitful parents and caretakers who attempted to cover up a baby murder by claiming SIDS (Sudden Infant Death Syndrome). Still today, it is not always possible to distinguish at autopsy between SIDS and accidental or deliberate asphyxiation with a soft object without circumstantial evidence that the infant had been intentionally victimized.

One telltale sign of possible criminal intent is when an episode of SIDS is preceded by one or more similar cases in the same family or in the charge of the same caretaker. At an astonishing extreme, as described in Chapter 4, Marybeth Tinning of Schenectady, New York, killed nine of her own children, not all at once in a murderous fit, but one at a time, over the course of more than a decade, in a deliberate and selfish maneuver to win attention and sympathy. Even though suspicions mounted following each infant fatality, it was not until the death of her ninth child, a healthy four-month-old baby girl named Tami Lynne, in December 1985 that Marybeth's pathetic crime spree was fully exposed. With improved methods for distinguishing SIDS from induced asphyxiation, it was determined through a careful autopsy that Tami Lynne had not died of natural causes, but instead had been suffocated. Despite the fact that implicating evidence from earlier deaths had long since been buried, there was enough direct and circumstantial evidence to charge and convict Marybeth with murder. In 1987, she was sentenced to prison for 20 years to life.

Bodies that are not discovered for weeks, or even longer, pose additional problems for forensics specialists to determine time and cause of death, as well as the identity of the victim. A body left exposed to the elements starts the long process of decomposition or putrefaction. After death, bacteria begin to escape from the gastrointestinal tract, specifically the bowel, compromising the entire vascular system. The body swells from internal gasses and the skin discolors. Putrefaction distorts facial features and fingerprints, often complicating identification of the deceased.

Depending on atmospheric conditions, the corpse will experience additional kinds of transformation. If lying in a damp area, a greasy soap-like substance—known as *adipocere*—will form on the skin as body fats go through chemical changes. In especially dry and airy conditions, however, the corpse will mummify rather than decompose as the skin darkens and hardens to a leathery texture.

Corpses undiscovered for longer time spans, particularly when exposed to carnivorous animals, eventually dissolve to skeletal remains. Even then, certain markers can be used to identify the victim. A forensic anthropologist can not only discern whether bones are human in origin, but also the age, race, and sex of the victim. The size, development, and wear of bones indicate certain age ranges. Additionally, race can often be classified based on the shape of the skull. Furthermore, through the process of "elaboration," the shape of the skull can also be used to project an image of what the victim may have looked like and can often hint at the geographical area of the victim or his/her ancestry. Gender may be evident from the structure of hip, pubic, and other bone structures. If all else fails, of course, teeth are often the sole means of identifying victims through comparison with dental records (usually by examining cavity fillings, dental work, etc.). These and other means of victim identification (including DNA as described below) may only provide an answer to the victim's identity, yet say little about who the perpetrator was.

DNA (deoxyribonucleic acid), the genetic basis for all inherited traits, has undoubtedly been the single greatest advance for law enforcement in solving cases and bringing criminals to justice. There is a unique DNA blueprint for everyone, except identical twins, that can be extracted from samples of human cells in saliva, skin, sweat, bone, and follicles of hair, but especially blood and semen. DNA typing can be used, therefore, not only to implicate a suspect, but also to exclude someone whose DNA does not match that found in crime scene evidence.

DNA molecules contain a genetic code, consisting of a lengthy sequence of four letters—A, T, C, and G, representing the four nuclear types (adenine, thymine, cytosine, and guanine). The letters occur in pairs—A is always associated with T, and C with G, and the pairs are arranged along a spiral-shaped structure known as the double helix.

A genetic code or "genetic fingerprint" present in DNA can be determined from small amounts of bodily tissue or fluid. Enzymes are used to cut the DNA into fragments or segments of the genetic code. These segments are separated and sorted by a lab process to form a pattern that looks like a grocery store bar code used for scanning prices. Currently, DNA analysis is of two types. The older method, RFLP (restriction fragment length polymorphisms), requires large amounts of genetic material to establish a clear-cut DNA code, and works poorly on partially degraded samples. For example, seminal fluid extracted from a victim's rectal canal is often genetically compromised by fecal bacteria. Its forensic value would be akin to a partial fingerprint. A newer approach, PCR (polymerase chain reaction), requires far less genetic material, as available samples can be replicated as needed. This approach still is sensitive to contamination of sample at the crime scene or even in handling at the lab.

Finally, genetic samples come in two types: nuclear and mitochondrial DNA. The former, from the nucleus of human cells, provides the unique genetic code, but cannot be extracted from certain human matter, such as hair. Mitochondrial DNA, from the surface of human cells, may not be unique but is rarely duplicated in large samples of individuals.

The probative value of a DNA match is unparalleled, especially in the opinions of jurors who give great weight to its scientific authority. Of course, this has also meant that scores of falsely convicted defendants have been freed upon retesting old crime scene evidence with new technology. The ability to identify genetically an unknown killer through DNA left at the murder scene does not, of course, guarantee that the donor will be identifiable from available records and DNA databanks. Launched in 1990, the FBI has maintained a computerized DNA database, known as CODIS (Combined DNA Index System). With all states submitting information to the national DNA index system, as of December 2006, genetic profiles of nearly four million convicted offenders were included in the database. Nearly all states have passed legislation permitting DNA data storage associated with convicted murderers and sex offenders; some states have broadened the guidelines to include other violent felons and even nonviolent criminals. Although expanding rapidly in scope, the database is far from complete in covering the entire offender population, not to mention those who have never been previously convicted of a crime.

Despite the singular value of DNA typing and matching, there remains a danger to civil liberties that will play out in years to come. The appellate courts will need to deliberate on constitutionally acceptable methods for using this compelling evidence. Investigating the murders of five women between 2001 and 2003, for example, the Baton Rouge police performed a rather controversial DNA dragnet in an attempt to locate the unknown serial killer. Hundreds of potential suspects were asked "voluntarily" to allow a swab to be taken from the inner cheek for the purpose of comparison with DNA recovered at the crime scenes. They were advised of their right to decline, of course, but also were informed that such refusal would result not only in a court order for the sample but public notification of their failure to cooperate. In addition, even after Derrick Todd Lee was arrested and charged with the crimes, at least one innocent subject sued the police in attempt to have his DNA returned rather than have it saved in the state police DNA data bank.[1]

While the scientific theory underlying DNA is unimpeachable and the methods of extracting genetic material from limited trace evidence is improving every year, the testing process is still performed by human beings who are not exactly infallible. Overburdened labs, poorly trained technicians, as well as mistakes in maintaining the integrity of DNA samples and record-keeping, have unfortunately resulted in more than a few erroneous results, from mislabeling of samples in Kansas to falsified records at a Florida lab. Errors and false reporting uncovered in 2003 at the overloaded and understaffed Houston crime lab were so bad that several employees were suspended or terminated and hundreds of tests were ordered to be redone.

More recently, the Massachusetts State Crime Lab was rocked by scandal when it was revealed that an experienced DNA examiner, besides maintaining shoddy records, had falsified DNA results leading to the conviction of numerous defendants. Not only did this necessitate retesting of evidence and retrials of defendants, but it places into question the extent to which juries can trustfully rely on such scientific evidence.

Another face of emerging technology involves data banks of weapon identifiers, rather than of those who use them. For more than a decade, for example, the Bureau of Alcohol, Tobacco and Firearms (ATF) has developed a gun tracing initiative in which firearms recovered in the process of criminal investigations can be traced through manufacturer, distributor and dealer records back to the first point of retail sale. Of course, what may have happened to the firearm after reaching the street (such as private resale or transfer through theft) is beyond the scope of the gun tracing program.

Representing another avenue of firearms examination, so-called "ballistics fingerprinting" is predicated on the fact that every gun is unique in the inner surface of its barrel, arising from the particular tool marks left during the manufacturing process as well as imperfections in the metals used. As a result, microscopic examination of fired bullet casings can potentially link not just two spent casings to each other as in traditional ballistic work, but shell casings to an exemplar from the gun coded into a data base shortly after production. The objective then is to maintain data bases of weapons sold, with serial numbers and other identifying information, for comparison with ongoing recoveries of ballistic evidence. Unfortunately, there is some question concerning the reliability and utility of the initiative, leaving aside issues of cost and data base availability. Some critics, for example, argue that offenders can alter the gun barrel or even that a certain degree of change in barrel surface occurs with each firing of a gun.

A more novel approach to investigating gun crimes involves acoustic sensors that can alert police departments within seconds of a gunshot and pinpoint the location of the incident. Presumably a speedy police response would then increase the possibility of apprehending the shooter or even save a gunshot victim with swift medical treatment. As of early 2007, more than a dozen cities across the U.S., including Washington, D.C., Chicago, and Oakland, have invested in this technology with some promising, though preliminary, results regarding rates of gun violence and arrest.

Clearance Rates

Despite the rapid improvement in forensic techniques, the success rate in clearing homicide cases has dropped in recent years, a trend that has put law enforcement under a certain degree of scrutiny from politicians and the media alike. As shown in Figure 13.2, whereas in the mid-1970s, four out of five homicides were solved, this rate dropped steadily through the mid-1990s and into this century, reaching its current low point at 62.6 percent.

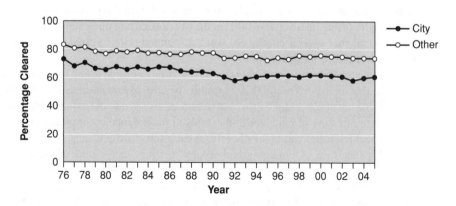

FIGURE 13.2   Homicide Clearance Rates by Location Type, 1976–2005

Some observers have questioned whether police personnel are doing a poorer job today or if they are just overwhelmed by a rising case load. The slippage in clearance, however, has much more to do with the changing nature of the case load, not the sheer number. As discussed in Chapters 4 and 5, there have been dramatic shifts in the pattern of homicide during the past quarter century—specifically, fewer spousal homicides and more murders involving younger assailants as well as strangers. Within the mix of cases that detectives must confront each year, there are simply fewer easy cases and more challenging ones.

While surely there are exceptions, spousal murders are frequently solved as soon as the perpetrator himself or herself calls the police to report the incident and often times to surrender. Or, if there is any attempt to escape justice, typically a telltale pattern of precipitants points directly to the current or former spouse or lover—a history of abuse or recent conflicts that friends and neighbors report. There may be a recent affair or a newly secured life insurance policy that gives the police all they need to determine the motive and thus the suspect.

When 27-year-old Laci Peterson of Modesto, California, eight months pregnant with her first child, disappeared on Christmas Eve, 2002, many of these same suspicious factors prompted the police, as well as a fascinated nation, to look squarely at her husband, Scott, as the prime suspect. The 30-year-old fertilizer salesman had been romantically involved with an attractive blonde massage therapist from whom he had concealed his marriage. In addition, Peterson had recently purchased a $250,000 life insurance policy on his wife, and was away alone on an all-day Christmas Eve fishing trip, without an alibi witness, when his pregnant wife reportedly vanished. Each of these implicating factors in isolation could be explained away as innocent; after all, many men have extramarital affairs without resorting to murder, and many decide to upgrade their insurance policies right before the birth of a child. But the confluence of these and other circumstantial factors was just too much for law enforcement authorities to ignore. Even without a "smoking gun," Scott Peterson was arrested in April 2003 and charged with double homicide as soon as DNA testing on the remains of a woman and a baby that had washed ashore in San Francisco Bay, not far from the location of his Christmas Eve fishing jaunt, were positively identified as Laci and her son Conner. A year later, in a closely watched and widely publicized murder trial, Peterson was convicted of first-degree murder in the deaths of his wife and unborn son.

At the other extreme, murders committed by strangers frequently have no clear-cut motive. If there are no witnesses to the attack, the pool of potential subjects of an investigation can be hopelessly endless. In addition, the gang-related and drug-related crimes among youthful offenders and victims, the kind that surged in the early 1990s, were shrouded within a code of silence. Although there may have been many accomplices and witnesses who knew exactly the one responsible for a drive-by shooting or a "sending a message" execution-style slaying, no one was talking to the police. Moreover, the notion that snitches would be dealt with tended to limit the cooperation that the police could expect.

Not only are the old and infirm particularly vulnerable to the malicious and self-serving misdeeds of murderous caretakers, as described in Chapter 8, but medical murders and hospital homicides pose special problems in terms of detection of foul play, suspect identification, and collection of probative evidence. Death among the elderly and terminal patients is more the norm than the exception, and so suspicions are slow to surface. Moreover, should an unusually high volume of deaths occur in a particular ward or on a particular shift, hospital administrators—charged with managing not just the well-being of patients but the financial health of the institution—are in a quandary. They may be reluctant to blow the whistle prematurely and without sufficient cause, not so much out of concern for a staff member whom they might suspect is up to no good, but out of fear of a lawsuit against the facility for negligence or just reluctance to stir up doubts surrounding the management of the hospital or clinic. Furthermore, when there is sufficient cause for an investigation, the physical evidence may be long buried, requiring the delicate task of seeking family permission for exhumation without any certainty that a criminal act had occurred. In addition, some of the remains may have been cremated and along with them any evidence of poisoning.

One particular class of offenders, featured in Chapter 7, which has challenged the skills of homicide detectives, is the serial killer. It is not that these murderers are particularly intelligent—as suggested by the fictional characters like Hannibal Lecter in *Silence of the Lambs* or Patrick Bateman in *American Psycho*. It is more a certain degree of cunning—cleverness and carefulness—rather than brilliance, that distinguishes these repeat and often prolific murderers from the rest.

A long-standing myth, commonplace in popular films and mystery novels, holds that serial murderers, at least at some level, wish to get caught. According to this view, serial killers—even the most sociopathic—actually do have a conscience strong enough to affect their behavior; they subconsciously leave clues to their crimes in order to get punished for their transgressions against humanity. This popular theme dates back years, at least to the 1946 case of William Heirens, the so-called Lipstick Killer, who scrawled a message for the Chicago police on the apartment wall of one of his victims, "For Heaven's sake, catch me before I kill more. I cannot control myself."

Unlike Heirens, most serial killers do everything they can to avoid getting caught. They are clever and careful—when it comes to murder they are fiercely resourceful. They methodically stalk their victims for the best opportunity to strike so as not to be seen, and they smartly dump the bodies far away so as not to leave any clues. The cool and calculating manner in which many sociopaths cover their tracks arises out of the fearlessness that characterizes this personality type. They respond unemotionally and without panic to the prospect of capture, undeterred by the risk of apprehension. A self-selection process—a survival of the fiercest—operates to separate the cool-headed men from the hot-tempered boys. If sexual predators like Jeffrey Dahmer or Theodore Bundy were not so good at killing and covering their trails, they would never have remained on the streets long enough to qualify as serial killers.

Murders committed by a serial killer, at least the methodical ones, are typically difficult to solve because of lack of an instrumental motive and useful evidence. Unlike the usual homicide that involves an offender and victim who know one another, sexually motivated serial murders are almost exclusively committed by strangers. Thus, the usual police strategy of identifying suspects—boyfriends, neighbors, or co-workers—by examining their possible motive, be it jealousy, revenge or greed, generally helps very little. With no such clear-cut motive, there are no immediate suspects.

In Gainesville, Florida, for example, a large task force investigating the murders of five college students in August 1990 had a wealth of crime-scene evidence for the lab to analyze, including pubic hairs and semen. For months, the task force operated a "pubes and tubes" strategy, collecting hair and blood samples from hundreds of "donors," just about anyone who possibly could have had a connection to the crime. But when seeking a stranger who had no prior relationship to the victims, this hunt for a killer was like searching for a needle in a haystack. The high-profile character of the Gainesville murders, furthermore, made for a particularly huge haystack of "suspects," as well-intentioned citizens from around the country phoned in the names of unscrupulous or sleazy people they thought might be involved.

While the Gainesville investigation team was fortunate to have plenty of clues—perhaps more than they needed, other serial murder investigations have very little evidence of a tangible nature to go on. The more successful serial killers transport their victims from the scene of the murder to a remote dumpsite or makeshift grave. The police may never locate the body and thus never determine that a homicide has occurred. Even if the bodies of the victims do eventually turn up at a dump site, most of the potentially revealing forensic evidence remains in the killer's house or car where the victim was slain; but without a suspect, the police do not know its location. Moreover, any trace evidence, such as semen within the vagina and skin beneath the fingernails, left on the discarded body tends to erode as the corpse is exposed to rain, wind, heat, and snow.

In 1988, for example, the police in New Bedford, Massachusetts, were stymied by a profound lack of physical evidence in their hunt for a killer of at least nine prostitutes and drug users. The unidentified predator had abducted his victims from the crime-ridden Weld Square area of town and discarded their remains along highways in southeastern Massachusetts. By the time the decomposed bodies were finally discovered, the police had enough trouble identifying the skeletal remains, much less the killer. After 15 years, this case remains unsolved; with the trail growing colder with each passing year, it will likely remain unresolved permanently.

In Gainesville and New Bedford, like many other serial murder sites, the police had little difficulty detecting the work of a serial killer from an alarming increase in similarly patterned murders or disappearances. Despite the fact that the police, alerted to a serial murder operating in the area, may heighten levels of surveillance, the killer may continue to tempt fate, believing arrogantly that he can outsmart the police. He persists in killing close to home or his workplace, staying within his comfort zone, knowing where he best can find and dump his victims as well as the best escape routes to avoid detection.

Many other serial killers, however, are able to obfuscate the serial pattern underlying their attacks by spacing them over time and distance. They can kill and dump one victim in Ohio, and then be in Indiana stalking the next victim by the time the police uncover any evidence of the previous murder. With the murderous carnage distributed far and wide, law enforcement, by virtue of its decentralized nature, may never discern the wide-ranging work of a single murderer. Even if the killings are consistent in style (similar victim type or method of killing), so-called linkage blindness becomes a significant barrier to solving serial homicides.[2]

VICAP and Profiling

To aid in the detection of serial murder cases—and specifically to address the linkage blindness problem, the FBI's Behavioral Sciences Unit in 1985 launched its Violent Criminal Apprehension Program (VICAP). VICAP is a computerized database for the collection and collation of information pertaining to unsolved homicides around the country. It is designed to flag similarities in unsolved homicides that might otherwise be obscured.[3]

VICAP was used successfully, for example, in identifying unsolved homicides linked to Rafael Resendez-Ramirez, the "FBI's Ten Most Wanted" fugitive who in 1999 traveled state-to-state by train committing robbery-murders along his route. Once it was determined that two Texas cases were linked to the same serial offender, the VICAP database was searched for similar incidents in other jurisdictions, leading analysts to a two-year-old Kentucky case that was eventually tied to the "railway killer" by DNA tests.

While an excellent idea in theory, VICAP has encountered significant practical limitations over the past two decades. According to former VICAP manager Gregory M. Cooper, "[the system is] potentially a very effective tool . . . as in any database, it's only as good as the amount of information in it."[4] Because of complexities in the lengthy and detailed data collection forms, cooperation from local law enforcement in completing VICAP questionnaires has been far less than satisfactory. Only three states—Alaska, New York, and New Jersey—mandate that police submit unsolved murder cases; overall, only about five hundred of seventeen thousand local law enforcement agencies participate in the VICAP initiative.

In addition to the missing data problem, pattern recognition is not as easy or straightforward as some may believe, regardless of how powerful the computer or sophisticated the software. Serial killers often vary their targets or method of killing, sometimes just to experiment with new approaches or even purposely to throw off the authorities. Because of these factors and despite a healthy dose of funding from the U.S. Congress, VICAP has failed to reach its potential. For example, of the twenty murders and assaults associated with the 2002 shooting spree committed by John Allen Muhammad and Lee Boyd Malvo—attacks in Washington, Arizona, Louisiana, Georgia, Alabama, Maryland, Virginia, and the District of Columbia—none was linked to the crime spree by VICAP.

The VICAP model rests on the assumption that offenders follow a specific pattern or signature—consistency in victim type, sexual rituals, style of killing, and so on—and that this can be discerned from a preset list of categories describing the victim, offender, and crime scene. Case similarities, however, cannot necessarily be adequately reduced to a set of questionnaire-type items.

During the 1990 investigation of the five grisly slayings in Gainesville, the task force was forced to look out of state for help in solving a murder case that dragged on for months without any of a large pool of potential subjects successfully tied to the crime scene through lab tests of blood and hairs. The critical lead eventually came from eight hundred miles away when a Shreveport, Louisiana, detective alerted the task force to a potentially related triple murder that occurred almost a year earlier. On November 4, 1989, 55-year-old Tom Grissom, his 24-year-old daughter Julie and her 8-year-old nephew Sean were found bound and stabbed to death. Julie Grissom, a college student, had been raped and her body posed in a sexually provocative manner, possibly for shock value. Her body was washed with vinegar, and the killer had apparently spent considerable time cleaning the crime scene of potential evidence.

Many experienced investigators inside and outside of the task force discounted this lead, focusing on certain dissimilarities. To them the cases were as different as day and night, literally: the Grissom murders in Shreveport had occurred in the late afternoon, unlike the early morning hours of the Gainesville attacks. Also, the Grissom murders did not reveal anything close to the level of brutality found in the mutilation and decapitation of the Gainesville victims.

Based on visual comparison of the crime scene photos, however, the Grissom murders appeared like they very well could have been committed by the same assailant as the Gainesville slaughters. The task force was impressed with the similarities—the use of duct tape to control the victims, cleansing of victims following sexual penetration, attempts to destroy evidence, similar provocative posing of bodies. As it happened, it was this link that directed the task force to consider 36-year-old Danny Rolling, hometown Shreveport, who was jailed in Ocala, Florida, on a robbery charge.

Needing more than just a Shreveport address to elevate Rolling to a high priority suspect, the task force sought physical specimens to compare with evidence recovered from the Gainesville crime scenes. Because Rolling was in custody, however, rules pertaining to search and seizure prohibited him from consenting to investigators' requests for blood and hair samples. By virtue of the coercion implicit by their confinement, jail and prison inmates cannot consent to searches. Further complicating matters was that the Shreveport address was insufficient to convince a judge to issue a warrant for a body search. By a stroke of good fortune, however, Rolling needed to have an impacted wisdom tooth removed by the dentist. The bloody tooth, once discarded as trash, was no longer Rolling's possession and could be submitted to the lab for DNA testing, an analysis that ultimately implicated Rolling as the Gainesville murderer.

Despite the problems encountered by the VICAP initiative, computers are clearly an indispensable tool in managing homicide investigations. Large-scale investigative task forces rely on them for information storage and retrieval. In a case that drags on for weeks or months, particularly when there are multiple victims and multiple crime scenes, the volume of information is unmanageable without the use of technology. This is especially true in high profile cases when the public is encouraged (often with promise of reward) to call information into a tip line.

The annals of law enforcement reveal many instances in which a large-scale investigation failed because certain key pieces of information were difficult to access, lost, or not relayed to the appropriate detectives. In recent years, software for indexing investigative data (including witness statements, tips, and field reports) was created and now allows detectives to query a database to link, for example, forensic analysis of tire tracks with a witness's statement about observing a truck leave the scene of a crime.

Of course, the computer is really only doing what police ordinarily do—tracking down leads and comparing information—but at lightning fast speed. Recent advances in information database matching and artificial intelligence have assisted law enforcement in drawing critical clues from seemingly disparate and incomplete sources. Designed by an Arizona-based software firm, a program called Coplink, for example, searches and matches arrest records, emergency calls to 9-1-1, motor vehicle registration files, and other existing databases to help police track down information in a timely fashion. Coplink was installed late in the DC sniper investigation, in fact on the very day when the police closed in on the two suspects in their blue Chevrolet Caprice at a rest stop off Route 95. Using a query about any person or vehicle identified within an hour of the shooting sites, Coplink flagged the fact that the same blue Caprice was stopped by police in multiple post-shooting roadblocks.

In addition to the VICAP clearinghouse, the FBI provides technical assistance to local law enforcement in attempting to solve open cases of suspected serial murder and other extraordinary crimes. Upon request, the FBI assembles an investigative profile of the unknown killer based on psychological clues left at crime scenes, autopsy reports, and police incident reports. Typically, these profiles speculate on the killer's age, race, sex, marital status, employment status, sexual competence, possible criminal record, relationship to the victim, and likelihood of committing future crimes.

At the core of its profiling strategy, the FBI distinguishes between "organized nonsocial" and "disorganized asocial." Based on an FBI study of 36 killers, 25 serial and 11 nonserial, typically the organized killer is intelligent, is socially and sexually competent, is of high birth order, is a skilled worker, lives with a partner, is mobile, drives a late model car, and follows his crimes in the media. In contrasting tendency, the disorganized killer is unintelligent, is socially and sexually inadequate, is of low birth order, is an unskilled worker, lives alone, is not particularly mobile, drives an old car or no car at all, and has minimal interest in the news reports of his crimes.[5]

According to FBI analysis, these two types tend to differ in terms of crime scene characteristics. Specifically, the organized killer uses restraints on his victims, hides or transports the body, removes the weapon from the scene, molests the victim prior to death, and is methodical in his style of killing. In contrast, the disorganized killer tends not to use restraints, leaves the body in full view, leaves a weapon at the scene, molests the victim after death, and is spontaneous in his manner of killing. The task of profiling involves, therefore, drawing inferences from the crime scene as to what the behavioral characteristics of the killer are.

The profiles are intended as a tool to focus on a range of suspects rather than to point precisely to a particular suspect. Even in meeting this limited objective, the profiles are not always successful. In Baton Rouge, months after the police had linked several murders to a serial killer, the task force released details of an FBI profile of the unknown assailant. The profile described the killer as a strong, 25- to 35-year-old man who would be awkward in interacting with attractive women. The task force also speculated that the killer would be white or Hispanic because of the race pattern in his victim selection. Derrick Todd Lee, a muscular 34-year-old, was eventually arrested for the crimes. Friends and neighbors described him as "disarmingly charming" and "easy to get along with." And, Lee is black.

The FBI's Unabomber profile, which guided the investigation of a series of bombings during the 1980s and 1990s, suggested that the perpetrator was in his mid-30s or early 40s, was a blue-collar worker with possibly some college education, and had resided in or around Chicago and later San Francisco. When Theodore Kaczynski was eventually captured, he was in his 50s, held a doctorate degree, and lived as a hermit in Montana.

Profiling is more an imprecise craft than an exact science. Behavioral inferences from the crime scene cannot be made with substantial reliability. An FBI reliability study revealed a 74 percent agreement rate in classifying crime scenes as organized or disorganized.[6] While this may seem impressive on the surface, it is actually deficient in view of the base rate of organized killers in the sample. Of 64 crime scenes classified in the FBI reliability study, 31 were organized and 21 disorganized, while nine were mixed and three indeterminable. Thus, the 74 percent agreement rate is not much better than a fixed "organized" response.

More to the point, the profiles have a very low rate of success in leading to the identity of a killer.[7] Thus, while psychological profiles work wonderfully in fiction, they are much less than a panacea in real life, even when constructed by the most experienced and skillful profilers like those at the FBI unit. Nevertheless, profiles are not designed to solve a case but simply to provide an additional set of clues in cases found by local police to be unsolvable. Moreover, one should not expect a high success rate in any event; only the most difficult and "unsolvable" cases ever reach the attention of the FBI unit.

It is critical, therefore, that we maintain some perspective on the investigative value of psychological profiles. Simply put, a psychological profile cannot identify a suspect for investigation nor can it eliminate a suspect who doesn't fit "the mold." Rather, a profile can assist in assigning subjective probabilities to suspects whose names surface through more usual investigative strategies (e.g., interviews of witnesses, canvassing of neighborhoods, and "tip" phone lines).

The craft of profiling came squarely under the spotlight during the fall of 2002 when full attention of the print and electronic media was focused on the DC area snipings. While all media outlets monitored the unsolved case, the cable networks in particular covered the case virtually around the clock, examining every possible angle in excruciating detail. Each network had their team of experts—criminologists, psychologists, former law enforcement personnel, and so on—to speculate, pontificate, and interpret each new wrinkle of the unfolding real-life murder mystery.

Among the many topics examined on-air was what kind of person could carry out the deadly assaults and so successfully evade the police. Unlike the usual process of profiling in which a wide variety of information is examined (crime scene photos, autopsy reports, investigative reports, etc.), for the TV profilers there was very little on which to base their speculations. The on-air profilers were not privy to much of the actual evidence that the task force kept under wraps; yet there were certain statistical patterns among sniper cases that generally helped to shape their speculations. While each of the analysts had their own unique perspective, there were some strong commonalities among their assessments. According to the experts, the shooter was likely a middle-aged, white male, possibly with a military background, and likely a loner. With no connection to the victims, targeted only because they happened to be at the wrong place at the wrong time, the sniper was likely expressing a grudge against all of society.

When the sniper case was finally solved, the media had a field day in scoring and second-guessing the accuracy of the very hunches they had solicited. While many features of the statistical profile were accurate, one glaring error was scrutinized. Not only were there two snipers, not one, but they were black, not white.

Some critics even suggested that the task force and the public at large were misled by the speculations of TV commentators.[8] "The important question is, was the orgy of speculation harmless—or was there a very dangerous undercurrent to it?" asked *Washington Post* reporters Paul Farhi and Linton Weeks following the suspects' arrest. "By saturating the public's consciousness with phantom images of thirty-something white men, did the media profilers distract attention from a more general and possibly open-minded search for the perpetrators? . . . If so, the media's performance raises a chilling possibility: that the suspects might have evaded detection for so long because witnesses were focusing too intently on media-created 'profiles' that didn't come close to the real thing."[9]

At no time, of course, did the profilers rule out the possibility of the killer(s) being black. In fact, one analysis of statistical patterns published in the *New York Times* noted that even though a majority of snipers are white (55 percent), as many as 43 percent are black.[10] Thus, statistically it was more likely that the sniper was white than black, but hardly a certainty. More importantly, there is no evidence whatsoever that the task force focused only on white suspects or that the public in any way patterned their daily lives to avoid white men. If anything, it was the white van theory, not the white man theory, that slowed and sidetracked the hunt for the DC sniper.

For weeks the police had alerted the public to a white van driven by the sniper, even distributing and posting on the Internet composite sketches of a white panel truck. Given the power of suggestion, eyewitnesses to subsequent sniper strikes reported seeing a white van speeding away following the attacks. Of course, there are so many such vehicles on the road that it is hard not to see one in any finite span of time. Plus, the mind can easily be tricked by preconceptions and prejudices—in the moonlight, gray, tan, yellow, and beige can all appear white when expecting to see white.

The FBI no longer prefers the term "profiling" to identify their serial offender tracking positions. The Bureau has had to contend with the negative connotation associated with racial profiling (for example, getting pulled over by the police because of "driving while black"), Hollywood's distortion of the job of a profiler (e.g., in *The Silence of the Lambs*) and perhaps most importantly with the fact that an analyst cannot offer expert testimony in court as a profiler. Agents can, however, offer expert testimony regarding crime scene staging; hence, the new moniker—Criminal Investigative Analysts (CIA)—who identify the personality and behavioral elements of the individual killer by looking at the crime scene. More often than not, elements of the crime scene are present in a killer's lifestyle (soliciting prostitutes, patronizing gay bars, etc.).

Also, contrary to some media portrayals of profilers/CIA, they typically work as a team, not as individuals. To build a profile, their analysis will include a visit to crime scenes (or photographs since, at the actual crime scene, law enforcement may not recognize the work of a serial killer), autopsy and crime lab results, investigative interviews and reports, descriptions and maps of the area around the killing, items taken by the killer, and dump sites. Adding to the tools that can be used by the crime scene analysts are fairly recent geographic profiling techniques that can identify a killer's home base by the addresses of the crimes.

Sightings and Visions

The fallibility of eyewitnesses has been the subject of much research. Seeing may mean believing for the eyewitness, but one must always take the accuracy of these observations with a healthy grain of salt. In an emotional state of panic, expectations and prejudices about what criminals look like can color perceptions. The mind tends to fill in missing information using whatever is available—what others at a crime scene report (collective recollections), what the police suggest through their questions, what the papers publish, and so on.

As an experiment of the effect of external validation on eyewitness confidence, Luius and Wells asked a group of subjects who had witnessed a staged theft to identify the perpetrator in a photo line-up.[11] After their identification, some of the eyewitnesses were told that another witness to the crime had picked out the same perpetrator; some were told that another witness had identified a different individual; and some were told nothing about the other witness. As expected, the degree of confidence that subjects claimed to have about their line-up identification was greatly impacted by the positive, negative or neutral feedback they received. More surprising is that those subjects whose confidence in their ability to identify the thief was enhanced or diminished by learning about another's recollection maintained their position even after being told that the information about the second eyewitness was incorrect because of a recording error. That is, their belief in what they saw conditioned in part by external validation or invalidation persisted even after learning that the validation was itself groundless.

At times, the technique of hypnosis has been used in an attempt to improve memory and recall, particularly when a traumatic experience of witnessing a crime may have compelled the mind to repress memory. But while hypnosis may be able to uncover recollections shrouded in pain, it cannot improve the lighting, line of sight, or even remove prejudice and bias in stored images.

While the therapeutic uses of hypnosis are well documented and widely accepted, forensic applications are much more controversial. Research on hypnosis indicates that the so-called "hypnotic trance" is little more than accepting the suggestions of a highly credible source. More important is that hypnosis increases the level of confidence but not accuracy in recalling events. For example, under hypnosis, witnesses to a crime involving a masked gunman have been asked to mentally remove the criminal's disguise and describe his face. Filling in the details on their own, these hypnotized subjects become convinced about the description they give. It may be a figment of their imagination, but one of which they are absolutely sure. In the same way, psychologists studying hypnosis have compared age regression with age progression. After first taking their subjects back several years in life to recall events at that time, they then take them forward into the future and ask them to describe what they are doing. Subjects tend to recollect the future in as much detail and certainty as they recall the past.

While the use of hypnosis to enhance memories of eyewitnesses, victims, and even perpetrators remains controversial, so does the use of psychic visions in homicide investigations. Rarely do investigators like to admit seeking or relying on the input of psychics, but in more than a few instances their input has been valuable.

Perhaps owing to the high profile nature of the case, the Gainesville student murder task force received more than a few tips from self-professed psychics, most of which were delegated with great skepticism to the lowest priority level. Early on in the investigation, the police received a call from a resident of Harrisburg, Pennsylvania, who claimed that she had had a powerful premonition, prompted by a television report of the crimes, that the killer's name was "Rollings." It wasn't until months later, when Danny Rolling catapulted to the top of the suspect list because of a DNA match between his blood and semen at the crime scenes that the investigators, tracking back through their computerized records for any mention of the suspect name, took note of this lead.

"I literally jumped up and said I know who it is," recalled Sharon Carroll, a 45-year-old office manager. "I really don't think they believed me." Carroll was later investigated for any possible connection to the murders. But no alternative explanation for her uncanny accuracy was ever found.

The Gainesville case notwithstanding, the investigative value of psychic visions is more the material for fictional accounts (as in Patricia Arquette's character in the TV series *Medium*), than reality. A number of self-styled crime psychics have made exaggerated, if not outlandish, claims of being able to locate missing bodies or help solve major crimes. Yet upon close scrutiny, many of their correct insights about various crimes appear to be a retro-fit of vague psychic clues to actual details.[12]

Working a Homicide in the Media Spotlight

As noted early on in Chapter 1, homicide cases receive an inordinate amount of attention in the mass media, especially so when a killer, possibly "armed and dangerous," remains at large. Growth and competition in the news industry has caused media saturation of certain breaking or continuing crime stories. At the extreme, during the nearly month-long investigation of the DC area sniper case in October 2002, the task force headquarters in Montgomery County, Maryland, became a makeshift media village. Virtually every major news organization was in residence, equipped with satellite trucks, tents, and power generators, as well as reporters and technicians, ready to go "live" with each new development in the case.

The task force, headed by Chief Charles A. Moose, obliged the information-hungry reporters and an anxious public with routine news conferences about the progress of the sniper manhunt. Not only was this relationship between the media and the investigation extraordinary in its closeness, but it marked a significant break for the usual guarded interactions between police and journalists.

Much of the time, exchanges between law enforcement handling a high profile case and the media attempting to respond to public fear or fascination are strained, if not distrustful. The police typically attempt to control the spread of information, especially certain details of the crime that are withheld for the purpose of validating confessions or interrogations of suspects. Seeking an advantage in covering a major story, reporters have been known to cultivate and even bribe inside sources in order to scoop the competition, although these scoops often turn out to be lacking in accuracy. The much maligned police investigation into the death of five-year-old JonBenet Ramsey, found on the morning after Christmas, 1996, in the basement of her Boulder, Colorado, home suffered significantly from constant pressure of politics and publicity. As Colorado and national media speculated endlessly about the case, and especially the role of her parents John and Patsy Ramsey, the local authorities had great difficulty managing the investigation under the constant media spotlight.

The tremendous pressure on the authorities to identify and capture JonBenet's killer, combined with the continuing and intense media focus on the decade-old unsolved case, created a "perfect storm" for some obscure false confessor to seize the limelight and enjoy his 15 days of fame. In 2006, John Mark Karr, 41, became a household name and suspect of the fortnight by professing his love for the slain girl and confessing his role in her death. With little more than the man's word, District Attorney Mary Lacy flew Karr first class from Bangkok to Boulder to face interrogation. Upon scrutiny, there were numerous holes and inconsistencies in Karr's tall tale, embarrassing the authorities and subjecting them to further charges of incompetence.

Notwithstanding the often contentious relations between cops and reporters, the media has on more than a few occasions been exploited by police to their advantage. In Sarby County, Nebraska, for example, the sheriff was able to challenge the killer through the media. Talking to reporters about the murders of two local boys, Sheriff Pat Thomas referred to the unidentified killer as "sick, spineless, [and] a coward" who didn't have the guts to pick on someone his own size. Little did Sheriff Thomas realize that the killer was closely following the progress of the investigation in the newspaper. Insulted by the sheriff's remark, 19-year-old John Joubert decided to prove he was more of a man than the sheriff had surmised. His next victim was a female adult who managed to break away from her assailant, take note of his license plate, and thereby help the police in making an arrest.

In the DC sniper investigation, the use of the media to further the police effort was more purposeful. Chief Charles Moose spoke directly to the perpetrators through his televised press conferences. At one point, he attempted to earn the trust of the killer by slamming the media for printing part of a note left at one of the shooting sites. Actually, his outrage was a good job of acting designed to make him appear like the killer's ally.

For their part, killers oftentimes reach out to the police and public through the mass media. Son of Sam frequently sent letters to *New York Daily News* columnist Jimmy Breslin, which would then be printed in the newspaper. The Zodiac killer, who terrorized the citizens of San Francisco during the 1960s and 1970s and was never caught, sent dozens of taunting letters to the police.

The police have often published written or verbal communications from an unknown perpetrator in the hope that someone will recognize the author. The most dramatic case was the Unabomber.

After more than a dozen years of serial bombing, the Unabomber went public. Perhaps feeling invincible after fooling the police for so long, the unknown bomber apparently wanted to send a message that would advance his anti-technology agenda. It began with letters sent to the *New York Times,* which were eagerly excerpted in the paper.

Emboldened by his continuing elusiveness, the Unabomber then sent to the press a 35,000 word manifesto, entitled "Industrial Society and the Future," insisting that it be published in a prestigious paper worthy of its content— the *New York Times* or *The Washington Post.* If his demand was not met, he would strike again: an odd and literal twist on the academic phrase "publish or perish."

Much hand wringing ensued at the *Times* and the *Post* about how to respond to the bomber's threat. Ostensibly for the purpose of public safety, the joint decision of the editors of the two papers, in consultation with the FBI, was to start the presses. On September 19, 1995, *The Washington Post* published a special section with the document in full. This set a potentially dangerous precedent. Would others in the future decide to threaten violence unless their letters or manuscripts were published? Of course, reasoned the paper, this was not the typical offender, but someone who had terrorized the nation for almost two decades. They only hoped that someone would read the text and recognize its author.

The curious decision was to print the manifesto in the weekday *Post*, attempting to satisfy the killer's demands in the most minimal way. The *Post* has far less circulation than the *Times*, and the daily substantially less than the Sunday edition. However, in the early-Internet days of 1995, the choice of location virtually guaranteed that no one in the San

Francisco or Chicago metropolitan areas—where the FBI believed the Unabomber had lived—would get hold of the daily edition of *The Washington Post*.

As the story unfolded, David Kaczynski did notice some similarity between the manifesto and his brother's ranting and raving about the evils of modern technology. Kaczynski contacted the FBI, leading to the eventual arrest of Theodore Kaczynski for the serial bombings. In the minds of many observers, the happy ending justified the controversial means. But David Kaczynski was actually tipped off long before the Post's publication of the manifesto by reading the letters excerpted earlier in the *New York Times*. Even if the *Post* had not published the manifesto, David Kaczynski would, in all likelihood, still have responded to the FBI's invitation for anyone to examine the manifesto, denying the killer his undeserved platform.

While forensic investigation, psychological profiling, and VICAP all play integral roles in trying to apprehend killers, there is no substitute for old-fashioned detective work and a healthy dose of luck. In some cases the police do get lucky because the killer slips up. He may begin to feel after awhile that he is invincible and that the cops cannot match his skill or cunning. By becoming complacent, lazy, and sloppy, he starts to cut corners and take chances, which leads to his ultimate demise.

In June of 1993, the police in Mineola, Long Island, indeed got lucky. Stopping a motorist in the middle of the night because of a missing license plate, state troopers discovered a woman's body in the back of the grey pickup truck. The driver, 34-year-old Joel Rifkin, was en route to dump the body of his seventeenth victim.

London's Colin Ireland thought he had all the bases covered, but ultimately he too hadn't worked out every important detail. Spanning several months in 1993, the 39-year-old Briton stalked and killed members of London's gay community without leaving so much as a clue. All of his five victims were gay men who engaged in sadomasochistic sex, enabling Ireland to bind and gag them at will. Hence, they were completely at his mercy.

Ireland was methodical. Before each and every murder, he emptied his pockets so that nothing would fall out and implicate him. Afterward, he spent hours wiping away the evidence, even destroying the clothes he wore at the scene of the crime. Despite his preparation and planning, however, Ireland made a major blunder. A security camera captured his presence as he walked behind his fifth and last victim at a subway station just prior to the murder. Seeing his photo reprinted in the newspaper, Ireland panicked and came forward to confess.

Frequently murderers are apprehended after being linked to crimes or violations having little apparent connection to their killings. Serial killer Theodore Bundy was captured after being stopped in Florida on a traffic violation, and New York's Son of Sam killer, David Berkowitz, was identified because of a parking ticket tagged on his car near one of his shooting sites. While in these and other cases the police appear to have capitalized on some degree of luck, they benefited because of their attention to detail. Bundy's arrest resulted from the good work and alertness of an officer simply doing his job. Similarly, the lucky ticket associated with Berkowitz's vehicle would not have surfaced had the detectives not decided to track down all violations issued near each of the Son of Sam homicides. As in many areas of life, you make your own luck.

ENDNOTES

1. Susan Finch, "Baton Rouge Man Sues for His DNA," *New Orleans Times-Picayune,* June 3, 2001, p. 1.

2. Steven A. Egger, "A Working Definition of Serial Murder and the Reduction of Linkage Blindness," *Journal of Police Science and Administration* 12 (1984): 348–357.

3. J.B. Howlett, K.A. Haufland, and R.K. Ressler, "The Violent Criminal Apprehension Program—VICAP: A Progress Report." *FBI Law Enforcement Bulletin* 55 (December 1986): 14–22.

4. Steve Ritea and Stephanie A. Stanley, "Why Didn't They Put the Pieces Together Sooner?" *New Orleans Times-Picayune*, June 1, 2003, p. 1.

5. Robert K. Ressler and Ann W. Burgess, "Violent Crime," *FBI Law Enforcement Bulletin* 54 (August 1985).

6. Robert K. Ressler, Ann W. Burgess, and John E. Douglas. *Sexual Homicide: Patterns and Motives.* Lexington, MA: Lexington Books, 1988.

7. Institutional Research and Development Unit, "Evaluation of the Psychological Profiling Program," FBI Academy, Quantico, VA, 1981.

8. Rachel Smolkin, "Off Target," *American Journalism Review*, December 2002.

9. Paul Farhi and Linton Weeks, "A Surprise Ending," *The Washington Post*, October 25, 2002, p. C1.

10. Jeffrey Gettleman, "The Hunt for a Sniper," the *New York Times*, October 15, 2002, p. A19.

11. C.A. Elizabeth Luius and Gary L. Wells, "Eyewitness Identification Confidence," in David Frank Ross, J. Don Read, and Michael P. Toglia, eds., *Adult Eyewitness Testimony: Current Trends and Developments.* New York: Cambridge University Press, 1994.

12. Joe Nickell, ed., *Psychic Sleuths: ESP and Sensational Cases.* Buffalo, NY: Prometheus, 1994.

14 Getting Away with Murder, or Not

"Prison is too good for them." "He'll be out on parole before the victim's body is cold." "The juvenile courts let kids get away with murder."

These are just a few of the kinds of allegations about the failures of the U.S. justice system that not only have become frequent fodder for radio talk shows and bloggers alike, but are used by aspiring politicians who wish to characterize their opponents as soft on crime. Apparently, the public seems to agree. According to a 2004 poll conducted by the National Opinion Research Center, seven out of 10 Americans feel that the courts are too lenient on criminals.

At times, of course, the getting away with murder perception may indeed be accurate. In an effort to protect the rights of the accused, criminals have on occasion received unreasonably lenient treatment from the courts, including the acquittal of apparently guilty defendants because of procedural irregularities. The important question, however, is whether this is the exception or the rule.

It is undeniable that public attention is drawn to the absurd. When the criminal justice system fails, it becomes a big news story and an opportunity for millions of Americans to stand in righteous indignation and to demand reform. It is not so newsworthy when cases follow the course that is intended by lawmakers. Yet one can surely trace the development of criminal justice as a piecemeal effort to respond to the latest high-profile cases, regardless of how common or representative they are.

The Insanity Defense

Many of the recent legislative changes in the criminal code have surrounded an attempt to prevent criminals from getting away with murder. On occasion, these reforms have enabled the law to stay in touch with a fast-changing society. For example, the historical traditions of English common law could hardly have anticipated regulations needed in the area of drunken driving or cyber-crime. Similarly, allowances for conditions like post-traumatic stress disorder or the battered woman syndrome have been responses to medical and sociological knowledge as well as public opinion.

Unfortunately, in many aspects of the criminal law, legislative reforms have come in response to perceived loopholes or deficiencies, which in fact were imagined or exaggerated. The law pertaining to the insanity defense and the associated not guilty by reason of insanity (NGRI) plea is surely a leading case in point.

Most people would agree that certain criminal acts committed by deeply impaired individuals may indeed be beyond their responsibility. If a parent stabs an infant daughter, acting under an hallucination that she is being smothered by the family dog (which is actually a stuffed animal), then the parent neither has any intent to kill nor is he or she a negligent caretaker. The homicide is excusable because it arises from a diseased state of mind.

Even English common law recognized madness as a defense against criminal responsibility. The first actual insanity trial occurred in 1724 England when Edward Arnold was charged with shooting Lord Onslow, whom Arnold had perceived was inside his "belly and bosom" and causing imps to keep him awake at night.

Over the past 200 years, legislatures and appellate courts have struggled with the meaning and definition of madness and have attempted various solutions to this elusive issue. Much of the time, however, these changes have been motivated by a perceived injustice in which insanity is seen to have allowed a defendant to get away with a crime. Perhaps it is more in theory than in practice that most people accept the validity of the insanity defense.

The historic McNaughtan rule, still used in some form in a majority of U.S. states, was more a response to public outcry than an attempt to fine-tune the law. In 1843, Daniel McNaughtan, a Scottish wood burner who was overwhelmed by delusions of political persecution by the Tory Party, attempted to assassinate English Prime Minister Robert Peel, instead mistakenly shooting his secretary, Edward Drummond. McNaughtan was found insane and thus not criminally responsible for the homicide, which so incensed Queen Victoria that she formed a panel of experts to rewrite the insanity law. The McNaughtan rule was designed to narrow the defense, especially for use by political "crazies" like McNaughtan.

The McNaughtan rule is often called the "right–wrong test." In order to be criminally responsible under this standard, a defendant must both understand the nature of his act and also know that it was wrong. Despite its widespread adoption, many legal experts were uncomfortable with the strictly cognitive dimension of the McNaughtan defense. That is, McNaughtan considered exclusively what the defendant was thinking, but nothing of his or her affect or emotional state.

As an alternative, the Irresistible Impulse test considers whether the defendant was deprived of the mental power or capacity to control his actions. This approach was developed in 1883 and was first used in Alabama three years later.

During the twentieth century, significant advances were made in the development of psychiatry and the understanding of human behavior (and misbehavior). Recognizing that mental illness could potentially affect the control mechanisms in ways poorly captured in existing definitions of legal insanity, the federal courts adopted the broadest definition embodied in the Durham rule, first formulated in New Hampshire in 1871. According to this approach, a defendant is not responsible if his or her criminal conduct was the product of a mental disease or defect. This rule was so broad and poorly defined that the number of insanity claims, including successful ones, rose precipitously. Defendants were alleging that their conduct resulted from such disorders as depression or even character disorders.

The turning point in American public opinion arguably came on March 30, 1981, when 25-year-old John W. Hinkley, Jr., attempted to assassinate President Ronald Reagan as he exited the Washington Hilton Hotel, a shooting that was captured on videotape and replayed on TV for weeks. Hinkley was so obsessed with actress Jodie Foster that he contrived the assassination plot to get her attention and win her affection for his courage. Just prior to taking a taxi cab to the assassination site, Hinkley mailed a letter to Foster outlining his plans and motivation:[1]

> I will admit to you that the reason I'm going ahead with this attempt now is because I cannot wait any longer to impress you. I've got to do something now to make you understand, in no uncertain terms, that I'm doing all of this for your sake! By sacrificing my freedom and possibly my life, I hope to change your mind about me. This letter is being written only an hour before I leave for the Hilton Hotel. Jodie, I'm asking you to please look into your heart and at least give the chance, with this historical deed, to gain your love and respect.

Perhaps because of the patent absurdity of his motivation, John Hinkley was successful in raising an insanity defense. Yet an ABC poll taken the day of the NGRI verdict found that 76 percent of Americans felt that justice had not been served by the outcome. The U.S. Congress and many state governing bodies apparently agreed and moved quickly to reform the law of insanity. Many legislatures adopted an approach contained in the American Law Institute's Model Penal Code, which took the best elements from both the McNaughtan and Irresistible Impulse rules and explicitly excluded character disorders.

The Model Penal Code definition of insanity states that "A person is not responsible for criminal conduct if at the time of such conduct as a result of mental disease or defect he lacks substantial capacity either to appreciate the criminality of his conduct or to conform his conduct to the requirements of law." The Model Penal Code approach was used in a majority of American states until the late 1980s, since which time the narrower McNaughtan definition has returned to favor.

More importantly, through recent reforms to federal and many state statutes, the burden of proof was transferred to the defense. Rather than forcing the prosecution to prove the defendant sane, the defense would have to demonstrate insanity with clear and convincing evidence.

These changes have severely limited the scope of the insanity defense, although many Americans still fear that legal insanity is a gaping loophole through which thousands of cunning criminals walk their way to freedom. This perception could not be further from the truth. For example, a 1991 study funded by the National Institute of Mental Health of felony cases in eight states determined that fewer than 1 percent of defendants attempted the insanity plea as a defense, and only 26 percent of these were successful.[2] In addition, in those rare instances when NGRI pleas are successfully invoked, most of the time they occur through a plea agreement between the prosecution and defense counsel, not from a jury verdict.

Juries are extremely reluctant to return an insanity verdict. To some extent, this may reflect the difficulties that some jurors have in understanding much of the complex and jargon-filled testimony delivered by psychiatric expert witnesses. Unable to intelligently weigh the conflicting conclusions reached by prosecution and defense experts, jurors may simply vote with their gut feelings and prejudices: "He did the crime, so how can he be not guilty even by reason of insanity?" Furthermore, laboring under the false notion that the insanity defense is tantamount to a pardon, juries are reluctant to return this verdict even in cases that most observers declare open and shut.

In 1994, for example, John Salvi murdered two receptionists during armed assaults on two Brookline, Massachusetts, abortion clinics in what appeared initially to be a politically motivated crime. Yet as his trial approached, it became clear to virtually everyone that Salvi's motivation for murder had more to do with mental illness than with any real desire to save the lives of unborn infants. He sincerely believed that he was the victim of a large-scale conspiracy to destroy Catholics. He told his parents that he had seen an evil bird in the family room of their home, and that he would stay up all night guarding against the presence of evil. He claimed to have watched a friend turn into a vampire. He ranted and raved about international plots to rob Catholics of jobs, to commit genocide against white people, and to destroy the Catholic Church. Despite the rather compelling evidence surrounding his severe illness, the jury was unwilling to acquit by reason of insanity. After his conviction, Salvi was sent to state prison where he later committed suicide, apparently by asphyxiating himself with a plastic trash-can liner.

It is quite possible for a person to be truly mentally ill yet legally responsible. That is, legal and medical definitions are not consistent in defining the forces that influence behavior. Kip Kinkel, who killed both his parents before his shooting rampage at Thurston High School in Springfield, Oregon, was, according to psychiatrists, deeply disturbed and possibly psychotic. The young murderer left this note near the bodies of his parents:[3]

> I have just killed my parents. I don't know what is happening. I love my mom and dad so much. I just got two felonies on my record. My parents can't take that. It would destroy them. The embarrassment would be too much for them. They couldn't live with themselves. I am so sorry.
>
> I am a horrible son. I wish I had been aborted. I destroy anything I touch. I can't eat. I can't sleep. I didn't deserve them. They were wonderful people. It's not their fault or the fault of any person or organization or television show. My head just doesn't work right. Fuck these voices inside my head.
>
> I want to die. I want to be gone. But I have to kill people. I don't know why. I am so sorry.
>
> Why did God do this to me? I have never been happy. I wish I was happy. I wish I made my mother proud, but I am nothing. I try so hard to find happiness, but you know me: I hate everything. I have no other choice. What have I become? I am so sorry.

In his taped confession to the police, Kinkel described voices in his head that encouraged him to kill. He was also suicidal, having taped a bullet to his chest just in case he needed one more round to take his own life. Shortly after his arrest, Kinkel rushed a police officer in a failed attempt to provoke him to shoot (suicide by cop).

Kip Kinkel initially entered an insanity plea but then withdrew it in favor of a plea of guilty as charged. During sentencing hearings, a defense psychiatrist testified that Kinkel had heard voices imploring him to kill. A neurologist also testified that Kinkel had holes in his brain, consistent with research findings into schizophrenic children. Notwithstanding the medical evidence, Kinkel was given a life sentence.

Perhaps the insanity defense is infrequently attempted because defense attorneys are well aware of what the public likely misunderstands: that is, that a NGRI verdict, whether negotiated by opposing sides or determined by judge or jury, is hardly a free walk for the defendant. In fact, defendants committed to a psychiatric facility for an indefinite period of time following an insanity finding tend to spend more time in confinement than they would have had they been convicted of the criminal charge. Though avoiding prison (where they don't belong), they don't "get away" with anything at all.

John Hinkley, Jr., for example, remains institutionalized, more than two decades after his unsuccessful assassination attempt, despite several attempts to win his freedom by claiming he is no longer ill. This is not the kind of lenient treatment that many ill-informed citizens screamed about following his trial. As a historical note, moreover, the infamous Daniel McNaughtan didn't get off as easily as the Queen of England had suggested. He died in an asylum some twenty years after he was spared the death penalty for his crime.

Finally, the insanity plea is also eschewed by some defendants because it stigmatizes them as crazy. Some offenders would far rather be considered bad than mad. This is especially true for criminals who act to further their own political cause. Being labeled insane signals that their point of view has no credibility and is just the product of a diseased mind. This is the reason perhaps that Theodore Kaczynski rejected his attorney's attempts to plead insanity. He may have felt that a claim of insanity would negate his anti-technology ideology, articulated in his lengthy manifesto that was published in *The Washington Post* under threat of continued bombings.

Unlike political fanatics who reject insanity as an option, in cases of murdering moms, the defense is often employed in attempt to excuse infanticides committed in the throes of postpartum psychosis. At times, the strategy has been successful, as in Andrea Yates's Texas retrial for drowning her five children. Apparently, juries are not as reluctant to spare a defendant with whom they may sympathize, notwithstanding the defenselessness of her young victims.

Despite its limited usage overall, many Americans call for the total elimination of the NGRI defense, and some state legislatures have complied. Three states (Utah, Idaho, and Montana) have abolished the defense. Thirteen states have instituted the guilty but mentally ill (GBMI) alternative. The GBMI option ensures that the defendant is confined in custody, yet because of the mental illness, he or she serves time in a psychiatric facility rather than a correctional facility.

Some legal scholars have also argued for the elimination of NGRI, but not for the same knee-jerk emotional reasons that seem to underlie the popular viewpoint. According to Norval Morris, for example, the not guilty by reason of insanity defense is simply unnecessary. If a mental disease is so profound that the defendant cannot form criminal intent, then he should not be convicted of a crime but should instead be civilly committed to a psychiatric facility.[4]

The problems associated with using hypnosis to improve the recall of eyewitnesses to crimes, described in Chapter 13, are compounded when applied to defendants in trials involving the question of legal insanity. The fact that hypnotized subjects can confidently recall, create, or alter their biographies casts doubt on the accuracy of memories. On the one hand, it is quite possible that a hypnotized subject will reveal painful yet accurate memories. On the other hand, subjects can fabricate events in their past if it suits the occasion, the context, or some ulterior motive.

Forensic psychiatrist Dorothy Otnow Lewis, for example, was hired by defense counsel in the Arthur Shawcross case to reveal his motivation and to support a plea of insanity in his trial for the murders of prostitutes in Rochester, New York. Based on sessions of hypnosis in which she age-regressed Shawcross for early memories of mistreatment, Lewis testified that Shawcross suffered from post-traumatic stress disorder brought on in part by experiences of abuse during his childhood. At first, he recalled having a normal upbringing and failed to reveal any abusive experiences. After lengthy and persistent probing under hypnosis, however, Shawcross finally "remembered" being sodomized by his mother with a broomstick and being forced to perform oral sex with her.

Did Lewis' discovery of suppressed and painful memories of abuse in Shawcross's background reflect an uncompromising effort to uncover the truth about deeply hidden secrets? Or did Shawcross finally give his examiner exactly what he figured she expected to hear? Either way, Shawcross's mother called her son a liar; and, given his attempt to save himself through the insanity plea, he certainly had very good reason to fabricate or exaggerate bad childhood experiences. We really can't know for certain, however.

In forensic work, the hypnotist deals with a subject who may have a stake in faking a hypnotic trance and divulging inaccurate information about himself and his past. The hypnotist can actually create the information through subtle and perhaps not-so-subtle suggestions to the subject. Thus, it is possible for an individual who may indeed have felt intimidated as a child to recall under hypnosis experiences of abuse, particularly if the hypnotist solicits such recollections and the subject has a self-serving interest in providing them.

The case of serial murderer Kenneth A. Bianchi provides another revealing example of how hypnosis has been exploited to find support for the child abuse explanation for murderous impulses. In 1977 and 1978, Bianchi and his cousin Angelo Buono abducted, tortured, raped, and murdered 10 young women, whose bodies they dumped along roadsides in the Los Angeles area.

Kenneth Bianchi's insanity defense was centered on the theory that he suffered from a multiple personality disorder (MPD), a psychiatric illness characterized by the presence of two or more distinct personalities sharing the same body. MPD is believed to stem from a history of severe child abuse. An abused child escapes from cruel parental treatment by developing a fantasy world of pleasure and kindness. At the same time, the angry and hateful feelings toward the abusive parent are stored in a reservoir that the child suppresses. In later life, the two perspectives—the loving and the hateful—split into their own personalities which compete for control. The angry "person" takes turns with various alter-egos for dominance over the same body.

If Bianchi was in fact a multiple personality, this could easily explain and reconcile how someone as seemingly nice as Bianchi could also commit the heinous crimes with which he was charged. Through hypnosis, a second personality surfaced—that of "Steve," a hostile, crude, impatient, and sadistic character who proudly claimed responsibility for the slayings. "Killing a broad doesn't make any difference to me," bragged Steve. Everything now made sense to the psychiatrists.

Bianchi was advised by his hypnotist that his medical history failed to include the kind of documentation of child abuse that would be needed to support his defense based on MPD. Hypnotized once more, Bianchi then recalled a dream about "a woman putting his hands over a kitchen stove fire while he was young." Finally, the psychiatrists had the evidence of abuse that was lacking!

As the court hearings on Bianchi's sanity approached, the MPD theory and the hypnotically included evidence began to crumble when subjected to external validation. Bianchi's mother did confess that she had threatened her boy, "See this fire? If I catch you stealing once more, I'll hold your hand over this stove." But she denied ever going further than a threat. Moreover, there was no evidence of burns or scarring in Bianchi's detailed childhood medical file. At best, the hypnotically included recollection was just a fearful memory transformed into an imagined event. At worst, it was the attempt of a pathological liar to escape justice.

Justice for Juveniles

Another gaping loophole, at least according to public opinion, surrounds the legal defense of youthfulness. From the English common law's "infancy defense," persons under the age of 7 could not be charged with crimes because of a irrefutable presumption that they lacked the ability to form criminal intent. For children between the ages of 7 and 14, the same presumption held, but it could be challenged or refuted based on evidence to the contrary. In common law, defendants older than 14 were considered no different from adults in terms of culpability or responsibility.

By the end of the nineteenth century, children's advocates in the United States had become deeply disturbed about the treatment of minors by the criminal justice system, and understandably so. Adolescents and youngsters were being prosecuted, convicted, and imprisoned in the same manner (and in the same institutions) as adults. Wanting to provide an alternative approach not just for young criminals but for incorrigible children as well, the so-called child saving movement successfully pushed for the nation's first juvenile court.[5] Established in Chicago in 1899, the new juvenile court was designed to take a therapeutic rather than punitive approach to handling youthful delinquents and status offenders. The process was to be paternalistic rather than adversarial.

The new approach to juvenile justice spread quickly, and through much of the twentieth century the juvenile court movement appeared to fare quite well. Over time, juveniles were afforded expanded rights (e.g., the right to an attorney), just like adults in criminal courts. By the 1980s, however, as rates of juvenile violence and murder, in particular, began to surge, politicians and the public alike questioned the role and appropriateness of juvenile court for these dangerous offenders of tender age.

A child found delinquent for committing a homicide or another serious crime would generally serve time within a juvenile detention facility until the age of majority (generally 18 years of age), or in some states a few additional years at the discretion of the judge. Under the assumption that wayward youths could be rehabilitated into law-abiding adults, juvenile sentences even for serious crimes were, for the most part, relatively short.

Even from the earliest years of the juvenile court system, the criminal courts were not completely willing to give up jurisdiction over all crimes committed by children. In part, the battle between the "kiddie courts" and the more prestigious and powerful adult courts was a political one over authority and turf.[6] More generally, in response to concerns that some youthful offenders were simply not amenable to treatment (as well as doubts about the efficacy of rehabilitation itself), waiver procedures allowed juvenile court judges to transfer particular defendants over to criminal adult court for prosecution and punishment. On a case-by-case basis, certain repeat, chronic, or violent youths were appropriately removed from the jurisdiction of juvenile court.

As the pressure upon the juvenile court to take a harsher stance toward murder and other serious offenses mounted, however, judges began deciding the transfer question even for first-time offenders, less on the basis of treatment amenability and more to satisfy public opinion. In 1986, for example, 14-year-old Rod Matthews of Canton, Massachusetts, was arrested for the murder of his classmate Shaun Ouillette; because of widespread outrage over the shocking and senseless crime, he became at that time one of the youngest children tried for murder in adult court.

Apparently, Matthews had made a hit list of possible victims, huddled with two buddies to determine the most deserving target, and then led his unsuspecting victim into the woods where he bludgeoned the boy with a baseball bat. Afterward, Matthews brought his friends to view the body and to show off his courage. Despite his young age and lack of any criminal record, the juvenile court judge waived jurisdiction over to the adult court in the face of intense pressure from the victim's family and the local media.

In March of 1989, 9-year-old Cameron Kocher shot and killed his 7-year-old neighbor as she rode on the back of a snowmobile. Kocher pled guilty to a first-degree misdemeanor of involuntary manslaughter and was on probation and court supervision until he turned 21. More recently, several Florida juvenile murders have been tried and sentenced as adults. Derek King, 14, and his brother Alex, 13, received eight- and seven-year prison sentences for beating their father to death with a baseball bat. Nathaniel Brazill, also 14, received a 28-year prison sentence for shooting to death his middle-school teacher.

In a closely watched Florida case, 12-year-old Lionel Tate was arrested in July 1999, for beating and stomping to death his 6-year-old neighbor Tiffany Eunick. Tate claimed that her death was an accident, occurring during rough-house play in which he was imitating wrestling moves he had seen on television. Although old enough to be prosecuted as an adult, Tate was deemed too immature to have final say in whether to accept a plea bargain for a lesser penalty that had been offered by the prosecution. Instead, his mother insisted on a trial, a trial in which Tate was convicted and sentenced to life in prison.

Widespread concern for the harshness of the outcome, an outcome that was prescribed by Florida law, may very well have been considered when an appellate court in 2004 overturned his conviction. Tate subsequently accepted a plea deal for second-degree murder, receiving a term of incarceration equal to time already served and 10 years probation. While the resolution was hailed by legal scholars, within nine months Tate violated the terms of his probation by staying out after curfew and was returned to jail. Released once again in late 2004 with an extra five years probation, Tate was unable to keep his nose clean. In May 2005, having by then reached the age of maturity, he was arrested for robbery and reincarcerated. Ending the long legal saga surrounding the troubled youngster, Tate was sentenced to 30 years in prison for violating his probation by possessing a gun and breaking a glass door at the Broward County Jail.

Unlike the judicial waiver strategy that many states have employed, the New York state legislature, reeling from a brutal double murder committed by a 15-year-old, decided to take matters into its own hands. In 1978, after 15-year-old Willie Bosket was sentenced to a maximum term of five years in Family Court for killing two men on the subway, the legislature passed the New York Juvenile Offender Law (also known as the "Willie Bosket Law") mandating that all youth as young as 13 who are charged with murder shall be processed in adult court and receive adult sentences unless there was compelling reason to move the case down to juvenile court.

How young is too young to hold children accountable? In New York, at least, nine year-old girls who kill are handled with a sensible measure of compassion. During Memorial Day weekend in 2005, Shanine K. (identity protected) of Brooklyn fatally stabbed her best friend, 11-year-old Queen Washington, during an argument over a rubber ball. Though charged with murder, Shanine pled guilty to second-degree manslaughter, and as a juvenile would serve a maximum of 18 months in a youth facility.

During the late 1980s and early 1990s, years after the Matthews and Bosket cases, juvenile murder rates rose sharply, and state legislatures responded with harsh measures. Rather than leave the waiver decision up to the judges, the wisdom of whose judgment was being questioned in the appellate court of public opinion, lawmakers generally proposed two alternative strategies: prosecutorial discretion and statutory exclusions. In the former, the determination as to whether to charge a youngster in juvenile or adult court is made by the prosecutor under the logic that this public official, elected by the citizenry, is more responsive to public mood than are judges appointed to the bench for extended terms. Alternatively, some state legislatures opted to write into the law exactly which offenses (e.g., homicides by offenders ages 13 and over) are excluded from juvenile court jurisdiction. Some states simply lowered the age of majority below the traditional 18 years old for all offenses. A few eliminated altogether the statutory lower bound on eligibility for criminal prosecution in adult court.

The 1990s saw rapid change in transfer laws across the country.[7] Between 1992 and 1997, 17 states expanded the range of offenses and lowered the eligibility age for judicial waiver. During these same years, 27 states expanded the list of crimes that were excluded from juvenile court jurisdiction, and seven states reduced the age when these exclusions kicked in. Eleven states increased the range of crimes and reduced the age limits when prosecutors could opt to file charges in either juvenile or adult court.

These changes have opened the floodgate wide for juvenile offenders to be charged and prosecuted in adult criminal courts. From 1985 to 1996, for example, the number of juvenile delinquency cases waived from juvenile to adult court, generally through decisions of the juvenile court judges, rose 47 percent, from 6,800 to about 10,000 annually. For violent offenses specifically, including homicide, the number of waivers more than doubled from about 2,000 per year to over 4,000 per year.[8] In addition to these more traditional transfers, many times more youngsters are being tried as adults arising from decisions by prosecutors to file cases in adult court or from statutory exclusions of cases away from juvenile court jurisdiction. As a consequence of the movement to prosecute juveniles as adults, the number of offenders under age 18 sentenced to serve time in an adult correctional facility also climbed, from 3,400 in 1985 to 7,400 in 1997.[9]

As the rate of youth violence diminished during the latter half of the 1990s, so did the number of juveniles prosecuted in adult court and subsequently sent to state prisons. After peaking in the mid-1990s, the number of juveniles admitted to prison fell 45 percent from 1996 to 2002.[10]

Despite the downturn in case flow, the youthfulness of certain offenders prosecuted as adults is still quite striking. In 1999, for example, Nathaniel Abraham of Pontiac, Michigan, was tried as an adult for murder surrounding an incident that occurred on October 29, 1997, when he was just 11 years old, making him one of the youngest children ever charged as an adult. Abraham reportedly shot a gun into some trees, hitting and killing 18-year-old

Ronnie Greene, Jr. Despite testimony from a defense witness that the defendant had the mental capacity of a 6-year-old at the time of the killing, Abraham was convicted of second-degree murder.

It is likely that the jurors had at least to some extent sympathized with the victim's family. To Ronnie Greene's relatives, in terms of their loss and anguish, it is largely irrelevant that the person who shot and killed him was a diminutive 11-year-old. To the families who lose a loved one, it matters not whether the perpetrator was 11 or 41; the victim is just as dead. In terms of this retributive notion of justice, juveniles and adults should arguably be treated no differently.

Furthermore, there are indeed certain repeat, violent, chronic, ruthless juveniles who have proved through their recidivism that they are not amenable to treatment. They may have been through the juvenile justice system time after time, but with little or no improvement in their character or behavior. As juvenile justice failures, these offenders can and perhaps should be sent to the adult system.

It could also be argued that not all juvenile offenders deserve adult-like punishment, even though they may commit an adult-like crime such as murder or rape. The inspiration for their vicious crimes often stems from their immaturity—for example, kids committing murder in order to impress their peers or even to fulfill a dare. We must fully consider the special nature of youthful offending—even murder. Teenagers may look like adults, dress like adults, act like adults, even shoot like adults, but they tend to reason like teenagers, not like adults.

Some recent evidence from neurological studies supports the view that juveniles have a limited capacity for understanding consequences. According to Deborah Yurgelun-Todd, director of Neuropsychology and Cognitive Neuroimaging at McLean Hospital, the frontal lobe portion of the brain, which controls the ability to think things through fully, does not tend to develop until late adolescence or young adulthood.[11] Indeed, it has long been recognized that teenagers are often impulsive—in a sense "temporary sociopaths." Thus, leaving aside the purely retributive notion of justice, teenagers may not deserve the same punishment as adults given their limited capacity for considering consequences. Diminished capacity should mean diminished punishability, especially for non-habitual offenders.

Making the juvenile justice system more just and punitive is one thing, but eliminating it, as some have proposed, is quite another. Expanding juvenile penalties and blending juvenile and adult sanctions for the most serious offenders will go a long way toward addressing public concern without entirely sacrificing young lives that could be salvaged. We need to be selective in how we prosecute juveniles, even juvenile murderers.

Most surprisingly, Judge Eugene Moore, upon sentencing Nathaniel Abraham following his adult conviction on a second-degree murder charge, chose not to follow through with an adult punishment. Rather than hand down a protracted term of incarceration, Moore sent the boy to a juvenile facility until the age of 21, at which time he would be released. The judge also boldly articulated his concern for the snowballing trend in America toward trying juveniles as adults as well as his view that we should not forsake the rehabilitative goal, particularly when children are involved.

Quite apart from the question of rehabilitation, many proponents of the movement to try serious juvenile offenders as adults are hoping to send a strong deterrent message to other youngsters who might contemplate attacking a classmate or neighbor. Yet, we cannot deal effectively with teen violence through the threat of the criminal justice system. The threat of punishment, no matter how harsh, frequently fails to deter kids who face the threat of violence and death every day in their classrooms and their neighborhoods. As far as they are concerned, the criminal justice system can just take a number and wait in line with all the other enemies out to get them. Plus, tending toward impulsive action, adolescents do not fully weigh the costs and benefits.

Often these are juveniles who think little and care even less about the future, who don't expect to live past their twenty-first birthday. The prospect of a long-term prison sentence or even the death penalty will not dissuade them in the least. Criminologists Simon Singer and David McDowall, for example, conducted an assessment of whether the landmark and widely publicized New York Juvenile Offender Law of 1978 (the "Willie Bosket Law") had any impact on deterring youthful offenders. By comparing trends over time both in New York and, as a comparison, Philadelphia, they found that the threat promised by the tough New York law did not have any impact in lowering rates of serious juvenile offending.[12]

Not only does the wholesale transfer of juveniles into the adult court make little sense theoretically, but on a practical level it does little good in reforming offenders. Criminologists Bishop, Frazier, Lanza-Kaduce, and White compared a sample of Florida juveniles who were tried and sentenced as adults to a control group of juveniles retained in the juvenile system, matched on a variety of offense characteristics and risk factors. Upon follow-up, Bishop and her colleagues found that those who had passed through the adult system actually had a higher rate of recidivism than the control group offenders.[13]

Although there are some special, atypical cases in which the crime is so heinous that the likelihood of release is remote, most juvenile offenders, even young killers, do get released from prison eventually, better or worse than when they entered. Several states utilize an alternative approach to just punishing children as adults by combining juvenile and adult punishments. In a so-called blended sentence, a youthful offender serves the first portion of his or her term in a juvenile institution and then, upon reaching an appropriate age, is moved to finish out his or her term in an adult correctional facility.

Capital Punishment

For many people in the United States, the critical question is not so much whether a juvenile or adult penalty is involved, but whether the penalty is substantial enough, regardless of age. Many critics are especially incensed that murderers, whether they are 14 or 44, can ever be paroled because for the victim, of course, there is no parole from death.

The debate over the appropriate penalty for those who take a life often fails to distinguish, unfortunately, between the various kinds of homicides that we discussed in Chapter 1 (that is, first- and second-degree murder, voluntary and involuntary manslaughter). Although most states do indeed allow parole, early release, good time, furloughs, and so on, for lesser forms of homicide, statutes on first-degree murder in most jurisdictions are hardly lenient.

Table 14.1 summarizes the penalties available state by state for first-degree murder convictions. As shown, three-quarters of the states currently have a death penalty in place,

TABLE 14.1   State Murder Penalties

		Life without parole	
		Yes (N = 48)	No (N = 2)
Death Penalty	Yes (N = 38)	AL, AZ, AR, CA, CO, CT, DE, FL, GA, ID, IL, IN, KY, LA, MD, MS, MO, MS, MT, NB, NV, NH, NJ, NY, NC, OH, OK, OR, PA, SC, SD, TN, TX, UT, VA, WA, WY	NM
	No (N = 12)	HI, IA, ME, MA, MI, MN, ND, RI, VT, WV, WI	AK

a matter that we will discuss more later, and as many as 48 states can and do incarcerate first-degree murderers for life without the possibility of parole.

The public, it appears, is grossly misinformed about the life without parole (LWOP) sentence. Citizens hear about killers released on parole (generally those convicted of manslaughter or second-degree murder) and assume that this is the norm for all convicted killers, even first-degree murderers. Northeastern University criminologist William Bowers, for example, conducted a telephone survey of 603 residents of Massachusetts, a state that has mandatory life without parole for first-degree murder. Only 3 percent of those interviewed were aware of the lack of parole eligibility for first-degree murderers.

A 2002 U.S. Department of Justice report on sentencing patterns for felony defendants provides some information on how homicide defendants are handled by the state criminal courts.[14] The average (median) sentence length for the nearly 9,000 defendants convicted in 2002 of murder or non-negligent manslaughter was 20 years; one-quarter of the defendants were given a life sentence or a death sentence. Furthermore, based on prisoners released from custody, parole-eligible killers are expected to serve nearly two-thirds of their sentence (or nearly 12 years on average) before release.

In addition, life sentences are increasingly coming to mean that a defendant will indeed remain locked up for life. Currently, one out of every four lifers (26.3 percent) is serving life without parole eligibility, compared to 17.8 percent in 1992.[15] These offenders cannot be released, except in the unusual instance of a commutation or pardon.

Fueled by a widespread misunderstanding of the penalty structure for murder convictions, as well as by concern over rising homicide rates, public support for the death penalty mounted steadily over the final quarter of the twentieth century. With this encouragement from the populace, the number of prisoners put to death has grown as well. As shown in Figure 14.1, the number of executions has risen fairly steadily since 1980. Whereas in the mid-1970s, the public opinion in this country was virtually evenly split on

FIGURE 14.1   Executions in the United States, 1930–2005

the appropriateness of capital punishment, by the end of the 1990s, support for the death penalty was overwhelming, with as many as three-quarters of Americans in favor of it. Apparently, some citizens simply view an execution as the only absolute guarantee against a convicted killer being released on parole, being commuted, or even escaping over the prison walls. In one recent national poll, only 4 percent of respondents believed that criminals sentenced to life incarceration would actually spend their lives in prison.

Arguably, no other aspect of the criminal law receives so much attention as capital punishment, despite its relatively minimal utilization. Even at its peak level of use in 1935 when nearly 199 convicts were put to death, murderers under a death sentence represented a tiny fraction of convicted killers and an even smaller portion of convicted criminals generally.

Notwithstanding its limited application, capital punishment is an issue that has been used as a litmus test for what kind of public officials we elect to office. For example, a case can easily be made that Democratic presidential nominee Michael Dukakis lost to Republican George Bush in the 1988 campaign because of his stand on capital punishment. Even though most death penalty cases (nearly 99 percent) fall within state, rather than federal, jurisdiction, the voting public was concerned about Dukakis's liberal anti-death penalty ideology.

Bill Clinton eased his way into the White House with a pro-death penalty stand. As the Governor of Arkansas, Clinton signed the death warrant for an inmate executed under less than ideal circumstances. Candidate Clinton left the Presidential campaign trail in 1992 to be present in Arkansas for the execution of Ricky Ray Rector, a severely brain-damaged black man who had killed a white police officer (and then shot himself in the head). Rector was obviously mentally retarded and/or mentally ill. He routinely howled like an animal in the days leading up to his execution, and did not understand what was about to happen to him. Rector even saved the cake from his last meal to have later. Although a decade too late to spare Rector's life, the U.S. Supreme Court in 2002 ruled unconstitutional the execution of mentally retarded prisoners.

As shown in Table 14.2, a majority of every sociopolitical segment of the population supports the use of the death penalty. No wonder that very few politicians who are opposed

TABLE 14.2   Public Opinion of the Death Penalty for Murder, 2005

Characteristics	Category	Favor	Oppose	No Opinion
Overall		64%	30%	6%
Sex				
	Male	70%	24%	6%
	Female	59%	34%	7%
Race				
	White	69%	26%	5%
	Nonwhite	49%	41%	10%
	Black	35%	56%	9%
Age				
	18 to 29 years	60%	36%	4%
	30 to 49 years	64%	29%	7%
	50 to 64 years	69%	25%	6%
	50 years and older	66%	27%	7%
	65 years and older	61%	31%	8%
Education				
	College post graduate	54%	41%	5%
	College graduate	62%	34%	4%
	Some college	69%	24%	7%
	High school graduate or less	66%	27%	7%
Income				
	$75,000 and over	64%	29%	7%
	$50,000 to $74,999	68%	26%	6%
	$30,000 to $49,999	68%	29%	3%
	$20,000 to $29,999	67%	26%	7%
	Under $20,000	57%	33%	10%
Community type				
	Urban area	59%	33%	8%
	Suburban area	66%	29%	5%
	Rural area	67%	25%	8%
Region				
	East	59%	35%	6%
	Midwest	64%	30%	6%
	South	68%	25%	7%
	West	65%	29%	6%
Political affiliation				
	Republican	77%	18%	5%
	Democrat	56%	37%	7%
	Independent	63%	31%	6%

Source: Kathleen Maguire & Ann J. Pastore, *Sourcebook of Criminal Justice Statistics,* Online Edition. Washington, DC: Bureau of Justice Statistics, Table 2.52, October 2005.

to the death penalty can get elected to public office, regardless of the strength of their record in other areas.

It is important to view these opinion levels with a whole shaker of salt. Although the sampling and data collection approaches are quite sound, the wording of such questions as "Do you favor or oppose the death penalty for first-degree murder?" may not fully elicit an accurate picture of public sentiment. First, public opinion varies considerably based on the exact nature of the first-degree murder. Whereas the rape, torture, and murder of a child may fully arouse the public's thirst for the supreme penalty of death, felony murders in which robbery victims are shot to death do not quite spark the same level of vehemence and vengeance.[16] More important, Americans may change their opinion depending on the alternatives—that is, the death penalty compared to what other punishment? Several polls have shown that when presented a choice of death penalty or life without parole, public support is almost evenly divided.[17] In fact, a May 2006 *USA Today*/Gallup poll determined that although two-thirds of the Americans still support capital punishment, by the slightest of margins—one percentage point—respondents preferred life without parole to the death penalty.[18]

Curiously, whereas much of our criminal law pertaining to homicide developed 200 years ago in an attempt to limit those offenders who could face the penalty of death, in recent years most changes in homicide statutes have been introduced to expand the number of capital crimes. Following years of protest and disfavor during which time a majority of Americans actually opposed the death penalty, a virtual moratorium on capital punishment started in the late 1960s and was formalized in 1972 when the U.S. Supreme Court struck down the death penalty. Based on arguments that minorities and the poor were more likely to be sentenced to death, the Court held (in *Furman v. Georgia*) that the death penalty was being applied in a capricious, arbitrary, discriminatory, and therefore unconstitutional manner. Importantly, the Supreme Court did not hold that capital punishment was inherently cruel and unusual but instead set out a process for how the death penalty could be administered in a fair and constitutional manner.

The Supreme Court also added in a later decision that the application of the death penalty must be in proportion to the seriousness of the crime: only the most grievous acts should qualify for the supreme penalty. Because of the proportionality notion, it could be ruled unconstitutional to execute rapists. There is, however, another more practical reason for eliminating rape as a capital crime. Despite the historical practice, executing a rapist may even encourage murder by removing any disincentive for the offender to kill his victim in order to prevent her from testifying against him.

In the wake of this landmark 1972 *Furman* decision, more than three dozen states hurried to redraft their murder statutes to include a death penalty consistent with the Court's framework. To pass constitutional muster, the guidelines for sentencing a defendant to death would have to be clearly defined. A first-degree murder conviction was not sufficient. In order to limit the potential for bias, states had to identify those aggravating factors that would warrant it and mitigating factors that would disqualify it. In addition, the trial would need to be bifurcated so that the fact-finding guilt phase of the trial would be separate from the penalty phase. Thus, should a jury find a defendant guilty of capital murder (murder in the first degree with one or more special or aggravating circumstances), the trial would then proceed to hear testimony about the most appropriate sanction, usually either death or life imprisonment.

Volumes have been written debating the utility and appropriateness of the death penalty. One controversy that has received the most attention is that of its general deterrence—that is, whether the existence of the death penalty discourages potential murderers from following through with the act. Could life be so precious even to hardened criminals that the ultimate penalty might dissuade them more than any other sanction?

Much of the early research on this topic, conducted through the mid-1970s, suggested that the deterrence argument was little more than wishful thinking. Comparative studies showed that death penalty states did not have lower homicide rates than similar neighboring states without such a law.[19] In 1975, however, economist Isaac Ehrlich surprised the criminological community and changed the legislative debate by claiming to have demonstrated through a sophisticated statistical analysis that each execution deters about eight homicides.[20]

On the wings of Ehrlich's provocative study, several states rushed to enact death penalty legislation. Death penalty supporters seemed finally to have some hard evidence with which to defend their point of view. It was not until several years later that critics of Ehrlich's research were able to identify the fatal flaws in his work. The most important was that Ehrlich's analysis mainly hinged on the fact that during the late 1960s and early 1970s, when the death penalty was rarely used (only three executions were staged from 1966 to 1976), the homicide rate soared. Yet other crimes soared as well, even those such as auto theft that had little to do with capital punishment. Clearly, other factors were responsible for the growth in crime during the 1960s and 1970s, including a homicide rate that doubled from 1963 to 1973.

By the time that Ehrlich's work and a few similar studies by a handful of his disciples were refuted, the United States had seen renewed support for capital punishment. By then, the pro-death penalty movement had gained so much momentum that the deterrence argument was no longer vital to undergird the pro-death penalty position.

On balance, therefore, the scientific evidence is fairly clear in showing that the death penalty fails to deter murderers—that is, any more than life imprisonment does. Those offenders who are not dissuaded from committing a murder by the prospect of being locked up for life also are not likely to be discouraged by the prospect of death. Thus, while the death penalty may deter in an absolute sense (even murderers fear death), in a relative sense it is no more of a deterrent than the life imprisonment alternative. The key term is prospect, or the perceived probability that the penalty will be applied. Those who act with deliberation, planning, and premeditation generally view their risk of apprehension as low. If one is not caught, there can be no punishment, regardless of what penalty is on the books.

Although life imprisonment may be virtually as powerful a deterrent, many Americans are concerned about their tax dollars being used unnecessarily and wastefully to house and feed convicted murderers for the rest of their lives. Yet, economic analyses have shown that the cost savings associated with removing a prisoner from a cell and executing him or her has been grossly exaggerated. Given the fixed overhead costs of incarceration— utilities, salaries, and maintenance, relatively little is saved by staging an execution. On the other side of the fiscal ledger, moreover, the cost of capital trials tends to be rather high. Given the life-and-death stakes, the necessary procedural safeguards in place in some states in an attempt to avoid a wrongful execution provide capital defendants with the best defense that the taxpayers can buy. Capital murder trials tend to be many times more costly than non-capital murder trials, given the complexity and length of these prosecutions. The process could be streamlined, of course, but at a very different cost—the possibility of executing an innocent person.

Of course, for many people, according to polls, the defining issue is justice or vengeance—an eye for an eye, a tooth for a tooth. According to a 1991 Gallup poll, one-half of the supporters of capital punishment indicated retribution as the primary reason for their position, well ahead of any other justification.[21] Many supporters insist, despite the lack of deterrence and the costliness, that it is the just punishment, not to mention a surefire way of preventing the offender from repeating his offense, outside or even inside prison.

The concern for racial discrimination, which motivated the 1972 moratorium on executions, no longer appears to sway public opinion or even today's conservative Supreme Court. In *McCleskey v. Kemp,* the justices reviewed and debated the results of a statistical study, offered by University of Iowa law professor David Baldus, based on over 2,000 murder cases in Georgia during the 1970s.[22] Bealdus's concluded that, even while controlling for a host of relevant factors, black defendants who killed white victims had the greatest likelihood of receiving the death penalty. Even so, the Court's majority dismissed the statistical correlation between race and sentencing, indicating that a defendant on appeal would need to demonstrate racial prejudice in his or her particular trial, not a statistical pattern in cases generally.

Under current operating procedures, there are actually more whites sentenced to death than blacks, both in absolute numbers and in relation to the homicide offending rates. As shown in Figure 14.2, the gap between the number of white and black prisoners sitting on death row nationwide has widened over the past thirty years since capital punishment was restored.

The pattern of racial discrimination is much subtler, however. Figure 14.3 shows rates of execution (executions per 1,000 cases) for victim/offender race combinations, by comparing solved homicides for the years 1977–2005 with executions through the end of 2005. Overall, regardless of race combination, there were 2.2 defendants executed per 1,000

FIGURE 14.2   Death Row Inmates by Race, 1968–2005

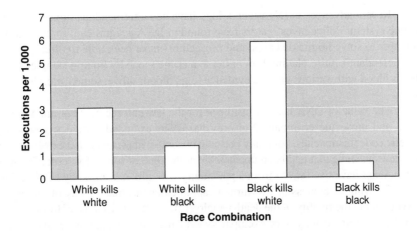

FIGURE 14.3 Executions Rates by Race of Victim and Offender, 1977–2005, Combined

known murderers. The differences according to race are, however, quite provocative and give different inferences when probing below the surface. The execution rate for white killers (3.0 per 1,000 offenders) is double that for blacks (1.5 per 1,000 killers). Furthermore, those who kill whites are five times as likely to be executed as those who kill blacks (specifically 3.5 executions per 1,000 killers of white victims as compared with 0.7 executions per 1,000 murderers of blacks).

But when examining the race combinations of offenders and their victims, an apparent injustice emerges. As Baldus found for Georgia cases from the 1970s, for the country overall, blacks who kill whites have the greatest chance of being executed (5.9 executions per 1,000), twice as high as whites who kill whites (3.1 executions per 1,000), four times higher than for whites who kill blacks (1.4 executions per 1,000), and, more disparately, nine times higher than for blacks who kill blacks (0.7 per 1,000).

Thus, although it may appear that black murderers are less likely to receive the death penalty, this is a function of the intraracial nature of homicide and the racism of a criminal justice system that places less value on black murder victims. When blacks kill whites, they are more likely than any other victim–offender dyad to receive the death penalty. Indeed, a long history of scientific research has exposed the racial bias associated with the use of capital punishment.

The death penalty is also less likely to be carried out against women than men. From 1977 through 2005, 993 men and only 11 women have been put to death in the United States. Clearly, the gender ratio for executions is far more lopsided than that for murder arrests.

Until very recently, the issue of age—specifically whether juveniles should be eligible for the death penalty—was hotly debated. But on March 1, 2005, abolitionists cheered when the Supreme Court announced, in *Roper v. Simmons,* that the death penalty for juveniles was unconstitutional, in violation of the Eighth Amendment's ban on cruel and unusual punishment. The decision ended a capital punishment practice in 19 states and took 72 minors off death row.

Recent advances in DNA technology have had a tremendous impact on the criminal justice system. Police investigators have found in DNA a significant forensic tool for their attempts to solve homicide cases, and prosecutors have been able to offer definitive proof of a defendant's guilt, placing him or her at a crime scene by linking samples of the defendant's blood with various genetic evidence (e.g., blood, saliva, semen, etc.) left at the crime scene.

The value of DNA has not just been for the law enforcement community in trying to catch and prosecute criminals. Not only has DNA excluded certain suspects because of genetic code mismatches, but many previously convicted prisoners have been exonerated by this new evidence that had been unavailable at the time of trial. Most critically, many death row inmates have been saved from a potentially wrongful execution by DNA technology.

Growing awareness of overturned capital cases has made many observers extremely nervous about the finality of the death penalty. Lifers, such as ex-boxer Hurricane Carter, can be released from custody once exculpatory evidence surfaces, but those who were executed have no reprieve. Governor George Ryan of Illinois, a state that has traditionally been willing to execute murderers, made history and headlines by calling a moratorium on executions until the reliability of capital prosecutions could be determined. Upon announcing this move, he noted that the 13 condemned prisoners removed from death row in recent years based on innocence was 1 more than the number of executions that the state had performed since the restoration of capital punishment. Then, just prior to leaving office, Governor Ryan commuted the death sentences of all 156 inmates on the Illinois death row (along with 11 others). Most of the sentences were reduced to life without parole.

Ryan's discomfort surrounding the possibility of egregious error in the application of capital punishment likely reflects why death penalty support has softened in this country since the late 1990s. The receding tide of support may not just be the result of plunging homicide rates, which helped make the public feel more secure. More fundamentally, in a nation whose system of jurisprudence honors and protects the rights of the innocent over all else, growing concern for wrongful executions may signal that the days of the death penalty are numbered.

For years, the United States has stood alone amongst Western nations in the practice of executing murderers. Our foreign peers—countries such as Australia, Canada, Finland, France, Germany, Italy, Netherlands, New Zealand, Norway, and the United Kingdom abolished capital punishment. Others, such as Mexico and Greece, have retained the penalty of death, but only for military crimes and high treason. Even the Russian Federation has imposed a moratorium on executions, although the provision for capital punishment remains on the books. Meanwhile, the United States is conspicuous among the list of nations imposing the death penalty for common murderers, a collection that includes countries like Afghanistan, China, Cuba, Iran, Iraq, and Saudi Arabia.

The rapid growth in the number of executions performed in this country during the 1990s has, however, been followed by a modest downturn at the start of the new millennium. In part this may reflect the decline in homicide rates in the 1990s, which would have reduced the number of new death sentences and may have lessened the public's desire for capital punishment. In addition, many Americans have reconsidered their position on death penalty because of the numerous cases of convicts who have been exonerated. The polls clearly tell a story of declining passion for capital punishment. Majority support for capital punishment, which had reached as high as 80 percent in the mid-1990s, has slipped steadily to 64 percent over the past 10 years.

On the other hand, there remains little chance that the United States Supreme Court will do much in the years ahead to change the law on capital punishment, especially with the conservative imbalance in its current membership. The Court has repeatedly held that, in general, the penalty does not violate the Eighth Amendment prohibition against cruel and unusual punishments nor the Fourteenth Amendment's equal protection clause. After having ruled unconstitutional the death penalty for mentally retarded offenders (*Atkins v. Virginia*, 2002) as well as to those who committed murder as a juvenile (*Roper v. Simmons*, 2005), there may be little of significance remaining for the Court in this arena.

Epidemic Thinking and Overresponse

Whatever the current climate of public opinion, perceptions and attitudes are quite volatile and can easily be altered by high profile events, regardless of their statistical prevalence. Crime rates may be at their lowest point in three decades, yet a particularly heinous episode of senseless violence, if covered extensively by the mass media, can quickly renew demands for tougher sanctions for criminals.

To suggest that the news media is overly reactive to extraordinary episodes is perhaps an understatement. Constantly seeking to increase their market shares, local and syndicated news outlets often treat the latest shocking murder case like a national catastrophe. More-over, there is a clear tendency to hype their coverage by declaring the crime as the latest epidemic to confront the American public. The logic seems to be that if it isn't a raging epidemic, then no one will pay attention.

Virtually ever year, the news media contributes to constructing a new crime growth curve. Very few Americans realize that the current crime rate is lower than it has been in thirty years. The mid-1980s witnessed a serial murder panic fueled by outlandish reports that as many as five thousand Americans were killed annually by these sexual predators. Next came a media-hyped scare in relation to carjackings, then home invasions, then sexual molestation in day care centers, then workplace killings, then road rage, then school shootings, then child abductions. Many of the episodes on which the media focused their attention and their cameras were real in their impact on victims, yet statements concerning the risk to others were often exaggerated.

Recent cases of missing children illustrate exactly how these so-called epidemics are invented. In February 2002, 7-year-old Danielle van Dam was snatched from her bedroom during the middle of the night, prompting a massive search of her San Diego neighborhood, as well as a nationwide appeal by her parents on the *Today Show* pleading her safe return. Three weeks later, however, the girl's charred and decomposed body was found near a small grove of trees east of San Diego. She had been abducted, molested, and murdered by her neighbor, 50-year-old David Westerfield.

"Bad things come in threes," it is said, and numbers two and three came in quick succession. In June, 14-year-old Elizabeth Smart was abducted from her bedroom while her younger sister watched in horror; nine months later, Smart resurfaced alive and well after having roamed with a nomadic husband and wife team of religious zealots. Her abductor, who called himself Emmanuel, was a self-styled prophet with a long history of delusions that included fantasies of multiple child brides. In July 2002, a month following Smart's disappearance, 5-year-old Samantha Runnion was kidnapped as she was playing with a friend in the yard next to her home; her body was found the following day with evidence that she had been sexually molested and asphyxiated. Alejandro Avila, age 27, was arrested and subsequently convicted in Runnion's murder.

Eager to jump on the latest and scariest crime trend, the news media declared kidnapping the newest epidemic. One media outlet dramatically labeled the long steamy months of 2002 as the Summer of Abduction. Having considered the possibility that these abductions signaled a new and ominous trend, journalists and news directors began searching news wires far and wide for any story of a disappearance or attempted abduction to fit and confirm the epidemic theory.

On Fox television, Bill O'Reilly, host of *The O'Reilly Factor,* cited an erroneous statistic that 100,000 children are abducted each year by strangers. Hurriedly doing the math, he also miscalculated there to be more than thirty such kidnappings a day. Actually, the mathematically correct calculation would place the daily count at about three hundred children, the host being off by an "O'Reilly Factor" of ten. If it were indeed the case that 100,000 children annually fall victim to stranger abduction, we would all likely be personally familiar with at least one such unfortunate child. Among a national population of fifty million youngsters under the age of 13, this prevalence of stranger abduction would translate to one out of every five hundred children. At this rate, an average size grade school would endure one stranger abduction each year. Stated in this way, the statistics seem more than a bit preposterous. Unfortunately, once these blatant exaggerations are stated as "facts" on one of the many 24-hour news channels, they are repeated and continue to contribute to uninformed policymaking.

Amidst the tremendous media hype about stranger-child abductions, some sober perspective on the scope of the problem would surely have calmed some nervous parents and outraged politicians. The most reliable and trustworthy estimates of stranger-child abductions are in the hundreds, not hundred-thousands. The national organization *Child Find,* for example, estimates that after removing parent abductions arising out of custody battles (the most common form) as well as attempted kidnappings, fewer than six hundred children are abducted by strangers each year. Furthermore, the majority of these youngsters are eventually found alive. The less fortunate victims who are slain by their abductors number about fifty per year.

Of course, the thought of any child being kidnapped, raped, and murdered is horrible, but in statistical terms it is hardly one of the greatest perils that children face on a daily basis—even if and when a serial predator is operating in the neighborhood. A child is more likely to be killed in a fall off of a bicycle than by being grabbed off the bike by a rapist/murderer; still, some parents are more apt to keep their children at home in protective custody than to enforce the use of the helmets. More children are killed each year by playing with their parents' loaded gun; yet, some parents are more apt to lock up their children for safekeeping than their firearms.

With fifty million children in the United States under the age of 13, the likelihood of any one ending up like Samantha Runnion is literally one in a million. For Samantha's family, of course, it matters not that her case is statistically exceptional. But for the rest of us, it matters a lot.

For the well-being of children, it is important that parents not pass along a sense of paranoia to their kids. Youngsters should not be made into prisoners of fear, constantly looking out for the boogeyman in a parked car. For society, it also matters—it matters that we resist the temptation to rush to enact legislation and public policy that is not well-conceived.

As with other imagined epidemics, the intense focus on the issue of child abductions faded somewhat by the close of 2002, as Americans moved on to the next issue of the day. But in so many of these instances, also left behind is some poorly conceived policy response hurriedly crafted amidst a climate of hysteria. Talk of an epidemic of workplace homicide with scores of disgruntled employees "going postal" may have enhanced efforts to support laid-off workers, but it also led to misguided efforts to profile unhappy workers rather than respond to their grievances. Widespread concern that our schools were populated by armed misfits who might "do a Columbine" may have forced educators to take issues such as bullying seriously, but it also resulted in serious infringements upon the rights of many innocent students caught up in zero-tolerance policies. In the final analysis (literally, for this book at least), the important lesson is to view with healthy skepticism any public policy proposed in the wake of extraordinary and ghastly episodes of murder and mayhem.

ENDNOTES

1. URL: www.law.umkc.edu/faculty/projects/trials/hinckley/letter.htm

2. L.A. Callahan, M.J. Steadman, M.A. McGreevy, and P.C. Robbins, "The Volume and Characteristics of Insanity Defense Pleas: An Eight-State Study," *Bulletin of the American Academy of Psychiatry and the Law* 19 (1991): 331–338.

3. Kip Kinkel, "The Killer at Thurston High," *Frontline,* 1999 www.pbs.org/wgbh/pages/frontline/shows/kinkel/

4. Norval Morris, *Madness and Criminal Law.* Chicago: University of Chicago Press, 1982.

5. Anthony M. Platt, *The Child Savers: The Invention of Delinquency.* Chicago: University of Chicago Press, 1969.

6. David S. Tanenhaus, "The Evolution of Waiver in the Juvenile Court," in Jeffrey Fagan and Franklin Zimring, eds., *The Changing Borders of Juvenile Justice: Transfer of Adolescents to Criminal Court.* Chicago: University of Chicago Press, 1999.

7. Patricia Tourbet and Linda Syzmanski, "State Legislative Responses to Violent Juvenile Crime: 1996–97 Update." Washington, DC: Office of Juvenile Justice and Delinquency Prevention, 1998.

8. Howard N. Snyder and Melissa Sickmund, "Juvenile Offenders and Victims: 1999 National Report." Washington, DC: Office of Juvenile Justice and Delinquency Prevention, 1999.

9. Kevin J. Strom, "Profile of State Prisoners under Age 18," 1985–97. Washington, DC: Bureau of Justice Statistics, February 2000.

10. Howard N. Snyder and Melissa Sickmund, "Juvenile Offenders and Victims: 2006 National Report." Washington, DC: U.S. Department of Justice, Office of Justice Programs, Office of Juvenile Justice and Delinquency Prevention, 2006.

11. Deborah Yurgelun-Todd, "Functional Brain Changes in Adolescents." Presentation at the Whitehead Institute for Bio-Medical Research, Massachusetts Institute of Technology, Cambridge, MA, June 1998.

12. Simon I. Singer and David McDowall, "Criminalizing Delinquency: The Deterrent Effects of the New York Juvenile Offender Law," *Law and Society Review* 22 (1988): 521–535.

13. Donna M. Bishop, Charles E. Frazier, Lonn Lanza-Kaduce, and Henry George White, "Juvenile Transfers to Criminal Court." Washington, DC: Office of Juvenile Justice and Delinquency Prevention, 1998.

14. Matthew R. Durose and Patrick J. Langan, "State Court Sentencing of Convicted Felons, 2002: Statistical Tables." Washington, DC: Bureau of Justice Statistics, 2005.

15. Marc Mauer, Ryan S. King, and Malcolm C. Young, "The Meaning of 'Life': Long Prison Sentences in Context." Washington, DC: The Sentencing Project, 2004.

16. James Alan Fox, Michael Radelet, and Julie Bonsteel, "Public Opinion on the Death Penalty in the Post-Furman Years," *New York University Review of Law and Social Change* 18 (1990–91): 499–528.

17. William J. Bowers, Margaret Vandiver, and Patricia H. Dugan, "A New Look at Public Opinion on Capital Punishment: What Citizens and Legislators Prefer," *American Journal of Criminal Law* 22 (1994): 77–150.

18. Gallup News Service, June 1, 2006.

19. Thorsten J. Sellin, *Capital Punishment.* New York: Harper & Row, 1967.

20. Isaac Ehrlich, "The Deterrent Effect of Capital Punishment: A Question of Life and Death," *American Economic Review* 65 (1975): 397–417.

21. A. Gallup and F. Newport, "Death Penalty Support Remains Strong," *The Gallup Poll Monthly* 309 (June 1991): 40–45.

22. David C. Baldus, Charles Pulaski, and George Woodworth, "Comparative Review of Death Sentences: An Empirical Study of the Georgia Experience," *The Journal of Criminal Law and Criminology,* 74 (1983): 661–753.

A NOTE ON DATA SOURCES

Except for the few instances where a source note is indicated, the information for nearly all tables and charts was drawn from a cumulative data file of the FBI's Supplementary Homicide Reports (SHR) for the years 1976 through 2005, the most recent year available at publication time. Compiled and reformatted by one of the authors (Fox), the complete data file is available at the National Archive of Criminal Justice Data of the Inter-University Consortium of Political and Social Research at the University of Michigan. In addition, these and many more tabulations and charts are maintained and updated on-line in *Homicide Trends in the United States*, at the Website of the Bureau of Justice Statistics.

The SHR provides incident-level details on location, victim, and offender characteristics for almost all homicides in the United States. Specifically, these data include information on the month and year of an offense; the reporting agency and its residential population; county and Metropolitan Statistical Areas (MSA) codes; geographic division and population group; the age, race, and sex of victims and offenders; and the victim/offender relationship, weapon use, and circumstance of the crime. For the years 1976–2005, contributing agencies provided homicide reports for 538,210 of the estimated 594,227 victims of murder and non-negligent manslaughter, and for 597,359 of the estimated 659,862 offenders.

Although national coverage is quite high (about 92 percent of homicides are included in the SHR), missing reports have been corrected using weights to match national- and state-estimated counts prepared by the FBI. The most significant problem in using SHR data to analyze offender characteristics, however, is the sizable number of unsolved homicides contained in the data file. To the extent that the pattern of missing offender data is associated with certain offender characteristics, ignoring unsolved homicides would seriously underestimate rates of offending by particular sub-groups of the population, distort trends over time among these same sub-groups, and bias observed patterns of offending. To adjust for unsolved homicides, a method for offender imputation has been implemented, using available information about the victims murdered in both solved and unsolved homicides. Through this imputation procedure, the demographic characteristics of unidentified offenders are inferred on the basis of similar homicide cases—similar in terms of the victim profile, weapon, circumstances, region, and year of the offense—that had been solved. In other words, offender profiles for unsolved crimes are estimated based on the offender profiles in solved cases matched on victim age, sex, and race as well as weapon, circumstances, region, and year. This imputation strategy was particularly useful in tracking offending rates over time.

Finally, several terms and homicide classifications were used throughout the book, particularly in tables and graphs presented in Chapter 3. These are defined as follows:

Intimate homicide: Killings involving spouses, ex-spouses, boyfriends/girlfriends, or homosexual couples

Family homicide: Killings involving spouses, parents/children, siblings, or other family members

Infanticide:	Victims under 5 years old
Eldercide:	Victims age 65 or over
Felony-murder:	Homicides involving rape, robbery, burglary, larceny, auto theft, arson, or vice law violations
Sex-related:	Homicides involving rape, prostitution, or other sex crimes
Drug-related:	Homicides involving narcotics law violations or arguments over narcotics
Gang-related:	Gangland or youth gang killing
Argument:	Homicides involving disputes over money, drugs/alcohol, jealousy, etc.
Workplace:	Homicides by employers or employees

INDEX